WHAT PUPILS SAY: CHANGING POLICY AND PRACTICE IN PRIMARY EDUCATION

Also available:

Sandra Acker: *The Realities of Teachers' Work*
Patricia Broadfoot *et al.*: *Promoting Quality in Learning*
Anne Convery *et al.*: *Pupils' Perceptions of Europe*
Paul Croll (ed.): *Teachers, Pupils and Primary Schooling*
Ann Filer and Andrew Pollard: *The Social World of Pupil Assessment*
Marilyn Osborn *et al.*: *What Teachers Do: Changing Policy and Practice in Primary Education*
Andrew Pollard with Ann Filer: *The Social World of Children's Learning*
Andrew Pollard and Ann Filer: *The Social World of Pupil Career*
Andrew Pollard *et al.*: *Changing English Primary Schools?*

What Pupils Say

Changing Policy and Practice in Primary Education

Andrew Pollard and Pat Triggs
with Patricia Broadfoot, Elizabeth McNess and Marilyn Osborn

CONTINUUM
London and New York

Continuum

The Tower Building	370 Lexington Avenue
11 York Road	New York
London SE1 7NX	NY 10017–6503

First published 2000

British Library Cataloguing-in-Publication Data
A catalogue record for this book is available from the British Library.

ISBN 0–8264–5061–x (hardback)
    0–8264–5062–8 (paperback)

Typeset by YHT Ltd, London
Printed and bound in Great Britain by TJ International, Padstow, Cornwall

Contents

List of Figures and Tables   vii

Preface *Jennifer Nias*   xi

Books from the PACE Project   xiii

Acknowledgements   xv

Part 1   The Primary Assessment, Curriculum and Experience Project

1. Introduction: The Context and Research Questions   3
2. Research Design and Data-Gathering Methods   18

Part 2   Classroom Change and Pupil Experience

3. Observed Changes in Classroom Practice   47
4. Pupil Perspectives on Curriculum Subjects   66
5. Pupil Judgements on the Curriculum   85
6. Pupil Perspectives on Teacher–Pupil Relationships   104
7. Pupil Perspectives on Classroom Assessment   132
8. Pupil Perspectives on Teachers' Teaching   155
9. Pupil Perspectives on Learning   180
10. Pupil Perspectives on Standardized Assessment   215
11. Case-Studies in Learning Disposition and Identity   241

Part 3   Research Questions Revisited

12. Major PACE Findings on Teacher and Pupil Experience   277
13. Developing Learning Disposition   292
14. Childhood and Education: Past, Present and Future   306

Appendices

1. Systematic Observation: Definition of Categories   317
2. A 'SAT Story': A Sample Comic Strip (completed by Kirsty Jones in
   relation to her science SAT in which she scored Level 3)   321
3. Target Pupils Participating in PACE for Three or More Years
   (by school, years of study and SAT results where known)   326

References   328

Name index   337

Subject index

List of Figures and Tables

Figures

Chapter 1
Figure 1.1   Changing dimensions of curriculum, pedagogy and assessment   11
Figure 1.2   Changing dimensions of teacher professionalism   12

Chapter 2
Figure 2.1   Major phases of data-gathering   22
Figure 2.2   The classroom studies timetable   30
Figure 2.3   A child observation schedule   32
Figure 2.4   An illustration from 'The SAT story' completed by Year 6 pupils in 1996   41

Chapter 3
Figure 3.1   From turbulence to continuity   48

Chapter 10
Figure 10.1   An extract from Laura's SAT story for her extension test in Mathematics   223

Chapter 11
Figure 11.1   Jessica's Key Stage 2 Writing SAT story   257–8
Figure 11.2   Scott's Key Stage 2 Writing SAT story   260

Chapter 13
Figure 13.1   Attributions of academic performance   295
Figure 13.2   A model of learning, identity and social setting   299

Figure 13.3   Complementary factors in pupil learning   305

Appendix 2   Kim's SAT story for her Science SAT   322–5

Tables

Chapter 2
Table 2.1   Research design: data to be gathered   19
Table 2.2   Sample schools by location and predominant social class of
               local communities   23
Table 2.3   Sample schools by size   23

Chapter 3
Table 3.1   Some contrastive aspects of liberal progressive and
               performance models in relation to schools and teachers
               (after Bernstein)   49
Table 3.2   Overall main curriculum content observed   50
Table 3.3   Proportions of time spent on 'basic' subjects and other
               subjects in a range of research studies (extended from
               Campbell and Emery, 1994)   52
Table 3.4   Main teaching contexts experienced by pupils   54
Table 3.5   Pedagogic contexts in systematic observation studies of
               teacher–pupil interaction in English primary schools   56
Table 3.6   Summary: pedagogic contexts in systematic observation
               studies of teacher–pupil interaction in Key Stage 2 of
               English schools by decade   56
Table 3.7   Child interaction   57
Table 3.8   Main types of pupil activity observed in classrooms   58
Table 3.9   Observed teacher activities   59
Table 3.10   ORACLE findings on teacher activity, 1976 and 1996   60
Table 3.11   Mode, purpose and frequency of assessment   61
Table 3.12   Significant assessment procedures used by teachers   63
Table 3.13   Some contrastive aspects of competence and performance
               models in relation to classrooms and pupils   65

Chapter 5
Table 5.1   Comparative 'league table' of pupils' favoured curriculum
               activities   86
Table 5.2   First and second choices in 'most liked' category for top
               five subjects   87
Table 5.3   First and second choices in 'least liked' category for top
               five subjects   87
Table 5.4   Criteria used in explanation for most liked activities and
               subjects   89
Table 5.5   Criteria used in explanation for least liked activities and
               subjects   92

Table 5.6   Rank order of criteria used in explanation for most liked
                 activities and subjects   96

Chapter 6
Table 6.1   Pupils' perceptions of their relationships with their teachers   105
Table 6.2   Boys' and girls' perceptions of their relationships with their
                 teachers   107
Table 6.3   Children's criteria for liking teachers   107
Table 6.4   Breakdown of the 'Interaction' category in pupils' criteria
                 for liking teachers   110
Table 6.5   Children's perception of who selects tasks at school   111
Table 6.6   Children's preferences for who chooses classroom activities 113
Table 6.7   Reasons given by pupils who preferred to choose activities
                 themselves   114
Table 6.8   Reasons given by pupils who preferred their teacher to
                 choose activities   118
Table 6.9   Pupils' answers to the question 'Do you have to do what
                 your teacher says?'   122
Table 6.10   Behaviour and personal characteristics of the ideal pupil   125
Table 6.11   Rank order of characteristics of the ideal pupil for each
                 school   126
Table 6.12   Girls' and boys' perceptions of the degree to which they
                 think they are like their teachers' ideal pupil   127

Chapter 7
Table 7.1   Responses of pupils to the question 'Do you like it when
                 your teacher asks to look at your work?'   133
Table 7.2   Self-assessment by pupils of being 'good at' reading,
                 writing, Mathematics and Science   140
Table 7.3   Children's responses to the question 'Why do you think
                 you are good at those things?'   142
Table 7.4   Children's responses to the question 'Why do you think
                 you are not so good at those things?'   144
Table 7.5   Rank order of categories used by the children to account
                 for attainment   149
Table 7.6   Major categories used by children in each year to account
                 for attainment   149

Chapter 8
Table 8.1   Children's awareness and understanding of teacher inten-
                 tions for learning activities   156
Table 8.2   Children's awareness and understanding of 'learning'
                 related to teacher intentions   159
Table 8.3   Pupils' responses to the question 'Does it matter if you
                 don't do things the way your teacher wants them?'   165

Table 8.4   Pupils' perceptions of the risks associated with not doing
              things the way their teacher wants   167
Table 8.5   Pupils' understanding of the basis for classroom groupings   175
Table 8.6   Pupils' feelings about the way their teachers grouped them   175
Table 8.7   Reasons behind pupils' feelings about how they are
              grouped   177

Chapter 9
Table 9.1   Factors that made pupils worried about their work   182
Table 9.2   What pupils were pleased with about their work   185
Table 9.3   Pupils' explanations of what happens when someone does
              their work really well   187
Table 9.4   Pupils' criteria for choosing people to work with   192
Table 9.5   When you seem to be concentrating are you sometimes
              really thinking about other things?   209
Table 9.6   What the children said they were thinking about when they
              were distracted   209
Table 9.7   Children's reasons for being distracted   211

Preface

Jennifer Nias

This and its companion volume (Osborn *et al.*, 2000) are important books. Grounded in data collected in the last decade of the twentieth century, they point forward to the twenty-first. *What Teachers Do* describes and analyses the response of English primary school teachers and headteachers, of all lengths of experience, to the changes in policy which followed from, and after, the Education Reform Act, 1988. *What Pupils Say* documents the parallel impact on the lived experience of pupils between 5 and 11. The focus of the books is the introduction of the National Curriculum and its associated assessment procedures, but because the Primary Assessment, Curriculum and Experience (PACE) project was longitudinal in its approach, they also take note of the changes in inspection procedures, school governance and funding which took place in the years 1989 to 1997. What emerges from the mass of quantitative and qualitative data which the project team accumulated is a vivid and disturbing picture of teachers' and pupils' evolving experience of the new requirements for curriculum, pedagogy and assessment; and of the cumulative effects of this experience upon their sense of autonomy, their motivation and their attitudes to, on the one hand, teaching and, on the other, learning.

The books are vivid because they draw extensively upon painstaking classroom observations and on sensitively conducted interviews with participants, as well as on appropriate statistical evidence. They are disturbing because they point up some of the unintended consequences of, and tensions within, the policies of three different governments, each intent on raising educational standards by the use of centralization and control together with an appeal to the power of competition and parental choice. The PACE evidence suggests that an apparent rise during the 1990s of measured standards in English, Mathematics and Science has been achieved by sacrificing, at least in part, some of the characteristics of teaching and learning in

English primary schools that have attracted the attention of visitors and researchers from over the world. Among these are a warm affective climate and encouragement of pupils' autonomy, creativity, activity and reflexivity. The curriculum has narrowed, despite the initial promise of the National Curriculum, sometimes bringing boredom in its wake. More fundamentally, the cumulative pressures of additional curricular content, of assessment, recording and reporting have eroded time for affective contact between teachers and pupils. Partly as a result of this, many teachers have begun to replace their sense of moral responsibility for their work, deriving from their relationship with individuals, with one of contractual accountability for the achievement of externally set targets.

Indeed, a theme running through all the project findings is the growth among teachers and pupils of an instrumental and pragmatic view of education. As pupils grew older they increasingly came to equate 'success' with producing what teachers wanted in the narrow curricular areas of reading, writing, Mathematics and, to a lesser degree, Science. In addition, they showed limited understanding of the learning purposes which their work was intended to fulfil. For their part teachers too, although in most cases reluctantly, began to define their own success in terms of their ability to meet performance targets over which they had little or no control. For both sets of participants schooling during this decade often became a question of task accomplishment, a process in which quality was constantly overtaken by quantity; teacher facilitation of pupils' self-defined learning goals by instruction; pupil activity by sitting, listening and writing; spontaneity, creativity and inquiry by satisfactory performance on school and national tests.

This pervasive instumentalism has had the further effect of creating a new type of differentiation between pupils and among teachers. One of the stated aims of all governments since 1988 has been to reduce the impact of economic and social class differences on access to, and the ability to profit from, education. The National Curriculum was conceived as 'curriculum entitlement' and the rhetoric of this aspiration has persisted. Similarly, the drive to raise standards in 'the basics' derives in part from a desire that all children should achieve equality of educational opportunity. Whatever the outcome in terms of test results of this emphasis by central government, the PACE project makes it clear that a new form of differentiation has replaced, or perhaps been added to, the familiar distinctions which are associated with social and economic status. Pupils who did well in primary schools during the 1990s and whose SAT results, especially at Key Stage 2, were satisfactory or better, were those who showed obvious signs of self-confidence and self-esteem as learners. Similarly, the teachers who rose above the pressures of constant modifications to curriculum and assessment, intensified workload, the need for new curricular knowledge, OFSTED inspections and media attacks were those whose self-confidence as teachers was not eroded or was, in some cases, enhanced by these policy changes. By contrast, pupils and teachers who experienced anxiety and loss of confidence when faced with what they perceived as their failure to meet externally imposed, and often apparently arbitrary, goals did not thrive under the new conditions. When such pupils could, they devised strategies to get by or to avoid overt censure, thus achieving some sense of control over their environment, if not over their learning. The toll among teachers who were anxious or lost professional self-esteem was more obvious. Illness and early retirement rose to unprecedented levels during this period, especially among the more experienced.

Of course, the confidence that one can succeed in meeting the standards set by others, or can successfully afford to ignore them, derives from many sources. Evidence from this project indicates the importance of support by other people. Teachers benefited from working in collaborative environments; pupils tended to receive support from teachers, but also, and crucially, from parents, peers and siblings. This further complicates the problem of how to achieve equality of opportunity. Differentiation based upon degrees of self-confidence, self-esteem (as teachers or learners) and support is not likely to be susceptible of easy solutions, especially in a social and political climate that favours competition and individualism.

As an instrumental view of schooling has gained ground in the minds of pupils, parents and teachers, a further tension in government policy has emerged. The present system of curricular instruction, external target-setting, regular assessment and measured outcomes encourages a performance view of the learner and the teacher. This is in line with the official doctrine that Britain's economic future depends upon the existence of a skilled, competitive and reliable workforce. *Mutatis mutandis*, this argument is little different from that used in the late nineteenth century to justify the curriculum, pedagogy and assessment of the elementary schools. But the social, economic and technological background from which school entrants come and into which leavers must fit has radically changed. Business leaders, politicians, educationalists and many parents are all aware that now and in the foreseeable future society and, more narrowly, economic enterprise needs citizens who are flexible, resourceful and capable of 'lifelong learning'. The evidence presented in these two volumes suggests that the structured pursuit of higher standards in English and Mathematics may be reducing the ability of many children to see themselves as self-motivating, independent problem solvers taking an intrinsic pleasure in learning and capable of reflecting on how and why they learn. It also highlights the fact that primary schools can strongly affect pupils' willingness as learners to take risks and to engage emotionally with their learning. Too great or inflexible an emphasis upon pupils as products may inhibit the emergence of a society whose members are also capable of acting as agents, wanting to learn, confident of their capacity to do so, responding to economic and technological challenges in active yet reflexive ways. There is little indication that politicians are yet aware of this tension in the goals which they espouse.

Similarly, the fact that their teachers have tacitly been defined as technicians whose skills can be judged against externally set criteria has reduced the sense of moral commitment which most feel to their work. It has been replaced by a narrower, more bureaucratic sense of accountability which, in its turn, may prove too limited and inflexible to meet the future needs of a 'learning society'. At the same time, those teachers who have retained a sense of moral responsibility for pupils often experience dysfunctional levels of stress, because they feel required to act in ways which they believe to be contrary to the latter's best interests.

Paradoxically, the answer to these apparent conflicts may also lie within the project data. Pupils have only one education and although their attitudes to it are influenced by parents and older siblings, they are less likely to question innovations than are teachers. The latter are older; their beliefs and values are more firmly established. Even if they have been teaching for only a short time, it may cost them a great deal in personal terms to alter or surrender these principles. *What Teachers Do* shows the ways in which a fluctuating number of 'creative mediators' have taken active, but selective, control of the changes imposed upon them, with the result that they have sometimes become makers rather than simply implementers of educational policy. These teachers and headteachers have retained their educational beliefs, and a sense of their professional efficacy and autonomy. In their classrooms and schools, instrumentalism is often reconciled with creativity, the fulfilment of external targets with affectivity and pupil-directed learning. It seems as if relatively small reductions in the pressures currently bearing upon teachers and pupils would free some learning time and space into which both could grow. If the imbalance between instrumentalism and individual development, between extrinsic and intrinsic motivation, were corrected, teachers might begin to regain their sense of professional autonomy and with it their feeling of moral, rather than contractual, accountability for their work. In their turn, pupils might become more concerned with their own learning and less with mere task-fulfilment.

The data presented in these volumes and the conclusions drawn from them are thought-provoking and potentially far-reaching in their consequences. These books are a fitting outcome from a decade of rigorous and insightful inquiry with which I have been glad to be associated. I hope that they will reach a wide and appropnate readership.

Jennifer Nias
University of Plymouth
July 2000

Books from the PACE Project

This book derives from the three phases of the Primary Assessment, Curriculum and Experience project (PACE), which ran from 1989 to 1997.

The value of the book may be enhanced by reading it in conjunction with the other PACE books, and the structure of these is as indicated below.

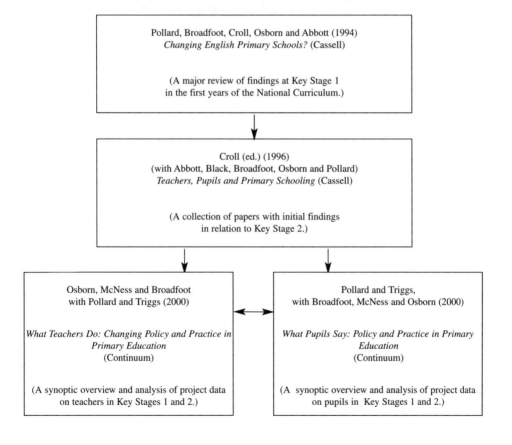

Pollard, Broadfoot, Croll, Osborn and Abbott (1994)
Changing English Primary Schools? (Cassell)

(A major review of findings at Key Stage 1
in the first years of the National Curriculum.)

Croll (ed.) (1996)
(with Abbott, Black, Broadfoot, Osborn and Pollard)
Teachers, Pupils and Primary Schooling (Cassell)

(A collection of papers with initial findings
in relation to Key Stage 2.)

Osborn, McNess and Broadfoot
with Pollard and Triggs (2000)

*What Teachers Do: Changing Policy and Practice in
Primary Education*
(Continuum)

(A synoptic overview and analysis of project data
on teachers in Key Stages 1 and 2.)

Pollard and Triggs,
with Broadfoot, McNess and Osborn (2000)

*What Pupils Say: Policy and Practice in Primary
Education*
(Continuum)

(A synoptic overview and analysis of project data
on pupils in Key Stages 1 and 2.)

As would be expected, there are many design and theoretical elements that are shared between our two parallel synoptic books reporting six years of fieldwork findings on teacher and pupil experiences. Their origins and the coherence of the project as a whole is reflected by some shared text, particularly in the introductions and chapters on research design.

A fifth book deriving from the PACE projects is being considered (Broadfoot and Pollard). Provisionally entitled *The Assessment Society*, this would address the emphasis on 'performance' within modern education, taking its influence on primary education as a case-study.

Members of the PACE teams have been engaged in other, closely related, projects. For international comparisons, see Broadfoot *et al.* (2000). For studies at a further level of detail concerning pupil 'life-stories' through primary schooling, with particular foci on learning, career and assessment, see Pollard with Filer (1996), Pollard and Filer (1999) and Filer and Pollard (2000).

Details of other publications from the PACE projects are available on the ESRC database, Regard, at http://regard.ac.uk (search on authors or the ESRC project reference numbers: R000231931, R000233891, R000235687).

Acknowledgements

The three phases of the PACE projects between 1989 and 1997 were each funded by the UK's Economic and Social Research Council. We gratefully acknowledge this support.

Pupils, teachers, headteachers and LEA staff have faced many challenging years since 1989, and yet they have found both the time to talk with us and the generosity to welcome us into their schools. Although they must all remain anonymous, we thank them.

We would like to acknowledge the support of many academic and teacher colleagues, in particular those of our Consultative Group, in discussing ideas, problems, strategies and the many other issues which arise during a longitudinal study of this sort. Jennifer Nias and Basil Bernstein have been particularly influential in the evolution of our thinking and our particular thanks go to the former for reading our manuscript and for providing a preface. Julie Anderson, Neil Simco and Colin Richards also commented very helpfully on this 'pupil' book. Felix Braun designed and produced the splendid 'SAT stories'. We are also grateful to the two universities from which the project derived (the University of the West of England and the University of Bristol) and to staff of the ESRC who have helped us in many ways throughout the programme.

We are also enormously grateful to our other colleagues who have been members of the PACE team at various stages – Dorothy Abbott, Paul Croll, Edie Black, Jenny Noble and Mike Taysum. Their work has contributed to the analysis which is reported in this book, and its companion volume. We have also had superb assistance from support staff during the project, including Jacquie Harrison, Viki Davies, Sheila Taylor, Sarah Butler, Elspeth Gray and Jenny Wills.

To Isobel and all other children growing up in the new millennium – who challenge us to provide an enriching and worthwhile education.

Part 1

The Primary Assessment, Curriculum and Experience Project

Chapter 1

Introduction: The Context and Research Questions

1.1 Changing times
1.2 The context for change
1.3 The Education Reform Act 1988
1.4 Developments under New Labour
1.5 The PACE project
1.6 A study of pupil experience
1.7 The structure of the book
1.8 Conclusion

1.1 CHANGING TIMES

Primary education in England and Wales will never be the same again. The Education Reform Act (ERA) 1988 was the most radical education legislation in half a century, and a decade of unremitting change followed it. As the tidal wave of new policy initiatives began to ebb, it revealed a shoreline in which many of the principal features had been rearranged – the role of the headteacher and the way schools were managed, teachers' priorities and ways of working together, curriculum content, teaching methods and forms of assessment. Perhaps to the casual observer, classroom practices and the activities of teachers and pupils may appear little altered. The constants of classrooms everywhere – talk, activity, display, busyness, a single teacher occupied with a large group of children – these remain the defining characteristics of formal education across the globe. For the present, notwithstanding the new learning technologies of the information society, schools and teachers, pupils and lessons are constants which we both recognize and understand. They are a familiar feature of our contemporary culture. All the more difficult, then, to appreciate the subtle yet profound redefining of the educational project that the introduction of the National Curriculum and associated initiatives has produced in

English primary schools; the changes in relationships between headteacher and staff; between the teachers themselves and between teachers and their pupils; and the product of these changes – different attitudes, different goals, different concerns, different skills. The result in the 1990s was an education system in which teachers' priorities in practice reflected a hard-won and often uneasy compromise between new obligations and an enduring vision that had its roots in a different era. For pupils, the new requirements introduced into their schooling a more specified curriculum, tighter framing of classroom life and a new level of assessment activity. On the other hand, it was 'still school', whether they answered to the idiosyncrasies of their allotted class teacher, or to a common, national statutory requirement. Compulsory schooling remained something 'done to you' – 'teach, teach, teach – learn, learn, learn', as one pupil put it.

The Primary Assessment, Curriculum and Experience (PACE) project was established in 1989 to monitor the impact of the momentous changes then occurring following the passing of the Education Reform Act 1988. Funded in three stages, 1989–92, 1992–4 and 1994–7, the PACE project was uniquely placed to document the unfolding story of change in primary schools and, in particular, the impact of the new National Curriculum and assessment requirements on headteachers, teachers and pupils. As Chapter 2 describes in detail, we chose a national sample of primary schools which afforded us access throughout the years of the project to collect information about the changes teachers and pupils felt they were experiencing, to document the evolving school experience of a particular group of pupils throughout the course of their primary schooling, and to observe these experiences for ourselves by sitting in classrooms and staffrooms. The project amassed an enormous quantity of material which provides a unique resource for both current and future analyses of English primary education in the final years of the second millennium. As with all data, its value is realized by exposing it to the filter of particular questions and to the subsequent interpretation of theoretical analyses.

In this book we present one such account. Its focus is on pupils and we report the experiences and perceptions of the first cohort of children to experience the National Curriculum from the start of their formal schooling, as it was progressively introduced in the 1990s. Our account is matched by that in the companion volume on teachers (Osborn *et al.*, 2000). Whilst faithfully reporting the evidence we have found, our goal is to go beyond mere description in order to analyse and explain; to understand and to assess the significance of the pupil perceptions that our data reveal. In this way, we hope that the case-study which this period of educational history represents can illuminate more enduring educational issues which must be confronted in any era.

Our aspiration then, is to generate insights into the relationship between educational policy, classroom practice, pupil perception and learning. We will particularly consider the issues of children's learning disposition and motivation, which are becoming so important in the new millennium. Further, we will use our findings to raise some questions about how, in modern English society, we conceptualize 'children' and 'childhood'. In summary then, this book addresses three key questions:

- How did pupils perceive and experience the introduction of the National Curriculum and assessment?
- Did the introduction of the National Curriculum and assessment facilitate or undermine the development of positive pupil learning dispositions?
- What is the significance of the recent education policy in terms of how children and childhood are understood in modern English society?

The rest of this chapter sets out the context both for the policy initiatives themselves and for the PACE research project. Then, arising from this analysis, we introduce in more detail the three key questions which are listed above. The chapter concludes with a review of the contents of the book as a whole.

1.2 THE CONTEXT FOR CHANGE

Educationalists in other countries are frequently amazed that there was no tradition of a national curriculum in England and Wales until the Education Reform Act 1988 was implemented. Previously, the only formal control of the content of education concerned the requirement to teach Religious Education, which had been established in the Education Act 1944. Historically then, England has been almost unique in not having a national curriculum. Instead it has traditionally relied on various kinds of assessment, particularly public examinations, to control the system. As in other countries the existence of so called 'high-stakes' public examinations at ages 11, 16 and 18 provided a powerful focus for schools which were otherwise free to make their own decisions about content. At primary school level, relatively far from the constraints of the exam system, teachers had considerable autonomy to develop their interests, commitments and particular areas of expertise. Further, 'topic work' and other integrated forms of curriculum planning flourished in the years following the Plowden Report (CACE, 1967). Overall however, there were significant problems in providing coherence, continuity and progression within the curriculum, with the result that children were sometimes exposed to the same content or activities on several occasions, whilst other curricular entitlements could be unwittingly neglected (HMI, 1978). Thus one of the main stimuli for the introduction of a national curriculum was the desire to provide a broad, balanced and coherent curriculum for the years between age 5 and 16, Years 1–10.

Other straws in the wind were also significant in prompting legislation. The 1980s had seen a growth in international economic competition. This, together with growing financial pressures and an increased demand for state institutions to be accountable, underpinned a desire to curb the professional autonomy of teachers and to replace it with a much greater measure of central control. A key ingredient in providing for such control was seen as the generation of comprehensive information about standards, about finance and about many different aspects of educational provision, hence the simultaneous and significant development of a variety of forms of monitoring of performance.

It was in the 1980s and 1990s too that a series of international surveys began to reveal how standards in England compared to those in other countries (e.g.

Degenhart, 1990; Keeves, 1995; Reynolds and Farrell, 1996). The Third International Mathematics and Science Survey (TIMSS) (Keys *et al.*, 1996) illustrates this kind of concern, showing as it did that English pupils apparently compare well with their peers in other countries on Science achievement, but are well down when it comes to Mathematics. How far it is appropriate to trust such statistics (see Broadfoot *et al.*, 2000) is perhaps less important than recognizing the effect of such high profile studies on policy-makers, who are keen to be seen to be responding to public concern about standards.

In addition to these general concerns, there were also a number of more specific developments. One of these was the 'fall out' from the virtual abandonment of eleven-plus testing with the advent of comprehensive schools during the 1970s. This development left primary schools free of almost any kind of formal curriculum or assessment control. It also meant that there was very little information about the standards being achieved in primary schools and in the lower years of secondary schools. Although the Assessment of Performance Unit had been set up in the 1970s to monitor national performance in particular subject areas, this was a spasmodic exercise and was not sufficient to reassure public disquiet.

Concern about education, and primary education in particular, grew throughout the 1970s. The publication of the 'Black Papers' (Cox and Boyson, 1975, 1977; Cox and Dyson, 1969) was an early manifestation but debate was fanned by the furore over the management and teaching at Tyndale Junior School (Dale, 1981). Other key events of 1976 were the publication of Neville Bennett's book, *Teaching Styles and Pupil Progress*, and Prime Minister Jim Callaghan's Ruskin College speech. Callaghan, with an eye on the public critique of 'progressivism', argued that the educational aims of the time were unbalanced. As he put it: 'The goals of our education are clear enough. They are to equip children to the best of their ability for a lively, constructive place in society and also to fit them to do a job of work. Not one or the other, but both.' The concern about the relevance and control of education continued following the 1979 election of Margaret Thatcher. New thinking by her education ministers, such as Sir Keith Joseph, and various New Right pressure groups, led to the publication of a White Paper, *Better Schools* (DES, 1985), and the actual legislation of 1988.

1.3 THE EDUCATION REFORM ACT 1988

The expressed aim of the Education Reform Act, a policy initiative almost unprecedented in its ambition and scope, was quite simply to raise standards. This was to be achieved by raising expectations about pupil achievement and through the imposition of a broad and balanced National Curriculum for all pupils to provide continuity and coherence in their learning experience. The introduction of the National Curriculum was complemented by provision for a standard and comprehensive assessment system. This national system was designed not only to measure the performance of pupils at the end of four key stages (Years 1–2, 3–6, 7–10 and 11–12), but also to make it possible for market forces to operate by providing a currency of information which would fuel competition between schools.

The original aim of the national assessment system was that it should provide formative and diagnostic information to guide teachers in the classroom as well as summative information for students, teachers and parents about the level of attainment of a given child at a given stage. Thus the government's Task Group on Assessment and Testing (TGAT, 1988) envisaged an elaborate criterion-referenced structure of attainment targets, and pupils' achievement was to be recorded and reported at the end of Key Stages 1, 2 and 3 by means of a combination of Teacher Assessment and results from externally provided Standard Assessment Tasks (SATs). At the end of Key Stage 4, external assessment was to be in the form of the newly introduced GCSE examination. Significantly, such a comprehensive national assessment system could, and subsequently did, provide attainment data with which to compare not only individual students, but also the results of their schools, of local education authorities and indeed of English schooling as a whole in comparative league tables. Slowly, the formative purpose of assessment waned in significance, and its role as a summative measure of performance became dominant.

Innovation on the scale described was likely to cause turbulence in any education system, and the English reforms were no exception. The PACE study (Pollard *et al.*, 1994; Croll, 1996) documented the anger and despair of teachers in the early 1990s as they struggled to implement both the National Curriculum and new assessment procedures. Both proved to be too demanding in terms of teachers' time and were perceived as being over-prescriptive. The National Curriculum was therefore reviewed by Sir Ron Dearing and a second version was introduced in September 1995. This 'slimmed down' the curriculum content and simplified the elaborate structure of criterion-referenced attainment into a simpler system of 'level descriptions' for 'best fit' assessment judgements and reporting. National tests were only statutory in the core subjects of English, Mathematics and Science and, for Key Stages 2 and 3, external markers were to be provided to lighten the load on classroom teachers.

The first PACE book, *Changing English Primary Schools?* (Pollard *et al.*, 1994), reported the project's findings concerning teachers' experiences with, and attitudes to, both the National Curriculum and the assessment system during the early years of this decade. It made clear that teachers found the workload of implementing the new requirements both an unacceptable burden in terms of the time required and equally unacceptable in terms of the prominence given to subject knowledge and the categoric assessment of pupils in terms of their levels of achievement. The 'child centred' commitment of primary teachers was still very strong at the time, with considerable support for 'topic work' and for the significance of developing close teacher–pupil relationships. Subject knowledge, however, was weak in a number of areas. Assessment practices were undeveloped, since primary schools in most parts of the country had had little, or no, tradition of formal assessment since the demise of the eleven-plus selection examination. Further, many teachers were ideologically opposed to conducting tests which they felt were neither meaningful nor helpful. However, as with subject knowledge, many teachers also lacked professional experience in conducting such formal assessments and thus were faced with the need to develop new skills in this respect.

In 1993 many teachers, suffering low morale from the sustained public critique combined with the work-pressure of the overloaded curriculum, refused to do the national tests on a formal basis. This revolt was initiated by English teachers at Key Stage 3 who were objecting to the content of the tests and their inevitable washback effect on curriculum priorities. However, the fact that the boycott rapidly spread into primary schools provides a good illustration of the extent of the antipathy towards national assessment and government policy that existed amongst primary teachers at that time. As *Changing English Primary Schools?* makes clear, the causes of this antipathy were at a number of levels. At the most obvious were issues of workload and time, and teachers objected strongly to a procedure that would take many days of effort for themselves and their pupils but would not, in their view, contribute to the facilitation of pupil learning. Beneath this though, were more fundamental concerns about the anticipated effect of such tests on the priorities and practices of English primary schooling. For instance, it was already clear that the well-established English tradition of controlling schools by means of external assessment requirements was being redeployed in a new and powerful way to impose a particular set of curriculum priorities on schools. Further, the steadily growing emphasis year by year on the use of national assessment results as an external indicator of school standards meant that the reliability of the information became increasingly important. In the context of the publication in the national media of 'league tables' of test results at school and LEA level, assessment procedures had to be rigorously controlled in order to ensure fairness in comparisons between schools. The consequence was a steady trend towards the use of formal, externally controlled paper and pencil tests at all levels, and with this came a washback on to the curriculum so that teaching and curriculum planning became increasingly designed to maximize test performance.

Another major development under the Conservative administrations of the 1990s was the introduction of the OFSTED school inspection system. Established through the Education Act 1992, this was designed to monitor and make public the quality of management, teaching and pupil attainment at each school. Once again, there was a rationale in terms of providing public information based on independent judgement, but the system was commonly seen by the profession as a vehicle for 'teacher bashing'.

Overall, the early and mid-1990s, the period of PACE data-gathering, were years of considerable tension between the government and the teaching profession, and this tension was only partially ameliorated by Sir Ron Dearing's review, which took effect in 1995. At the end of the period, teachers eagerly anticipated a new start from a more sympathetic government.

1.4 DEVELOPMENTS UNDER NEW LABOUR

When the Labour government came to power in May 1997 the White Paper, *Excellence in Schools*, was rapidly published, and it was evident that the pace of new education policy-making was to continue. However, there was a reappraisal of focus and priorities, and this resulted in a new concern for social inclusion and an ever-increasing emphasis on the basics of literacy and numeracy. Indeed, in January 1998 the Secretary of State for Education, David Blunkett, announced that some of the requirements of the primary National Curriculum were being suspended for the next two years to enable more time to be spent on these 'basics' prior to a comprehensive revision of the National Curriculum. Thus, although schools were 'expected' to continue teaching History, Geography, Design and Technology, Art, Music and Physical Education, only English, Mathematics, Science, Information Technology and Religious Education remained as required subjects. In the other subjects the content and the amount of coverage was left to the discretion of schools. The goal of this initiative to suspend and focus the National Curriculum was expressed in terms of the government's desire to ensure that all children would leave primary school equipped with the necessary competence in the basics of literacy and numeracy. On the other hand the focus on 'the basics' of literacy and numeracy was criticized for undermining the previous commitment to a broad and balanced curriculum.

In 1999, plans for a new revised National Curriculum were published. This *Curriculum 2000* (QCA, 1999) was the result of much more extensive consultation with classroom teachers than previous versions, but the radically slimmed-down curriculum that had earlier been envisaged to give more scope for teachers' professional judgement did not materialize.

New Labour also increased pedagogic prescription through the competency requirements of the Teacher Training Agency, the frameworks of the Literacy and Numeracy Hours, the naming and shaming of 'failing' schools and the specification of school inspection. Such developments, in combination with the gradual development of sophisticated target-setting systems for schools and local education authorities and the linking of teachers' classroom performance to salary enhancement, have ensured that primary school teaching has become increasingly framed by requirements and pressures that are external to the school itself.

Such policy development following the period covered by the PACE study represents a continuation of the major themes which we have identified. There are differences between the Conservative administrations and that of New Labour, but remarkable continuities also remain. We believe that this means that the policy-significance of the study remains, and we will try to draw this out at the end of the book.

1.5 THE PACE PROJECT

The overall goals of the PACE project were broad: to describe the impact of the English National Curriculum and to evaluate its significance for pupils, teachers and the process of education as a whole. Its focus was on the process of change in primary schools; its origins and progress; its management and effects.

Expressed in terms of specific objectives the PACE project sought:

- to monitor changes in teachers' practices and pupil experiences in terms of curriculum, pedagogy and assessment;
- to investigate the consequences of national policies and mediating effects which are associated with teacher perspectives, cultures and behaviour and, in

particular, their perceptions of professional responsibility; and,
- to investigate the consequences of national policies and mediating effects which are associated with pupil perspectives, cultures and classroom behaviours.

Whilst our first priority was to describe and analyse the impact of the Education Reform Act on primary schools, we also aimed to consider the changes in primary schooling as an illustration of wider social developments. In particular, we came to see the changing focus of education policy as a reflection of the tensions between modern and 'post-modern' society, with new priorities and new forms of contestation, regulation and discourse. Our study has a strongly empirical flavour, and we feel a responsibility to fully report the patterns of opinion, behaviour and practice which we have recorded. However, we have also attempted to theorize these findings and set them in the wider context of social change.

After eight years of study we now have a comprehensive picture of the changes which took place for pupils, teachers and headteachers. In this book we focus particularly on pupil experience during the turbulent years of the early and mid-1990s; on their classroom experiences and perspectives. This book, and its partner volume on teacher practices and professionalism, aim both to describe the developments in primary education that have taken place and to understand them as part of wider social developments at the end of the twentieth century. A further proposed synoptic PACE volume, *The Assessment Society* (Broadfoot and Pollard), will have as its central focus an analysis of the impact of recent policy changes in assessment. It will explore the nature of contemporary educational discourse as a case-study of underlying trends in society and, in particular, of the significance of the gradual establishment of the new hegemony of 'performance' which the PACE project has documented.

Given that from its inception, the PACE project aspired to describe and, crucially, explained the nature of the changes taking place; it was also concerned with evaluating their significance, both for the business of education specifically and more generally, for the nature and conduct of social life. In 1994 we described the PACE project as 'one of the many stepping stones in the quest to understand the nature of the educational enterprise and hence, how to provide for it most effectively in a changing context' (p. 4). Thus our research was designed to help understand the origin and significance both of the policy initiatives imposed by government and those which are the product of the attempts by teachers and headteachers to reconcile these requirements with their professional values and understandings. Why were these policy initiatives set in motion in the England of the late 1980s and what, ultimately, is likely to be their significance for the nature and quality of pupils' learning?

From the outset, the work of Basil Bernstein has proved particularly apposite as a foundation for our theoretical interpretations. The capacity of Bernstein's conceptualization to embrace curriculum, pedagogy and assessment, and its concern with power, knowledge and consciousness as key variables, enabled us to integrate the diverse perspectives of the PACE project into three core themes which we identified as 'values', 'understanding' and 'power'. We also used Bernstein's well-established concepts of classification and framing to develop various cubic representations, facets of which portray the different, but interrelated trends which have taken place in primary schools over the period. Thus, for instance, our early data suggested that classroom life reflected the move to a more classified, subject-based curriculum, increasingly controlled and framed forms of pedagogy, and more explicit and categoric forms of assessment (see Figure 1.1).

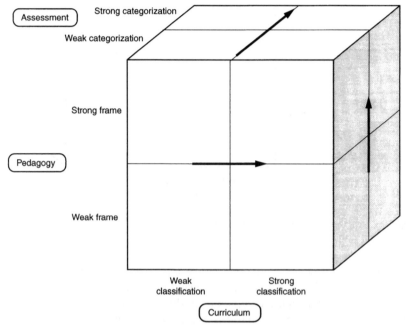

Figure 1.1 Changing dimensions of curriculum, pedagogy and assessment
Source: Pollard *et al.*, 1994, p. 238.

Similarly, the demands on teachers and the nature of teaching also changed. Professional autonomy became more constrained, accountability pressure grew, and teachers' views of their own professional responsibilities began to become more pragmatic. Over time there was a gradual acceptance of the National Curriculum and assessment, particularly as older teachers retired, new teachers were inducted into a new set of professional expectations, and the worst excesses of prescription were moderated. Teachers also began to recognize the value of subject knowledge, and to see it as complementing the previous emphasis on children constructing their own understandings. We conceptualized these developments as shown in Figure 1.2.

In a subsequent PACE book, edited by Croll (1996), we explored at greater length the ways in which these changing characteristics of the organization and delivery of primary education in this country were being experienced and managed by those affected. It reinforced the salience of values, understanding and power as key themes in the explanation of both the rationale for the changes that were being imposed and teachers' responses to them.

We argued that schools, as well as teachers and pupils, are 'embedded in a

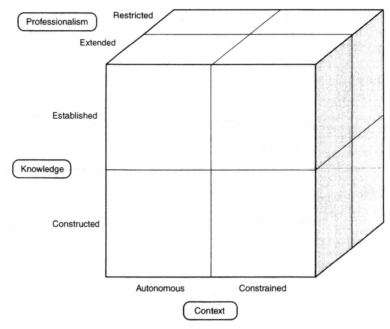

Figure 1.2 Changing dimensions of teacher professionalism
Source: Pollard *et al.*, 1994, p. 237.

dynamic network of personal identity, values and understandings that are constantly developing in the light of internal and external interaction, pressure and constraint' (Croll, 1996, p. 156). Because of this, policy directives are translated into classroom practice through a series of 'mediations'. Such mediations, we argued, should not be conceptualized in engineering terms as a series of articulated levers that relay a load through the structure. Rather, they are the creative reinterpretation by the actors involved at each successive stage of the process of delivering education. Once again, Bernstein's analysis of the pedagogic code and its power to define, and hence control, provided a powerful theoretical model with which to examine the significance of the changes documented in the PACE data (Broadfoot and Pollard, 2000).

Now, at the end of the empirical phase of the longitudinal study as a whole, we have tried to produce both a comprehensive descriptive picture of how things have changed in primary schools since 1989 and an analysis that highlights the significance of these developments.

1.6 A STUDY OF PUPIL EXPERIENCE

This book focuses on the experiences of pupils in English primary schools following the implementation of the Education Reform Act. In tracking a sample of children from the first cohort to experience the new National Curriculum and its associated assessment procedures, we have explicitly attempted to document and analyse the impact of the legislation *from the pupil perspective*. Thus, irrespective of the intentions of the politicians, officials and other policy-makers, how were the new requirements actually experienced by pupils – the end-point consumers?

How did pupils perceive and experience the introduction of the National Curriculum and assessment?

We believe that this is an important question in its own right, for the period from age 5 to 11 is a phase of life which should have as much intrinsic quality and value as any other. Notwithstanding the legitimate case to be made, we argue that childhood should not simply be seen as a period of preparation for adulthood. Here, of course, we trigger a long-running debate about social and educational priorities. In terms of primary education, Blyth (1965) was among the first to contrast the 'traditions' of elementary and developmental education, which date from the 1800s and before. Reflecting the elementary tradition, the Education Act 1870 was intended to provide 'cheap and efficient' mass instruction in basic skills, and pressure for its introduction was underpinned by the workforce needs of manufacturing industry, the extension of the franchise and the perceived need to 'civilize' the working classes. In contrast, the developmental tradition of Rousseau, Pestalozzi, Froebel and others reached its zenith in the Plowden Report of 1967. 'Child centred education', or 'progressivism', reflected strong value commitments and considerable idealism which became transformed into a powerful professional ideology. This has, in the past twenty years, been the subject of successive rounds of critique and moral panic fostered by politicians, journalists and others.

As we argued in the first PACE book (Pollard *et al.*, 1994), these 'echoes of the past' still influence modern primary education. The goals of the Literacy and Numeracy Hours are a direct link to the elementary tradition prioritizing basic skills, albeit now updated to draw on modern understanding of teaching–learning processes and appropriate use of Information Technology. As is evident from the companion PACE volume on teachers (Osborn *et al.*, 2000), the developmental tradition can still be traced in the beliefs and value-commitments of many teachers who continue to prioritize their 'caring' role and to derive much personal pleasure from children's individual development and achievement. Indeed, the developmental tradition remains underpinned by the way in which 'childhood' is idealized and sentimentalized in English culture – despite the evidence that, for many young people, childhood is increasingly challenging.

As we have seen, the context in which the National Curriculum and assessment were introduced was characterized by a strong discourse linking education to international competitiveness and asserting its 'accountability'. Such concerns articulate closely with the elementary tradition and were reflected in the content and structure of the curriculum. Children's opinions were not sought, and there was no apparent awareness in government circles of children's rights (Alderson, 1999; Franklin, 1995). If it is accepted that children do have legitimate fundamental rights and that primary schooling is a period of life which should have intrinsic value and quality, then it is appropriate and necessary to ask hard questions about the consequences of the introduction of the National Curriculum from the perspective of children.

Did the introduction of the National Curriculum and assessment facilitate or undermine the development of positive pupil learning dispositions?

Our second concern in analysing our data and shaping the arguments within this book accepts the responsibility of primary education to prepare children for their future roles in modern society. For instance, we welcome the New Labour government's emphasis on 'lifelong learning' and pose the question of how primary education, following the introduction of the National Curriculum, contributes to the goal of a population which is positively disposed to learning throughout life. This is an important addendum to the basic skills agenda. Indeed, we may perhaps imagine literacy and numeracy being joined by the new goal of 'learnacy' (Claxton, 1999). We believe that a commitment to lifelong learning requires the identity of the learner to become deeply embedded in the curriculum and process of learning itself – a process which has been illustrated in the detail of young children's lives by Pollard with Filer (1996). In an increasingly complex society, successful lifelong learners need to be open, reflexive and resourceful. Their sense of self and of personal capability must therefore embrace these attributes and pupils' experience of schooling needs to foster them. Some, however, have identified a tension between this goal and the pressure to improve basic skills through direct instruction. Indeed, it is possible that the constraints of an over-prescriptive curriculum could actually undermine the development of independent thinking and a positive disposition to learn. For instance, Quicke (1999) draws attention to the 'reification of subjects, strong boundaries between courses and highly ritualised and hierarchical teacher–learner relationships' that characterize new National Curriculum provision. He argues that:

> Far from being involved personally, learners are confronted with an 'impersonal' subject, the 'ultimate mystery' of which can only be 'revealed' after an apprenticeship stretching long into the future, and attainable only by those who stay the course and can properly access the subject ... Pupil's approach is basically instrumental.
>
> (p. 12)

This is an issue of enormous significance because it raises the possibility of a deep fracture at the heart of education policy. Is the rhetoric of lifelong learning undermined by the reality of over-prescription in curriculum, pedagogy and assessment?

The present book has also been designed to illuminate a third, and broader, issue concerning the way in which childhood is structured within our society at the turn of the century.

What is the significance of recent education policy in terms of how children and childhood are understood in modern English society?

For millions of years humans have grown and learned, as Blyth (1984) put it, through the fundamental process of interaction between 'development' and 'experience'. Thus our biological make-up and our interaction, in the broadest sense, with our environment produces change and evolution. Any education system represents an intervention in this basic process by the decision-makers of a particular time and place. In so doing, their actions tell us a great deal about how childhood and children are perceived – in particular about beliefs concerning their nature, needs and value for both the present and the future.

The rapidly evolving sociology of childhood raises some important issues here. First, 'childhood' is seen as a structural and social form. Thus, whilst it clearly denotes a period of life for particular individuals; knowledge, practices and experiences of childhood must also be seen as being historically located and socio-culturally sustained. As Corsaro (1997) puts it:

> For children themselves, childhood is a temporary period. For society, childhood is a permanent structural form or category that never disappears even though its members change continuously and its nature and conception vary historically ... As a structural form, childhood is interrelated with other structural categories like social class, gender and age groups. Thus, the structural arrangements of these categories and changes in these arrangements will affect the nature of childhood.
>
> (pp. 4–5)

This is enormously important for in recent years there have been considerable changes and challenges in family structures, wealth, housing, health and other social arrangements in the UK and other Western societies. We need to understand pupils' school experiences in that context. However, the social form of modern English childhood has been changed enormously by the introduction of the National Curriculum and associated educational innovations. Never before has there been so much centralization and standardization in education policy across the country. Never before have there been such explicit attempts to define what children of particular ages should know, do and understand.

Because children are, literally, the human resource on which the future of the country depends, the provision which is made for them also says a lot about how a society perceives its own future. What then does the English National Curriculum say about our future? How do children perceive it, and which children does it benefit? Did the introduction of the National Curriculum really support the development of 'flexible, lifelong learners', or was it closer to a preparation for a low-pay, low-skill economy?

The sociology of childhood makes a fundamental assumption that children have 'agency' in relation to the world in which they live. They thus both construct their own cultures and contribute, in one way or another, to the production of the wider world. In one sense, this assumption underpins the whole of this book and our commitment to document pupil 'experience' and pupil 'voice'. The bulk of the book does this in relation to curriculum, relationships, assessment and learning, through the vehicle of quotations from our extensive database of pupil interview responses. Occasionally we also offer case-study vignettes which attempt to convey a more holistic view of children's lives.

1.7 THE STRUCTURE OF THE BOOK

The book has been structured into three parts:

Part 1, 'The Primary Assessment, Curriculum and Experience Project', of which this chapter is one element, introduces the context, aims, rationale, research questions, design and methods of the study. It thus frames and explains the nature of the PACE study as a whole, whilst also drawing attention to the particular goals of the present book. Chapter 2 provides many technical details on the research design and could be bypassed by readers keen to engage with our substantive results. However, strengths and weaknesses of our design are reflected in the book as a whole, so the chapter provides a helpful overview. Some further detailed methodological information is provided in Appendix 1.

Part 2, 'Classroom Change and Pupil Experience', is the substantive core of the book. We describe and analyse our findings thematically and try to provide a cumulative demonstration of how key issues in pupil experience interpolate their perspectives.

Chapter 3 aims to establish the major characteristics of the classrooms of the early and mid-1990s in which children were expected to work and learn. What was the pattern of curricula requirements? How did teachers teach? What was the effect of new assessment procedures? To answer these questions we draw on some of the major findings from our companion volume on teachers (Osborn *et al.*, 2000) and we then review six years of systematic observation data on pupil behaviour and experiences in classrooms. These data are related to work by other researchers to construct an overall picture of 'what had to be coped with' by pupils in these classrooms.

Chapters 4–10 then present a thematically-based analysis of the full range of PACE data on pupil perspectives. These chapters range from pupil views of curriculum subjects to their more general criteria for evaluating the curriculum; from perspectives on teacher–pupil relationships to views on teacher aims and expectations; from pupil perceptions on classroom assessment to their experiences of SATs. In all cases, they consider the issue of children's learning and attempt to trace how pupils' classroom experiences may enhance or constrain learning. Chapter 9 focuses specifically on pupils' views on their own learning. The logic of these chapters is that they cover the substantive ground of curriculum, pedagogy and assessment – the three 'message systems' that Bernstein identified in educational practice as reflections of dominant educational ideologies and codes (Bernstein, 1975, 1996). However, we address them with particular awareness of their implications for learning.

Chapter 11 provides some illustrative, integrative case-studies of pupils and classroom processes. It thus offers a more holistic insight into the effects of the patterns and practices that have been identified in previous chapters.

Part 3 of the book, 'Research Questions Revisited', takes stock of the findings and significance of the study as a whole in relation to pupil learning and experience. Chapter 12 offers a concise summary of the substantive findings of both this book and its companion volume, and begins to theorize these results and relate them to other research. The strength of instrumentalism in children's approach to learning, and the lack of deeper, intrinsic forms of engagement, are particularly commented upon. Chapter 13 explores how our findings articulate with other social psychological work on learning. In so doing, particular attention is drawn to the effect of schooling on the development of learning disposition and engagement as a 'lifelong learner'. A constructive critique of government policy is offered, and reference is made to the insights of an associated ethnographic study, the *Identity and Learning Programme*. Finally, in Chapter 14, readers are invited to stand right back from the detail of the PACE study and to take stock. Are, we ask, present patterns of childhood and schooling really desirable? How, we challenge, should we educate our children for the future?

1.8 CONCLUSION

The last decade has seen considerable struggle over educational values, under-standings of teaching and learning, and over the exercise of power. Successive governments have challenged the teaching profession and have, by and large, been successful in bringing about system-wide change. In the late 1990s there were some popular successes – most notably rising attainment as measured by SAT scores in the core curriculum. However, along the way there has also been considerable teacher stress, an overloaded curriculum, the introduction of centralized assessment and inspection systems, and subtle changes in the nature of teachers' professional commitment.

The PACE project was not just concerned with policy change. Nor was it simply about pupils' or teachers' experiences within classrooms. Rather, it concerned the relationship between policy and experience; the ways in which the 'reformed' education system, its schools, curricula, pedagogies and assessments, impacted on and shaped the subjective, lived experience of teachers and children. Our companion volume analyses the consequences of the introduction of the National Curriculum and assessment as it affected primary school teachers. Given the stresses produced, it poses the core question of whether, when the dust eventually settles, it will all have been worth it.

The present volume on pupils has a similar purpose. Throughout the 1990s, children have continued to make sense of their schooling in relatively pragmatic and instrumental ways, as perhaps they have always done. But, we must ask whether this is good enough in the world of the twenty-first century. Could the introduction of more structure and prescription into curriculum, pedagogy and assessment have had the unintended consequence of reinforcing poor pupil motivation and undermining commitment to lifelong learning?

Chapter 2

Research Design and Data-Gathering Methods

2.1   Introduction
2.2   The data-gathering schedule
2.3   The national sample of schools, classrooms, teachers and pupils
2.4   The advance questionnaire to teachers
2.5   Structured interviews with teachers
2.6   Classroom studies
2.7   Assessment studies
2.8   Statistical analysis
2.9   Doing research as a collaborative team
2.10 Conclusion

2.1 INTRODUCTION

This chapter outlines the research design of the PACE project and its implementation over the eight years of the project's duration from 1989 to 1997. It considers some of the methodological challenges which emerged, together with the ways in which the team attempted to resolve them. In the concluding part of the chapter we discuss some of the issues which arose as part of the collaborative work of a team of five researchers over such a considerable period of time.

As we saw in Chapter 1, PACE aimed to monitor the impact of the curricular and assessment structures introduced by the Education Reform Act 1988 for primary schools, teachers and pupils. There was a particular focus on teacher and pupil perspectives and on classroom practices and experiences, though we also gathered data on school policies and management. In developing our research design we were considerably helped by Bernstein's conceptualization of three educational 'message systems' – curriculum, pedagogy and assessment. He argues that these message systems convey the 'education codes' of their particular society (Bernstein, 1975,

1990, 1996) and thus signify values, priorities and understandings. Table 2.1 represents our design embracing national policy, school contexts and classroom contexts, with our particular focus on teachers and pupils and on curriculum, pedagogy and assessment.

Table 2.1 Research design: data to be gathered

The national policy context
↓
The local government context
↓
Change and experience in the school context
↓
Change and experience in the classroom context

	Teachers	Pupils
Curriculum		
Pedagogy		
Assessment		

The particular focus of the project was a sample of children drawn from the first cohort of children to experience the National Curriculum from the beginning of their schooling in the Year 1 class throughout their primary school careers until the end of Year 6 at age 11. These children were studied from Year 1 onwards, together with their class teachers and headteachers. The design of the research had to take into account the complexity of changes being introduced at every stage and the need to obtain a variety of data from different sources. The design also had to allow for continued analysis of the themes outlined in the introduction of curriculum and pedagogy, assessment, pupil experience and teacher professionalism and, at each phase of the research, to build on existing sources of data from the earlier phases.

As we discussed in the Chapter 1, the project was wide-ranging from the start and it became even more complex as the phenomenon of almost continuous educational change evolved in the 1990s. A considerable variety of data collection procedures were used in the research in an attempt to capture the processes involved in multiple innovation (Wallace, 1991). Over the eight years of the study personal interviews with headteachers, teachers and children were one of the most important sources of data. These included both open-ended and structured questions. The early interviews with children included special techniques of 'embedded interviews' involving visual stimuli and discussion of activities which the researcher had observed earlier (Pollard *et al.*, 1994). Self-completion questionnaires were used with teachers in order to collect demographic and career data and also for attitude scales and similar data. Other procedures included observation in classrooms using both systematic, quantitative procedures and qualitative approaches with open-ended or partially structured field-notes. Sociometric data on children's friendship patterns and tape-recordings of teachers' interactions with children were also collected. These methods are described in more detail in later sections of this chapter.

Throughout the three phases of the study the major priority was to map the educational experiences of a pupil cohort as they developed within the new structures. The core of the PACE study was thus a longitudinal study of 54 children from nine schools drawn from across England as they moved through their schools. These children, their classrooms and teachers were studied in some detail over the years. However, to meet the objectives of the PACE study we needed to balance the need for a highly detailed study of children's and teachers' experience of the National Curriculum and assessment with the desirability of also having representative data from a broader sample. The nine classroom study schools were therefore embedded in a larger sample of schools drawn from across the country in which a larger number of teachers and headteachers were interviewed.

Since the longitudinal element was designed with the aim of following, as far as was possible, the same children throughout their primary school experience, the focus on their teachers was on a largely different population over the course of the study. In each round of interviews we talked to teachers of the year groups in which our target children were currently placed. This design enabled us to chart teacher perspectives throughout the primary school during this period of rapid, multiple change. However, we needed a cross-sectional element in the study in order to examine change in teacher perspectives. Therefore, during PACE 2 we returned to the same schools to interview a sample of Key Stage 1 teachers two years on, so that comparisons could be made between teacher perspectives in 1992 and 1994. We were also fortunate in that a number of teachers in the sample stayed with their pupils for several years as they moved through the primary school. This made possible several qualitative case-studies of individual teachers which analysed changes in perspectives as the reforms moved into successive phases (Osborn, 1996a, 1996b; Osborn *et al.*, 1997).

Regarding the tracking of change over a longer period, we designed many of our research instruments so that our new, post-ERA data on classroom practice in primary schools would be broadly comparable with earlier studies such as the ORACLE research (Galton *et al.*, 1980), the Junior Schools Project (Mortimore *et al.*, 1988) and the Bristaix project (Broadfoot *et al.*, 1993). The latter project was based on comparisons between teachers in France and England regarding their views of professional responsibilities in the mid-1980s. During the 1990s further international comparisons were made possible by a directly comparable project which used the PACE teacher data together with questionnaires and interviews with teachers in France, following recent policy reforms (Broadfoot *et al.*, 1996). Similarly, regarding pupils, our work was enhanced by other, parallel studies by members of the team. In particular, Pollard and Filer's longitudinal ethnography of children from age 4 to 16, with its foci on learning (Pollard with Filer, 1996), strategic biographies (Pollard and Filer, 1999) and assessment (Filer and Pollard, 2000) have provided insights for our interpretation of PACE data. In PACE 1 and 2 we specifically developed a 'federated network' of related research projects. This enabled us to link into other studies on the impact of the National Curriculum being conducted by researchers, some of whom were working alone in smaller-scale studies. The PACE study aimed to provide a broader contextualization for some of these other studies through ongoing debate and exchange of papers, together with a linkage at the level of findings. As such work on the initial implementation of the ERA was completed and published, we focused more on interpretation of our own data.

The PACE project was thus designed to track pupil experiences and monitor change on a very wide front, though not least amongst the project aims was the concern to analyse and theorize the new developments. Whilst taking the view that all social science is inevitably somewhat inexact, our task has nevertheless been to gather data as carefully as we can and to analyse it to provide a meaningful interpretation of developments since the Education Reform Act 1988. This will, we hope, have as much policy-relevance for government as it does for teachers.

In the sections of this chapter which follow, we provide more details on data-gathering methods, beginning with an outline of the data-gathering schedule and an explanation of how our national sample of schools was drawn.

2.2 THE DATA-GATHERING SCHEDULE

The study was organized in three phases: PACE 1 from October 1989 to December 1992, PACE 2 from January 1993 to December 1994, and PACE 3 from January 1995 to August 1997. This made it possible to request funding within the relatively limited budget of the Economic and Social Research Council (ESRC) research grants scheme. Some of the problems which arose for the team because of the need to obtain funding in this way are discussed in the concluding section of this chapter.

The major phases of data-collection are shown in Figure 2.1 which provides an overview and illustrates both the longitudinal and cross-sectional features of the research design.

In each phase of the project there were two rounds of interviews and questionnaires to a large sample of teachers, and two rounds of classroom and assessment studies using multiple data-gathering methods.

2.3 THE NATIONAL SAMPLE OF SCHOOLS, CLASSROOMS, TEACHERS AND PUPILS

Through careful sampling design the study aimed to provide data which was broadly representative of schools, teachers and pupils across the whole of England. At its most general level our analysis was derived from 150 teachers and headteachers in 48 schools in eight English local education authorities. At its more specific level it was based on the perspectives and practices of nine teachers for each year of the study (54 classrooms and teachers being reported over the whole study) and six children in each school moving through their primary school careers in those classrooms (a total of 54 pupils). Given the enormous national significance of the innovation being studied, and not least its cost, it would have been desirable to have a larger sample. However, given this impossibility and the scarcity of funding for educational research, we took steps to attempt to ensure that our sample represented a full range of primary school practices and circumstances.

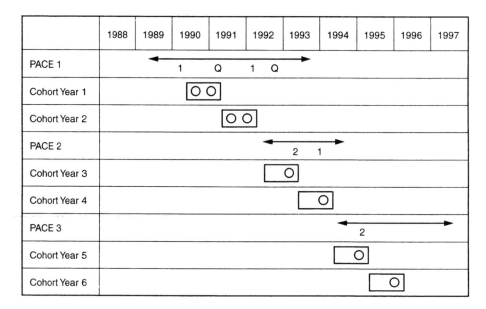

O　Classroom or assessment studies
1　Key Stage 1 teacher and headteacher questionnaires and interviews
2　Key Stage 2 teacher and headteacher questionnaires and interviews
Q　Questionnaires on assessment to teachers and headteachers

Figure 2.1 Major phases of data-gathering

The main LEA and school sample

An initial strategy, following ESRC advice, was to sample in local education authorities which were regarded as having 'positive support structures' for the implementation of the National Curriculum. A comparison of different types of support at LEA level was not one of the project's aims and it was felt this strategy could reduce some extraneous variables from our data-gathering. After consultation with HMI and others we identified eight such LEAs, aiming for a balance in terms of socio-economic factors, urban/rural areas and a geographical spread in the north, Midlands, south-east and south-west of England, as well as making some allowances for ease of access. The chief education officer in each LEA was approached in the first instance for permission to carry out the research in their authority and, with permission obtained, local primary inspectors were designated as liaison officers.

To identify schools within each local education authority, a random sample of twenty infant schools or departments was drawn from a sector of the LEA which had been nominated by local advisers as being broadly representative of the LEA as a whole. From each of these lists, six schools were then selected to reflect different socio-economic locations and distinctive features such as religious denomination or styles of internal organization. Overall, in producing the final selection of 48 schools, the aim was to obtain a sample that encompassed the considerable variety of educational approaches that currently exist within primary schools. Schools with separate infant departments and schools where infant and junior sections were integrated were both chosen in order to explore any differences which these organizational variations might have produced. Infant schools which were not attached to any one junior school were excluded in order to ensure the capacity for longitudinal study.

The sample schools were classified broadly in terms of location and social class and this is shown in Table 2.2.

Table 2.2 Sample schools by location and predominant social class of local communities

	Number	Percentage
Rural, mixed social class	9	19
Urban, settled working/lower middle-class	13	27
Inner city, deprived working-class	15	31
Urban/suburban middle-class	7	15
Urban, mixed social class	4	8
Total	48	100

The spread of the sample in terms of school size was as follows:

Table 2.3 Sample schools by size

Number on roll	Number	Percentage
Under 150	12	25
151–350	29	60
351–650	7	15
Total	48	100

When, at the end of PACE 2, the target pupils left infant schools to move into separate junior schools an additional sample of 20 schools was generated. These were in the same broad socio-economic catchment areas as their linked infant schools.

The school sub-sample

In the light of analysis of data collected from the advance questionnaire and first round of interviews, a sub-sample of nine schools was selected for more detailed and observational study in our 'classroom studies' and 'assessment studies'. Two of these schools were in a relatively accessible area for the research team and one was in each of the other LEAs. We attempted to achieve a school sub-sample reflecting the range of socio-economic circumstances, school size and responses to change which we had found, but it cannot be claimed to be strictly representative. Negotiations regarding access moderated our initial selection to avoid problems such as major building works and staff illness. The result was that our final sub-sample was not quite as well-balanced as had been hoped. For example, both small rural schools and Roman Catholic schools were over-represented in terms of their occurrence nationally.

Nevertheless, the sub-sample schools did, we feel, reflect most of the common characteristics and circumstances of English primary schools. Brief details of the sub-sample schools are as follows:

St Bede's was a Roman Catholic Primary school of 230 pupils in an established suburb of a medium-sized city in the south of England. It opened in the early 1970s and was built to a single-storey open-plan design around a central courtyard which had recently been developed with the help of the PTA into an environmental area with plants and a pond. Inside the building dividing walls had been gradually added to mask classes from noise coming from cloakrooms and corridors which were also used as teaching spaces. Outside there was a large playground with climbing apparatus, grass and trees. As a denominational school it had a wide catchment area and children were bussed to and fro each day. The school had close links with the local parish and the parish priest was a frequent visitor. It was popular with parents. The approach was fairly traditional – pupils were organized in year groups, routines and values were clearly established and the ethos was cohesive. Most children wore school uniform. The school was led by a strong, experienced (female) headteacher and the atmosphere in the staffroom was noisy and good humoured.

Kenwood Infant School was situated in very similar surroundings in the same city as St Bede's. It was built early this century and was set in a concrete playground, relieved by a new nature area. It had a well-stocked library and resource rooms. There was an emphasis on good behaviour and on making progress, and considerable effort was made to involve children in planning their own work. Children transferred to the nearby Kenwood Junior School at age 7. Like the infant school this was a large and somewhat rambling urban school situated on an estate which was mainly council houses but with some private housing. The school also served families from surrounding areas of private terraced housing. The 331 children, organized in year groups, were mostly from white working-class families. There were very firm school structures in place with strong central control emanating from the (male) headteacher and a tightly defined timetable. Staff turnover was very rapid reflecting the conflict which existed between the staff and the headteacher. A new (male) head was appointed in Year 6 of the project.

Meadway First School was an open-plan single-storey primary school built in the 1970s. It was set in a metropolitan inner-city housing estate and was surrounded by high-rise blocks of flats. The area suffered from high unemployment, significant crime rates and considerable vandalism. The school was light, airy and attractively decorated with children's work and other displays, and its pupils and staff reflected the multi-ethnic character of the local community. Amongst the teachers there was a high degree of joint planning, but their efforts often had to be directed towards the behavioural needs of the children. Ancillary support staff were provided to help with this.

During the course of the project, the LEA reorganized its schools from first/middle/secondary to primary/secondary. As a consequence, the pupils in our sample moved in Year 3 to Meadway Junior (previously a middle school) where the staff, led by a very long-standing and experienced (female) head, was also ethnically mixed. This school, located only a few yards from the infants, occupied two large Victorian red-brick buildings beside the road and shared an adjacent games field. Pupils in

Years 3 and 4 (the Lower School) were taught in one building and Years 5 and 6 (the Upper School) were taught in the other. At the time of the study there were 235 pupils on roll which was below capacity and allowed spare rooms to be used for a variety of purposes. There was a strong emphasis on behaviour, effort and achievement and a very public reward system. The pedagogy tended to be teacher-centred, and behaviour was often challenging. 50 per cent of the pupils had special needs statements. There were support staff for both special educational needs and English as a Second Language. The school made considerable efforts to involve parents in its work.

Greenmantle Primary School was located in a market town in central southern England where traditional agricultural occupations coexisted with modern light industry. Its buildings were a mixture of Victorian and newer architecture with a scatter of temporary classrooms. The playground, though small, had plenty to interest the children. Most of the 270 children lived in the town or close by. The school was popular locally and a high proportion of the pupils had prosperous, professional family backgrounds. It acquired grant maintained status during the project. Pupils were organized in mixed-age classes throughout; teaching methods were fairly traditional and with a good deal of positive reinforcement. In Years 5 and 6 the model was semi-secondary: pupils from three classes were set for Mathematics, English and PE; for some other subjects they were taught by 'specialists' from the three teachers. The school was led by a strong (male) headteacher and a supportive deputy (also male).

St Anne's was a Roman Catholic primary school in one of the country's least affluent LEAs in the north of England. The school population of 270 pupils (plus a nursery class) was drawn from a large council estate of very disadvantaged families. There was a high take-up of free school meals. Many parents were unemployed and some children were on the 'at risk' register or closely supported by social services. Some were living with extended family members – grandmothers, relatives or friends – rather than with their own families. The school had a caring, close-knit family ethos, deriving in part from its Roman Catholic philosophy. This provided a stabilizing influence which, in the early years of the study, was reinforced by daily visits by the local priest and by the assemblies led by the (male) headteacher who had grown up in the city.

Although the school was in a highly disadvantaged area, its surroundings were not unpleasant. The main building was between 40 and 50 years old and had a new wing which was attached to the Catholic church next door. It was surrounded by a concrete playground, but behind this were large green playing fields and trees which belonged to the Catholic comprehensive which many of the children would eventually attend. Unusually, pupils in the study were taught by male teachers for five of the six years. Classes in Key Stage 2 were mixed-age, with high achievers taught with older pupils. Teaching at Key Stage 1 was normally fairly structured around particular 'topics', while allowing for pupil choice of activities for part of each day. At Key Stage 2 lessons were structured by the subject timetable with strong teacher direction and little choice of activity for pupils.

Orchard was a small rural primary school of 116 pupils located in a pleasant village in central England. The school was an attractive purpose-built modern building, surrounded by trees and fields. During the course of the study an extension housing a new library and other facilities was added. The school was very popular amongst local parents who were mainly employed in the professions, business and farming. Because of its reputation, built up by the (female) head who led the school when the study started, children were drawn from a wider area of neighbouring villages and were either bussed in or driven to and from school by parents. Parental expectations were high and pupils were well-motivated. Because of the school's small size, all the children were in mixed-age classes, some of these spanning three year groups. The three class teachers, all female, had considerable classroom autonomy and teaching methods were varied. Both the staff and the headteacher knew the children's families well, and the relationship between home and school was relatively close. During the course of the study there was a change of headship and a new (male) headteacher, who had been a deputy in a neighbouring school, took over. The school continued to enjoy a high reputation in the local community.

Lawnside Primary School was set in a village near a large Midlands conurbation. The population consisted of a mixture of commuters and local families with agricultural connections. The school was opened in the 1930s and conditions were cramped with a small original building, a brick structure and temporary classrooms. During the course of the project a new school was built on the site which pupils and teachers moved into at the beginning of school year 1995. In Year 6, at the move, the school population was 186 with a planned expansion to 500, including a nursery. Pupils came from the immediate locality but were also brought by car from the surrounding area. Children eligible for free school meals or with special educational needs were in single figures. All children had English as a first language. The school was welcoming and provided for a number of travellers' children from a nearby site. Pupils were taught in mixed-age classes spanning two years; all those in the study were taught by female teachers. The long-standing (male) head had led the school's expansion. The ethos was caring and structured. School uniform was almost universally worn and parents were supportive.

Valley was another rural school set in a traditional village in the south-west of England. The core of the school was stone-built Victorian but there were modern extensions and two portable classrooms and good facilities. The school had a small playground, imaginatively equipped, a netball pitch and a large playing field. It had a strong Christian ethos and close relationship with the village church and rector. The local population was a socio-economic mixture including local farming families and professional people who worked in nearby small towns. The school attracted its 111 pupils from largely middle-class and professional backgrounds from the village and the surrounding area. The level of support was high and parents and other local residents acted as adult helpers. Uniform was limited to a sweatshirt. The school was led by an experienced (female) teaching head who shared a class of pupils in Years 4 to 6 with a part-time teacher. The small, all-female staff worked closely together and teaching methods were eclectic.

Audley Infant School was built between the wars. It was somewhat overcrowded but busy and well-resourced. The location was an industrial village in the north-west where there was little unemployment compared with the surrounding area. Nevertheless, few local people were particularly affluent. There was a fairly high degree of teacher control, but children were allowed a degree of freedom within tasks. Children transferred to the neighbouring Audley Junior School at age 7. Audley Juniors amalgamated with the infants' school in Year 5 of the project to form a new primary school. The amalgamation was associated with a period of disruption and uncertainty over staffing. In Year 6, as well as the head (male) and deputy the school had nine teachers, with one exception, all female. The school was housed in an old Victorian building with a tarmac yard front and back and a small playing field. It had a mixed social intake of 207 pupils plus a nursery, drawing the children mainly from lower-middle and working-class families. The curriculum was taught mostly as separate subjects.

All schools and LEAs were provided with outlines of the project's aims, design and ethical guidelines. As the project progressed they received project newsletters and occasional papers and eventually copies of the books. They were also aware that ongoing findings were being disseminated to policy-makers and that the research might have an influence on the review of the National Curriculum which took place in the latter phases of the research. At a time when they had so many other demands and pressures on their time it is particularly remarkable that none of the schools wanted to withdraw from the project. We have been grateful for the very high degree of support and cooperation which they have offered. Pseudonyms are, of course, used in this book for all LEAs, schools, teachers and pupils.

The pupil sample

In each year of the study we focused our observation and interviews on six children from one class in each of the nine schools – 54 pupils per year. These children were initially selected by relating a list of random numbers to each class list. However, there was some turnover of sample pupils from year to year, either because of family mobility or pupil absence from school during the particular annual period of our data-gathering, and this effect was particularly marked in Years 1 and 2. In such circumstances the targeted pupil was replaced by a child of the same sex, and as similar as possible in terms of socio-economic background and attainment. In phases two and three of the project, where possible, gaps were filled by pupils previously in the sample to maintain the longitudinal data set. Overall, of the original 54 children, we have data for four or more years for 49 of the total sample (see Appendix 3), and these children account for 74 per cent of our total of observations and interviews.

In total 87 children, 43 boys and 44 girls, participated in the study as target pupils for observation and interview over the six-year period. Of these children, 54 per cent of the total sample were drawn from families in which the wage-earner was in a skilled or non-skilled manual occupation, with 46 per cent being non-manual. Ninety-three per cent were White. Six UK-born Black children participated in the study over the period, five of whom were from Meadway. Overall teacher ratings classified 7% of the sample as being of 'low' attainment, 16% 'below average', 32% 'average', 29% 'above average' and 15% 'high', and this distribution was broadly confirmed by SAT scores in both Year 2 and Year 6.

Many other children were interviewed in relation to SATs. For instance, in Years

2 and 6 over 100 interviews were conducted. In Year 6, in each school the six target pupils were interviewed plus six other pupils identified as higher and lower achievers. In addition, in Year 6 almost 270 'SAT Story' comic strips were completed by pupils from the classes being studied (see p. 39 for further details).

In the following sections we discuss sampling methods in more detail with regard to each method of data-gathering. We begin with a brief description of our methods for gathering data from teachers, further detail on which is available in the companion PACE volume (Osborn *et al.*, 2000).

2.4 THE ADVANCE QUESTIONNAIRE TO TEACHERS

During the three phases of the study there were four rounds of questionnaire surveys of the teachers and headteachers in our main sample of 48 schools.

In 1990 an initial 'advance questionnaire' was distributed by post to the main sample of 48 schools. This was designed to gather evidence of headteacher and class teacher perceptions on topics such as accountability, professional responsibility and educational aims as well as providing background information on age, gender, length of teaching experience and so on. In the first instance, questionnaires were completed by headteachers and by teachers of reception and Year 1 classes since the children who would later form the cohort to be studied were at that time in reception classes. For cross-sectional comparative purposes, identical questionnaires were again distributed and completed two years later, in the Summer Term, 1992 when heads and teachers of Year 1 and Year 2 classes took part. Questionnaires were distributed again at the beginning of PACE 2 to teachers of Years 3 and 4 and their headteachers and, finally, at the beginning of PACE 3 to teachers of Years 4, 5 and 6 and their headteachers. The inclusion of Year 4 teachers once again was designed to provide a cross-sectional comparison.

2.5 STRUCTURED INTERVIEWS WITH TEACHERS

Overall, five rounds of interviews took place with the teachers and headteachers in our 48 schools. First, in the same 48 primary schools, a round of interviews was conducted in the Summer Term, 1990. In each school, the headteacher, the teacher of the reception class and a Year 1 infant teacher took part. The interviews, which took approximately one hour, were based on a structured schedule, but many questions were open-ended and exploratory. They aimed to explore staff perceptions of the impact of National Curriculum requirements on their own work and on the life of the school as a whole.

The main areas of discussion were:

- Headteachers' perceptions of the changes needed and their strategies for providing for these.
- Teachers' perceptions of the impact of National Curriculum and assessment

arrangements on the curriculum and pedagogy of the school as a whole and of their own individual classrooms.

- Perceived changes in pupils' responses to schooling both in their attitudes and in their learning.
- Teachers' responses to the preparation they had been given to help them meet the novel requirements being placed upon them.

Similar interviews and questionnaires were again completed two years later in the Summer Term, 1992 when headteachers and teachers of Year 1 and Year 2 classes took part. The core of the interviews remained unchanged to make it possible to trace changes taking place in teachers' perceptions during the study period. Further rounds of interviewing took place in summer of 1993 with teachers of Years 3 and 4 and their headteachers; in 1994 when we revisited the Key Stage 1 teachers in order to provide for direct cross-sectional comparison; and in the autumn of 1995 and early 1996 when we interviewed Year 4, 5, and 6 teachers.

2.6 CLASSROOM STUDIES

Detailed case-studies of individual classrooms from the nine case-study schools provided the next element of data-collection. These began in the Year 1 classrooms in 1990 and continued every year through Years 2 to 5, ending after we had studied the Year 6 classrooms in 1996.

All the sub-sample classrooms selected for closer study were visited for a full week during each successive year. This phase of the research included gathering of documentary evidence, qualitative observation, systematic observation and interviews with pupils and teachers. The research focused primarily on curriculum and pedagogy whilst assessment processes, although observed and recorded, were the prime focus for a separate element of the study. This is discussed in section 2.7.

When the sample school and class had been identified according to the criteria discussed earlier and cooperation had been agreed, the headteacher and class teacher were sent an overview of the week's data-collection plan (see Figure 2.2). Six children from each of the nine classrooms were sampled (see p. 27 for more details).

The classroom study data-collection plan set up a schedule for each day, which provided blocks of time for particular types of data-gathering and ensured efficient sequencing of the process. Prior to the visit by a member of the research team, each teacher was asked to provide copies of key documents: the class list, a curriculum plan and sociometric data collected from all the children in the class. The latter, and each of the other major data-gathering methods used in the classroom studies, are described in more detail below.

Sociometry

Each child was asked to write the names of three friends within her/his own class on a sheet specially designed for this purpose. These were later used to complete a sociometric grid showing children's friendship patterns and group membership.

| In advance | *Ask for:* | Class list
Curriculum plan
Sociometry | |
| | *Give:* | Overview of research intentions for week | |

During week	a.m.	p.m.	Other
Monday	Field notes	Teacher interview Field notes	In evening: analyse sociometric data, consider friendships in relation to pen sketches
Tuesday	Teacher audio-recording Systematic observation of two children and teacher (child A + B + teacher)	Two child interviews (A + B) Systematic observation of two children and teacher (child C + D + teacher)	
Wednesday	Recording and observation as Tuesday (child C + D + teacher)	Interviews with child C + D Observation as Tuesday	Over lunch etc. on Tuesday, Wednesday and Thursday: hold general discussions with teacher
Thursday	Recording and observation as Tuesday (child E + F + teacher)	Interviews with child E + F Observation as Tuesday (child A + B + teacher)	
Friday	Field notes Contingency time	Teacher interview	

Figure 2.2 The classroom studies timetable

Field notes

Field notes were relatively open-ended. The aims were to provide a rich and detailed account of the various routine procedures and phases of a school day and, at other times in the week, to record any particularly interesting or theoretically significant events, statements or activities.

Systematic observation

Systematic observation was carried out during the mornings and afternoons of the three central days of the week of classroom study so that a wide spread of activities could be observed. Break times were not observed. Each of the six 'target children' in each class was observed during both a morning and an afternoon and a rotational system was used to focus successive periods of observation on target children and the teacher. Observations were recorded on coding forms relating to a ten-minute period (see Figure 2.3). Six minutes of systematic observation, using a ten-second interval, were followed by four minutes of contextualizing notes.

When focusing on the teacher, the observer coded 'child interaction' and 'teacher activity' simultaneously at ten-second intervals.

When a pupil was being observed, the observer coded 'child activity' and 'interaction' at all ten-second intervals. 'Teacher activity' was recorded only when the target child was directly interacting with the teacher or with another adult.

The sheet also carried a list of 'curriculum context' categories – English, Maths, etc. – and another of 'pedagogic context', including class teaching and individual and group work. These were recorded at the end of each six-minute observation period in terms of the 'main' or 'part' aspects of the curriculum and pedagogic context. Where more than one curriculum context or pedagogic context had been observed, both 'main' and 'part' were used. More qualitative contextualizing notes were completed immediately after the timed recording and these were structured by the headings of curriculum, pedagogy, interactions/relationships, assessment, other/general.

Child interviews

Each target child was individually interviewed following the period during which they had been a focus for classroom observation. The aim here was to complement observational data with material on pupil perspectives so that explanatory analyses could be attempted. These interviews provided the major source of the data reported in this book.

Child interview questions were structured and covered the following areas:

- Discussion of an observed curriculum task in which they had participated
- Views of curriculum subjects
- Child culture and friendships
- Views of curricular activities
- Views on pupil control
- Views on hierarchy in achievement
- Views on teacher assessment and responses
- Views on relationships with the teacher

This framework of topics was sustained throughout the project, whilst the children aged from 6 to 11 years old. However, there was some minor adjustment to the wording or technique of posing questions. Thus 'views of curriculum subjects' was

Figure 2.3 A child observation schedule

Note: teacher observation sheets contained no 'child activity' categories and listed 'teacher interaction' rather than 'child interaction'

PACE CHILD OBSERVATION

Observer	Teacher	Pupil year	LEA
....	....	....	....

Target child	Pupil code	Time	Date
....	....	....	...../...../.....

Child activity

Child interaction

Teacher activity

Child activity

Child interaction

Teacher activity

CHILD ACTIVITY		CHILD INTERACTION		TEACHER ACTIVITY	
TE	Task engagement (apparent)	O	Alone	I	Instruction (curriculum)
TM	Task management	TC	With teacher in whole class	C	Control (behaviour)
D	Distracted	TO	With teacher in one-to-one	D	Direction (task management)
B	Both distracted and TM	TG	With teacher in group	A	Assessment (explicit)
A	Assessment (explicit)	AO	With other adult one-to-one	E	Encouragement (support, facilitating)
W	Waiting for teacher	G	With individual girl		
X	Waiting (other)	B	With individual boy	N	Negative (discouragement, criticism)
O	Out of room/sight	X	With a group of boys		
R.	Reading to teacher	Y	With a group of girls	R	Hearing children read
		M	With a mixed group	O	Other

PEDAGOGIC CONTEXT

	Main	Part
Class teaching		
Individual work		
Co-operative group work		
Group with teacher		
Other (specify)		

CURRICULUM CONTEXT

	Main	Part
RE		
English		
Maths		
Science		
History		
Geography		
Music		
Art		
Physical Education		
Technology		
Personal and social		
Non-curriculum		

Observer	Teacher	Class	LEA	Date	Target Child	Time
☐	☐	☐	☐	☐☐☐☐☐	☐	☐☐☐

NOTES:

Notes to yourself where necessary

Curriculum
Classification
(strength of subject boundaries)

Pedagogy
Framing
(control over pacing and organisation of tasks)

Interactions/Relationships

Assessment

Other/General

approached in a very open-ended way at Key Stage 1 and was made more structured for Key Stage 2. Occasionally new questions were introduced, particularly in PACE 3 when we sought to generate pupil narratives on learning and assessment experiences.

In the early stages of the project the children interviewed were very young – mostly aged 6 – and it was particularly important to establish and maintain rapport and interest. If necessary, interviewers would thus rephrase questions and if the child appeared to lose concentration break off and complete the interview later. Most children appeared to enjoy the interviews and throughout the study many requests for interview were received from children not in the sub-sample.

To begin each interview an attempt was made to embed the interviews in pupils' immediate experience. Thus for the first questions the researcher and the child discussed some work produced during a classroom activity which had been observed earlier. Children were then asked whether they felt the activity was enjoyable and the reasons for their judgement, and what they saw as the teacher's reasons for giving them the activity. Pupils were also probed on the topic of engagement and distraction in relation to school work. Thus, the questions posed included:

- Could you tell me about what you were doing?
- Did you like doing it?
- Why is that?
- Why do you think your teacher wanted you to do it?
- When you are working at something like that and you seem to be concentrating, are you sometimes really thinking about other things?

The children were asked for their views of their own attainment at major curriculum activities – reading, writing, Mathematics, Science – to which they responded in terms of 'good/OK/not so good'. This section of the interview concluded with:

- Are you particularly good at other things in school? If so, what are they?
- Why do you think you are so good at those things?
- Are there things which you don't think you are very good at? If so, what are they?
- Why do you think you are not so good at those things?

The next set of questions referred to child culture, polarization, stigma and views of self. While the children were in Years 1 to 3, for orientation purposes they were shown the illustration of a playground scene on the cover of the Puffin book *Please, Mrs Butler* by Allan Ahlberg (1984). This shows clearly discernible friendship groups and typical playground activities. Children were then asked to confirm their friendships, to describe activities in their playground and school and explain more about their peer relationships. The questions posed included:

- I think you are friendly with … aren't you? (pre-prepared from sociometric data)
- What sorts of things do children in your class do in the playground?
- Which sorts of things do you like doing best in the playground?
- What sorts of things do you like doing best out of school?
- Are there any children in your class who you don't like playing with, or do you enjoy playing with all of them? Can you tell me why that is?
- Do you think other children like playing with you? Why do (or don't) they like to play with you?

- Are there children in your class who you particularly like to work with? Can you tell me why that is?
- During this year, have you been involved in the school in any special ways?

Further questions in PACE 1 were based around a picture book which the PACE team had produced. Again this was an attempt to embed the interview in contexts which would be familiar to the children, in this case discussion of a picture book. The book began with a double-page collage of bright illustrations of children engaged in twelve different classroom activities, derived from the Ahlbergs' Picture Puffin *Starting School* (Ahlberg and Ahlberg, 1988). The activities shown varied from core curriculum subjects to expressive areas and children were asked about their curricular likes and dislikes and the reasons for these.

These questions were followed by others on pupil and teacher control of classroom activities. Other illustrations, some commissioned for the study, were used to stimulate pupils' responses to questions on differences in attainment at school and to elicit views on hierarchy in achievement.

To examine children's views on aspects of teacher assessment, an illustration was used of a teacher talking to a child about his work. The feelings of the child in the picture were discussed. Children were then asked about their own feelings when the teacher looked at their work and about teachers' responses to their work. The last questions in the child interview dealt with children's views on their teacher and relationships with her or him. Another picture from *Starting School* was used showing a whole class sitting with a teacher and children were asked how they got on with, and what they liked best about, their teacher.

As the children grew older, and particularly in Years 5 and 6, interviewers made less use of embedded techniques and more of direct discussion. For instance, views on the frequency of different curricular activities were collected by asking pupils to indicate 'a lot', 'a bit' or 'not much' to a list covering a wide range of common classroom activities. The preferences of children were then probed by asking:

- Which two of these subjects or activities do you like doing *best*?
- Which two do you like *least*?
- Why do you like (first positive choice) ... better than (first negative choice) ... ?

Pupils' views on classroom framing and control were investigated by asking three very open questions:

- Do you choose what you do at school or does your teacher decide for you mostly?
- Do you like it best when you choose or when your teacher decides?
- Why is that?

A further group of questions was designed to highlight the extent to which the children were aware of the achievements of others and their explanations for this. In asking these questions, we were particularly seeking indicators of differentiation and explanations for it. We asked:

- Are there some children in your class who do particularly well at school work?
- Are there some who don't do so well?
- Why do you think some people do better at school work than others?
- If a new child came to be in your class, what sort of a person do you think your teacher would like?

A further group of questions concerned assessment and learning. We wanted to gather data on how children felt about routine classroom assessment activities and about the role of their teachers. We tried to reassure them that they could 'open up' on the topic with a short preamble: 'Some children seem pleased when the teacher looks in their books, but others seem worried'. We then asked:

- Do you like it when your teacher looks at your books?
- How do you feel (when your teacher looks at your books)?
- What happens if someone does their work really well?
- Does it matter if you don't do things the way your teacher wants them?

In PACE 3 we specifically tried to tap into issues of risk, ambiguity and the affective as well as cognitive challenges of learning. With a tape running, and hoping for a narrative account, we asked them:

- Can you tell me about a time in the juniors when you felt very pleased because you'd done some difficult work?
- Can you tell me about a time in juniors when you felt worried about your work?

Our final set of questions was focused on the children's perception of their teachers and their relationships with them. Again, we were particularly looking for the concepts and criteria that underlay the pupils' answers, and we were aware of pupil concerns about teacher power.

- How do you get on with *your* teacher?
- What do you like best about your teacher?
- Do you have to do what she/he says?
- How do you feel about that?
- Can you tell me about a time when you got told off, but didn't think it was fair?
- If you could imagine your 'ideal' /'perfect' teacher, what would he or she be like?

The interviews were recorded in longhand and then typed. Additionally, in Years 5 and 6 interviews were taped and selectively transcribed. Analysis was initially undertaken using the Ethnograph, a computer programme for processing qualitative data. However, this was later abandoned in favour of relational databases (Superbase and then MS Access) capable of integrating qualitative interview data and data on attainment, social class and sociometric status with the quantitative results of the systematic observations.

Teacher interviews

Structured interviews with the class teachers took place on the first and last afternoons of the observation week. Notes were made on a schedule during the interviews, but the whole conversation was also tape-recorded for transcription.

The first day's interview was aimed at obtaining the following:

- Pen sketches of target children
- Brief descriptions of attainment, behaviour and social relationships of each child
- Curriculum plans
- Details of the procedure for the allocation of work to children
- Normal routines of the teacher's morning

The last day's interview covered:

- Teacher assessment
- The teacher's views of work and changing role
- The teacher's views of pupil control of learning
- The teacher's views of relationships with children

Unstructured discussions throughout the week supplemented these pre-specified interviews. Observers took whatever opportunities arose to seek clarification or ask questions suggested by observation or field notes and teachers' views were written up in full as soon as possible afterwards.

Tape-recorded interaction

In some classes, teachers agreed to carry small cassette recorders fitted with throat microphones for some teaching sessions. Tapes were not transcribed in full, but extracts were used for analytical purposes in conjunction with field notes to provide a more detailed picture of pedagogy and of teacher–child interaction.

Analysis of classroom studies data

As with all other elements of data-gathering in the PACE study, responsibility for data-analysis was shared and data-analysis sheets were produced to record and summarize results for circulation amongst the team. Sociometric diagrams were completed for each class, revealing sociometric status and the membership of friendship groups. Systematic observation data were entered and analysed using SPSS (Statistics Package for the Social Sciences). Questions from both child interviews and teacher interviews were distributed amongst team members for initial analysis and tabulation.

In each round of data-gathering, the analyses from the various empirical aspects of the classroom studies were compared and integrated together where possible.

Sociometric data, attainment data, teacher interview data and systematic observation data were entered on the same Access database. This provided for a degree of methodological triangulation and a more multifaceted analysis. For instance, teachers' views of children's achievement levels could, in principle, be compared with pupil perceptions on both their own and their classmates' attainments, related to other data from the pupil interviews and then linked to patterns which had been produced from the systematic observation of teacher or pupil classroom behaviour. Field notes and transcripts of tape-recorded teacher–pupil interaction were also used to augment emerging analysis. The possibilities of such analysis were considerable, but there were also significant technical difficulties in interpreting the scale and variety of data on a year-by-year basis. The data became most meaningful at the end of the study when the patterns and trends of six years of data were apparent.

2.7 ASSESSMENT STUDIES

Key Stage 1

During the early part of the Summer Term, 1991, Year 2 classes in the nine schools of our sub-sample were visited for two days each while SATs were in progress. This meant that pupils who were one year older than our longitudinal pupil sample, and their teachers, were observed and interviewed while the first round of SATs took place. This was our first use of an anticipatory cross-sectional strategy (section 2.1) and was designed to enable us to make comparisons of change as our main pupil cohort experienced the SATs in the following year and to monitor piloting of SATs.

Observers watched whichever SATs teachers had chosen to carry out in the data-gathering period and the unit of analysis was taken to be the SAT as a complete classroom episode. An attempt was thus made to observe each SAT in operation from beginning to end and to record, using field notes, as much detail of the interaction and classroom processes as possible. Following SAT observation, interviews were conducted on an individual basis with as many as possible of the pupils who had experienced the observed SAT.

During the 1992 assessment study the process was similar but this time the cohort of pupils on which we focused was that of our continuing study. This was, in other words, our third major period of sustained observation and interviews with these children. This time data were gathered for three days in each classroom and qualitative observations were more focused. Again, as many pupils as possible were interviewed. Observers made sure that these included the six target pupils in each class. Further details of the data-collection processes follow.

Classroom observation during the SATs

Observers used open-ended observation methods, making field notes and written records of teacher–child and child–child conversation and other interaction, whilst recording at intervals brief notes on such pre-selected categories as preparations for the SAT, arrangements for the rest of the class, extra help, if any, provided for the teacher and post-SAT events. Various SATs were observed in use. However, when the same SAT was observed in different classrooms it was possible to examine the effect of different styles of teacher presentation and of physical circumstances on the perceptions and performance of pupils.

In the 1992 assessment studies there were some adjustments to the data-gathering programme to increase standardization of data. Schools were also asked if observers could be present when one specific SAT, Maths 3, was carried out. It was thus possible to record, for an apparently 'standardized' test situation, the effects of different contexts and interaction.

Interviews with teachers about assessment

Teacher interviews were structured in both rounds and covered such areas as teachers' perceptions of the role assessment should have in infant classrooms, the relative degree of value they found in SATs and in Teacher Assessment, and the support they were given in carrying out the process. Further topics covered were their perceptions of their pupils' experience, including the question of whether National Curriculum assessment procedures reinforced a sense of academic hierarchy amongst the children and whether they took steps to address this issue. Interviews conducted one year later during the second SAT period differed only slightly from the first set, so that changes in perceptions could be tracked.

Interviews with pupils about assessment

Children were asked about whether they had enjoyed the tasks observed, how they rated their own performances and those of their classmates, whether they discussed the work at home and how they saw the purpose of the tasks carried out. These data were coded and entered on our database for analysis.

Assessment questionnaires

After the completion of the 1991 and 1992 SAT procedures, all 48 schools in the main PACE sample received questionnaires for all teachers involved in carrying out SATs. The response rate was 92 per cent of schools in 1991 and 81 per cent in 1992. Teachers were asked to note, using five-point scales, their views of the degree of difficulty in organizing the tasks, the degree of value they attached to the results, the support they received within their schools and the reactions of their pupils. Headteachers were asked an open-ended question about the experience of the process in their schools. Both quantitative and qualitative material was therefore available for analysis on this major innovation.

Key Stage 2

Since the arrangements for the Key Stage 2 SATs which our cohort of children took in 1996 were significantly different, a different research strategy was required. The

Key Stage 2 SATs involved pencil and paper tests, centrally set and taken on a prescribed day. The 1996 SAT study was therefore designed to focus on a number of rather different key issues. These included issues of continuity and progression, investigating the extent to which teachers used assessment data to work towards continuity and individual matching in curriculum provision. In particular we were concerned to investigate teachers' changing assessment practices at Key Stage 2, especially in Year 6; how far assessment requirements were influencing teaching, learning and classroom priorities; and the overall impact of the prevailing assessment climate on pupils and their sense of themselves as learners.

To gather data for the study, researchers spent time in each of the nine PACE classroom study schools during Key Stage 2 SAT week in May 1996. They observed tests across the subject range, making field notes on the preparation and application of the SAT, together with what they observed as the children resumed their normal timetable. Some SATs were tape-recorded. The English writing SAT was observed in all nine schools concurrently and gave useful data on comparability.

Researchers then returned to the nine schools the following week to interview in each case the Year 6 teacher, the cohort of six target pupils, together with an additional six Year 6 children. The additional children were chosen to create a sample of equal numbers of high attainers, average attainers and low attainers.

Additionally, all of the children in each of the classes from which data had been gathered completed a cartoon story-based questionnaire eliciting their feelings at each stage of taking the SAT. For instance, prompts included:

- On the way to school I was thinking ...
- I looked at the paper to see what I had to do. I thought ...
- While I was doing the test ...
- After it was over, I talked to my friends ...
- I thought about what I would say when I got home ...
- I thought about what people at home would say to me ...

Figure 2.4 is an example of one of the illustrations, and a full copy of a 'SAT story' forms Appendix 2. These cartoon stories were completed with teachers' support as soon as possible after the end of SATs – often on the final day itself or at the start of the following week. We were aware that use of this particular genre might mean that children tended to respond stereotypically. However there was sufficient overlap between this data source and the interviews and observations to suggest that the responses could be considered as a reflection of authentic pupil experience.

Finally, after the completion of the Key Stage 2 SATs, a postal questionnaire was sent to all schools in the larger sample of 48 to be completed by teachers who had been involved in the Key Stage 2 testing. This replicated the assessment questionnaire that had been used in 1991 and 1992.

2.8 STATISTICAL ANALYSIS

Tests of statistical significance were used in connection with our teacher interview

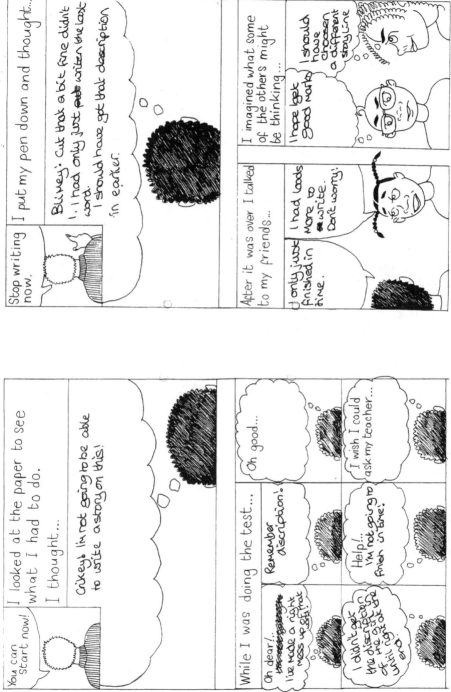

Figure 2.4 An illustration from 'The SAT story' completed by Year 6 pupils in 1996

and questionnaire data (see Osborn *et al.*, 2000). However, these were not used in the case of the pupil interview data because the overall samples of children in each year are relatively small and are neither consistent nor independent of one another. In many cases figures from year to year refer to the same children, but since there was some natural drop-out and replacement of pupils within the sample, the groups are neither identical nor totally independent of one another.

2.9 DOING RESEARCH AS A COLLABORATIVE TEAM

The research design, data-collection and analysis procedures outlined above were an excellent resource and provided a data-set of unusual range and richness. However, the scale and magnitude of the research, together with the nature of the task we had to undertake, raised a number of issues which had to be confronted while working as a collaborative team over the six years of the project. From the point of view of the research design, there were two related problems.

First, there was the issue of multiple innovation (Wallace, 1991). Whilst the phenomenon we set out to study – change in primary school classrooms following the introduction of the National Curriculum and assessment – had itself several dimensions, these were set in an even wider context of many other changes. These included local management of schools, the roles of local education authorities, school inspection requirements and the introduction of OFSTED, school account-ability structures, teacher appraisal systems and the introduction of the market philosophy to education through open enrolment, opting out and publication of league tables of assessment performance. The project team could not address the ramifications of all these issues, yet nor could we ignore them. Our solution to this dilemma was to attempt to liaise with other research teams and to maintain awareness of the wider social, political and historical context in which our study was set, whilst maintaining our prime focus at the classroom level. The study can thus contribute to a holistic understanding of the many facets of change in the 1990s but its contribution, whilst necessary and perhaps unique, is not sufficient to embrace the full complexity of the system-wide innovation which has occurred.

The second major challenge to our research design concerned when, how and from whom to gather data which would be as nationally representative as possible and also provide valid indications of trends in perspectives, classroom practices and provision. Of course, research resources are always limited and judgements are always required to identify the most worthwhile data-gathering strategies and scheduling. However, in this case, these routine decisions were complicated further by the continuing process of change. The study had to aim for as much comparability as possible and yet at the same time respond to evolving policy change. We also needed to take into account the increasing age and sophistication of the children who were at the heart of the study, so that comparability of research instruments sometimes needed to take second place to the need to talk to children in an appropriate way. Therefore, with the child interviews we aimed for continuity of topics, rather than continuity in the way questions were framed.

Another set of issues were related to the nature of the project itself and the consequences for the researchers within it working as a collaborative team. Initially the study was located within two institutions, the University of the West of England and the University of Bristol, with two of the directors located at UWE and one at Bristol. One full-time contract researcher was based in each institution. Later the project team moved entirely to the University of Bristol when one of the directors left the city and the other became a professor at Bristol. The logistical challenges of working in two sites and then later moving all the data and resources plus half the project team to Bristol were considerable. In addition there were other issues to be resolved deriving from the differences in cultures of the two institutions, financial arrangements, computer systems and, indeed, the different research paradigms held by some members of the research team. The latter provided both a creative and a constraining tension.

Other issues derived from the nature of the funding of social science research in the UK. This had implications for the way in which the project was designed, for the career structure of both the contract researchers and the directors, and for maintaining continuity in the team. The relatively limited funds available for social science research meant that the research had to be designed in three consecutive phases and as three separate projects which would both provide a basis for a subsequent stage and be self-contained and complete in themselves if no further funding were to become available. This created the necessity to leapfrog strategically from one project to another without knowing until near the end of one phase whether further research would be funded. As in all such funded projects, the conditions of the professional researchers' employment were uncertain so that there were times when members of the team were compelled to follow up other career opportunities in order to maintain continuity. The directors of the research were also undertaking a wider range of responsibilities, leaving a greater load of fieldwork and other responsibilities for the contract researchers. Some of these tensions will be familiar to the participants in any funded research project but others may have been relatively unusual and particular to a longer-term longitudinal project.

All these conditions, together with the natural progression of team members' careers and life-cycles over a six-year period, meant that there were considerable changes in the research team during the life of the project. When the research drew to a close only two of the directors and one senior researcher remained from the original team. There had been three other part-time research associates plus a consultant working on the research in the interim. The complexity of the project sometimes posed problems for new team members joining later. They needed to get a grasp fairly quickly on what had gone before and to have time to acquire feelings of ownership in the research.

However, there were a number of ways in which we attempted to resolve these issues which may be of interest to other research teams. First, the team meetings and the way in which responsibilities were allocated attempted to build on individuals' strengths and expertise and to allocate themes and tasks in accordance with these. For example, different team members took prime responsibility for one or other of the major themes of the project, pupil and classroom experience, teachers' professional perspectives, whole-school change, and assessment. These were followed through, where possible, throughout the life of the project and also carried through into writing responsibilities.

There were particular methodological issues involved in teamwork of this nature. Because of the relatively large number of researchers involved the research needed to have a very structured focus, discussed and agreed in team meetings. Research instruments had to be carefully designed to ensure comparability from one researcher's classroom to another, and after intensive rounds of data-collection there were brainstorming and mind-mapping sessions in which the whole team participated and in which emerging issues from the fieldwork fed into a number of themes and where the beginnings of a conceptual framework began to emerge. Earlier parts of this chapter described the data-analysis sheets which were used and circulated among the team so that everyone had a grasp of new issues emerging.

Different members of the team took responsibility for the fieldwork in particular classroom study schools and maintained their contact with the school, as far as possible, throughout the life of the project. This relationship played a considerable part in the trust and goodwill which was built between the researchers and the schools, so that, as noted earlier, all the study schools remained with the project throughout in spite of many other pressures they were experiencing.

2.10 CONCLUSION

The procedures outlined above provided large quantities of varied data allowing for analysis on several levels. Some of the problems they posed for the research team working over the eight years of the project have been discussed.

Throughout the research there was a potential risk that the scale of empirical work would steer the project towards description of change, rather than providing the foundation for analysis and theorization. As one of very few independently funded social science projects on changes in primary schools following the Education Reform Act, we felt that we had a particular responsibility to stand back from simple evaluation of the innovation and to attempt to discern and articulate more fundamental developments and consequences.

In this we were able to build on some of our previous work. One of our major theoretical concerns was the influence of external constraints on teachers' professional perspectives and here it was possible to develop work from the ESRC project: Teachers' Conceptions of their Professional Responsibilities in England and France (Bristaix) (Broadfoot *et al.*, 1993) and later from other related work. Another theoretical issue centred on teacher–pupil interaction and strategies in classrooms, on which we were able to develop the work of Pollard (1985) and others in tracing the changes in classroom practices adopted by teachers and children as they responded to new curricular and assessment arrangements. For complementary insights on learning and 'pupil career' through their primary schooling we drew on the longitudinal ethnography of the Identity and Learning Programme (ILP) of Pollard and Filer (Filer and Pollard, 2000; Pollard and Filer, 1999; Pollard with Filer, 1996).

At the end of the eight years of the PACE project we have described how primary schools have changed substantially. Additionally, we have also tried to present the challenges for learner engagement within primary schools, and to pose questions for future policy and practice.

Part 2

Classroom Change and Pupil Experience

Chapter 3

Observed Changes in Classroom Practice

3.1   Introduction
3.2   Curriculum contexts
3.3   Pedagogic contexts
3.4   Assessment
3.5   Conclusion

3.1 INTRODUCTION

In Chapter 1 we saw how the PACE project was established to monitor and analyse the impact of the Education Reform Act 1988 on teacher and pupil experience in primary schools. The origins and impact of that key legislation and of the other Education Acts which followed it were reviewed. We argued that underlying successive waves of legislation was a model in which higher educational standards were to be delivered through greater curriculum specification, targeted and coordinated whole-school management, the development of teacher subject knowledge, whole-class instruction and higher quality instructional skills, assessment of pupil performance, reporting of results, school inspection, and increased accountability of teachers and schools to parents and the public generally. We characterized this overall conception as a model for the 'delivery of performance'. It was, and is, a logical, system-wide reform to which enormous resources have been committed.

However, in the first report of the PACE research (Broadfoot and Pollard, 1996; Pollard *et al.*, 1994) we documented how *mediation* of policy occurred at various levels of the education system. Thus we represented 'external turbulence' and initiatives at the policy level becoming transformed into relative 'internal continuity' at the level of pupils' classroom experience (see Figure 3.1 below).

For our present analysis at LEA and school levels, we rely on the parallel PACE book on teachers (Osborn *et al.*, 2000) which includes an account of changes in

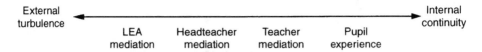

Figure 3.1 From turbulence to continuity

school organizational forms, management styles, teacher accountabilities and conceptions of professionalism within English primary schooling over the period of study. At its most analytical, this can be represented as a development from practices associated with post-war 'liberal progressive' ideologies of primary education, towards those associated with modern 'performance' models.

For instance, Table 3.1 highlights the organizational and professional tensions and changes which are reported in our companion volume (Osborn *et al.*, 2000).

We summarized this transition with regard to primary teachers' perspectives and practices as follows:

> In broad terms, the PACE study tells a story of both change and continuity since the passing of the Education Reform Act 1988. The many changes have centred on a progressive loss of professional freedom to determine what and how to teach, which has resulted in perceived loss of creativity and more or less grudging compliance on the part of teachers. The climate of increased managerialism, based on targets and performance indicators, served to reinforce this compliance and to encourage a sense of commodification in the pursuit and judgement of learning outcomes. Where teachers were conscious of such an increased instrumentality in their teaching, this was often experienced as a source of conflict. However, other teachers, either as individuals or as groups, were able to integrate these new pressures into their existing professional values. These have in turn become the basis for a new 'professionality', which is a synthesis of past and present ideologies.
>
> (Osborn *et al.*, 2000, p. 232)

The task of the present chapter is to look beyond the contextual factors of school organization, management and teachers' work and to directly focus on the nature and extent of continuity and change at the classroom level. What was the classroom impact of the progressive introduction of the 'performance' model through the early and mid-1990s? In particular, we will be concerned with curriculum, pedagogy and assessment as three key elements of classroom life.

Most of the data that we report in this chapter are quantitative. They are drawn from successive phases of the PACE study in which systematic observation has been a key technique used to record classroom behaviours and practices (Croll, 1986). In addition, as appropriate, the chapter also draws on and makes comparisons with studies by other primary school classroom researchers who have worked with quantitative data such as Alexander, Campbell, Croll, Galton and Mortimore. We start by considering the curriculum.

3.2 CURRICULUM CONTEXTS

Readers of the companion PACE book on teachers (Osborn *et al.*, 2000) or of other studies of the impact of the National Curriculum on primary education in the 1990s

Table 3.1 Some contrastive aspects of liberal progressive and performance models in relation to schools and teachers (after Bernstein)

	LIBERAL PROGRESSIVE 'COMPETENCE' EDUCATION	'PERFORMANCE EDUCATION'
SCHOOLS AND TEACHERS	*'Invisible management' with relative professional autonomy*	'Visible management' with relative professional regulation
Organizational form	Professional, with flat management structure. Control through self-regulation, socialization and internalization of norms	Mechanistic, with hierarchical structure and bureaucracy. Standardization for control and coordination
Management style	Collegiate, with emphasis on proficiency, dialogue and consensus. Informality in relationships	Managerial, with emphasis on efficiency and target setting for results. Greater formality in relationships
Teacher roles	Teachers as facilitators, with affective dimensions seen as intrinsic to the teaching role	Teachers as instructors and evaluators, with emphasis on cognitive and managerial skills
Teacher professionalism	Professional covenant based on trust, and commitment to education as a form of personal development. Confidence, sense of fulfillment and spontaneity in teaching	Professionalism as the fulfillment of a contract to deliver education, which is seen as a commodity for individuals and a national necessity for economic growth. Less confidence, fulfillment and spontaneity in teaching
Teacher accountability	Personal and 'moral' accountability	External and contractual accountability, backed by inspection
Whole school coordination	Relative autonomy and informal teacher collaboration	Formal school planning, with 'managed' collegiality

(Acker, 1999; Campbell and Neill, 1994a and b; Croll, 1996; Galton, 1995; Galton *et al.*, 1999; National Union of Teachers, 1991; Nias *et al.*, 1992 ; Webb and Vulliamy, 1996b; Woods, 1995) will recall the extent of research which documented curriculum overload, assessment 'unmanageability' and teachers' attempts to come to terms with the unfolding situation. For many, 'conscientiousness' led to extremely long working hours and work intensification. The concern to maintain holistic, child-centred educational principles and a nurturing self-image in the face of new requirements posed dilemmas and challenged the values of many primary school teachers throughout the period of the PACE study.

The first main requirement of the Education Reform Act concerned the introduction of the National Curriculum structure of subjects and statutory orders. Such content specification challenged not only previous commitments to integrated 'topic work', but also teacher expertise and the use of classroom time. Table 3.2 records the 'main' curriculum content coded over the entire six years of the PACE research. These codes reflect the judgement of the researchers and were made at the end of each six-minute observational period in relation to the curriculum context in which each observed teacher or child had been engaged.

Table 3.2 Overall main curriculum content observed (percentages)

	Year 1 1991	Year 2 1992	Year 3 1993	Year 4 1994	Year 5 1995	Year 6 1996	
	1990–1	1991–2	1992–3	1993–4	1994–5	1995–6	Average
The core curriculum							
English	37.6	33.1	27.4	32.3	24.1	25.4	29.7
Mathematics	14.1	16.9	19.8	21.8	17.6	23.0	19.0
Science	7.1	9.0	9.4	6.1	16.3	12.9	10.2
Total core curriculum	58.8	59.0	56.6	60.1	58.0	61.3	58.9
Other non-core subjects							
Art	8.5	2.2	6.6	2.6	6.9	3.3	5.0
History	2.9	0.0	6.3	1.8	3.8	7.4	3.8
Technology	4.4	3.2	1.2	1.0	2.1	2.5	2.4
Physical Education	2.6	3.2	2.3	3.3	0.6	1.9	2.3
Music	2.4	2.8	0.8	2.8	1.5	2.7	2.1
Geography	0.3	0.2	1.6	5.1	6.1	0.8	2.4
Total non-core subjects	21.1	11.6	18.9	16.7	20.9	18.4	17.9
Religious Education	0.7	3.8	1.5	4.0	2.5	1.9	2.4
No main curriculum subject	19.4	25.6	23.2	19.3	18.5	18.4	20.7

Source: PACE 1, 2 and 3 systematic observations of pupils and teachers
Sample: 54 children and nine teachers in nine classrooms over each of six years
Date: Summer 1990 to Summer 1996
Note: The observational figure for Physical Education is low because sampling was classroom-based only. However, it does reflect some class lessons in school halls where data-gathering opportunities were constrained.

As Table 3.2 reveals, the core curriculum of English, Mathematics and Science was dominant in the classrooms observed. Irrespective of the age of the pupils being observed, it took approximately 60 per cent of all observed time throughout the period. However, it is also apparent that an early emphasis on literacy gave way to a significant growth in the time spent on Mathematics and Science. This can be related to public pressures through the period and the schedule for the introduction of assessment in Science, but it was to lead later to public concern that the teaching of reading was being undermined by the National Curriculum. Our sampling and data-gathering methods were not appropriate to accurately record the very small amounts of time which the non-core subjects appear to have struggled to secure. Indeed, as the main focus of the curriculum, they managed only 18 per cent of observed classroom time throughout Key Stages 1 and 2. Religious Education was similarly small in its impact, averaging 2 per cent of time. However, this was augmented by acts of collective worship which were not recorded by systematic observation.

For 21 per cent of observed time over the six years, no main curriculum subject was recorded, and this provides an indication of the extent of combined subject work. The particular emphasis on basic literacy probably explains a relatively low figure in Year 1, but combined subject work was significantly higher in Years 2 and 3. However, it decreased again during 1994–6, when the target pupils were in Years 5 and 6. At this time, public pressure to increase subject teaching was particularly strong. When subjects were combined, the most common subject 'parts' recorded were: English (14%), Art (7%), Mathematics (7%), Science (6%) and History (6%). Music (1%) and Geography (2%) were rarely observed as parts of the curriculum context. These data suggest that 'topic work' and integrated curriculum study were not strong features of the primary classrooms studied. The PACE teacher book records teacher perception of a major increase in single-subject teaching at the top end of Key Stage 2, and a dramatic fall in integrated topic work.

Whilst the rhetoric associated with the introduction of the National Curriculum had emphasized provision of a 'broad and balanced' curriculum, and specialist subject working parties had created detailed programmes of study for each subject, primary school teachers felt constrained by the core curriculum. This is very understandable given the emphasis of criticism from politicians and the media. Thus national debates focused on 'basic skills'. Further, public tests of pupil performance, through which teachers and schools were to be held accountable to parents, constantly drew teachers back to English and Mathematics. This is an echo of the old 'elementary school' tradition, as Alexander (1984), Campbell (1994) and Blyth (1998) have argued, and it is interesting to trace the balance in the taught curriculum over the past 20 years.

Table 3.3 shows findings from a range of studies focused on the percentage of recorded time in which 'the basics' of English and Mathematics were the main curriculum context. Although a health warning on the direct comparison of such a wide range of findings is necessary (particularly regarding the 'other subject' category in which a variety of classification systems have been used), the overall impression remains that there has been relatively little change in the dominance of the old 'elementary school' curriculum of English and Mathematics. However, there was a decrease of the 'basics' in 1994–5, which were widely regarded as being 'driven out' by the attempt to make the curriculum 'broad and balanced'. Indeed, the decrease was matched by the introduction of a new Science curriculum in that year, which was exceptionally measured at 16 per cent of curriculum time. The concerns aroused at the time contributed to the New Labour government's determination, following the 1997 election, to 'streamline' the curriculum to enable a prime focus on literacy and numeracy.

Of course, there is evidence that many school pupils are not overly concerned about the particular subject content they are required to study (Goodnow and Burns, 1985). More important may be the question of what they are actually expected 'to do' in terms of writing, reading, listening, talking, making, etc. PACE did not collect observational data of this sort (although, as we will see in subsequent chapters, pupils had much to say about these activities), but two other relevant sources of indicative information are available about English primary schools in the

Table 3.3 Proportions of time spent on 'basic' subjects and other subjects in a range of research studies (extended from Campbell and Emery, 1994)

	Basic 'main' subjects	Other subjects
Bassey (1978) Junior	54	46
Bennett *et al.* (1980) Infant	53	25
Bennett *et al.* (1980) Junior	48	39
Galton *et al.* (1980) Junior	49*	51
DES Primary Staffing Survey (1987) Junior	49	51
Tizard *et al.* (1988) Infant	52*	40
Alexander (1992) Primary	52	48
Campbell and Neill (1992) Infant	51	39
Campbell and Emery (1994) Junior	49	45
Meyer *et al.* (1992) Primary/Elementary	50	50
PACE 1990–1, Year 1, Infant/Key Stage 1	52	31
PACE 1991–2, Year 2, Infant/Key Stage 1	50	26
PACE 1992–3, Year 3, Junior/Key Stage 2	47	30
PACE 1993–4, Year 4, Junior/Key Stage 2	54	27
PACE 1994–5, Year 5, Junior/Key Stage 2	42	40
PACE 1995–6, Year 6, Junior/Key Stage 2	48	35

Sources: Campbell and Emery (1994) with their recalculations from original sources asterisked, and PACE 1, 2 and 3 systematic observation, Years 1–6, 1990–1 to 1995–6
Note: The PACE data are scaled combinations of teacher and pupil percentages of 'main curricular context'.

early part of the period. Thus Alexander (1997) reports data gathered between 1986 and 1990 in Leeds which shows 33% of overall pupil time spent in writing, 28% working with apparatus, 24% reading, 20% listening or looking, 19% drawing, 18% collaborating, and 14% 'moving about'. Galton *et al.* (1998) report from the INCSS study of small rural schools in the early 1990s and offer 33% listening, 28% writing, 17% observing, 10% drawing , 7% reading and 5% talking. Specific comparisons are difficult, but there is no doubting the major activities of listening, observing and writing. There is every indication from PACE findings on curriculum and pedagogy, based on teacher and pupil observational and interview data, that the preponderance of such pupil activities grew further as the implementation of the National Curriculum developed through the 1990s.

Across the PACE study, year by year and as a whole, there was no indication of gender differences in the subject balance of the curriculum that boys and girls were observed to experience. However, there was some evidence that children from families where parental employment had been classified as 'manual' were likely to spend more curriculum time on English and Mathematics. Time spent on English was particularly high in inner-city and estate schools. This finding may be related to the teacher perception that the National Curriculum had benefited lower attainers less than other pupils (see Osborn *et al.*, 2000).

In summary, it seems on the basis of observational data that for many years pupils in English primary schools have experienced relatively similar proportions of time on the 'basic' subjects of English and Mathematics. This appears to be the historic elementary school curriculum, which is sustained by predominant cultural expectations of 'what school is for'. Within this, curriculum time spent on Mathematics increased as the cohort moved from Year 1 to Year 6. Following its introduction in 1989, Science began, variably, to establish itself as a 'core subject'. However, observations indicate very small proportions of time spent on other curriculum subjects in the early 1990s, despite the existence of specific statutory content requirements. Nevertheless, from teacher interview data we know that the time given to other subjects was planned with increasing thoroughness as schools developed whole-curriculum planning schemes in attempts to maximize continuity and progression between classes (Osborn *et al.*, 2000). There was also an increase in the use of explicit timetabling and, later, in 'setting' pupil groups by subject attainment both within and across classes.

The implications of all this were profound. Whereas it had once been commonplace for teachers to espouse a conception of children exploring integrated topics across subjects, 'appropriating' knowledge and 'constructing understanding' (Armstrong, 1980; Egan, 1988; Kelly, 1994; Rowland, 1984), the curriculum of the early 1990s became increasingly structured and controlled. In terms of Bernstein's analysis, there was a clear move from integration towards the specific classification of knowledge in the form of subjects. In essence, teachers felt required to deliver specific content to pupils. Indeed, the issues of 'overload' and 'manageability' were only partly resolved by the Dearing Review which took effect from 1995, for the demands of formalized assessment and the pressure to formalize pedagogy remained. Through the six years of the PACE study, a third of teachers feared that their relationships with pupils were being adversely affected by the challenges of the National Curriculum, a figure which rose to 58 per cent in 1992–3 when the pressure was at its highest (see Osborn *et al.*, 2000). Despite these concerns, pupils, at the end point of the line of command, received and responded to the curriculum tasks and challenges with which they were presented, as we will see in Chapters 4 and 5.

3.3 PEDAGOGIC CONTEXTS

PACE pupil observation data of main teaching contexts in the 54 classrooms studied over the period is shown in Table 3.4. It is important to remember that in our observational system 'whole-class work' included activities such as discussions and storytime, as well as more direct, expository instruction, and that PACE data record teaching contexts as our pupil cohort moved through their primary schools, rather than permitting direct comparisons of change in classrooms of children of the same age.

In studying Table 3.4 it is notable how whole-class work gradually decreased from Year 1 to Year 5, before rising again in Year 6. Group work fell very distinctively from almost a fifth of pupil experience in Key Stage 1 to well under a tenth throughout Key Stage 2. Compensating for the overall decrease in whole-class and group work was the very significant rise of individual work, again with a distinctive step difference in each key stage. These proportions of recorded classifications reflect classroom processes, and the typical Key Stage 1 lesson pattern of beginning with an

Table 3.4 Main teaching contexts experienced by pupils (percentage of observed time)

	Year 1 1991	Year 2 1992	Year 3 1993	Year 4 994	Year 5 1995	Year 6 1996
Whole-class work	33.9	31.6	31.2	26.6	25.9	30.3
Group work	19.1	18.4	7.2	7.2	8.4	5.6
Individual work	42.0	40.8	51.3	52.9	54.8	52.9
Parts of each	5.1	9.2	10.4	13.3	10.8	11.1

Source: PACE 1, 2 and 3 pupil systematic observation
Sample: 54 Years 1–6 classrooms in nine schools in eight LEAs
Date: Summer 1991 to Summer 1996

interactive 'carpet session' and then dispersing to groups or individual assignments can be contrasted with Key Stage 2 lessons in which teachers were typically observed to introduce information through some form of whole-class teaching and then follow with tasks to be completed by each pupil individually. The explanation given for this pattern of working at Key Stage 2 concerned the amount of content to be covered and the need to provide differentiated practice. Group work was only really significant in Key Stage 1, and in Key Stage 2 it was not considered effective at 'covering the ground'. From the pupil perspective, these data suggest a fairly consistent experience of being introduced to new knowledge by the teacher and then being set individual follow-up tasks. In the very few cases where attempts at 'cooperative group work' were observed, they exclusively involved high-attaining pupils in schools serving more favoured socio-economic communities.

We have data from the teachers on the ways in which they organized seat-place groups within their classrooms and it is evident that attainment, ability, friendship and age were continuously important considerations. However, gender became a particularly significant factor as the children reached Year 6.

PACE findings on teachers have demonstrated the ways in which they felt their pedagogy had changed following the introduction of the National Curriculum and assessment, and in the light of pressures from ministers and the media during the early 1990s. There had been an initial period of adjustment as the National Curriculum was introduced, with a great deal of work going into learning about new curriculum content, teacher assessment and SAT assessment requirements and improving planning and record systems. Teachers reported that, with reluctance, they were having to restrict pupil autonomy because of the amount of subject content and standards of attainment that were now required. For instance, a teacher quoted by Osborn *et al.* (2000) said:

> I think they (the pupils) should have more (autonomy) than they've got. It's been my experience that children have learnt more when they're interested in something. Some of the topics that we are being forced to teach are really not that interesting for 10–11-year-olds. For the time we spend doing them, they don't get enough out of it.
>
> (p. 133)

Teachers consistently described themselves as using a mixture of teaching methods. Indeed, the idea of 'fitness for purpose' in selecting teaching strategies became a vital defence of professional judgement following the publication of the 'Three Wise Men' report (Alexander *et al.*, 1992). This urged an increase in whole-class teaching to more effectively convey subject knowledge – 'the most powerful tools for making sense of the world which human beings have ever devised' (p. 17). Whilst this report was a key event in the pedagogic debate of the 1990s, it can also be located in the continuous flow of criticisms of primary school teaching methods that developed from the 1970s' critique of Plowden and 'progressivism'. Pressure for more 'traditional', whole-class teaching has been sustained over many years and is aligned with a discourse that links primary school pedagogy to issues such as basic skills, educational standards, economic competitiveness and the moral foundation of 'the British way of life'.

In the light of these contextual issues it is interesting to compare PACE findings with those from other studies, although there are considerable technical difficulties in so doing because of variations in the classification and observations systems used. Table 3.5 summarizes findings from key studies over the past twenty years.

This type of table is fraught with technical difficulties, as Galton *et al.* (1999) acknowledge. There are variations in the samples, focus on teachers or pupils, instruments and analyses, and it is extremely difficult, if not impossible, to unravel

Table 3.5 Pedagogic contexts in systematic observation studies of teacher–pupil interaction in English primary schools (rounded percentages)

	Teacher interacts with		
	Individuals	Groups	Whole class
ORACLE (Galton *et al.*, 1980)			
1976–7 58 Y3–6 classes	72	9	19
40 Y3–6 classes	69	15	16
PRISMS (Galton and Patrick, 1990)			
early 1980s infant classes	61	13	26
small schools junior classes	58	16	26
One in Five (Croll and Moses, 1985)			
early 1980s 32 Y4 classes	51	18	30
School Matters (Mortimore *et al.*, 1988)			
mid-1980s 50 Y4 classes	67	9	23
50 Y5 classes	63	11	24
INCSS (Galton *et al.*, 1998)			
early 1989–9 junior classes	65	10	25
PACE			
1991 9 Y1 classes	41	23	36
1992 9 Y2 classes	42	22	36
1993 9 Y3 classes	55	10	35
1994 9 Y4 classes	60	8	32
1995 9 Y5 classes	61	9	30
1996 9 Y6 classes	55	8	37
ORACLE 20 years on (Galton *et al.*, 1999)			
1996 28 Y4, Y5 and Y6 classes	48	16	35

Source: Galton *et al.*, 1999 with additional PACE 1, 2 and 3 systematic pupil observation
Sample: 54 Years 1–6 classrooms in nine schools in eight LEAs
Date: Summer 1991 to Summer 1996

them all. The PACE data given here *combine* teacher and pupil observations where 'main teaching contexts' were recorded – some 90 per cent of all observations. It is therefore not identical to the data in Table 3.4 because that table reports pupil data only and also includes observations in which 'part' pedagogic context was coded in relation to some combination of individual, group and whole-class work. Over the study such observations amounted to over 10 per cent of the whole, and may indicate that the simple classification system is too crude to reflect more varied pedagogic practices that may be emerging.

Nevertheless, the cumulation of broadly similar data in successive studies is thought provoking. For instance, Table 3.6 summarizes *by decade* the previous data for interaction with children aged 7 to 11. Over the three decades it appears that individual work, though still very significant, has dropped from its 70 per cent high-point in the 1970s, and various forms of group work have also fallen away. In their place has been the resolute growth of interaction as a whole class. Indeed, the 1970s figure appears to have almost doubled by the 1990s. This appears to be an exceptional demonstration of the influence of changes in education policy and practice.

These data seem to resonate with the perspectives of experienced primary school teachers who, when reflecting on their professional biographies (Acker, 1999; Nias, 1991; Osborn, 1996a; Woods, 1995) felt that change had been considerable. PACE findings suggest that Key Stage 2 pupils of the 1990s still spend most of their time on individual work assignments, but there was twice as much whole-class teaching as there had been in junior schools twenty years previously.

The interaction of target pupils was coded every ten seconds during periods of observation. The aggregated results are shown in Table 3.7, which provides clear evidence about the experience of pupils in terms of the people with whom they interacted in the classrooms of the 1990s. Of course, it echoes the data considered above on the overall pedagogic context. Thus we find that working alone was the predominant experience for pupils, particularly in Key Stage 2, whilst interacting with the teacher as part of the class, or talking with other individuals (often in adjacent seat-places) were also relatively commonplace. Group work was a significant part of children's experience in Key Stage 1, but was relatively unusual when our sample passed through Key Stage 2. Interacting on a one-to-one basis with the teacher was an unusual experience throughout, and averaged only 3.4 per cent of classroom time over the six-year period.

Table 3.6 Summary: pedagogic contexts in systematic observation studies of teacher–pupil interaction in Key Stage 2 of English schools by decade (rounded percentages)

		Teacher–pupil interaction	
	Individuals	Groups	Whole class
Av 1970s	70.5	12.0	17.5
Av 1980s	60.8	12.8	26.4
Av 1990s	56.3	9.8	33.7

Source: Galton *et al.*, 1999 with additional PACE 1, 2 and 3 systematic pupil observation

Table 3.7 Child interaction

	Year 1 1991	Year 2 1992	Year 3 1993	Year 4 1994	Year 5 1995	Year 6 1996	Mean
Alone	26.6	35.1	44.3	45.8	47.7	44.9	40.7
With individual children	14.8	12.7	15.5	14.6	14.9	16.9	14.9
With other children in a group	13.0	7.3	5.4	7.3	8.0	8.1	8.2
With teacher in whole class	30.6	32.9	25.9	22.8	21.7	24.3	26.4
With teacher in group	10.0	6.3	2.6	2.7	2.1	2.1	4.3
With teacher one to one	2.5	3.3	3.2	4.7	3.7	2.9	3.4
With other adult one to one	1.2	0.9	0.6	0.2	0.3	0.1	0.6
Not recorded	1.3	1.6	2.6	1.1	1.7	0.6	1.5

Source: PACE 1, 2 and 3 systematic pupil observation
Sample: 54 Years 1–6 classrooms in nine schools in eight LEAs
Date: Summer 1991 to Summer 1996

Beyond the broad overview of interaction are some finer, but important patterns. For instance, lower-attaining children were more often observed to be involved in group work and they did not work alone as much as other children. However, our analysis revealed no differences by social class. Our data confirmed that boys and girls tend to interact with others of the same sex, and suggested that boys had slightly more one-to-one interaction with their teachers, particularly in Years 5 and 6. However, low-achieving boys received four times more teacher contact than low-attaining girls – reflecting, as we shall see, greater encouragement, instruction and disciplinary control. On the other hand, high-attaining girls had no less than eight times the overall level of teacher attention of low-attaining girls. This suggests that, despite recent concern over the school attainment of boys, low-achieving girls might be at greater risk of being permitted to drift through their classroom lives, causing little trouble but wasting their potential.

Just one-third of children's classroom time was spent in some form of interaction with the teacher or other adult – leaving no less than two-thirds remaining where pupils were either alone or interacting with other children. This is a consistent pattern and provides a clear indication of why friendships and peer relationships are so significant to primary school pupils. Having friends to share work with and to talk to is vital to accomplishing each day in the primary classroom.

Remarkably however, the relatively low levels of interaction with their teachers did not seem to mean that the observed children failed to engage with their learning tasks. This was monitored by coding 'pupil activity' during observations, again at ten-second intervals. Table 3.8 reports the aggregated results.

The overall task engagement figure of 60 per cent is identical to that found by Galton *et al.* in 1976 and 1996. This is interesting, because the doubling of whole-class interaction over that period seems to have had no overall impact on the amount of pupil engagement. Nevertheless, PACE data record that there was an overall increase in task engagement as the target pupils moved through their schools. There were also two step-reductions in 'waiting for teacher' which suggest possible changes in pedagogy at the end of Key Stage 1 and as the children entered Year 5. In Year 6 a

Table 3.8 Main types of pupil activity observed in classrooms (percentages)

	Year 1 1991	Year 2 1992	Year 3 1993	Year 4 1994	Year 5 1995	Year 6 1996	Mean
Task-engaged	55.3	58.6	59.5	60.8	56.9	67.8	59.9
Task management	12.8	12.7	12.7	13.0	14.3	11.3	12.8
Distracted	21.0	18.3	20.5	18.9	23.9	17.8	20.1
Waiting for teacher	8.4	8.8	4.5	5.1	2.9	2.1	5.2
Other	2.5	1.7	2.8	2.2	2.0	1.0	2.0

Source: PACE 1, 2 and 3 systematic pupil observation
Sample: 54 Years 1–6 classrooms in nine schools in eight LEAs
Date: Summer 1991 to Summer 1996

particularly high level of task engagement was recorded (68 per cent), with low levels of task management, distraction and waiting for the teacher. This was also the year in which the highest level of whole-class pedagogic contexts was observed (37 per cent) and a time when the pressure of Key Stage 2 SAT assessments became extremely high. Both teachers and pupils took the challenge seriously, particularly as they approached the period of the tests.

As reported in the first PACE book (Pollard *et al.*, 1994), our data suggest that task engagement and task management tend to vary together in English classrooms, and that 'distraction' has remained relatively stable for many years at around 20 per cent of observations. This is a high inference observational category, but data across studies is relatively consistent. Given the fact that pupils were either alone or interacting with other children, rather than the teacher, for two-thirds of the time, the level of distraction might be judged to be relatively low. Although in Year 5 the level of distraction reached 24 per cent, the overall impression is that primary school pupils of the 1990s were very hard-working. The total time-on-task (task-engaged and task management) was consistently over 70 per cent of available time. These data do not suggest that English primary schools are characterized by children 'doing what they want' and 'playing all day', as some media images have sought to portray them.

In our observations, boys were more distracted and less task-engaged than girls. Indeed, in every year except Year 2, our data show girls having higher levels of task engagement than boys – with an exceptional excess of 8 per cent in Year 6. Analysis based on peer status was also illuminative. Each of the children in the sample were assigned to one of four categories of peer status each year on the basis of sociograms derived from asking pupils to secretly nominate three children in the class they most like to play with. As peer status fell, distraction increased – probably as less popular children sought attention from their peers. When peer status was high, task engagement also increased, perhaps as more socially secure children sat and worked with their friends. A similar pattern emerged in relation to the three categories of socio-economic status against which each child's family background was coded – non-manual, skilled manual and unskilled manual. Children in non-manual families were the least likely to be distracted and the most likely to be task-engaged. However, the factor most strongly and consistently related to levels of distraction was attainment. Distraction increased steadily as attainment fell, and a rise of task engagement was associated with increasingly high levels of attainment.

As we previously reported (Pollard *et al.*, 1994) there were significant variations between schools. In schools serving families in more challenging socio-economic circumstances, there were higher levels of distraction, task management and waiting for teacher. It appeared simply to be much harder for teachers to settle their classes into the smooth patterns of task engagement that were achieved by some schools in more affluent communities.

This chapter is focused on the classroom experiences of pupils, but teacher behaviour is perhaps a very important factor in this. 'Type of teacher activity' was coded every ten seconds during periods of teacher observation. A relatively simple classification system was used which, in particular, highlighted a distinction between task instruction, task direction and disciplinary control (see Appendix 1 for more details). As Table 3.9 reveals, the six years of the PACE study revealed some significant developments.

Table 3.9 Observed teacher activities (percentages)

	Year 1 1991	Year 2 1992	Year 3 1993	Year 4 1994	Year 5 1995	Year 6 1996	Mean
Instruction	37.2	45.5	46.0	40.0	60.2	63.4	49.6
Direction	35.8	32.5	31.6	38.2	24.2	20.9	30.0
Control	10.4	6.0	6.8	5.9	6.1	5.7	6.7
Assessment	7.2	3.9	5.6	6.9	5.2	5.3	5.7
Encouragement	5.1	6.4	4.3	4.3	2.2	1.1	3.7
Hearing children read	4.0	5.4	5.2	3.4	1.2	3.1	3.6
Negative	0.2	0.4	0.6	1.2	0.9	0.6	0.7

Source: PACE 1, 2 and 3 systematic pupil observation
Sample: 54 Years 1–6 classrooms in nine schools in eight LEAs
Date: Summer 1991 to Summer 1996

In particular, the amount of 'task instruction' rose dramatically in Years 5 and 6, to around 60 per cent of teacher activity compared with approximately 40 per cent in Years 1 to 4. About half of this time replaced task direction activities, perhaps suggesting that this was a lesser concern for teachers of older pupils. Understandably, hearing children read also decreased as they grew older, but so too did teacher activity coded as 'encouragement'. This was always a small percentage, but it gradually fell from 5 per cent in Year 1 to just 1 per cent in Year 6. Overall teacher activity concerned with disciplinary control was fairly consistent, averaging some 7 per cent.

Teacher activity was also coded during child observation when the teacher interacted directly with the target child. As we saw above, one-to-one pupil–teacher interaction amounted to just 3.4 per cent over the whole study. However, on such occasions the proportion of task instruction was particularly high at 63 per cent.

In the case of Key Stage 2, Galton *et al.* (1999) offer further insight into the trends which have been reported above. Using a four-part categorization system to record 'questions', 'statements', 'silent interaction', and 'no interaction', they compared original 1976 ORACLE data on teacher activity with that gathered through a 1996 replication. Table 3.10 sets out their comparative results.

Table 3.10 ORACLE findings on teacher activity, 1976 and 1996

	1976 – All	1996 – All
Questions	12.0	16.2
Statements	44.7	59.2
Silent interaction	22.3	12.2
No interaction	21.0	12.4

Source: Galton *et al.*, 1999, p. 30.

As with PACE, these data describe a considerable increase in the proportion of teacher activity spent in active instruction, with the combination of questions and statements rising from 57 per cent to over 75 per cent. Primary classrooms thus appear to have become more intense places pedagogically, with a higher proportion of time being used by direct teacher instruction. Indeed, Galton *et al.* argue that the shift towards more whole-class teaching has 'largely been taken up, in absolute terms, by an increase in the amount of talking at pupils through statements' (p. 27). Additionally, Galton *et al.* report a doubling in the proportion of closed questions from 1976 to 1996. Such questions embody relatively low levels of cognitive challenge and do not call for elaborated replies.

Despite such changes in the absolute amount of instruction, there are also signs of continuities in pedagogic method. For instance, Galton *et al.* (1999) suggest that the ratio of questions to statements has not altered greatly over the past twenty years – with three and a half times more statements being made than questions asked at both their points of data-gathering. Alexander's work from the CICADA project also suggests that, despite significant curriculum changes, there has been remarkable 'resilience at the deeper levels of pedagogy' (1995, p. 111). Overall, these findings suggest that pupils in the 1990s experienced an increasing proportion of instruction and whole-class teaching. However, as Galton *et al.* put it: 'the pattern of teachers' discourse at the level of questions and answers has remained relatively stable (p. 28) ... Teaching in today's primary schools ... is very much a matter of teachers talking and children listening' (p. 33).

Expressing this in Bernstein's terms, it appears clear that the framing of pupil activity through teachers' classroom pedagogy has tightened over the past twenty years. Classroom practice in primary schools is more intense and more teacher controlled. Pupils are less autonomous in their use of space and time and in their choice of activity. This pattern is reinforced by data on the PACE sample of pupils moving through their primary schooling. Gradually, from Year 1 to Year 6, the extent of teacher control and classroom framing increased. In part, as we have seen, this may be attributed to new curriculum requirements and pressures from the media and government ministers, to which teachers felt the need to respond. However, the tightening of frame can also be seen as a response to new assessment and inspection requirements – issues to which we now turn.

3.4 ASSESSMENT

Whilst curriculum addresses 'content' and pedagogy focuses on 'process', assessment is concerned with the exercise of 'power' in respect of performance. As we shall see in Chapter 7, primary school pupils are extremely aware of this fact, and the ways in which teachers undertake assessment within school classrooms is thus a vital feature of their lives.

In the first PACE book (Pollard *et al.*, 1994) we constructed a framework for considering a transition in the forms of assessment that appeared to be occurring (Table 3.11).

Table 3.11 Mode, purpose and frequency of assessment

	Assessment to support the construction of knowledge	Assessment to monitor the acquisition of established knowledge
Mode	Covert/intuitive	Overt/explicit
Purpose	Encouragement/guidance	Accountability
Frequency	Continuous	Intermittent

In the liberal-progressive discourse of child-centred constructivism, assessment was conceived for formative purposes, but assessment practices were rarely made explicit. Indeed, at the level of actual practice, teacher perspectives of pupils were formed through intuitive pragmatism, based on day-to-day experiences of children but without systematic evidence. However, teacher views were nevertheless very significant because of the anticipated link between the expectations of others and performance, deriving from studies such as Rosenthal and Jacobsen (1968), or more broadly, through the 'hidden curriculum' (Jackson, 1968; Snyder, 1971). Abbott (1996) studied teacher expectations and judgements of pupils using PACE data gathered in the first four years of the study and found that there was a close relationship and continuity from year to year between the views of performance held by teachers and those of the pupils themselves. However, there remains the question of whether the behaviour or the expectation came first.

The introduction of more rigorous assessment of subject knowledge, as specified by the new National Curriculum, represented a move in the direction of overt and explicit assessment. Following TGAT (1988) there were to be two forms of assessment – Teacher Assessment (TA) and Standard Assessment Tasks (SATs). To provide clear sets of assessment criteria, the National Curriculum was expressed with Levels, Attainment Targets and statements of attainment for each subject. In the very early 1990s many teachers hoped to be able to develop TA as formative assessment and to build it as an integral part of their classroom practice. However, the demand for 'consistency' in comparative assessments (SCAA, 1995) generated an enormous demand for detailed paperwork as teachers attempted to develop record-keeping systems and 'collect evidence' to support their judgements. As each subject was successively introduced, the scale and complexity of the activity threatened to overwhelm teachers, and Gipps *et al.* (1995) reported that teacher assessments in these early days often remained intuitive rather than being evidence-based. From

1990, when end-of-Key Stage SATs began to be piloted and implemented, their requirements for standardization challenged the values of many teachers at the classroom level. Thus the degree of explicit and categoric judgement required and the summative form of SAT testing contrasted with the previous intuitive provisionality. Further, the fact that assessment data was required for publication to parents as part of new school accountability measures was seen as an attack on teacher professionalism. There were thus a variety of reasons why teachers' initial reactions to assessment requirements were generally negative.

However, the existence of new requirements could not be denied and teachers gradually began to develop more skills and confidence in Teacher Assessment. Processes of inter-school moderation were established as part of this, and such activities were extremely important in exchanging ideas and sharing experiences. Over time, there was a gradual mellowing of teacher resistance to externally imposed assessment. Thus comparing PACE 1993–4 data with that for 1995–6 shows a halving of negative and a doubling of positive feelings about Teacher Assessment (Osborn *et al.*, 2000). This change in teacher perceptions of assessment had important consequences in the classroom because more explicit assessment activities started to become built into class routines, particularly for older pupils. For instance, the Year 3 teachers studied by Gipps *et al.* (1995) reported the use of assessment level information for devising individual work programmes and differentiation in their classrooms, for forming task groups and for planning topic work and other curriculum activities. PACE data suggest a trend towards a range of more categoric assessment procedures (see Table 3.12). The most significant finding is the doubling in the use of routine spelling, Mathematics and other standardized tests between 1993–4 and 1995–6, although there was a fall in listening/observing and less oral questioning in the same period.

In the summer of 1992 we observed the Key Stage 1 SATs being taken by the pupils in our study. As reported in Pollard *et al.* (1994), these tests were extremely problematic. Apart from the enormous workload that they demanded of teachers, they were too weakly integrated into the curriculum to provide diagnostic

Table 3.12 Significant assessment procedures used by teachers

	1993–4 Years 1, 2	1995–6 Years 4, 5 and 6
Listening/observing children	70.5	52.3
Tasks planned specifically	63.6	51.6
Regular spelling tests	33.0	60.9
Pupil self-assessment	23.9	33.6
Selection portfolio work	20.5	28.1
Oral questioning	19.3	10.9
Regular Maths/tables tests	18.2	43.8
Standardized tests	9.1	15.6

Source: PACE 2 and 3 teacher interviews
Sample: 92 Years 3–4 teachers, 128 Years 4–6 teachers in 48 schools in eight LEAs
Date: Autumn 1993, Autumn 1995

information and were insufficiently reliable to provide sound evidence on performance. However, despite the opposition of teachers, the tests were developed in each successive year and they undoubtedly became more manageable. In addition, as is reported in Osborn *et al.* (2000), there is evidence that teachers developed more self-confidence and skill in conducting assessment over the period. There was considerable professional development activity through sharing ideas and experiences of assessment, Key Stage coordination and involvement with inter-school moderation processes. Indeed, Gipps *et al.* (1995) provide a positive summary of changes among Key Stage 1 teachers over the period:

> We believe that we have offered evidence that ... teachers have redirected the focus of their teaching and this has been reflected in improved national assessment results in the 'basic skills'. Greater care in planning, close observation of children and a more detailed understanding of individual progress impacting on teaching were reported by over half of our headteachers ... Many of our Key Stage 1 teachers have moved away from intuitive approaches towards more systematic, evidence-based techniques. The SATs have acted as a training device and group moderation has broken down barriers.
>
> (p. 187)

However, by the summer of 1996 when we collected evidence on the implementation of the Key Stage 2 SATs, there were some less positive indications. In particular there was evidence of assessment targets becoming increasingly 'high-stakes' as schools felt exposed to political, parental and media critique and vulnerable to new inspection processes. In consequence, very concerted efforts were being made to increase pupil performance. This often took the form of an increased amount of revision and preparation for testing in Year 6 – 'teaching to the test' – and there were also indications of a 'washback' effect into earlier year groups of younger children. The tests at Year 6 were thus beginning to have an effect on teaching and pupil experience throughout Key Stage 2.

This capacity of assessment to distort a whole curriculum has been noted many times before (Broadfoot, 1996), indeed Bernstein (1996) has characterized assessment as the purest form of the 'pedagogic device'. It is thus a considerable source of power in framing, constraining and directing the curricular and performance focus of routine classroom processes.

3.5 CONCLUSION

This chapter has set out key findings from PACE observational data to indicate how the 'performance' model had began to affect classroom practice in primary schools of the early and mid-1990s. In terms of our cubic representation of the three key 'message systems' of classroom life – curriculum, pedagogy and assessment (Figure 1.1) – the directions of change continued to be clear. Thus, despite the initial attempt to broaden the *curriculum*, we saw a reassertion of the 'basics' and the core subjects of English, Mathematics and Science. This reassertion was particularly driven by external pressures for accountability in these subjects. There was also a sustained trend towards teaching single subjects, and this eventually culminated in the Literacy and Numeracy Hours initiatives of the late 1990s. Whole-school curriculum planning provided much tighter sequencing and progression within subjects.

Regarding *pedagogy*, we reported a doubling of children's time spent in whole-class interaction compared with the 1970s, although almost 60 per cent of time was still spent in individual task work. There remained very little one-to-one interaction with the teacher. Children were task-engaged for 60 per cent of the time, but this rose to 68 per cent in Year 6 when SAT pressure began to be felt particularly strongly. There was a very significant growth in the proportion of teacher time spent on instruction (37 per cent in 1991, Year 1; to 63 per cent in 1996, Year 6), and this finding is reinforced by Galton's work showing a doubling in the proportion of closed questions used by teachers between 1976 and 1996. Setting was developing at the end of our period of study, and this continued the trend towards more tightly framed pedagogic practices. Overall, classroom practice became more intense and more teacher controlled.

Assessment became an accepted part of primary school practice over the period of our study – a fact which reflects considerable ideological and professional accommodation by teachers. Commitment to implicit and formative assessment was gradually eroded by workload and new external requirements. As the significance of assessment results increased for both teachers and schools, there were increasing signs of curricular and pedagogic adjustment through 'teaching to the test' and of the 'washback' effect of Year 2 and Year 6 SATs spreading further through schools. Gradually, the expectation that pupil performance would be measured and reported in explicit, categoric and public ways became accepted.

Having noted these developments, we must also acknowledge the deep continuities in primary school practices which also existed. The basic elementary school curriculum has dominated primary schools for over 150 years. Teachers have always been in ultimate control and have certainly dominated classroom talk. Teachers' assessments and judgements have always been a key source of their power, to which pupils must respond. Classrooms remain much the same in terms of appearance. However, having said that, the available evidence clearly shows changes in the degree of curriculum classification, pedagogic frame and assessment categorization. They have tightened and become more specific. Further, this is a system-wide development which has come about as a result of clearly stated national policy. The changes which have been recorded by PACE and other studies are the result of progressive waves of systemic 'reform'. There has been a sustained political commitment to alter the nature of education provision for young children and, whilst the fundamentals of classrooms remain, policies designed to ensure the 'delivery of performance' have had an undeniable effect.

In this context, the contrastive analysis of pedagogic discourse offered by Bernstein (1996) and developed by the PACE team (Pollard *et al.*, 1997a) is compelling. We represent it in Table 3.13 below.

This representation highlights different conceptions of appropriateness in a variety of pedagogic domains – pupil autonomy, the use of classroom space, time and activity, evaluation and assessment, classroom control and the nature of pupil products. Although originating in Bernstein's rather abstract theorizing, the framework finds considerable resonance in the PACE data-sets. Such theorizing

Table 3.13 Some contrastive aspects of competence and performance models in relation to classrooms and pupils

	LIBERAL PROGRESSIVE 'COMPETENCE EDUCATION'	'PERFORMANCE EDUCATION'
CLASSROOMS AND PUPILS	*'Invisible pedagogies', with weak classification and frame*	*'Visible pedagogies', with strong classification and frame*
Autonomy	Considerable	Limited
Space	Flexible boundaries and use	Explicit regulation
Time	Flexible emphasis on present experiences	Strong structuring, sequencing and pacing
Activity	Emphasis on the realization of inherent learner capabilities through subject integrated and learner controlled activities, such as projects	Strong control over selection of knowledge and explicit promotion of specialized subjects and skills
Evaluation and assessment	Emphasis on immediate, present qualities using implicit and diffuse criteria	Emphasis on correct products or capabilities using explicit and specific performance criteria
Control	Relatively 'invisible', with control inhering in interpersonal communications and relationships	Explicit structuring and systems for classification, setting and differentiation through instruction
Pupil products	Pupil products are taken to indicate a stage of cognitive, affective or social development. Teachers 'read' and interpret learner products using specialized professional judgement and knowledge	Pupil products are simply taken to indicate performance, as objectified by grades. Teachers instruct and assess using nationally defined procedures and criteria.

also has considerable propositional value, posing questions to be addressed. In particular, we now turn to the question of pupil perspectives and motivation in relation to learning. How did pupils adapt to the new performance-orientated curriculum, pedagogies and forms of assessment? What were pupil perspectives on classroom life in the new era? Answering these questions is the goal of the next eight chapters.

Chapter 4

Pupil Perspectives on Curriculum Subjects

4.1   Introduction
4.2   Children's views of the core curriculum
4.3   Children's views of the non-core subjects
4.4   Conclusion

4.1 INTRODUCTION

In Chapter 3 of this book we reported our analysis of the quantitative data drawn from systematic observation in the classrooms of our target schools. We asked 'What was the classroom impact of the progressive introduction of the "delivery of performance" model of education through the six years of the PACE study?'. The next eight chapters take up this question and consider it from the perspective of the pupils in those classrooms. In this chapter we look at what the children told us about the subjects that made up the National Curriculum they experienced. We concentrate on their accounts of *what* they were taught and their perception of how much time they spent learning core and non-core subjects. Where appropriate we make cross-reference to what teachers told us and what we observed.

Chapter 2 gave an overview of the PACE research design and methodology. The data we deal with here were gathered during interviews with our target pupils. In the PACE 1 interviews we gained insights into the curriculum as the children experienced it by showing them a collage of typical activities from an infant classroom and asking them to tell us which of these sorts of things they did in their class. From this we derived a list of thirteen activities and calculated the nominations each had received. In Key Stage 2 the list was expanded to 29 curriculum activities. In the PACE 2 and 3 interviews the pupils were shown the list and, using categories derived from their own language use, they were asked whether they felt they did these activities or subjects 'a lot', 'a bit' or 'not much'. They were given the opportunity to add any activity they felt was missing and to answer 'not at all' if they thought the activity never appeared in their curriculum. Using the same list, the children were then asked in each year of the study to tell us the two curriculum activities they 'liked best' and the two they 'liked least' and if possible to tell us the reasons for their choices. The data relating to their curriculum preferences are discussed in detail in Chapter 5; here references to their likes and dislikes are used to develop discussion of subject content.

4.2 CHILDREN'S VIEWS OF THE CORE CURRICULUM

In Key Stage 1 (Pollard *et al.*, 1994) the children clearly perceived a curriculum dominated by 'the basics'. They were most strongly aware of English, in the guise of 'stories', 'reading' and 'writing'. These three activities accounted for 30 per cent of the nominations made in response to the question 'Which of these sorts of things do you do in your classroom?'. Maths (by that name) also figured largely (19 per cent of nominations). The children were much less aware of 'Science' as a curricular subject (this accounted for only 2 per cent of the nominations although it featured as 8 per cent of our systematic observations). However, overall, there was a close match between the children's perception of curriculum balance and our classroom observations where 60 per cent of observed time was devoted to the core subjects.

In Key Stage 2 this perception of a strong emphasis on 'the basics' was sustained. The children interviewed in our target schools certainly felt that they were doing 'a lot' of Maths and English activities. Our systematic observations in classrooms suggest that this perception was an accurate reflection of pupil experience where, in Years 3 to 6, English and Maths accounted for between 42 and 54 per cent of the observed time. In both phases of Key Stage 2 teachers from our larger sample of 48 schools said they felt they were doing more Maths and English. The pupil responses do not suggest that they were aware of any increase, simply that these activities consistently figured most strongly in their experience.

Among our pupils, awareness of Science remained weak until Years 5 and 6 when there was a marked increase in the amount of time reported for 'writing about Science' and (to a less extent) for 'doing Science investigations'. A similar increase was also evident in our classroom observations of time spent on Science over that period (see Table 3.2). To provide a more detailed picture of what the children told us about their experiences of the core curriculum we look at each subject in turn.

English

To identify 'English' in the primary curriculum was not a straightforward task. Reading, Writing, Talking and Listening, the four strands of the English National Curriculum, appeared in classrooms in many forms and guises, some of them cross-curricular. The children found it relatively easy to know and say when they were engaged with Mathematics, but English for them involved a range of activities referred to by a variety of names. For example, pupils (often in one class) referred to having exercise books/folders for 'writing', 'stories', 'language', 'grammar', 'handwriting', 'English workbook', 'Longman', and 'spelling'. With this in mind we drew up for each key stage a list of activities to discuss with the children using as far as possible familiar formulations.

There was considerable variation in the perception of time spent on different activities but the rank ordering remained fairly consistent. In Year 6, for instance, the activities mentioned as occurring 'a lot' by over half of the group were: reading to yourself (74 per cent); spelling (65 per cent); writing other than stories (57 per cent). To organize discussion of the data we will use the National Curriculum strand headings.

Reading

The account of reading given by the children is particularly interesting in the light of the development of the Literacy Hour and its subsequent introduction into all primary schools in 1998. In general terms, the model of reading development experienced by the PACE children involved reading to the teacher, one-to-one, and reading to yourself. Reading to the teacher was the dominant activity in Key Stage 1 and at the beginning of Key Stage 2. In Year 3, for example, almost all pupils reported spending time reading to the teacher (61 per cent a lot; 28 per cent a bit). This fell away sharply in Year 4 with fewer pupils (35 per cent) reporting doing it a lot and more (26 per cent) not much or not at all. Spending less time reading to the teacher was a marker in reading progress which the children were aware of and there was considerable status in doing less reading of this kind, in having 'finished the scheme' and becoming a 'free reader'. In answering this question some children differentiated themselves: 'I don't read to my teacher but other people do'.

In Key Stage 2 the picture of reading which emerged from most of the children's comments, positive or negative, was still one defined by a hierarchy of difficulty.

> I like it. I've got loads of books at home. I like big books and try to pick them out 'cos they've got lots of stories and it shows you can read well.
>
> (Dawn, Year 3, Kenwood)

> I like it. I'm on the hardest book in our class.
>
> (Jan, Year 6, Valley)

> I don't like reading to the teacher. I don't know how to read and some words I get muddled up with other ones. When I get words muddled up I have to take them home to practise them.
>
> (Jacquie, Year 5, St Anne's)

Reading development was largely vested in pupils continuing to read alone. Most pupils thought they did this 'a lot' and regular daily silent reading times on class timetables suggest the source of this perception. However it is worth noting that the perception of having 'a lot' of time given to this activity fell from 90 per cent in Year 5 to 74 per cent in Year 6 which suggests that time for reading alone was the core curriculum activity which was most squeezed in SATs year. Thus children, apart from those who were still reading to their teacher, had less time for the silent reading which, in theory, was relied upon as a major vehicle for their reading development. Teachers resorted to the strategy of encouraging children to read at home, although aware that this would not operate in the same way for all pupils.

The statements made by pupils suggested little, if any, awareness of time spent monitoring, reviewing or discussing what they had read or might read, or of specifically promoting and developing the activity of reading for a variety of purposes. In Years 5 and 6 two-thirds of the group said they did this 'not much' or 'not at all'. Some quite explicitly referred to the fact that they had not found books that gave them a satisfying read and would extend their reading experience:

> Sometimes when I've done loads of reading I don't like it. When I start I think 'This is going to be great' but after I've done a lot it isn't really.
>
> (Lucy, Year 3, Lawnside)

> I don't like reading to myself unless it's a Roald Dahl book. His books are funny.
>
> (Trevor, Year 5, Valley)

In general, the accounts of the children provide little evidence of awareness of progression in reading beyond a basic competence.

Outside of reading to the teacher and reading alone, pupils were less clear about other activities associated with reading development. The concept of 'reading lessons', now so evident in the form of the Literacy Hour, was one that few children recognized. Reading was something you 'did' rather than something you learned or were taught. Indeed, pupils' responses suggest that in Key Stage 2 teacher time was allocated only to those who were having problems with reading. In Year 3, 43 per cent of pupils put reading lessons in the 'not much' category with 13 per cent 'not at all'; in Year 4, 51 per cent said 'not much' with 27 per cent 'not at all'. The children also made no mention of teaching or lessons related to the reading of non-fiction However, they did recognize doing English exercises from books or worksheets – in Year 6, 46 per cent said they did this 'a lot' and 43 per cent 'a bit'. This concurs with what we saw in the teachers' planning where there was growing evidence of regular timetabled slots for work from published scheme books, cards and photocopied worksheets on comprehension, vocabulary, grammar and punctuation. If we assume these were planned to contribute to reading and writing development, it appears that, for reading at least, the children perceived these as separate activities rather than related to the reading of other texts at school and at home.

Listening to stories and other kinds of texts read aloud was another aspect of reading readily recognized by the children. In Years 3 and 4 two-thirds of the children thought their teachers read to them a lot and only 10 per cent suggested this happened not much or not at all. However, awareness of 'being read to' dropped sharply in Years 5 and 6 – another area of the curriculum vulnerable to the squeeze on time. A very similar pattern of responses emerged in both these years with less than half of our pupils indicating that this happened a lot, and over a quarter that this was something their teachers did not much or not at all. There was, however, considerable variation between schools. In some schools, children's responses indicated an apparent school-wide commitment to reading aloud that was on the whole sustained through all six years. In other schools, children's experience seemed to reflect the relative enthusiasm individual teachers felt about this activity. In one school for instance, after two years in which children were unanimous that they were read to a lot, they reported not much of this in Year 5. But in Year 6 the majority felt they were being read to a lot again. In three of our schools the children's responses indicated that teachers reading to the class had virtually disappeared from the curriculum in Year 6.

Writing

As might be expected, writing as an activity figured very large in the children's perceptions. In all years over 50 per cent of the children thought they did a lot of writing and the percentages for 'not much' writing were very small. They thought they did less writing stories in Years 5 and 6 but their estimations of time spent writing for other things remained high. In contrast to reading, the concept of 'lessons about writing' was more clearly established for most of the children. In Year 3 just over a third thought they had these 'a lot' and another third, 'a bit'. Lessons in handwriting were similarly perceived in Year 5 but figured less strongly in Year 6. However, spelling was well-established in pupils' consciousness in Year 6 with 65 per cent thinking they did it a lot and 35 per cent, a bit. Although a concern, spelling was not the aspect of writing which provoked most comment. The children were far more exercised about handwriting, its size and neatness.

> I'm not that good at handwriting. I write a bit big sometimes. I don't do joined-up that much, only if it's posh work to go on the wall.
>
> (Dean, Year 3, Kenwood)

> Joined-up is hard – I get letters wrong then.
>
> (Kevin, Year 6, Audley)

They also disliked having to practice it:

> Handwriting is boring – all you do is go up and down, up and down.
>
> (Polly, Year 3, Valley)

> With handwriting you don't get to do much, it's boring.
>
> (Tom, Year 3, Greenmantle)

In general, English activities, in contrast to Mathematics, were not strongly liked or disliked. However, when children did express a view it was usually related to some aspect of writing and more likely to be negative. The act of writing for many of our target children was painful, threatening and not enjoyed at either key stage.

In Key Stage 1 the labour of 'getting the words', holding the pencil, forming letters and spelling correctly was amplified by the problem of thinking of something to write, being neat, writing an acceptable amount and getting finished in time.

> Writing is hard.
>
> (Dean, Year 1, Kenwood)

> I like doing the picture. I don't like the writing. It's difficult to write the letters.
>
> (Kim, Year 1, St Bede's)

I'm always slow at writing.

(Sean, Year 2, Greenmantle)

Writing takes me a long time because the spellings trouble me and I can't rush it. Mrs P wants it done quick. I was doing a piece of writing about rain. That's our project at the moment. I don't like writing. I feel I'm never going to get it done.

(Patrick, Year 2, Orchard)

If we get our writing really spidery we have to write it again – in Maths we just rub it out.

(Abel, Year 2, Valley)

I was writing about a squirrel. (Did you like doing that?) No, because sometimes you don't know what to write.

(Corrinne, Year 2, Meadway)

The responses of Key Stage 2 developed the themes of Key Stage 1. Children were still concerned about the amount that was expected and the time and effort involved in transcription, especially if this involved writing things out again:

News takes ages and if you don't write much the problem is Mrs D writes 'Where were you all the weekend? In bed?'.

(Eliot, Year 3, St Bede's)

We have to write it in rough then copy it and it might be really long and it takes too long.

(Olivia, Year 4, Lawnside)

I just don't like writing; I don't like doing lots of it. Writing out stories – there's so much of it.

(Jessica, Year 5, Kenwood)

I liked doing the activity. I didn't like writing it out.

(Esther, Year 6, Greenmantle)

The negative connotations of some sorts of writing are made very clear by these examples of the many comments that placed activities that were liked in opposition to activities that required writing:

I like doing things like making a light bulb work with a battery and wire. I don't like writing, you have to write long stories.

(Robin, Year 2, Valley)

Writing makes my hand hurt and I have to put special cream on it. I like cookery because you don't have to use pencils.

(Gavin, Year 4, Orchard)

In PE we are allowed to move around and make up things. We have a choice and we just move to the music. I don't like topic work because of all the writing we have to do.

(Jan, Year 5, Valley)

We can see here the opposition between being active in learning – making, doing, moving – and the pressure to record. We explore this further in Chapter 9 on pupil perspectives on classroom learning. However there was one form of writing – writing stories – that constituted an exception to all this. Although a few children disliked writing stories because it took a long time or because they couldn't think what to write, far more relished the freedom this kind of writing gave them to exercise their imaginations and to enjoy some creative play.

> Writing stories – I get ideas and I write it really fast and it's enjoyable.
>
> (Haley, Year 3, St Bede's)

> In Science Sir tells us what to do but when we write stories we can make up our own minds.
>
> (Samantha, Year 4, St Bede's)

> I like writing stories – it's imaginative. When you write about other things you have to think about that thing and you can't imagine anything.
>
> (Lucy, Year 4, Lawnside)

> We had to write a story suitable for a 5-year-old. I like writing stories and I've got the book of *Bambi* at home so I chose that. I like the bit when he says 'No, Flower' and 'No, Skunk'.
>
> (Kelly, Year 4, Orchard)

> I like writing stories about stuff that's happened or I want to happen. In handwriting you've just got to write on the sheet and that's quite boring.
>
> (Ewan, Year 5, Kenwood)

Strongly evident here is the sense that writing stories gave the children some sense of having made their own choices and of being in control. Opportunities for this kind of autonomous expression were few in the later years of Key Stage 2 as curriculum coverage became a priority. The children's perception that they did less story writing in Years 5 and 6 suggests that scope for their own writing was reduced as writing controlled by the teacher and grounded in teacher-led tasks increased.

Talking and Listening

In PACE 3, to get an impression of the attention being given to oracy skills and of the amount of talk for learning children thought went on in their classrooms, we asked them about 'having discussions about any subject'. In general, pupils perceived less time for subject-based talk as they moved to the end of Key Stage 2. The percentage of children who thought they discussed things 'a lot' decreased from 41 per cent in Year 5 to 37 per cent in Year 6. In the same year over half of the pupils thought they spent only 'a bit' of time having discussions. The increasing emphasis on literacy which emerged as the PACE study progressed, combined with the weight of content in subjects which made up the rest of the curriculum, appear to have led to a weak perception of the talking and listening strands of English. Certainly the pupils in our study were not aware of explicit attention to the development of communication skills and reported less time for developing understanding through interaction with others. Of the four strands of the National Curriculum for English, two have a much higher profile in pupils' minds.

However, as with 'being read to', perceptions of 'discussion' varied between schools. Lawnside emerged as the most 'talkative' school in both years with no children recording 'not much' for this activity. At Valley and Orchard there was a perceived increase in the amount of time for this kind of interaction. These are all small rural or semi-rural schools with mixed-age classes and a high socio-economic status intake. They were also, as we will see, schools which more than others in the sample retained a greater degree of integration between subjects in planning the curriculum. In contrast, at St Bede's, Kenwood Junior and Audley Junior, all large urban schools with more structured timetables, the children perceived a reduction in the amount of discussion they experienced in Year 6.

Overall the data communicate a sense of classrooms with little (and in some cases increasingly less) time for talk as a learning activity. This reflects, as we have seen in Chapter 3 and will continue to see as this and the following chapters unfold, an experience of curriculum that was increasingly tightly framed, with the emphasis on individual work and writing.

Mathematics

On the list of activities offered to the children Maths appeared as 'Maths with sums', 'Maths with problems and games' and, in Year 6, 'Mental Maths/Maths in your head, e.g. tables'. In Key Stage 2 'Maths with sums' was the most clearly perceived and dominant of all the curriculum subjects and activities. Between 80 per cent and 90 per cent of pupils in Years 3 to 6 thought they did 'a lot' of it. In Year 6, 60 per cent thought they did 'a lot' of mental Maths and 30 per cent did 'a bit'. This is a shift in perception from Key Stage 1 where reading and writing activities figured most strongly. The strong awareness of Maths in Key Stage 2 is consistent with our systematic observation data which show a steady increase in the percentage of time spent on Maths, although this never exceeded the time observed for English.

Although 'Maths with sums' was immediately and unanimously acknowledged as an activity, 'Maths with problems and games, etc.' was less consistently perceived. Teacher evidence suggests that in general 'applied' or 'practical' Maths was decreasing in Years 5 and 6. The dominance of structured schemes/worksheets was the result of a perceived need to stress basic concepts and manipulation for SATs. Overall, the children's responses confirm this. There was a decrease in those who thought they did 'a lot' of 'Maths with problems and games' from 41 per cent in Year 4 to 24 per cent in Year 6. There was, however, variation between schools. Orchard and Lawnside reflected the general downward trend. At St Anne's, where awareness of this kind of activity was never very strong, the children in Years 5 and 6 were hardly conscious of doing any 'Maths with problems and games'. At Audley Junior there was a marked decrease in awareness of this kind of activity in Year 6. In contrast, perceptions at Meadway Junior and Valley were consistently quite high from Year 4. Individual children's perceptions also varied. High-attaining children more frequently reported that they did a lot of 'Maths with problems and games', thus suggesting that use of this aspect of the Maths curriculum was one way in which teachers differentiated their provision. This pattern was particularly evident where children were set across classes for Maths.

The changing nature of the experience of Maths is illustrated by contrasting quotations from Year 3 and from Years 5 and 6. In Year 3 Maths for many children still included a practical element which was enjoyed:

> It's fun to be measuring and seeing how high and that.
>
> (Tom, Year 3, Greenmantle)

> It's been fun figuring it out. Nearly all our work is like a puzzle.
>
> (Ewan, Year 3, Kenwood)

In the later years of Key Stage 2 Maths was seen as something that came around regularly, was a serious sitting down activity and involved work books by which progress was measured.

> Usually you just sit there doing Maths.
>
> (Carol, Year 5, Orchard)

> We do a Maths sheet every day.
>
> (Susie, Year 6, St Anne's)

> We have to do set pages and I don't find it easy to do.
>
> (Juliet, Year 6, Greenmantle)

The children were also aware of the status of Maths in comparison with other activities and of teachers' expectations that they would get through the work alone and in silence. The following quotation provides an example of a child constructing different categories of work – 'serious' Maths contrasted with more relaxed and chatty technology. In the phrase 'it's not so bad' there is also a sense of the relative pressure associated with the two activities:

> They prefer you to get on with your Maths but with models it's not so bad, you can talk to your friends.
>
> (Sharon, Year 5, Greenmantle)

As we will see later in this chapter and in Chapters 7 and 10 on assessment, many children placed themselves into one of two groups – those who were confident they could do Maths and those who felt they couldn't. Interestingly it was often both very high and very low attainers who felt confident about Maths. Some very low attainers enjoyed the security of differentiated work which they could 'get right' and many would happily have 'stayed on it all day'. This contrasts sharply with their feelings about writing activities where their shortcomings were all too clearly manifested. It was those 'in the middle' who were more likely to experience Maths as problematic and worrying in the demands it makes:

> Maths I sometimes get muddled and might have to stay in at play, so Maths is more worrying. Sometimes if you can't use a calculator it goes on for days and days.
>
> (Eliot, Year 5, St Bede's)

> I don't know what we are doing and I just don't like it. I find it hard and I don't understand it.
>
> (Geoffrey, Year 5, Orchard)

> Maths they give you hard sums and sometimes you get so worried you don't know what you are doing.
>
> (Carol, Year 5, Orchard)

However Maths was frequently enjoyed and described as 'good fun' and 'just good'. 'Getting it right' was as appealing and satisfying as 'not understanding', 'getting stuck' or 'getting it wrong' was distressing. Interestingly it was also the curriculum activity in which the children seemed most aware of their mental processes and spoke about them in ways that did not occur in, for instance, their comments about writing: 'it makes your brain work', 'you have to think in your head', 'I like using my brain', 'I just like sorting out the answers', 'I like solving problems'.

Science

In Key Stage 1 the children were hardly aware of 'Science' as something they were learning about, though they were engaging in a variety of Science-based activities. The Key Stage 2 story in relation to Science appears to inherit this issue of discourse but also reflects, perhaps, the pace at which schools introduced National Curriculum Science and the varied confidence of teachers in tackling this area of the curriculum. In Years 3 and 4 the children's perceptions of how much Science they did matched almost exactly their perceptions of time spent on painting. In Year 3 almost half of our pupils reported that they did 'not much' or no Science. However in Year 5 (when our questionnaire indicated that teachers felt they were doing more Science) there was a sharp rise in pupil awareness of this subject. This is matched by our systematic observation data which in Year 5 shows an increase (from 6.1 per cent to 16.3 per cent) in time devoted to Science. By Year 6, 82 per cent of pupils were evenly divided between thinking that they did 'a lot' or 'a bit' of Science.

In Year 6 we asked the children to consider how much time they spent 'writing about Science' and 'doing investigations'. The responses indicate that they saw themselves as spending less time doing investigations than writing. This may be read as another indicator of teachers responding to the pressure of time, the quantity of content to be covered and the shift in assessment to content knowledge rather than process skills and understanding. Mandy, recounting her experience of Science in Year 4, encapsulates some of the dilemmas of this approach to learning.

> Science is hard – you have to find things out and it takes you a long time to figure things out.
>
> (Mandy, Year 4, Audley)

It seems likely that teachers, with less time available, felt unable to sustain investigational Science and resorted to a higher proportion of direct instruction.

The children exhibited some ambivalence about the reduction in investigational Science. Doing investigations created opportunities for the active involvement and sociability which, we have already seen, they saw as positive.

> I like doing experiments but I don't like writing about it afterwards because you don't feel like writing after something exciting, you feel tired.
>
> (Lucy, Year 4, Lawnside)

> It's more fun. You get to do experiments – more things to do and you can have a chat with your neighbours.
>
> (Melanie, Year 5, St Anne's)

> Science is OK when you do experiments.
>
> (Amanda, Year 6, Kenwood)

However, it did not lessen the demands for writing afterwards:

> I like doing investigations but I don't like writing conclusions.
>
> (Simon, Year 6, Valley)

The children also discovered that being taught, rather than finding out, did not reduce the requirement to write things down.

> In Science you have to, like, write things down and it gets very boring after a while. I used to like it when I was in the infants and we did less of it. Now we do it quite a lot. You do Science every week and it gets really boring. This week we're doing about mammals and it gets boring 'cos we've done quite a lot of it now.
>
> (Jeremy, Year 5, Kenwood)

> In Science you just have to copy down what the teacher says.
>
> (Mandy, Year 6, Audley)

With this emphasis on recording it is perhaps not surprising that only 2 per cent of children in Years 5 and 6 chose Science as their most liked subject. Far more (19 per cent in Year 5 and 9 per cent in Year 6) nominated it as their least liked subject. Simon, Lucy, Jeremy and Mandy, whose comments appear above, all reached Level 4 for Science at the end of Key Stage 2. However, the pressure to record and recall information which they described appeared to have killed their enthusiasm for the subject. There is arguably a discrepancy here between the curriculum as intended and Science as received. There was not enough time for learning through investigation and the pressure on transmitting content knowledge for assessment produced demands for copying and other writing which created boredom rather than interest and excitement.

4.3 CHILDREN'S VIEWS OF THE NON-CORE SUBJECTS

We were interested to discover whether the teachers' view that there had been a squeezing of non-core subjects had been perceived by the pupils. We looked to their reports of how much or how little they felt they had engaged with these subjects to suggest the degree with which they had been sustained within the experienced curriculum.

Physical Education, Art, Music

The most striking finding in PACE 1 was the very strong showing of PE in the responses. It received 24 per cent of the children's nominations (a little more than Maths) although it represented only 3 per cent of our systematic observation time. In discussing this difference (Pollard *et al.*, 1994) we argued that children's perception of a curriculum subject is influenced by the subjective feelings aroused by the activities associated with it. PE, we suggested, was mentioned because it was seen as a source of enjoyment, a release from 'work' in the form of Maths, reading and writing.

In Key Stage 2, PE was perceived less strongly than Maths and English but was seen as taking more time than any other non-core subject. In Years 3 and 4 half of the sample thought they did 'a lot' of PE. This fell to a third in Years 5 and 6 but over the whole period only a very small percentage of children reported that they did 'not much'. This is interesting when set beside the view, expressed in 1995 by a quarter of the Key Stage 2 teachers in our larger sample of 120 from 48 schools, that they were doing less PE.

PE and Art, as we will see in Chapter 5, were the 'most liked' subjects in Years 5 and 6. Although children's awareness of PE activity was relatively high, Art was reported consistently across the years as occurring 'not much' by nearly half the pupils (a little over a third thought they did it 'a bit'). In contrast to PE, which had a regular place in the timetables of all classes we observed, Art/Painting was less frequently planned into the weekly programme and often occurred alternating with 'Craft', 'Design', or Cookery. Our analysis of questionnaire returns from the larger sample of teachers showed also that nearly a third thought they were doing less Art. The children's responses confirm this and indicate their sense of how little they experienced an enjoyable activity. The picture does not change markedly if we include the children's reports of the amount of Drawing they experienced. Drawing, an activity which featured in many curriculum areas, appeared much less strongly in Years 5 and 6 in comparison with Years 3 and 4 – 70 per cent thought they did a lot of it in Year 4 but this fell to 26 per cent in Year 6. We may be seeing here the consequences of a change in pedagogy – less of 'doing a picture' as part of the learning process – as the children got older and also with a premium on time.

With regard to Music, pupil perceptions of the amount they encountered varied considerably across Years 3, 4 and 5. For example 5 per cent of pupils in Year 5 thought they did no Music at all and 22 per cent thought they did a lot. This pattern also occurred in the other years. By Year 6 over half the sample thought they did 'a bit' of Music. There was noticeable variation between schools – Audley Junior was consistently perceived as the most 'musical' and St Bede's the least. In other schools pupils reported changes in the amount of Music they experienced from year to year. In Year 4 at Greenmantle, for instance, Music was much more strongly perceived than in other years. In St Anne's awareness of Music in the curriculum declined over Key Stage 2; in Lawnside it grew. The picture is further confused by the fact that in commenting on Music there is more variation between the perceptions of pupils in the same class and the same year than for most other subject areas. These variations may be partly explained by the differential arrangements made by schools for pupils who have instrumental lessons. Year-on-year differences appear also to reflect the expertise and enthusiasm of individual teachers.

In contrast to Music, Singing figured largely in the curriculum perceived by our pupils and there was more unanimity in the responses from each class. This can be mainly accounted for by the fact that they all experienced regular class or whole-school singing practices/hymn practices, frequently identified by schools as a vehicle for delivering the Music curriculum where teachers felt less confident.

The children's reports of their experience illustrate quite clearly the squeezing of 'creative' activity. If PE managed to retain a regular place in the timetable, the identity of Art was diluted in many of our schools and children did not encounter it with any regularity. The Music curriculum, similarly, was experienced differently and haphazardly; it was most clearly recognized in whole-class or whole-school singing lessons and practices.

History, Geography

Children's perception of the Humanities was varied. History was most strongly perceived in Year 4 when 40 per cent of the children thought they did 'a lot'. However in Year 5 over 80 per cent of the pupils divided equally between feeling they did only 'a bit' or 'not much'. In Year 6 there was a slight strengthening with 51 per cent thinking they did 'a bit' of History and 32 per cent 'not much'.

The following quotations convey something of how the children in our sample experienced History in Key Stage 2:

I like TV programmes on Vikings.

(Samantha, Year 3, St Bede's)

I like reading and finding books in the library about people long ago.

(Ewan, Year 3, Kenwood)

In History she often asks us things and we don't know much about it.

(Kate, Year 4, Greenmantle)

History you get to learn more stuff about the old days.

(Jacquie, Year 4, St Anne's)

In History we're doing about the olden days which I don't find very exciting.

(Theresa, Year 6, St Anne's)

With History you have to be quiet and work.

(Laura, Year 6, Orchard)

With History it's a lot of cutting and sticking into our books. And then you have to write a lot and it's hard to remember.

(Kim, Year 6, St Bede's)

Geography was less strongly perceived than History in Years 3 and 4. Children were more equally aware of it in Years 5 and 6, although there were still fewer pupils who thought they did 'a lot'. Geography figured high in the list of least liked subjects.

Geography is a bit boring – we only have worksheets and maps and sometimes I forget what he's saying.

(Jane, Year 4, Meadway)

I don't find Geography fun, just find it boring.

(Rosie, Year 5, Lawnside)

Geography I don't really like because it's all about different countries and we don't do a lot of it but when we do you're supposed to know a lot about it.

(Harriet, Year 6, Valley)

Geography's plain boring – the world, your route to school.

(Jane, Year 6, Meadway)

You have to find different places in Geography and I don't like that.

(Samantha, Year 6, St Bede's)

I don't like doing all the maps.

(Maura, Year 6, Audley)

The lack of enthusiasm for History and Geography evident here in what the children said is disturbing. In particular in Years 5 and 6, the combination of lack of time and weight of content appeared to have created a situation in which children did not feel they were engaged with these subject areas in any meaningful way. The expectation that they would 'know' or remember, a sense of alienation from the material, the perceived superficiality of tasks and activities have combined to produce a verdict of 'boring'.

Topic work

The research evidence from the 1970s and 1980s indicates that, although the basics of English and Mathematics were being taught in primary schools as single subjects, other subjects, in particular History, Geography and the Arts, were planned into the curriculum around an integrating topic (Alexander, 1984). In reporting our findings from Key Stage 1 (1990–2) we suggested that the implementation of the National Curriculum had brought about a move from integrated work towards more highly classified subject teaching. In PACE 1 we did not ask the children about 'topic'. As they moved into Key Stage 2, where this term was more firmly established in the pre-National Curriculum discourse, we added it to the list of curriculum activities we invited them to talk about. The children's responses indicated that in Year 3 the concept of learning through 'topic' was well established in six of the nine schools in the project. However, as PACE continued, children spoke less of 'topic' and were more likely to use a subject classification. Even where 'topic' remained in their discourse this was frequently attached to a subject focus – 'our History topic', 'our Geography topic'.

For these pupils, however subject-based the content, the term 'topic work' signalled *a way of working*. Their perception of 'topic' was related to activity which involved group work, collaboration, talking, researching in the library, watching videos and above all a lot of writing. Some children responded positively to this and chose 'topic' as their most liked curriculum activity. In doing so they mentioned finding this 'interesting', or 'easier', or providing an opportunity to be active. Others found much to dislike in this process – the difficulties of collaborating, the pressure of time, the demands on writing skill and for outcomes. We discuss this in more detail in Chapter 9.

Meanwhile, looked at school by school, we begin to see some variety in children's perceived experience of 'topic work'. This variety appears to reflect school-wide decisions as well as the decisions about their teaching made by individual teachers. In four of the project schools (Lawnside, Valley, Orchard and Kenwood Junior) children in Years 5 and 6 still had a clear sense of topic featuring prominently as a way of delivering the curriculum and the term was current in the classroom and used by teachers and children. In Kenwood, for instance, there was a 'termly topic'. In Lawnside a 'History topic' on Egypt was used to integrate work in Art and Mathematics.

In two other schools (Greenmantle and Audley Junior) children reported a decrease in time spent doing topic work. In Meadway Junior the use of topic as a vehicle for curriculum planning was not strongly evident in pupil responses throughout Key Stage 2. This quotation from one teacher interview reflects what the teachers reported about exclusively subject-based planning in these schools.

> It's become ... more concerned with getting through quotas and lessons, not even trying to get through topics any more ... it's a Geography lesson ... a History lesson.
>
> (Year 3 Teacher, Audley)

Less consistency in the children's reported experience of topic work was apparent in two schools (St Anne's and St Bede's). Here the children's responses indicated an experience of marked and erratic shifts from year to year in the extent to which their teachers were incorporating a topic approach in their curriculum planning.

The period of the PACE research was one in which the concept of integrated topic-based planning was undergoing radical revision. The variations reported by the pupils may be simply a reflection of language use – the degree to which teachers ceased or continued to refer to particular approaches to subject work as 'topic'. It seems clear from the overall sense of what teachers and pupils were telling us that any semblance of integrated teaching had disappeared from almost all of these primary classrooms. At Valley the teaching head commented, 'cross-curricular links are less – it's the weight of content, of facts to be covered'. At Kenwood Junior in Year 5 the teacher commented on the shift to subject-based teaching: 'I don't think you can get through the work without doing it.'

Design Technology

As a result of the National Curriculum, Technology/Design Technology became much more sharply focused as a curriculum area. During the period of the PACE research it was high-profile and the subject of much staff development. The inclusion at that time of Information Technology within this area increased the demands on schools for resources and teacher expertise. Our analysis of the teacher questionnaires of 1995 indicates that teachers thought they were giving more time to Technology. Pupil responses indicate a different perception.

The data indicate that 'Technology' was very weakly perceived with well over 50 per cent of the children in Years 3 to 6 thinking they did 'not much' or 'none' of this kind of activity. Because in our experience not all children habitually used the label 'technology', the list, which was constructed using their terminology, also included 'making models', 'construction' and 'cooking'. Even when we add these to 'technology' the picture does not change significantly. Most striking was the sharp drop in consciousness of this curriculum area in Years 5 and 6. This may in part reflect the increasing focus on subjects to be tested and the lowering of status for a subject that in the early years of the National Curriculum had assumed almost parity of importance with the core.

In four of the nine schools the children thought they did 'not much' or no Design/ Technology activities. This may in part have been a consequence of the fact that in these schools Technology (DT) appeared on the timetables linked with 'Art' and 'Craft' and sometimes 'Cooking'. In schools where awareness was stronger Technology was specifically timetabled in addition to those other curriculum areas.

However, even though they thought they did little Technology, the children frequently cited it as a 'most liked' subject. The reasons given were invariably some variation on 'you can make things'. This was usually accompanied by some reference to 'fun', 'play' and/or 'doing stuff'.

In the school where it was most strongly perceived in Key Stage 2 (St Anne's) the details the teachers gave of their approach suggest why it registered so powerfully with the children. The Technology curriculum in the school was resourced from a trolley which moved around the classrooms. The trolley was equipped with construction kits, Lego, Polydrom, plasticene and tools such as paper, glue, card, felt tip pens and Lego technic. 'We have a rota of activities based around it,' the Year 4 teacher explained. The Year 5 teacher described the day his class had the trolley as 'a messy doing day' when the children were organized differently 'in friendship pairs and allowed to move'. Asked how much free choice the children had in Year 6 their teacher referred to Technology as the one example he could give:

> They get a loose-based sort of task, for instance produce a model that will move over a certain distance, carrying such a weight or whatever. Again that's not always quite so rigid. They have free time with that to explore the different construction kits that we use and come up with their own models. That's about it to be honest. It's not very rigid. Minimal.
>
> (Year 6 Teacher, St Anne's)

In this non-core, unassessed area these teachers seemed to feel the pressure for outcomes less. They could allow the children more autonomy, take a more relaxed approach to pupil grouping, encourage collaborative rather than individual learning, and engage with mess and doing. The children responded positively. We can see a similar reaction in other schools:

> I like Technology because it's good fun and we make lots of different things every week.
>
> (Janet, Year 5, Greenmantle)

> Making models is fun to do and not hard; people can always help me making models.
>
> (Sharon, Year 5, Greenmantle)

We want to suggest that in all the schools where children mentioned Technology positively, they felt their teachers' relaxation; but although they constructed it in opposition to 'work', there was often a positive sense of achievement and a motivation to complete when they referred to the work they produced in this area.

I like making things and feeling proud of what I have made. If you don't finish and you have some free time because you have finished all your work you can ask sir if you can finish your model and he will probably say 'yes'.

(Eliot, Year 5, St Bede's)

Information Technology

In the context of a new millennium and an increasing focus on Information Technology in schools it is interesting to consider the perceptions of 'using a computer' conveyed by the children in the PACE study. This activity was added to the list in Year 3. It was most strongly perceived in Year 5 when 33 per cent thought they used a computer 'a lot', 48 per cent 'a bit' and only 19 per cent 'not much'. In Year 6 the perception reverted to the pattern evident in Years 3 and 4 where around 80 per cent of the children considered they did 'a bit' or 'not much' (fairly evenly shared between the two categories). Children in seven of the nine schools said they did less work with the computer in Year 6 than they experienced in Year 5, arguably another indicator of their sense of the narrowing of curriculum experience in Year 6 as teachers responded to the impending SATs.

However, this overall pattern conceals noticeable variations between schools and pupils. In a curriculum area which is increasingly identified as crucial to life chances, the experience as reported by the PACE sample of children provides an illustration of the issue of entitlement as it operated in the mid-1990s.

Replies of the children at Orchard, Lawnside and Kenwood reveal a high awareness of using a computer across Key Stage 2. This contrasts with Audley Junior where in Year 4 five of the six pupils in the sample reported that they never used a computer. In Year 5 there was an increase but by Year 6 they returned to telling us that computers figured 'not much' or 'not at all' in their curriculum. These variations in perception can be seen as a consequence of availability and disposition of resources. At Lawnside, for example, there was a computer in every classroom. In Year 6, with a move into a new building, computers were even more widely available in and out of classrooms and pupils were encouraged to use them whenever possible. At Audley Junior the children explained that they did not use the computer much because all their computers had been stolen again. Their teacher commented 'We're not brilliantly well off for resources ... If I'm doing work on the computer I end up sending children to different rooms and asking if anyone's using that computer, which can inconvenience the person who's working in that room ... if a child gets stuck they ... ask whoever's in there with them'.

Allied to the availability of hardware, access to teacher expertise also plays a part in the variations in experience the children described. An example of this is provided by the Year 5 class at Meadway where uniquely all the pupils thought they used the computer 'a lot'. In the term in which they were interviewed it was these children's turn to have the computer permanently in their classroom. In addition their class teacher was the coordinator for Design and Technology and confident about building computer activity into the curriculum.

Variations in perceptions of individual pupils in the same school can also be accounted for by pupil expertise. Using a computer was often defined by teachers as a voluntary activity; pupils who were competent and confident (and frequently had their own PCs at home) tended to do more, thus reinforcing an already existing imbalance of advantage. However, there was also evidence in our observations of competent children teaching others.

4.4 CONCLUSION

Our conclusions in relation to the curriculum as perceived by the pupils remain as they were at the end of the first two phases of the PACE project – despite the National Curriculum's commitment to breadth and balance, for our target group the 'basic' subjects of Mathematics and English were dominant in their perception of the curriculum they experienced across all six years of the study. In Key Stage 1 reading and writing activities figured most prominently in their minds. In Key Stage 2 there was a shift and pupils were most sharply aware of Mathematics. Reading in Key Stage 2, except for those not making progress, was perceived mainly as silent reading rather than as direct teaching. Writing as an activity loomed large in their experience and was generally disliked except for some when perceived as story writing.

This emphasis is much as it was before the introduction of the National Curriculum. In addition we can see that attempts by designers of the National Curriculum to redefine balances within core subjects have had little impact on pupil perceptions. In English, pupils were very aware of literacy activities; speaking and listening, in contrast, were rarely, if ever, explicitly perceived as a focus for development. Similarly in Mathematics, discussion, practical activities and problem solving were low-profile in comparison with the dominant 'Maths with sums'.

Science, which acquired a new status as the third core subject, was slower to establish itself in pupils' consciousness. Here too the emphasis on learning processes evident in framework documents declined, rather than grew, in pupil awareness. In Year 6, for example, there was a fall in the children's awareness of Science as investigation.

Outside core subjects, our target pupils experienced a squeezing of the creative curriculum. Breadth and balance, it appears, were compromised by the powerful and increasing emphasis on core subjects and national testing, and also by the weight of content to be covered. There is also evidence in the children's accounts of varied access to the curriculum in Music and Information Technology. We suggest this is caused by variation in availability of resources and teacher expertise.

The tightening of the curriculum frame observed in PACE 1 and 2 continued and in the later stages of Key Stage 2 the children reported a very subject-based and teacher-determined curriculum. Relevant here are data, not yet discussed, on pupils' experience of 'free choice'. In Year 6, 58 per cent reported 'not much' free choice and 9 per cent none at all. Only 7 per cent thought they had a lot of free choice. 'Choosing' was generally understood as happening in time allocated for 'finishing off'. Teachers told us that they placed developing autonomy, confidence and independence in learning fairly high in their priorities. However, the children's reported experience of the curriculum shows little match with this aspiration. In their estimation of how much free choice they had in the curriculum, the children reported strong and increasing teacher control across Key Stage 2.

There was evidence that these pupils valued opportunities for making their own learning decisions but saw this as happening rarely and mainly in connection with non-core subjects, in particular Art and Technology. In general, their accounts convey a strong sense of the weight of content they were expected to engage with, the demand for writing that this produced, and the pressure for outcomes. As children moved to the end of Key Stage 2 they reported a curriculum in which the core subjects were powerfully present and which they experienced mainly through sitting, listening and writing rather than through activity.

Themes and issues raised in this chapter are discussed further in subsequent chapters on learning and assessment. In the next chapter we continue to develop our account of the curriculum as experienced by the pupils and look in more detail at children's changing attitudes to the curriculum.

Chapter 5

Pupil Judgements on the Curriculum

5.1   Introduction
5.2   Attitudes to the curriculum
5.3   Children's explanations for their curriculum likes and dislikes
5.4   The influence of gender and achievement on pupils' preferences
5.5   Conclusion

5.1 INTRODUCTION

In Chapter 4 we reported pupil perspectives on the subjects that constituted the curriculum they received. This chapter continues the analysis by looking in detail at children's changing curriculum preferences, their likes and dislikes and the reasons they gave to explain their choices. As explained in the introduction to Chapter 4 the data were gathered in interviews with the target pupils in which they talked with us about a list of curriculum subjects and activities. Using the same list, the children were then asked in each year of the study to tell us the two curriculum activities they 'liked best' and the two they 'liked least' and if possible to tell us the reasons for their choices.

As we established in Chapters 3 and 4, pupils in the study experienced an increasingly tightly framed, subject-based and teacher-controlled curriculum. As Key Stage 2 progressed they became more aware of the extent of curriculum content and the demand for written outcomes. It is with this context in mind that we continue our consideration of what the children told us.

5.2 ATTITUDES TO THE CURRICULUM

Our already published accounts (Pollard *et al.*, 1994, Croll 1996) show that as children moved from phase one of the project (Key Stage 1) into phase two (Years 3 and 4) interest in and enthusiasm for the core activities of Mathematics, Reading and Writing increased so that all these were high on the list of children's preferences. The PACE 3 data complete this picture of pupils' perspectives on the curriculum they were experiencing. We can now see the pattern that emerges from the results over the whole period of the project. As before, we have produced league tables of pupil preferences based on the rank order of the net score when the percentage 'best liked' was set against the percentage 'least liked' for each subject or activity in each year.

Table 5.1 Comparative 'league table' of pupils' favoured curriculum activities (net rank)

Year 1	Year 2	Year 3	Year 4	Year 5	Year 6
PE	PE	Maths	Maths	PE =	Art
Painting	Maths	Singing	Drawing	Art =	PE
'Home'	'Home'	Read to teacher	Writing	Technology	Teacher reading =
Sand	Painting	Writing	Singing	TV	Topic =
Stories	Singing	PE	Teacher reading	Choice	TV =
Singing	Reading alone	Drawing	PE		
Construction	Construction	Teacher reading	Topic		
Reading alone	Reading lesson	Topic	Read to teacher		
Reading lesson	Sand	Reading alone	History		
Science	Science	Science	Reading alone		
Writing	Stories	History	Music		
Maths	Writing	Technology	Technology		

Source: PACE 1, 2 and 3 interviews
Sample: 54 children in Years 1–6
Date: Autumn 1990 and 1991, Summer 1993, 1994, 1995 and 1996

We see here a startling turnaround in children's attitudes in the final years of Key Stage 2. In contrast to the first two years of Key Stage 2 where all the core curriculum subjects featured, with Maths, Reading and Writing appearing in the first three places, Years 5 and 6 show children reverting to the activities (PE and Art), that they nominated as favourites in Year 1.

This is a very decisive move. Of the sixteen subjects mentioned by the children in Years 5 and 6 only five ended up with a net positive rating. We can explore more of this marked attitude shift in the second half of Key Stage 2 if, instead of a league table of net results, we look at the straight rank order in percentage terms of their likes and dislikes in these years.

Each year the children had the opportunity to nominate two subjects in the most/least liked categories and all of them in Years 5 and 6 found this easy to do. The effect of putting these two choices together to produce a rank order of these categories confirms the trend we have already seen in Table 5.1, but also allows us to identify more clearly those subjects that were liked least and those that were chosen as both most and least liked.

Table 5.2 First and second choices in 'most liked' category for top five subjects (percentages) (PACE 3)

| | Year 5 | | | Year 6 | | |
	1st choice	2nd choice	Total	1st choice	2nd choice	Total
Art	20	22	21	30	20	25
PE	22	9	16	20	13	17
Maths	18	13	15	16	11	13
Technology	15	7	11	4	15	10
Writing	7	7	7	5	9	7
Topic	4	9	6	4	7	5

Source: PACE 3 interviews
Sample: 54 children in Years 5 and 6
Date: Summer 1995 and 1996

As these tables show, in these years there was considerable unanimity among the pupils in our sample about both liked and disliked subjects. Table 5.2 allows us to confirm the strength of the swing towards Art and PE. In Year 5, 42 per cent of the 'most liked' preferences were for these subjects and this rose to 50 per cent in Year 6. In addition, only one or two pupils nominated these subjects as disliked.

Table 5.3 First and second choices in 'least liked' category for top five subjects (percentages) (PACE 3)

| | Year 5 | | | Year 6 | | |
	1st choice	2nd choice	Total	1st choice	2nd choice	Total
Geography	11	13	12	18	13	16
History	7	15	11	9	15	12
Maths	22	2	12	19	4	11
Science	19	15	17	9	8	8
Writing	7	5	6	5	7	6

Source: PACE 3 interviews
Sample: 54 children in Years 5 and 6
Date: Summer 1995 and 1996

Net ranking conceals pupils' nominations of their 'least liked' subjects. In Table 5.3 we can see again the tendency for our target group to mention the same subjects in both years. Science, Geography and History between them account for 37 per cent of negative first choices in Year 5 and 36 per cent in Year 6. These subjects also were rarely nominated as 'most liked'. However it is interesting that in Year 6 the general dislike of Geography increased but Science was less disliked.

Rank ordering, unlike net ranking, also reveals those subjects that were both most liked and least liked. We can see that Maths figured strongly in both categories and that, exceptionally, it was a clear first choice for those who disliked it. This is perhaps not unexpected for a subject which differentiates very clearly through categoric and overt assessment. However, as we have seen in the previous section and will note again later in this chapter when we discuss the attitudes of low and high achievers, this was not a simple division between those who could do Maths and liked it and those who could not and did not. Writing attracted similarly polarized responses, if to a lesser extent. A closer look at the Writing category reveals that positive views of Writing were associated with writing stories, negative views with 'writing for other things' and with technical features of writing. The fact that Reading appears as neither strongly liked or disliked reminds us, as we saw in Chapter 4, of how low this activity was in pupils' awareness.

In seeking to better understand pupils' preferences we need to look to the reasons they gave for their choices. In the next section we focus our analysis on these explanations.

5.3 CHILDREN'S EXPLANATIONS FOR THEIR CURRICULUM LIKES AND DISLIKES

In each round of data-collection when the pupils were asked which subjects they liked most and least, they were also asked to give reasons for their choices. Responses for all years were coded separately for 'most liked' and 'least liked'. Six constructs were used to code the children's criteria for their choices:

- success/ease – fail/hard
- interesting – boring
- activity – constraint (on physical activity)
- autonomy – constraint (on freedom of choice)
- educational (mention of learning/challenge/future value) – not educational
- fun – no fun

Children frequently commented on only their positive or negative choice. Reasons were more frequently given for liking than disliking. In many cases what the children said implied a bipolar construct but we have coded only what was said. As the children got older they were more likely to offer a cluster of reasons for the things they liked. We have therefore used multiple codings and taken account of this in our discussion.

Criteria for liking

Table 5.4 Criteria used in explanation for most liked activities and subjects (percentages)

	Year 1	Year 2	Year 3	Year 4	Year 5	Year 6
Success/ease	8	19	34	21	20	16
Interesting	23	27	23	21	28	26
Activity	28	25	11	5	17	15
Autonomy	13	4	8	12	11	7
Educational	0	15	8	12	4	7
Fun	28	10	16	29	20	29

Source: PACE 1, 2 and 3 interviews
Sample: 54 children in Years 1–6
Date: Autumn 1990 and 1991, Summer 1993, 1994, 1995 and 1996

The consistent high placing of 'interesting' from Year 2 confirms the well-recognized importance to children and teachers of the experience of being intrigued, fascinated, surprised in determining engagement in learning. Not surprisingly, children were rarely able to be very articulate about their 'interest' but the sense of positive liking is clear in their statements.

> I like writing 'cause it's interesting.
> > (Polly, Year 1, Valley)

> 'Cause painting's interesting 'cause of what you paint.
> > (Martin, Year 3, Lawnside)

> I like watching TV. It's more interesting. I don't know why.
> > (Ian, Year 5, Meadway)

> I just like writing stories.
> > (Simon, Year 5, Valley)

> I like Maths, I just like doing it.
> > (Amanda, Year 5, Kenwood)

In some cases the ability to 'be interested' depended on individual predilection, frequently nurtured at home or in other extra-school activity:

> I like building things – I do it at home.
> > (Frances, Year 3, St Anne's)

> I have lots of music at home and it doesn't get boring.
> > (Laura, Year 5, Orchard)

As might be expected, 'interesting' often occurred in conjunction with other codes. Sometimes the children linked it with 'fun'. We were particularly interested to consider the meanings that the word 'fun' held for pupils.

'Fun' appeared sometimes as a single criterion. Where it was part of a bundle it was linked most with 'activity' and 'autonomy' and less frequently with 'interesting'.

Liking something because it was 'fun' was also linked in children's explanations with seeing it as play, finding it enjoyable because you could 'have a laugh', sometimes because it was sociable and you could 'have a chat':

> Choosing – you can do whatever you want. It's more fun.
>
> > (Kelly, Year 3, Orchard)
>
> It's fun because you can get your face mucky and stuff.
>
> > (Sean, Year 4, Greenmantle)
>
> Maths – you can do more things. You can have fun. With English you can't.
>
> > (Kevin, Year 5, Audley)
>
> Science is more fun. You get to do experiments – there are more things to do and you can have a chat with your next door neighbours.
>
> > (Melanie, Year 6, St Anne's)
>
> I like Art because it's a time when you can splash on paint and do whatever you like – it's good fun.
>
> > (Jan, Year 6, Valley)

The link between 'fun' and 'activity' was strong as the children moved into Key Stage 2 and offered more complex explanations. In Key Stage 1 'activity' alone was a justification for liking; mostly this related to PE but also to opportunities to move around the class. As we have seen, in the later years it was more likely to appear in conjunction with 'fun', 'autonomy' and 'interesting'. In Key Stage 2, while children still liked opportunities to be physically active, whether in PE or just not sitting down, some also felt positively about opportunities to be active in their own learning:

> You get more fun in Maths like cutting out and sticking.
>
> > (Eliot, Year 3, St Bede's)
>
> You can do a lot more things like measure water, weigh things.
>
> > (Neil, Year 4, Audley)
>
> I like Technology because it's good fun and we make lots of different things every week.
>
> > (Juliet, Year 5, Greenmantle)

Related to this is the 'educational' category. This figured most strongly in the middle years. Here the coded responses in general reflected children's received notions that some things are 'good for you'. This declined later in Key Stage 2 though there were some children who appeared to be reflecting on their learning processes.

> PE keeps you really fit and healthy.
>
> > (Sean, Year 2, Valley)
>
> History. You get to learn more stuff from that.
>
> > (Jacquie, Year 4, St Anne's)
>
> Because you can work things out for yourself.
>
> > (Jessica, Year 4, Kenwood)
>
> It's a good way of learning, learning how to do things, how to make something.
>
> > (Lucy, Year 6, Lawnside)

I like using my brain.

> (Mandy, Year 6, Audley)

Spelling because you learn better how to spell; when you get to High School you have to learn how to spell and how to read.

> (Shona, Year 6, Meadway)

Those who were most keen on opportunities to think hard, work it out for themselves and who appeared to be aware of learning processes were, in general, high achievers and more likely to be girls. The consistently low ranking of reasons that could be classified as 'educational' is an indicator of the extent to which the children in our sample rarely understood the reasons behind the educational experiences to which they were exposed. This point is discussed and illustrated further in Chapter 8.

Finding a subject easy became gradually more important through Key Stage 1 and was the most frequently given reason for liking in Year 3. From that point success/ease was less important in determining liking than 'fun' and 'interesting'. Pupil priorities were changing. In opposition to fail/hard various combinations of 'fun', 'activity' and 'autonomy' appeared. The meanings encoded by the 'autonomy' category also shifted as pupils moved up the school. In Year 1 'choosing' was part of the classroom discourse and was associated with the opportunity to do something enjoyable. In Key Stage 2, as we have seen, the opportunities for autonomy to be applied as a positive criterion were limited and this may explain its relatively low ranking. But it was clearly valued by those who mentioned it as a positive factor and its absence regretted when explaining something not enjoyed. Many pupils' reasons for choosing Art and PE related to the scope they provided for choice or individuality.

In PE we move around and we are allowed to make things up. We have a choice.

> (Jan, Year 5, Valley)

Also in Key Stage 2 reasons cited for liking indicated that some pupils were applying more strategic thinking, making references to opportunities to choose subjects and activities so that difficulty could be avoided, to make and do rather than sit and write a lot, and to work sociably rather than alone:

Singing 'cause you don't have to write.

> (Susie, Year 4, St Anne's)

Making models 'cause it's fun to do and people can always help me.

> (Sharon, Year 5, Greenmantle)

With Art you don't have to do any work – just paint and draw.

> (Frances, Year 6, St Anne's)

These more negative reasons for liking provide a natural bridge to children's explanations for disliking subjects.

Criteria for disliking

The picture here is much clearer and more consistent than that for subjects and activities about which pupils felt positive. The children were agreed that they disliked subjects and activities because they found them difficult, boring, physically constraining or lacking opportunity for autonomy.

Table 5.5 Criteria used in explanation for least liked activities and subjects (percentages)

	Year 1	Year 2	Year 3	Year 4	Year 5	Year 6
Fail/hard	55	52	76	50	52	46
Boring	20	16	18	35	36	40
Constraint (physical)	20	32	6	0	0	11
Constraint (no autonomy)	5	0	0	11	9	3
Not educational	0	0	0	4	3	0
Not fun	0	0	0	0	0	0

Source: PACE 1, 2 and 3 interviews
Sample: 54 children in Years 1–6
Date: Autumn 1990 and 1991, Summer 1993, 1994, 1995 and 1996

Across all the longitudinal data, we found that success (or the lack of it) and the perceived ease (or difficulty) of an activity were particularly mentioned when children were discussing the subjects they liked *least*. Finding an activity or subject too hard, not succeeding in or being good at it, getting confused and not understanding (the 'fail/hard' category) were used to account for half or more of pupils' choices in all years. This becomes more marked if we also take into account the tendency for children who are finding something difficult to label it 'boring'. This category frequently carried an implied opposition to 'success/ease'. For instance,

> I never like Maths problems – it's the way they are. Boring.
>
> (Rosie, Year 6, Lawnside, low attainer in Maths)

In Key Stage 2 'boring' loomed progressively larger as a criterion for dislike. However, as we have already suggested, we have to consider the many possible constructions to be placed on the use of 'boring'. In this sample it seemed to be used in three ways: first, as in the previous quotation, as a disguised reference to or explanation of lack of success (a version of 'fail/hard'); second, to indicate processes which were not enjoyable such as repetition or copying:

> In handwriting all you do is go up and down, up and down.
>
> (Polly, Year 3, Valley)

> It's just listening to stories I've heard five times before. Boring.
>
> (Rupert, Year 5, Lawnside)

> Boring. We just have to copy. We don't have questions. He just tells us the answers.
>
> (Celia, Year 6, Meadway)

The third application of 'boring' was to express an intrinsic dislike of the subject – a genuine opposition to interest:

> Doing about the olden days which I don't find very exciting.
>
> (Theresa, Year 6, St Anne's)

> I do like singing but the music I like, not the school's music.
>
> (Corrinne, Year 5, Meadway)

> I don't like Geography, I'm not that sort of person. I'm the sort that likes Art and Music.
>
> (Lucy, Year 6, Lawnside)

Dislike of an activity was also associated with the constraints placed on physical activity. In Key Stage 1 children complained of being crowded and uncomfortable for storytime on the carpet, especially when the stories were long.

> You have to sit on the carpet and it hurts your legs.
>
> (Hugh, Year 1, Lawnside)

> You have to sit on the carpet and listen or you get told off.
>
> (Olivia, Year 2, Lawnside)

This was more important to the children at this stage than finding the activity boring. In Key Stage 2 children also expressed a dislike of having to sit still for long periods; this was often associated with writing tasks or listening to teacher reading stories.

> You have to sit down and it's tiring.
>
> (Geoffrey, Year 3, Orchard)

> You have to just sit there in silence.
>
> (Jeremy, Year 6, Kenwood)

> You have to be quiet and work (contrasted with expressing yourself and making a noise in Music).
>
> (Laura, Year 6, Orchard)

> You're not using your body – just pen, pencils, colours and rubber.
>
> (Corrinne, Year 6, Meadway)

The 'constraint (no autonomy)' category was used when children expressed a particular dislike of having no choice. This appeared much less often than references to physical constraint as a reason for dislike. When it did, it referred to strongly teacher-framed activity:

> Sir tells us what to do – we can't make up your own minds.
>
> (Samantha, Year 4, St Bede's)

> You've just got to write what's on the sheet.
>
> (Ewan, Year 5, Kenwood)

> In reading – you have to do it out loud.
>
> (Dawn, Year 4, Kenwood)

It also referred to activity which was perceived to offer less possibility of personal engagement:

You have to write about that thing – you can't imagine anything.

(Lucy, Year 4, Lawnside)

The category 'not educational' was rarely used to explain dislike. Where it did children referred to a subject as being 'a waste of time' or knowing it already or having done it before.

Pupils' reasons for liking or disliking frequently clustered around specific subject areas. Analysis of this provides us with another perspective on the children's report of their experience.

Links between subjects, activities and criteria

The core curriculum

Mathematics figured more prominently in pupils' choices than the other core subjects. Many of those who selected Mathematics as their most liked subject did so because they found it easy or saw it as a subject where they could succeed. It was not until Key Stage 2 that Mathematics began to be extensively disliked because pupils found it difficult. Mathematics showed the largest cluster of responses coded 'educational' and some children considered it was fun. Equal numbers of children chose Mathematics and English for being interesting.

There were fewer choices, positive or negative, for English than Mathematics. Pupils who selected English as a most liked subject were less likely to explain this by reference to how easy they found it. Of the negative choices English had most mentions. It attracted a third more 'fail/hard' references than Mathematics. These, in contrast to Mathematics, were spread across both key stages and most frequently associated with problems in writing, or, less often, reading. 'Constraint' was most associated with listening to stories and having to sit and write. English (writing again) was also categorized as 'boring'.

Science barely showed as a most liked subject. It came third behind Mathematics in being disliked because pupils found it difficult.

The non-core curriculum

Art, PE and Technology received most nominations for being liked. The criterion of activity was, not unexpectedly, associated very strongly with PE (the highest coding for a single subject). This was also used as a reason for liking Art and Technology. This trio of subjects also attracted the highest scores for 'fun', and Art and Technology were seen as 'interesting'. Art scored highest for 'autonomy' and was also perceived as easy.

Apart from Art, PE and Technology, the only non-core subjects to make any noticeable appearance were History and Music, chosen most for interest. Geography and RE followed English in being most often categorized as 'boring', though all subjects except PE were considered boring by someone. Similarly all subjects (except History) were disliked by some children because they found them difficult.

In summary

The core curriculum featured prominently in children's likes and dislikes where the reasons given were to do with succeeding or failing. English, Mathematics and Science, in that order, received most nominations where dislike was explained by some reference to difficulty. Art (the most liked subject in Year 6) was the only non-core subject where children used this category to explain their choice. It was liked because it was easy to succeed in.

The children's comments in Key Stage 2 indicated that what made them dislike Science, Geography, History and RE was the weight of information presented to them which they had to learn. The teacher's success or otherwise in linking the children's experience with the curriculum was especially apparent when the children were talking about their preferences in Geography and History. This determined whether or not they found the subject 'interesting'. The amount of writing they had to do in these areas (including topic) also affected their response.

At this point it may be helpful to look at some examples of the reasons the children gave in Years 5 and 6 for their positive and negative choices as an illustration of the way they were constructing their experience.

Pupil preferences in Years 5 and 6

In Technology we get to make things and I like construction. In Maths we have to do sums.

(Ben, Year 5, Greenmantle)

Technology, I like making things and feeling proud of what I have made. Maths, sometimes I get muddled and might have to stay in at play so Maths is more worrying.

(Eliot, Year 5, St Bede's)

In Art I really like drawing. I never get bored of that. In Science you have to remember everything and write it up and I get bored of writing.

(Martin, Year 5, Lawnside)

'Cos PE is fun and Science is not. In Science you have to like write and stuff and in PE you haven't.

(Scott, Year 6, Kenwood)

Art is fun and you can draw different things and shade things in and draw real life pictures. You sometimes have choice. With Maths we have to do set pages and I don't find it easy to do.

(Juliet, Year 6, Greenmantle)

Art is fun, you get to choose; PE as well. In topic work you just keep it piling on and on. When you finish one piece there's another five more to do. You just have to do it again and again and again.

(Ewan, Year 6, Kenwood)

I like watching TV because I don't have to write.

(Harry, Year 6, St Bede's)

With PE you're allowed to do stuff like games. With spellings all you have to do is try to spell ... 'Cos I can't spell.

(Susie, Year 6, St Anne's)

Music's good, it's fascinating. RE's very boring we just have to copy. We don't have questions, he just tells us the answers.

(Celia, Year 6, Meadway)

I can really understand Maths. I'm quite good at it. Geography just gets boring.

(Brian, Year 6, Audley)

These few examples illustrate the range of criteria pupils were using for making their choices, positive and negative. They liked activities that they found interesting and understandable, that gave them a chance to have fun, and to be active and exercise some choice. They disliked things they found hard, or which involved a lot of writing, routine and repetition. It might be argued that this is a not unusual response for 10- and 11-year-olds but there is, in addition in these comments, a sense of being weighed down by the amount of work, the requirement to remember, and the cost of not knowing what to do or how to do it that we believe marks a change from pre-National Curriculum primary education.

We can develop this argument by looking at shifts in the ranking of criteria used by the pupils across the six years of the project. We are interested here in apparent changes in pupils' views of the curriculum they experienced and in considering what can be inferred from their explanations of their attitudes and priorities.

Table 5.6 Rank order of criteria used in explanation for most liked activities and subjects (PACE 1, 2 and 3)

Year 1	Year 2	Year 3	Year 4	Year 5	Year 6
Fun	Activity	Suc/Ease	Fun	Interest	Fun
Activity	Interest	Interest	Interest	Fun	Interest
Interest	Suc/Ease	Fun	Suc/Ease	Suc/Ease	Activity
Autonomy	Educational	Activity	Autonomy	Activity	Suc/Ease
Suc/Ease	Fun	Autonomy	Educational	Autonomy	Autonomy
Educational	Autonomy	Educational	Activity	Educational	Educational

Source: PACE 1, 2 and 3 interviews
Sample: 54 children in Years 1–6
Date: Autumn 1990 and 1991, Summer 1993 and 1994, Spring 1995 and 1996

The rise and fall of the use of 'success/ease' to determine liking is most intriguing. In Year 3 the preoccupation with activity and the preference for not having to sit still had receded in importance. Instead we see some of the classic signals associated with 'becoming a junior'. Children liked the things they succeeded at and found easy and interesting. We have argued in previous accounts of the PACE research (Pollard *et al.*, 1994; Croll, 1996) that this congruence between pupil and teacher concerns reflected in part natural shifts in priority as the children got older, but also the tighter framing of curricular activity and the increased emphasis on evaluation. In Year 3 the children appeared to have accepted this emphasis and applied it as a criterion. The strength of this acceptance is evidenced by the very high percentage of children who also used 'fail/hard' as a criterion for their *least* liked curricular activity – 76 per cent, the highest in all six years (see Table 5.5). From Year 4, however, children were once again asserting the importance to them of 'fun'. In Year 6, as in Year 1, opportunities to have fun, to be active, move about, and not sit down for long periods were the most welcome and valued. Throughout Key Stage 2 we have evidence of increasingly tight framing of the curriculum and in Year 6 the focus on evaluation was very strong. The consequence of this appears to be that the concerns of many pupils in Year 5, and even more in Year 6, were not congruent with their teachers' emphasis on performance. They were not happy about the goals and priorities being set for them or the ways in which they were being pursued. However, this does not mean that they were unaware of attainment. After Year 4 more pupils consistently cited both ends of the success/ease – fail/hard construct when explaining their choices. For some pupils the division between success and failure, finding work hard or finding it easy, was becoming much clearer and more sharply defined. In Year 4 all of those who used both poles were low attainers, but in Years 5 and 6 low, average and high attainers were all included among the children who represented their preferences in this way. What is of interest here is that the subject a large number of pupils identified as liked because it provided opportunities for success was Art. In opposition to this they placed core curriculum subjects which they found difficult. We seem to have here a picture of classrooms in which many pupils did not experience the core curriculum with any pleasure. Instead children were enjoying anything that gave them relief from the pressure to perform. In addition, the focus on performance appears to have produced a pedagogy which the children found unattractive.

We are now faced with the question of whether or not the picture painted here reflects the experience of all pupils In the next section we analyse the data from the point of view of gender and attainment.

5.4 THE INFLUENCE OF GENDER AND ACHIEVEMENT ON PUPILS' PREFERENCES

In order to gain more understanding of what these likes and dislikes tell us about how different children experienced the curriculum, we looked at all six years of our data to discover whether there were differences between the choices made by boys and girls and by low and high achievers.

Boys' and girls' perspectives on the curriculum

We found no consistent patterns across all six years for positive preferences which were related to gender. However, some differences began to emerge in Years 5 and 6. In this period significantly more girls than boys preferred Art/Painting. In Year 6 more boys than girls selected Mathematics as a most liked subject. This was a turnaround for the girls who in Years 4 and 5 had nominated Mathematics as 'most liked' slightly more often than the boys.

As with other variables, patterns emerge more clearly in relation to the pupils' choices of subjects and activities they *disliked*. Boys in general disliked English activities more than girls. The detail reveals that from Year 4 boys consistently disliked Writing. However, this general dislike of English, and of Writing in particular, was less evident among the higher-achieving boys. Girls did not mention Writing negatively in Year 5 or Year 6. In contrast, the number of girls choosing Mathematics as 'most disliked' increased as they moved up the school; in Year 6 it was the subject girls mentioned most in this category. This was in spite of the fact that the girls in our sample attained higher in Mathematics at Key Stage 2 than the boys: of the 35 per cent who attained Level 4 20 per cent were girls and 15 per cent boys. Furthermore, although there were equal numbers of boys and girls who attained Level 5, only one girl maintained her nomination of Mathematics as 'most liked' subject into Year 6. The attitude of these high-achieving girls to Mathematics is developed below and in a case-study in Chapter 11. Here we note that we appear to be seeing the beginnings of a pattern still evident in the secondary phase.

Girls consistently disliked Science more than boys did until Year 6 when antipathy, generally less evident in this year, was more evenly divided between the sexes. In Years 5 and 6, girls disliked Geography much more than boys did; their antipathy was particularly marked in Year 6 when it shared top place as 'most disliked' with Mathematics. Boys consistently disliked Singing more than girls who did not mention it negatively after Year 3; in Year 6 this sample of boys expressed particular dislike of Singing.

We made it clear to the children in our interviews that they did not have to nominate a subject they disliked. It is interesting that dislike began earlier for the boys in our sample who began to nominate things they disliked from Year 2. It was Year 4 before all the girls were doing this. In general, the data show the girls in the study as apparently more compliant and accepting of classroom activity, more prepared to 'get on' with things. The idea of different dispositions to learning is further discussed and illustrated in Chapters 9, 10, 11 and 13.

The influence of attainment

We were particularly interested in examining the relationship between pupils' attitudes to the curriculum and their levels of attainment. For the purposes of this analysis we used the Teacher Assessments of attainment which we collected each year for the target children. Teachers were asked to rate each child in the class for attainment using a scale of 1 to 5. The assessments for the target children were entered on the PACE database. In addition, in some cases we also used the end-of-Key Stage 2 assessments.

Preferences of higher achievers

The children assessed by their teachers as high attainers in PACE 1 favoured a curriculum which was a blend of the 'basics' and creative activities: Painting, Writing, Mathematics, Reading, Singing and PE. They did not select 'home corner play', 'sand', 'water' or 'construction'. They seem to have assumed an orientation to things classified in classroom usage as 'work' rather than 'play'. It may be that they were focusing on activities they perceived as having high status, and for which they would receive praise and increased self-esteem. It may be that they were bored by the lack of stimulus and interest provided by 'play'. Do our data of the explanations children gave for their choices provide any evidence of the influence of their dispositions to learning on their early achievement?

In Year 2 three high-attaining girls all chose Mathematics as a favourite subject. Their explanations reveal very different motivations. Kate told us why she preferred Mathematics to dressing up:

> I like sums because they are hard and I have to think. Other things don't take enough time and I get bored when I've done all my jobs.
>
> (Kate, Year 2, Greenmantle)

There is a strong sense here of Kate seeking and responding to cognitive challenge. Laura's explanation of her preference for Mathematics over construction also implied an idea of challenge but more notable is the commitment to long-term aims which she could already articulate:

> Because you can work harder and I'm going to go to college. You have to work hard for that. That's why I like Maths.
>
> (Laura, Year 2, Orchard)

Laura, then, liked Maths because it was 'hard work'. In contrast, Alice's explanation for liking centred on the ease with which she could accomplish the Maths and reading tasks she was given.

> I like reading stories 'cos most words are easy, and Maths has easy answers.
>
> (Alice, Year 2, Lawnside)

Kate, Laura and Alice were in the study throughout. Already at this very early stage they were exhibiting very different dispositions and motivations. Although all three were among the girls who attained Level 5 in the three standard assessments at the end of Key Stage 2, only Laura maintained a consistent preference for Maths right through to Year 6. One of the case-studies in Chapter 11 tells the story of these three pupils and their changing attitude to Maths in more detail.

Of the core curriculum subjects, Maths was mentioned positively and negatively in all years much more frequently than English or Science. An analysis of high achievers' comments about Maths enables us to develop the exploration of differing attitudes to this subject begun in Chapter 4 and continued earlier in this section. This also provides an indication of which aspects of subject learning high achievers found attractive in the later stages of Key Stage 2.

Of the twelve pupils who attained Level 5 in Maths at the end of Key Stage 2, four consistently cited Maths as a most (or second most) liked subject each year they were interviewed. They enjoyed the success, found it easy, but also liked working hard and saw doing Maths as fun. They were also among the few children who specifically mentioned liking Maths with problems as well as sums.

> 'Cos you work harder and it's more interesting. You get better at it. When I've finished my Maths she gives me more Maths. She knows I like doing it – it's my best subject. I do Maths at home.
>
> (Laura, Year 4, Orchard)

> I find Maths challenging – the teacher's always giving us harder and harder things to do so it's not boring. She's going to the centre and keeps bringing back hard Maths for us. I seem to have got a system going.
>
> (Brian, Year 5, Audley)

It was only among this small group that we found any indication of intrinsic motivation. The data indicate that for our target group high attainment in Maths was not necessarily associated with liking the subject. Among the other pupils who attained Level 5, there was a steady decline in the tendency to identify Maths as a liked subject and a marked fall off in Year 6. For instance, a group of pupils who had chosen Maths as a most liked subject fairly consistently in previous years selected different subjects in Year 6. Until then they had referred to enjoying being good at Maths, sorting out the answers and solving problems. By contrast, in their SATs year many chose Art and PE for the opportunity to be active:

> It's a time when you can splash on paint and do whatever you like, it's good fun.
>
> (Jan, Year 6, Valley)

> You get to run instead of just sitting there in silence.
>
> (Jeremy, Year 5, Kenwood)

Their experience of Maths had apparently ceased to be enjoyable. Indeed, for one pupil whose story we tell in Chapter 11, high attainment was achieved against a background of consistent dislike.

If we turn to look at the high achievers in English we see different issues emerging. Of the nine children who gained Level 5 in English, seven were girls and two were boys. Of these, three girls nominated an English activity as 'most liked' in Year 6. Only one of the three had liked English consistently through Key Stage 2, the other two nominated English for the first time after several years with Maths as their favourite activity. Alice, whose Year 2 comment about liking Maths because it was easy is quoted above (p. 99), was one of these. The experience which lay behind her change of preference suggests one direction in which we might look to explain the attitudes of these high achievers. She had recently been involved in a class newspaper project where she had taken her turn as editor. This had involved a considerable degree of autonomy which she had relished. This enthusiasm for autonomy is evident in a different form in the choices of other high achievers. The English activity they nominated was 'writing stories' which they distinguished from other kinds of writing that they sometimes found tedious. They enjoyed writing stories for the freedom it gave them to use their imaginations and create a world they could control.

What picture of the attitudes of high-achieving pupils is suggested by this analysis? There are indications here that a few of these pupils in our target group acquired an intrinsic interest in subjects they excelled at. High achievers also enjoyed autonomy when it was available. However for most, their experience, especially in Year 6, was frequently demotivating. Enjoyment of core curriculum subjects appeared to be ebbing (in contrast to the enthusiasm evident in Years 3 and 4). Strongly favoured subjects with high attainers in Years 5 and 6 were PE and Art. This seems to indicate support for the argument that the pressures of the National Curriculum and its assessment created a climate where even higher-achieving pupils favoured subjects which provided opportunities to be active and where assessment was not overt. The one exception to this for some of the children was the mention of writing stories, an activity with the potential to meet their twin desires for autonomy and escape.

Preferences of lower achievers

The children assessed by their teachers as low achievers in PACE 1 favoured a curriculum in which PE was the most prevalent choice. These children liked to be active: 'I like running around', 'There's more fun, more running about', 'Cause you can run around'. They were also generally in agreement about their other choices: playing in the home corner, dressing up, sand, painting and building/construction. The reasons they gave indicate that at this early stage they were already using a construction of work/play and hard/easy. The reasons they gave included: ''Cause you can play', ''Cause you don't have to do no work', 'It's easier', 'It's more easy doing it', ''Cause you don't have to do so much work and that stuff', ''Cause it's more fun'. The attitude and disposition to learning evident here may be a reflection of their comparative immaturity, but it is in stark contrast to that of their peers assessed as being higher achievers.

These early indications are sustained in the reasons lower achievers gave over the whole period of the research. The data indicate pupils' increasing awareness of their attainment and dislike of subjects where they encountered difficulty. They were positive about subjects and activities which provided opportunities for routine or avoidance; in short, anything which reduced the anxiety brought about by problems in learning. Like their high-achieving peers they enjoyed Art and PE for the freedom of choice, the activity and the ease with which they could succeed.

The data on attitudes to Maths again provides us with the clearest illustration of these factors. Maths was chosen as both 'most liked' and 'most disliked' by low attainers. In Year 6, those pupils who mentioned Maths and attained Level 2 or 3 divided almost equally between those who said Maths was their most disliked subject and those who nominated it as most liked. Those who said it was their favourite subject saw it as a refuge from more open-ended tasks like writing. They enjoyed the security its routines could provide and with differentiation they enjoyed a degree of success. The lowest achievers in our sample were in this category.

Maths with sums is fun. You can't have fun with English, you can't.

(Kevin, Year 5, Audley)

I like sum work – things you have to find out. It's fun, working in your head, learning how to do times tables, division.

(Kyle, Year 6, Meadway)

You can do Maths for ages.

(Philip, Year 6, St Anne's)

I like numbers, working from the book.

(Jacquie, Year 6, St Anne's)

The low achievers who *disliked* Maths mainly attained Level 3 at the end of Key Stage 2. They disliked Maths because of the difficulty it presented them with, and the anxiety and uncertainty they felt as a result.

In Maths they give you hard sums and sometimes you get so worried that you don't know what you're doing.

(Carol, Year 5, Orchard)

Maths. I don't know what we're doing and I just don't like it. I find it hard. I don't understand it.

(Geoffrey, Year 5, Orchard)

I'm no good at Maths. Sir tries to explain but I still can't do it.

(Samantha, Year 5, St Bede's)

These examples suggest that pupils whose attainment was below average but who were not the lowest attainers felt greater anxiety about their performance and more exposed.

Looking beyond Maths, the reasons given by lower achievers for disliking subjects encompassed similar factors: facing failure, feeling confused and uncertain, the labour of writing.

Science gets on my nerves and I'm not always sure what to do in Science.

(Haley, Year 5, St Bede's)

In Science you like have to write stuff and in PE you haven't.

(Scott, Year 6, Kenwood)

Reading to the teacher. When I get words muddled up I have to take them home and practise them.

(Jacquie, Year 5, St Anne's)

Spelling. 'Cos I can't spell. And writing stories. When I'm finished I want to go to sleep – it's so tiring.

(Susie, Year 6, St Anne's)

Subjects and activities which attracted positive rating from lower-attaining children were, as we have suggested, those where they felt confident and competent or where they could avoid things they disliked doing and found difficult.

Technology. You can spend all morning making things and not having to write.

(Kevin, Year 4, Audley)

Free choice – you get to do what you want and you can choose drawing.

(Jacquie, Year 5, St Anne's)

I'm a good drawer. I like doing the things I do best.

> (Eliot, Year 6, St Bede's)

I like drawing. I draw all the time.

> (Samantha, Year 6, St Bede's)

I like drawing pictures and all sorts of things about drawing 'cause I'm more talented at it.

> (Ian, Year 6, Meadway)

The contrasts and similarities between higher and lower achievers will be developed further in subsequent chapters as we focus on relationships with teachers, assessment and learning.

5.5 CONCLUSION

Over the six years of the study there were radical changes in children's stated preferences for curriculum activities. In Years 5 and 6 there was a noticeable turning away from taking pleasure in core curriculum activities which had headed their popularity poll in Years 3 and 4. A net ranking shows that children's preferences for subjects and activities reverted to those of Year 1 – PE and Art – with the addition of Technology, TV watching and listening to stories. In short, to those activities associated with physical and expressive activity, entertainment, little demand for writing, and low-stakes assessment.

The most common criteria for explaining positive choices involved fun, activity and autonomy. The explanation most frequently given for disliking a subject or activity was that it was hard, difficult to succeed at, or offered the experience of failure. However, the experience of success was not necessarily associated with liking. Many children expressed little enthusiasm for the core curriculum subjects in which they achieved high scores in the end-of-Key Stage 2 assessment. In addition, even where children expressed interest in subjects, the perceived burden of the pressure to recall and record, combined with the lack of opportunities for personal control, was demotivating for many. Low achievers in particular experienced considerable anxiety and fear of their failure being exposed.

It is difficult to avoid a sense of children in flight from an experience of learning that they found unsatisfying, unmotivating and uncomfortable. This is evident in the data from all our schools. In attempting to explain this we do not propose a simple cause and effect, but we argue that the children's attitudes to the curriculum were rooted in their classroom experiences and that these reflected the pressure created by the National Curriculum and its assessment. In the following chapters we unpack this argument further as we consider what the children told us about their relationships with their teachers and their experiences of learning and assessment.

Chapter 6

Pupil Perspectives on Teacher–Pupil Relationships

6.1   Introduction
6.2   Pupil relationships with teachers
6.3   Pupil perceptions of classroom control
6.4   Pupil preferences for autonomy or task direction
6.5   Pupil acceptance of teacher control and authority
6.6   Pupil perception of the ideal pupil
6.7   Pupil perception of the ideal teacher
6.8   Conclusion

6.1 INTRODUCTION

Chapters 4 and 5 focused on pupils' perspectives of the curriculum. We described children's lack of engagement with many subjects or curricular activities, particularly when they felt constrained by prescribed content, increasingly oppressed by demands for outcomes and with little opportunity to pursue a personal or individual route to learning.

The intrinsic 'interest' of the curriculum is clearly important to pupils, but relationships with their teachers – the subject of this chapter – are arguably of even greater influence on their overall experience of classroom life. The key reason for this concerns the authority and power of the teacher. Pupils are subject to this power and are expected to conform to teacher requests concerning all aspects of behaviour and learning activities. On the other hand, children are not completely powerless themselves, having the particular advantage of large numbers. Teachers must also recognize that they can only demonstrate their effectiveness through the successful attainments of their pupils, so pupils do have some leverage. In any event, at the start of each year, a process of negotiation generally produces a set of understandings about classroom relationships and ways of working together. One aspect of this are the 'rules', both tacit and explicit, by which classroom behaviour is 'framed'.

The concept of 'frame' (Bernstein, 1971) has been one of the key analytical dimensions in recording changes in primary school pedagogy and classroom practices across the six years of the PACE research. We use it to refer to the extent to which activities are structured by power relations and expectations. Where frame is strong then behaviour is bounded. Where it is weak there is more scope for self-determined and autonomous activity. As we have already seen, this is an important dimension for children's personal evaluation of the quality of their classroom experience.

In this chapter then, we address pupil–teacher relationships, the idea of frame and the operation of power through the analysis of various interview questions, ranging across the six years of our data. We begin with a general overview of relationships, before probing further into perceptions of classroom control and preferences for autonomy or task direction. Some of these findings offer interesting insights into pupil attitudes to risk. Towards the end of the chapter further light is shed on these issues through an analysis of children's perceptions of the 'ideal pupil' and 'ideal teacher'.

6.2 PUPIL RELATIONSHIPS WITH TEACHERS

In each year of the study we asked children directly 'How do you get on with your teacher?' The answers were coded 'positive', 'neutral', 'negative' or 'ambivalent'. It is a tribute to primary teachers' commitment to the quality of relationship with pupils in their class that in most years more than half the answers were unequivocally positive. The responses coded 'neutral' were less enthusiastic but still mainly positive and encompassed phrases like 'all right', 'OK', 'OK but not brilliant', 'not bad'. Meaning here was encoded as much by tone and body language as by what was said. Statements coded 'negative' included, for example 'not at all', 'we have arguments', 'he shouts at me a lot'. The 'ambivalent' code was used for 'it depends ...' and 'sometimes but ...' constructions.

Table 6.1 Pupils' perceptions of their relationships with their teachers (percentages)

	Year 1	Year 2	Year 3	Year 4	Year 5	Year 6
Positive	57	48	63	63	58	50
Neutral	35	46	22	31	33	31
Negative	2	4	4	2	0	4
Ambivalent	0	0	11	4	9	15
Don't know	2	0	0	0	0	0
No data	4	2	0	0	0	0

Source: PACE 1, 2 and 3 child interview data
Sample: 54 children in each of Years 1–6
Date: Autumn 1990 and 1991, Summer 1993, 1994, 1995 and 1996

The very low percentage of negative responses confirms the success that teachers were having in establishing and maintaining relationships with pupils. They will be reassured by this statistic as their evidence to us indicated that they feared other pressures were compromising what they believed was a central feature of their role (Osborn *et al.*, 2000). However, by Year 6 the more extended expressions of ambivalence had reached a peak. These reveal more of the complexities of classroom relationships and indicate something of the basis for pupils' judgements about 'how well they got on with their teacher'. Indeed, their perception of the importance of attainment ('getting things right') and behaviour ('being good') as a route to securing teacher approval, the need to negotiate teacher moods, and their concern with 'fairness' were all evident, as these examples show:

> OK but if she's in a bad mood and you go asking her questions she shouts – so you've got to ask her at the right time.
>
> (Mandy, Year 5, Audley)

> Sometimes – when I don't (get on well with him), Sir blames me for something I never done. He can be strict, but he's a good teacher to work with.
>
> (Wesley, Year 5, Meadway)

> She's all right sometimes but when we've not done enough work she gets mad; then she's normally mad for the rest of the day.
>
> (Theresa, Year 6, Audley)

> Depends on her mood. When she's in a nice mood I get on. Sometimes she shouts and then no-one gets on with her.
>
> (Laura, Year 6, Orchard)

> It depends – if I've been bad or good. If I've been good she's OK, but if I've been bad she treats me the same but not the same.
>
> (Harry, Year 6, St Bede's)

> All right most of the time, but not when she's in a bad mood.
>
> (Hugh, Year 6, Lawnside)

> OK. I think she thinks I'm a bit slow. She makes comments.
>
> (Kim, Year 6, St Bede's)

> He's kind, but I don't like it when he shouts. I feel a bit worried sometimes.
>
> (Malcolm, Year 6, St Anne's)

Some of these statements are from pupils whose behaviour and attitude presented teachers with a frequent challenge. Some are from cooperative high achievers. The pervasive refrain of teachers' moods may well reflect the tensions and pressures which many teachers said they experienced, especially in Year 6 as standardized assessment approached.

Further analysis of the data shows interesting variations in the perceptions of boys and girls. Our report of phase one of the PACE research showed 63 per cent of girls expressing positive feelings about their teachers compared with 43 per cent of boys (Pollard *et al.*, 1994). We see a striking reversal of this trend in the final years of Key Stage 2.

We can see from Table 6.2 that in Years 3 and 4 there was an increase in the percentage of positive responses from both boys and girls. However in Years 5 and 6,

Table 6.2 Boys' and girls' perceptions of their relationships with their teachers (percentages)

| | Years 3–4 | | Years 5–6 | |
	Boys	Girls	Boys	Girls
Positive	54	71	62	47
Neutral	32	22	28	36
Negative	4	2	2	2
Ambivalent	10	5	8	15

Source: PACE 2 and 3 child interview data
Sample: 54 children in each of Years 3–6
Date: Autumn 1990 and 1991, Summer 1993, 1994, 1995 and 1996

though negative feelings continued to remain relatively rare, girls were expressing more neutral and ambivalent feelings about their teachers. Boys' responses, in contrast, continued to be positive as they moved through the school.

We might speculate here on girls' greater linguistic ability to express ambivalence and to articulate more subtle shades of feeling in relationships. In addition, girls mature faster and in Year 6 some of those in our sample appeared to be developing more complex, critical and detached views of classroom experience. This analysis also reflects the traditional view of boys as less complicated in their feelings, more accepting of the status quo and quicker to forgive and forget. However, as we shall see later, by Year 6 boys were also beginning to construct positive images of non-conformity.

In order to gain a better understanding of pupils relationships with their teachers we asked each year 'What do you like best about your teacher?'. The analysis of their responses shows how the factors which children saw as important changed or stayed constant.

Table 6.3 Children's criteria for liking teachers (percentages)

	Year 1	Year 2	Year 3	Year 4	Year 5	Year 6
Personal	11	15	3	0	0	1
Interest	33	24	20	20	16	3
Ease	6	2	5	0	3	2
Choice	11	7	10	3	0	2
Interaction	24	44	55	69	80	89
Don't know	9	4	7	8	1	3
No data	6	4	0	0	0	0

Source: PACE 1, 2 and 3 child interview data
Sample: 54 children in each of Years 1–6
Date: Autumn 1990 and 1991, Summer 1993, 1994, 1995 and 1996

Table 6.3 dramatically shows the nature of their interaction with their teachers was of paramount importance for the children in the study. This became increasingly dominant, even surpassing the 'interest' of the activities provided which, though the second most mentioned factor, declined in importance. Being given 'easy work' was barely mentioned, probably because it was perceived as happening very seldom. Interest in teachers' looks, appearance, dress, or voice was hardly mentioned after Year 2, and at the same time having 'choice' ceases to be mentioned – arguably because this was not something that teachers offered in any meaningful way.

In order to investigate the children's preoccupation with interaction we developed further categories for this criterion and applied them, using multiple coding.

- 'Interaction – personal' – used to identify pupil statements that referred to the interpersonal qualities of teacher–pupil interaction, for example:

Talks to me when I'm feeling unhappy.

(Kate, Year 2, Greenmantle)

Nice and kind.

(Sam, Year 4, St Bede's)

Makes us laugh.

(Melanie, Year 4, St Anne's)

Nice to talk to.

(Amanda, Year 4, Kenwood)

Really understanding – like if we had a problem you could go to her.

(Jeremy, Year 5, Kenwood)

If we've done something we're upset about she comes and comforts us.

(Richard, Year 5, Valley)

Very friendly.

(Juliet, Year 5, Greenmantle)

- 'Interaction – instruction' – used to categorize references to interaction that related specifically to teaching and learning, for example:

Shows you things and you can get an idea what to do.

(Polly, Year 2, Valley)

Always explains the piece of work clearly.

(Alice, Year 3, Lawnside)

Doesn't get cross if you say you don't understand.

(Ben, Year 4, Greenmantle)

When we are doing work she tries and tell us in a language we understand and when you ask a question she can usually give you a very good answer.

(Rupert, Year 5, Lawnside)

Makes things funny instead of hard.

(Olivia, Year 5, Lawnside)

Walks about and checks on your work so you do better work.

(Scott, Year 5, Kenwood)

If she gives us really hard work she comes and helps us.

(Dawn, Year 5, Kenwood)

If you get stuck on something she helps you.

> (Juliet, Year 5, Greenmantle)

A good teacher, teaches me things I've never known.

> (Haley, Year 6, St Bede's)

Understands when we're going wrong. Doesn't shout. Explains it like *we* would tell it.

> (Brian, Year 6, Audley)

Gives me hard sums to do when I want and feel a need for them.

> (Neil, Year 6, Audley)

If you put your hand up, says 'Come straight away to see me'.

> (Laura, Year 6, Orchard)

Always tries to make work exciting. Tries to make it interesting.

> (Lucy, Year 6, Lawnside)

Explains things well and if you want help she helps you enough so you can understand it.

> (Jan, Year 6, Valley)

She keeps chasing you up and making you work hard, 'cos if she didn't I would just sit back and do nothing probably.

> (Jeremy, Year 6, Kenwood)

- 'Interaction – control' – used where the responses made reference to the teachers' management of behaviour, for example:

Doesn't tell me off.

> (Kim, Year 2, St Bede's)

Tells people off for being naughty.

> (Olivia, Year 2, Lawnside)

Has eyes in the back of her head. She calls out 'X why aren't you getting on with your work?'

> (Ewan, Year 3, Kenwood)

If you've been naughty, will give you another chance sometimes.

> (Jeremy, Year 4, Kenwood)

Doesn't get mad with me.

> (Theresa, Year 4, Audley)

Doesn't shout someone's name out – she'll talk to them – she might take them into the corridor and talk to them there.

> (Alice, Year 5, Lawnside)

Only shouts a little bit.

> (Corrinne, Year 5, Meadway)

Gives you chances. If you do it again on the final chance, he'll punish you.

> (Wesley, Year 5, Meadway)

If you are being silly and you know what to do but just can't be bothered she does get a bit angry. She's very fair.

> (Kate, Year 5, Greenmantle)

She never shouts.

(Martin, Year 6, Lawnside)

This coding was then used to analyse the responses in the broad Interaction category.

Table 6.4 Breakdown of the 'Interaction' category in pupils' criteria for liking teachers (percentages)

	Year 1	Year 2	Year 3	Year 4	Year 5	Year 6
Personal	14	21	26	41	47	49
Instructional	6	18	21	19	21	33
Control	4	5	8	9	12	7
Total	24	44	55	69	80	89

Source: PACE 1, 2 and 3 child interview data
Sample: 54 children in each of Years 1–6
Date: Autumn 1990 and 1991, Summer 1993, 1994, 1995 and 1996

The importance for the children of interpersonal interaction over instruction or control is clear. Kindness and friendliness in their teachers was consistently liked by children in all years. Making jokes, having a laugh and being fun became increasingly mentioned from Year 4 onwards and made up a third of the mentions in the 'personal' category in Year 6. However, in Year 6 there was an increase in the value placed on instructional interaction when, as we have already noted, there was a marked reduction in the importance of the interest of curriculum activity. Some pupils were apparently becoming very aware of the requirement to learn, irrespective of being interested, and were more aware of their teachers' instructional skills. The teacher's ability to explain things and the willingness to help when work was difficult or pupils 'got stuck' was mentioned increasingly frequently in Years 5 and 6. Higher-attaining pupils mentioned their teachers' instructional qualities more than lower achievers who were more likely to continue to value the ability to make learning interesting.

Where pupils mentioned more than one category of interaction, the concept of 'understanding' was most evident. They liked teachers who empathized with their feelings, whether these were to do with personal problems with friends, bullying or home difficulties. They also liked teachers who could understand and be patient with them as learners.

The infrequent mention of liking teachers for reasons associated with control is perhaps not surprising. What was noticeable was that very few pupils liked teachers because they were not strict. In Year 6 especially, more liked teachers because they kept them and others in order and made them work. The teacher behaviour mentioned most specifically was shouting: pupils liked teachers who didn't shout, or didn't shout much.

In this chapter, we are interested in the exercise of power in classrooms. At this point we shift the focus to pupils' views of who has control of curriculum activity.

6.3 PUPIL PERCEPTIONS OF CLASSROOM CONTROL

We wanted to know what, from the pupils' perspective, actually happened in their classrooms. Who in their view was in control? Their answers to the question 'Do you choose what you do at school or does your teacher choose?' indicated a very high degree of perceived teacher control – virtually 100 per cent in Years 4, 5 and 6. The very small percentage of children in Years 4 and 6 who indicated that they felt that both teachers and pupils were involved in the choosing made it clear from their additional comments that they were referring to a limited amount of choice for pupils in connection with topic or with 'finishing off' work. Other pupils from the same classrooms indicated a clear perception of dominant teacher control.

Table 6.5 Children's perception of who selects tasks at school (percentages)

	Year 1	Year 2	Year 3	Year 4	Year 5	Year 6
Teacher	59	80	98	98	100	96
Children	13	2	2	0	0	0
Both	26	16	0	2	0	4
No data	2	2	0	0	0	0

Source: PACE 1, 2 and 3 child interview data
Sample: 54 children in each of Years 1–6
Date: Autumn 1990 and 1991, Summer 1993, 1994, 1995 and 1996

The perception of increased teacher control in Year 2 prompted us to add a question to the Year 3 interviews. We asked 'Do you get as much choice now as you did in your class last year?' and probed the response by asking 'Why do you think that is?'. The questions were repeated in Year 4.

In Year 3, at the start of Key Stage 2, 76 per cent of the pupils told us that they had less choice than in Year 2. In Year 4 this fell to 57 per cent, but 30 per cent reported having the same amount of choice which for the majority meant no change from none: 'We didn't have any last year', 'There was no choosing last year and it's the same this year'. The children's clear view that their teachers were in control was not shifted by any subsequent probing questions. Choice, if it appeared at all, did so in limited and specific areas of activity; for example, choice within tasks for topic work, what happened when 'work' was completed, 'finishing off', or the last session on Fridays.

The reasons advanced by the children for this reduction in pupil choice were the same across all the schools in the study. It was seen as a natural accompaniment to moving into the juniors. A selection of explanations from Year 3 responses indicate the model of learning and of pedagogy that the children shared.

> In the little classes they don't do much work 'cos they are little and it takes them a long time.
>
> (Helen, Year 3, Orchard)

> When we were infants we were not expected to do as much as when we're juniors.
>
> (Alice, Year 3, Lawnside)

In the infants they don't give work that's really hard. If it's hard you didn't have to do it. In the juniors you've got to do it even if you don't know how to.

(Dawn, Year 3, Kenwood)

When you are little you can do easy work – we have to learn more now.

(Ameer, Year 3, Meadway)

It's a higher class and you have to do higher work and learn more about life – when you're younger you just have to learn to colour.

(Stella, Year 3, Valley)

When you go higher you have to do more work and you have to do harder work to get ready to go to middle school.

(Kyle, Year 3, Meadway)

Older children work harder to learn a lot more.

(Simon, Year 3,Valley)

It's harder work and more jobs to do; because it takes longer we have to do more.

(Kate, Year 3, Greenmantle)

The teacher thinks we'll choose babyish and easy things to do so we'll never learn.

(Amanda, Year 3, Kenwood)

'Cos we've grown up and what we should do is listen to the adults.

(Scott, Year 3, Kenwood)

They're younger – juniors have to be taught more.

(Samantha, Year 3, St Bede's)

Thus as the children saw it there was more free choice in the infants because expectations were lower and there was less to learn. Getting older meant harder work and more to learn so that they could progress through the educational system. Work took more time and there was less choice because choice is associated with 'play' and easy work. Increased teacher direction and control were natural concomitants to accomplishing the learning task for 'a junior', already anticipating the move to secondary school.

This Year 3 view was confirmed in Year 4 with for some an even greater sense of teacher control.

In Year 3 you could play when you finished – now you have to do more work.

(Dawn, Year 4, Kenwood)

Most of the time we have to do the work ready for going into the next year.

(Mandy, Year 4, Audley)

Now we are going up to the top class Mrs X wants us to know what it's like to do a lot of work.

(Harriet, Year 4, Valley)

I think you get less choice as you go up.

(Sean, Year 4, Greenmantle)

We're getting older now so the teacher has to decide.

(Tom, Year 4, Greenmantle)

You've got to learn more. In the senior school I expect you never choose.

(Haley, Year 4, St Bede's)

Being in the infants was remembered as a less 'serious' and pressured time. 'We were a lot younger then', said one 8-year-old. 'In the juniors you have to do more work – you can't play as you used to,' said another. There was some sad speculation: 'Because they liked us so much they let us choose in the little classes,' and one view of the process as essentially consistent:

It was the same then and now – they both just tell you.

(Sam, Year 3, St Bede's)

6.4 PUPIL PREFERENCES FOR AUTONOMY OR TASK DIRECTION

Given the pupils' perception of dominant teacher control of task and activity which we have seen, we were interested to know what they felt about this in relation to their own preferred way of working. In each year of the study we asked the 54 children in our longitudinal cohort 'Do you like it best when you choose what to do or when your teachers chooses?'. Again the data show interesting variations and shifts in pupils' views.

Table 6.6 Children's preferences for who chooses classroom activities (percentages)

	Year 1	Year 2	Year 3	Year 4	Year 5	Year 6
Teacher	30	33	53	35	37	46
Myself	63	61	39	61	44	48
Both	2	4	8	2	13	4
Don't know	2	0	0	2	2	2
No answer	3	2	0	0	4	0

Source: PACE 1, 2 and 3 child interview data
Sample: 54 children in each of Years 1–6
Date: Autumn 1990 and 1991, Summer 1993, 1994, 1995 and 1996

Almost two-thirds of the pupils in Years 1 and 2 recorded that they preferred to control their own activities. In Year 3 the swing was towards preferring teacher to choose, mirroring the acceptance of and accommodation towards becoming a junior which we have already seen in their remarks on reduced choice. However, in Year 4 there was a strong swing back to 'choosing myself' and by Year 6 pupils were fairly equally divided in their preferences.

We can learn more about their attitude to learning by looking at the reasons they gave for their preferences.

Perceptions of pupils preferring to choose for themselves

Table 6.7 shows the analysis of responses using multiple codes. The percentages here and in Table 6.8 are based on the total of pupils in each year who gave reasons for their choices.

Table 6.7 Reasons given by pupils who preferred to choose activities themselves (percentages)

	Year 1	Year 2	Year 3	Year 4	Year 5	Year 6
Because I can choose better	27	33	25	38	35	29
Because I can avoid things	4	23	9	10	9	9
Because it's more fun	20	5	9	10	8	9
Don't know	6	2	0	0	0	2
No data	2	0	2	2	3	3
Other	5	0	0	0	0	0
Total percentage	64	63	45	60	55	52

Source: PACE 1, 2 and 3 child interview data
Sample: 54 children in each of Years 1–6
Date: Autumn 1990 and 1991, Summer 1993, 1994, 1995 and 1996
Note: These are percentages of reasons given by the whole cohort in each year

The greatest number of reasons given by the children were associated in various ways with having autonomy over their learning ('I can choose better'). For all ages, this meant being able to choose things they liked doing best. When they talked of 'best' subjects some, but by no means all, children appeared to be constructing an association between 'what I like' and 'what I'm good at'. The opportunity to succeed was clearly welcomed but being in control also involved more varied motivation. For some it was a question of spending time on an activity that they were getting less experience of than they wished. They were, in addition, aware of the importance to learning of mood and inclination, of 'feeling like doing it'. Some examples illustrate the range of reasons the children advanced:

Because I can choose my very best things I like doing.

(Tom, Year 1, Greenmantle)

'Cos I can do my Maths. It makes me feel good 'cos I know them.

(Kim, Year 2, St Bede's)

Miss don't know what I like best.

(Wesley, Year 2, Meadway)

She sometimes chooses what you don't like.

(Gavin, Year 3, Orchard)

Because I can choose my best subjects.

(Neil, Year 4, Audley)

I like writing stories and sometimes Sir doesn't let us write stories.

(Samantha, Year 4, St Bede's)

'Cause I like getting the Technology trolley.

(Malcolm, Year 4, St Anne's)

You get to do what you feel like doing.

(Lucy, Year 4, Lawnside)

I always choose to draw; I like drawing.

(Philip, Year 5, St Anne's)

Because we like what we are doing. We don't necessarily like what we are doing with the teacher.

(Alice, Year 5, Lawnside)

You have to do exactly what he says when he chooses but not when you choose.

(Jacquie, Year 5, St Anne's)

Some of the things that Mrs S chooses are not all that interesting. Some of the things that we choose do help us a lot and they are interesting.

(Richard, Year 5, Valley)

When we choose we will like it because we wouldn't choose to do what we don't feel like.

(Harriet, Year 6, Valley)

We get to do what we want. I just do things I know a lot about.

(Kevin, Year 6, Audley)

Teacher might choose something that you really don't want to do. You choose the one you feel better and more confident doing and you want to do.

(Tom, Year 6, Greenmantle)

You can choose things the teacher wouldn't normally let you – I'd choose reading in the library and the computer.

(Carol, Year 6, Orchard)

However, in addition to these explanations there was another clearly identifiable strand of responses to do with children wanting to choose because it would give them more control over *how* they learned, particularly in the management of time which was perceived as a scarce commodity. They were aware of the pressure to get things done and felt there was not enough time to do some things properly, nor enough time for them to learn as they would like. Often they wanted more time than their teachers might like to give them. This could be seen in some children in Key Stage 1 but emerged much more prominently as they got older.

It's better if you want to change activities and you don't have to ask.

(Owen, Year 1, Valley)

Because you don't have to wait.

(Simon, Year 1, Valley)

So I can do the day before's things and catch up.

(Andrew, Year 3, Orchard)

'Cos sometimes Miss says do your Maths when you want to finish your topic – and the other way around.

(Amanda, Year 5, Kenwood)

'Cos say, like, you have English and you are really up-to-date – you feel like going on with your topic because you might be behind.

(Jessica, Year 6, Kenwood)

Because if you have stuff to catch up on you can do it when you want. Sometimes you have loads of pieces of topic work to do and you get fifteen minutes – and then you go straight to Maths for about an hour.

(Ewan, Year 6, Kenwood)

Stage 1 of the PACE research used the codes 'autonomy', 'interest', and 'ease' to analyse these data. After 'autonomy' and 'interest', the third most mentioned factor for the Year 1 and 2 children who preferred to choose for themselves was connected with the ease of the activity. In recoding all six years of data we identified instead answers where the children said they would prefer to choose in order to *avoid things*. For the most part these were things they saw as *too hard*:

'Cos sometimes the teacher chooses us to do a little bit hard work.

(Samantha, Year 1, St Bede's)

Because sometimes Mrs X's jobs are things I don't like, don't want to do or am not very good at, because it might be too hard.

(Kate, Year 2, Greenmantle)

She chooses writing and it's really hard. She gives us a lot and I get really tired.

(Hugh, Year 2, Lawnside)

She might just say 'Go and draw a picture like one of those (Tudor) houses' and it's hard to do.

(Abel, Year 2, Valley)

If I don't like it I might get it wrong and I won't like it.

(Helen, Year 2, Orchard)

'Cos sometimes I'm hopeless at computers. I like it when I can choose something else.

(Melanie, Year 3, St Anne's)

Mrs L sometimes gives us hard stuff that takes all day to do.

(Olivia, Year 3, Lawnside)

The teacher chooses hard stuff and I choose easy stuff.

(Scott, Year 4, Kenwood)

What he tells us to do gets a bit hard.

(Kim, Year 4, St Bede's)

Sometimes the things which our teacher chooses I get mixed up with and I don't know how to do it.

(Harry, Year 6, St Bede's)

In our coding the 'more fun' category was used where children very strongly indicated that choosing themselves would deliver more enjoyable experiences or where they expressed dissatisfaction with what the teacher provided. As might be predicted the oppositions 'work–play' and 'fun–boring' were evident and there are connections here with the 'avoid' category (children labelling challenging and difficult activities as 'boring') as well as desire for 'ease' and congenial activity with friends.

Miss gives us boring things.

(Celia, Year 1, Meadway)

When we choose we don't work, it's fun.

(Lynn, Year 1, Orchard)

'Cos I can play with me mates.

(Malcolm, Year 2, St Anne's)

You do things that are fun and easy.

(Kim, Year 3, St Bede's)

Basically what the teacher tells us to do is the most boring thing I can think of.

(Ben, Year 4, Greenmantle)

Teachers nag at you like they're supposed to if you're naughty and we have to have our books ready and that.

(Eliot, Year 4, St Bede's)

Teacher chooses all boring things – work.

(Frances, Year 6, St Anne's)

I'd do lots of fun stuff, not boring.

(Jane, Year 6, Meadway)

In summary, the reasons pupils gave for wanting to have control of what tasks and activities they tackled were varied. Many wanted to choose in order to avoid difficulty or to have more fun. There is overlap between the categories in that a number of those who claimed they could 'choose better' were in fact looking for a curriculum where they would not be faced with challenge or be exposed to the risk of failure. However, there is also evidence that some children saw choosing for themselves as a way to get a broader curriculum with more of the things they enjoyed. Most telling are the aspirations of those pupils who wanted to choose in order to have more control of their learning processes and who, in addition, implied that much of what they experienced failed to motivate them.

Perceptions of pupils preferring teacher choice of tasks and activities

We see in Table 6.8 the children valuing their teachers' ability and effort in providing them with activities that engage their interest. They are also increasingly aware of their own limitations in this area and of the ability of the teacher to protect them from the preferences of other pupils.

When we go home at night and she sorts something out it's usually good.

(Lance, Year 2, Orchard)

You do more things when Miss chooses.

(Alice, Year 2, Lawnside)

Table 6.8 Reasons given by pupils who preferred their teacher to choose activities (percentages)

	Year 1	Year 2	Year 3	Year 4	Year 5	Year 6
Because it's more interesting	18	19	25	14	18	13
Because it's easier	0	3	15	9	9	11
Because teacher knows best	7	7	12	9	15	19
Don't know	2	2	0	2	0	0
No data	7	4	3	4	3	5
Other	2	2	0	2	0	0
Total percentage	36	37	55	40	45	48

Source: PACE 1, 2 and 3 child interview data
Sample: 54 children in each of Years 1–6
Date: Autumn 1990 and 1991, Summer 1993, 1994, 1995 and 1996
Note: These are percentages of reasons given by the whole cohort in each year

Sometimes I like a surprise for what I'm doing.

(Dean, Year 2, Kenwood)

When we choose you think it's going to be exciting, but in the middle it isn't and it gets boring.

(Kyle, Year 3, Meadway)

She's got good ideas. The children would choose History; I don't like that.

(Dawn, Year 3, Kenwood)

'Cos she gives us hard work and it's interesting.

(Laura, Year 4, Orchard)

When Miss chooses she usually makes it more interesting. When I choose there's nothing there to make it interesting.

(Rupert, Year 5, Lawnside)

If we choose it would be stuff like going outside and the teacher thinks of new things to do.

(Sam, Year 5, St Bede's)

He chooses better, 'funner' things.

(Melanie, Year 6, St Anne's)

Analysis of responses from the early years of the study produced signs of the children adopting more instrumental strategies to accommodate the progressive challenges they faced in school as they got older. This was confirmed by the later data. Even when they were commending their teachers' imaginative ideas, they often added comments that indicated a need for a strategic approach and a desire to be clear about what they had to do. For instance:

'Cos sometimes she lets us do Art – most of the time if we say it we're not allowed.

(Mandy, Year 5, Audley)

She always thinks of good things that we like to do. She has a timetable. I want a copy so
I know what I'm doing.

(Brian, Year 3, Audley)

The evidence for increasing instrumentality is strong in the categories 'because it's
easier', 'because it's better for me/teacher knows best'. In Key Stage 2 these reasons
become as important (and in Year 6 more important) for pupils than having
activities that were interesting. If the teacher chose it was 'better for me' because it
offered the security of knowing what to do and what was required. Increasingly, as
children moved into Years 5 and 6 their answers indicated a perception of learning as
something possessed by the teacher – teachers knew what they had to learn so it was
better to let them decide what should be done. Greater prescription of the curriculum
and the introduction of categoric assessment in Year 6 appears to have produced a
strategic teacher-dependence in the pupils in our sample.

Because we won't know what we are doing if the teacher doesn't tell us.

(Sean, Year 1, Greenmantle)

She makes it clear to us what we have to do.

(Alice, Year 3, Lawnside)

She knows which Maths pages are right for us; if you did it yourself you'd go wrong.

(Simon, Year 3, Valley)

We don't really know what to choose but if he tells us we know what to do.

(Sam, Year 4, St Bede's)

It might not be as educating as what Miss chooses.

(Richard, Year 4, Valley)

I just like it when Miss decides because you really know what to do, 'cos she explains it.

(Jessica, Year 5, Kenwood)

'Cos he picks all the right things, and we don't.

(Susie, Year 5, St Anne's)

If we choose we might not be learning what our teacher makes us work for.

(Theresa, Year 6, Audley)

If the teacher chooses you get to learn more than when you're choosing.

(Stella, Year 6, Valley)

If we choose it might be something we've already done or are good at or like.

(Guy, Year 6, Valley)

The children believed their teachers made sure they didn't 'do the wrong thing' and
saved them from a natural tendency to avoid work, go off-task and be over- or
under-ambitious:

'Cos we don't know what we're doing and we might only choose our favourites. She gives
us Maths sheets.

(Dean, Year 3, Kenwood)

I usually choose stupid things.

(Amanda, Year 4, Kenwood)

He finds hard work and we can only find easy work that you can do in a minute.

(Kyle, Year 4, Meadway)

They choose the right stuff, like Maths. I wouldn't choose it otherwise.

(Susie, Year 4, St Anne's)

Because when I choose I might not get a lot done because I like talking a lot. We always have a lot to do so I have to get around to doing it.

(Dawn, Year 5, Kenwood)

If I ever choose it will probably go a bit over the top and be difficult to finish.

(Juliet, Year 6, Greenmantle)

Because if she lets us do whatever we want we will just play games and not learn anything because we won't do any work. But the teacher will give us Maths and English and a good selection and then we can learn a lot.

(Simon, Year 6, Valley)

Because sometimes we choose things that we're not very good at or are a load of rubbish.

(Richard, Year 6, Valley)

The children's answers also showed a clear-sighted grasp of the 'realities' of their classroom life. In giving us reasons why it was 'easier' when the teacher chose the activities, they touched on aspects of classroom management and of learning processes in a way that was essentially pragmatic. Pupils had problems with choosing so it was better if they didn't as it wasted time. If they did choose there would be problems with access to resources, with finding people to work with, with having to do what someone else had chosen, and with all the attendant noise and movement.

I don't know what to choose on planning sheets. They all look good and only three people are allowed in the shop at one time so you can't do what you want to do.

(Ewan, Year 2, Kenwood)

'Cos other people can't take things that you want and you get time to do it.

(Brian, Year 2, Audley)

We don't have to waste time asking her if we can't think what to do.

(Eliot, Year 3, St Bede's)

If she says to everybody 'You can choose' you find someone else is doing what you wanted. Sometimes I can't think of what to do.

(Jan, Year 3, Valley)

It makes a lot of noise when people choose. It makes me get headaches.

(Theresa, Year 5, Audley)

Then there aren't a lot of people rushing to different places. We are all in one place doing the same thing.

(Laura, Year 5, Orchard)

Most of the time if we wanted to do something that's our own idea we wouldn't have the stuff.

(Shona, Year 5, Meadway)

When the teacher decides there is not a big noise, everything goes quietly – no-one is saying 'What shall we do? What shall we do?'

(Laura, Year 6, Orchard)

I can never make up my mind if I have to decide.

(Alice, Year 6, Lawnside)

He can make a decision. I'll take forever.

(Celia, Year 6, Meadway)

Because I don't have to sit and decide and take ages thinking – I like to have set work so that I can get on and do it and not hum and ha about it.

(Jan, Year 6, Valley)

In summary

The reasons pupils gave for preferring their teachers to choose involved both trust in their teacher's professional skill to provide interesting activities and a strategic acknowledgement that letting the teacher choose was easier and more practical. In addition, as the end of Key Stage 2 approached, there was evidence that for these pupils in the context of the National Curriculum choosing for yourself was just too risky. Teachers knew what had to be learned and it was understood that the costs of following personal inclination could be high.

We close this section with some examples of pupils who wanted to share control with their teachers:

When our teacher chooses we find things out as well as having fun. I like it when I choose because I know what I want to do.

(Juliet, Year 5, Greenmantle)

Sometimes the teacher has good ideas, specially in Art and Technology, but sometimes it's nice to do what you want yourself.

(Kate, Year 5, Greenmantle)

When I choose I like doing fun stuff. When teacher chooses, sometimes it's fun stuff; sometimes it's hard work.

(Hugh, Year 5, Lawnside)

6.5 PUPIL ACCEPTANCE OF TEACHER CONTROL AND AUTHORITY

The degree to which control could be shared and the opportunities perceived by pupils to be available for teacher–pupil negotiation were of interest in relation to classroom management and control of behaviour as well as curriculum. In this connection we asked pupils each year 'Do you have to do what your teacher says?'. In PACE 3, we also invited them to tell us how they felt about this. We can see from Table 6.9 the high level of teacher control in this area perceived by our sample.

Over the six years of the study the percentage of children answering an unequivocal 'Yes' fell from 94 per cent in Year 1 to 76 per cent in Years 5 and 6.

Table 6.9 Pupils' answers to the question 'Do you have to do what your teacher says?' (percentages)

	Year 1	Year 2	Year 3	Year 4	Year 5	Year 6
Yes	94	83	89	85	76	76
Sometimes	6	15	11	11	24	24
No	0	0	0	4	0	0
No data	0	2	0	0	0	0

Source: PACE 1, 2 and 3 child interview data
Sample: 54 children in each of Years 1–6
Date: Autumn 1990 and 1991, Summer 1993, 1994, 1995 and 1996

However, this was accompanied by a balancing increase in those reporting that they had to obey 'most of the time' or 'sometimes'. Older children appeared more aware of the possibility for negotiation and of how different situations and activities produced varying requirements for conformity in their classrooms.

In Years 1 and 2 of the study, as Polly succinctly summed up 'We do what we're told and we're told what to do' (Polly, Year 1, Valley). However, the additional comments children made when answering this question indicated that they were very aware of the possibilities for the exercise of teacher power. Teacher anger and shouting was to be avoided, as was being 'told off' or sent out to the headteacher. In particular they were concerned about being shown up, shouted at, told off and isolated from their peers:

> Children that are naughty she shouts at them.
>
> (Noel, Year 1, Kenwood)

> If you don't you stand in the book corner and you're not allowed to leave or talk.
>
> (Samantha, Year 1, St Bede's)

> If I get told off I go red.
>
> (Darren, Year 2, St Bede's)

> Or she'd tell you off. If someone is really naughty they have to go to the office and see (headteacher).
>
> (Sam, Year 1, St Bede's)

> Otherwise she gets angry and sends you out.
>
> (Kate, Year 2, Greenmantle)

As the children got older they increasingly offered supplementary illustrations of the degrees of teacher control they perceived. To gain a better understanding of the level of acceptance of teacher authority, in Years 5 and 6 we specifically asked the children 'How do you feel about doing what your teacher says?'. Overwhelmingly they indicated that they accepted it (66 per cent in Year 5, 70 per cent in Year 6). The following examples illustrate their thinking about this:

> I don't mind – some people moan about it and then they get told off.
>
> (Sean, Year 5, Greenmantle)

He's the teacher; we can't answer him back. It's cheeky, we shouldn't answer him back. It doesn't annoy me; that's the way it goes.

> (Melanie, Year 5, St Anne's)

I don't like it but I have to do it. I'm not really bothered any more.

> (Samantha, Year 5, St Bede's)

When you come to school he's in charge of you for the day. When you go home you get all your free time.

> (Wesley, Year 5, Meadway)

It's fine – she's not demanding – you don't have to do it straight away.

> (Hugh, Year 5, Lawnside)

It's OK. I just get on – it's how you get on with it.

> (Kelly, Year 6, Orchard)

It's all right. I *expect* it.

> (Gavin, Year 6, Orchard)

I don't mind, I'm used to doing what people tell me.

> (Tom, Year 6, Greenmantle)

She's a very fair teacher – we have to do mainly what she says.

> (Lucy, Year 6, Lawnside)

There is a strong sense here of children who have learned to live with 'the way it is', who have accepted a particular construction of the role of 'teacher'. There are also indications of a tacit negotiation between teachers and pupils. For the pupils, acceptance was conditional on factors such as 'fairness', teacher personality or a level of demand they found acceptable. However, among the reasons given for acceptance of teacher authority, the fear of exposure, when expressed, was still strong:

> If she has to say it about five times you get sent outside. I feel scared. If she (the head) comes out of the office to ask why you're there you feel nervous – else me mum'll be coming in.
>
> (Mandy, Year 4, Audley)

There was also still a desire to avoid being shouted at and suffering the effects of the teacher's bad moods – 'I do ... so he doesn't get a nark on' (Melanie, Year 5, St Anne's) – and evidence of a strategic conformity to avoid unwanted outcomes – 'I like doing what the teacher says, otherwise you get more homework if you don't finish. I like getting it over and done with. I don't like homework' (Laura, Year 6, Orchard).

Some of the pupils' responses (less than 10 per cent) were unequivocally positive:

> It's fine. We've come here to learn; we should respect our teachers. They're teaching us how to learn. If we are going to mess around and do nothing what's the point of coming to school?
>
> (Rosie, Year 5, Lawnside)

> It's OK because he's the teacher. He knows lots of things about us and about other things like History and Art. If we don't do what he says we're bound to get it wrong – we're not

as smart as Sir yet.

(Kyle, Year 5, Meadway)

If you don't you'll be told off. I know that at the end of the day I will learn something and get a good job so I may as well listen and learn for my benefit.

(Harriet, Year 6, Valley)

She knows what's best for us.

(Ewan, Year 6, Kenwood)

I feel fine – it wouldn't be fair not to. If I was a teacher I would want people to do what I said.

(Brian, Year 6, Audley)

Less than 5 per cent of the responses were totally negative:

I don't really want to do what he says all the time. I feel not very pleased.

(Samantha, Year 5, St Bede's)

Normally we don't get to do the things we want to do at the right time. I don't feel good. I want to do the things I want first.

(Neil, Year 6, Audley)

I hate it – doing what other people say.

(Jane, Year 6, Meadway)

Far more responses (15 per cent in Year 5 and 18 per cent in Year 6) were coded as ambivalent. Although there was a greater acceptance and pragmatism in response to teacher power, there was also a growing ambivalence, even suppressed hostility for some children. This ambivalence related to different facets of teacher control – selection of curriculum activity, pedagogic processes, management of behaviour.

Sometimes I don't want to but I have to. I have to stand by the wall if I've done something I shouldn't. I want to draw but I can't. I have to do horrible Geography.

(Ian, Year 5, Meadway)

If it's something good I do it. If I was getting into a good book and I had to take the register I'd get angry.

(Jane, Year 5, Meadway)

I feel sad sometimes because I don't like the work – it's a bit boring.

(Martin, Year 5, Lawnside)

Sometimes I feel that he is bossy and sometimes I feel that it is good he is making us work.

(Harry, Year 5, St Bede's)

Sometimes I want to say something important to my friends – she shouts at me.

(Mandy, Year 6, Audley)

You have to stay in at break if you haven't done it and do it again if you haven't done it right. It's not fair if you really don't get it and don't understand. It is fair if you haven't worked.

(Geoffrey, Year 6, Orchard)

When she says 'History' I think 'rubbish'. I really hate it. Sometimes I feel mad; but sometimes I can understand her.

(Kate, Year 6, Greenmantle)

From their comments it is clear that many of the children indicated considerable respect for the role of 'teacher' and for their teachers as individuals. However, there was only one example offered of open negotiation of control between teachers and pupils:

Sometimes if she wants you to get something, but you say you're busy, she sends someone else to get it.

(Theresa, Year 5, Audley)

6.6 PUPIL PERCEPTION OF THE IDEAL PUPIL

An indication of pupils' views of their teachers' priorities was gained by asking in Years 5 and 6 for a description of the kind of pupil the teacher would most like to see joining the class. As Table 6.10 shows, pupils' awareness of attainment and ability did not feature highly in the characteristics they attributed to an 'ideal pupil'. This is particularly interesting in the light of our previous observations (and those we will make in Chapters 7 and 9) about the salience of end-of-Key Stage assessment. In fact, only 11 per cent of the 226 coded statements featured statements about being 'good at work' or about 'ability'. Slightly more (18 per cent) were concerned with being 'hardworking', 'getting down to work', 'getting on' and 'finishing'. The remaining majority (71 per cent) was made up of a mix of characteristics all of which related to behaviour, personal qualities or social skills.

Table 6.10 Behaviour and personal characteristics of the ideal pupil (percentages of total codings)

Hardworking	18
Obedient, well-behaved, not naughty	17
Quiet, doesn't talk	14
Nice, helpful, kind, caring, pleasant	13
Good at work, able	11
Polite, doesn't answer back	8
Sensible, responsible	6
Sociable, mixes well, good in groups	5
Listens	4
Other	4

Source: PACE 3 child interview data
Sample: 54 children in Years 5 and 6
Date: Summer 1995 and 1996
Note: Multiple codings were made for these answers

It is clear from this table that pupils perceived that their teachers placed great importance on the child's contribution to the social climate of the classroom. In very few cases was 'learning' included in their characterizations. For example, the 'ideal pupil' was seen as:

A hardworking, kind person that gets on well with people, good mixing and is well-behaved.

(Dawn, Year 5, Kenwood)

A person that doesn't fight a lot; someone that's not lippy.

(Kyle, Year 5, Meadway)

A nice person, caring, helps people. Like when someone falls over, goes and helps them up. Someone who comes to watch us at football, supports us, cheers us on.

(Hugh, Year 5, Lawnside)

Not too noisy, not rude, sensible, not shout out, would mix with others, would be friendly.

(Richard, Year 6, Valley)

Someone sensible.

(Esther, Year 6, Greenmantle)

Very polite. Not clever – Mrs W doesn't think they have to be clever. Someone who listens.

(Lucy, Year 6, Lawnside)

Someone with good manners, not cheeky. Good at working, but doesn't matter if they're not brilliant. I don't think she would mind.

(Kim, Year 6, St Bede's)

There was considerable variation in the weightings given to different characteristics by pupils in different schools. There is an indication of the particular school or classroom ethos which teachers were aiming to encourage in Table 6.11 which gives the rank order of characteristics cited for each school.

Table 6.11 Rank order of characteristics of the ideal pupil for each school

	First 'ideal'	Second 'ideal'	Third 'ideal'
Greenmantle	Quiet	Skilled	Hardworking
Kenwood Junior	Helpful & caring	Obedient	Quiet
Lawnside	Helpful & caring	Obedient	
Audley Junior	Hardworking	Obedient	Quiet
Valley	Hardworking	Quiet	
St Bede's	Obedient	Hardworking	Polite
Orchard	Obedient	Hardworking	Attainment
St Anne's	Obedient	Helpful & caring	Attainment
Meadway Junior	Attainment	Hardworking	Obedient

Source: PACE 3 child interview data
Sample: 54 children in each of Years 5 and 6
Date: Summer 1995 and 1996
Note: Characteristics which represented less than 15 per cent of the coded utterances in each school have not been included

We see here the strength of pupils' perception at Kenwood and Lawnside that what their teachers valued and liked was children who were helpful, kind, caring and pleasant. Evidence from the teacher interviews confirms that these indeed were teachers who, though concerned about performance, were anxious to retain the traditional primary school emphasis on the whole child. In contrast Meadway, an inner-city school with many social and behavioural problems, set out to cultivate an achievement culture. Here the children who saw the ideal pupil as 'smart', 'clever', 'intelligent', and 'good at work' were average or higher achievers themselves. Low achievers at this school thought their teachers would be more concerned to have pupils who were not rude or aggressive, who got on with the work and did as they were told. At Greenmantle pupils were very aware of their teachers' interest in classroom processes. The ideal pupil would 'get on well with other children', 'work well in groups and with partners', 'join in games and activities', 'not want to tell everyone how much they know in group discussions', 'be able to make their mind up and not annoy the teacher', and 'only puts their hand up if it's urgent'. In this school the children in Years 5 and 6 were grouped for different subjects and thus were taught by more than one teacher each day. This focus on working practices, on being sensible and responsible, may be a consequence of a requirement to adjust to regular changes of teacher.

The children were therefore experiencing very different classrooms. They were equally divided in Year 6 when we asked each of them how much they thought they were like the ideal pupil they had just described. Table 6.12 illustrates:

Table 6.12 Girls' and boys' perceptions of the degree to which they think they are like their teacher's ideal pupil (percentages)

	Yes	No	Quite	Don't know
Girls	22	17	17	0
Boys	9	18	15	2

Source: PACE 3 child interview data
Sample: 54 children in Year 6
Date: Summer 1996

As we can see, girls were much happier to define themselves as being like the ideal pupil. Some boys were particularly concerned to construct an identity for themselves which was in opposition to the ideal. Ewan, for instance described the ideal pupil as 'a nice, sensible, quiet, boring one ... someone that we'd all hate'. He saw himself as the complete opposite: 'being sensible is boring ... Everything I do I like to make it fun. If I'm bored with something I try to make it funner'. By implication he was telling us that he believed that this also made him someone that everyone (except his teacher) liked. We saw evidence of this construction of a social identity in opposition to the desired classroom norm in several other boys. Jeremy, for example, saw the ideal pupil as 'someone that's good – gets on with their work, quite quiet, probably like a girl or someone'.

Luke was not alone in associating ideal characteristics ('teacher's pet') with girls, rather than boys. His response, rejecting any likeness for himself, associated him firmly with 'the lads': 'When I'm with my mates I mess about. I talk too much'. Here already it seems are the beginnings of the association of non-conformity with masculinity, which is the focus of attention in relation of underachieving boys in the secondary phase. However, we also found some evidence of this in the girls' answers. Most girls who saw themselves as different did so by acknowledging some shortcoming: 'I don't work very well because sometimes I find the work difficult' (Juliet, Greenmantle). 'Sometimes I don't listen' (Kate, Greenmantle). 'I'm noisy and I'm not always a very kind person' (Jessica, Kenwood). 'I do work but sometimes I get bored before I finish' (Haley, St Bede's). Mandy and Jane, in contrast, though both high achievers and well-regarded by their teachers, did not want to be seen as conformist:

> No. I'm talkative. I like having a laugh. I don't like listening to teachers.
>
> (Mandy, Audley)

> Not at all. I'm smart but I don't get on with my work straight away. I like talking. I'm not a goody goody.
>
> (Jane, Meadway)

Nevertheless, these observations aside, it is notable that almost two-thirds of our sample agreed to some degree of match between themselves and the pupil they saw as their teacher's ideal.

We have seen in this section something of the great variety of classroom climate experienced by the pupils in our sample and their very different perceptions of teacher priorities. In the next section we see how unanimous they are about their view of the ideal teacher.

6.7 PUPIL PERCEPTION OF THE IDEAL TEACHER

The pupils' construction of their ideal teacher is strongly consistent with the characteristics they said they liked best in their own teachers. It is notable that between them and over the four years we asked this question, the children named 38 of their present or past teachers as examples of the ideal. Teachers in all nine schools were named, some of them many times.

> Like Mr A. He's a good teacher. He picks the right stuff for us.
>
> (Susie, Year 4, St Anne's)

> I don't need to imagine 'cos Mrs G is the perfect one. She joins in a game like rounders.
>
> (Scott, Year 5, Kenwood)

> A teacher like Mr B – he's strict and that's what teachers are meant to be. He's fun with children, doesn't get annoyed ... The work he gives us is quite hard, some is OK.
>
> (Haley, Year 5, St Bede's)

> Like Mr H. He's very kind and when you get in trouble he wasn't too hard on you. If a teacher's hard on you, you get more and more uptight and then lose your temper.
>
> (Kyle, Year 5, Meadway)

Like Mrs D really. She's funny but strict and I like that.

(Eliot, Year 6, St Bede's)

Like Mr J. He has a laugh and a joke. He explains work to you so you get it and he's sporty as well.

(Geoffrey, Year 6, Orchard)

Mrs W – she's fun and caring and good to speak to.

(Hugh, Year 6, Lawnside)

These descriptions contain many of the factors that were important to most children. A composite of our pupils' ideal, with factors in descending order of importance would look like this:

> Above all the ideal teacher is 'kind and nice; someone who likes you', is 'funny' and ready to 'have a laugh' ... He or she (sometimes boys specified a male and girls a female teacher) would give a choice so that pupils could do the things they liked more often and 'not always have to do everything like is on the National Curriculum'. This teacher would not shout, lose his or her temper or be moody; s/he would be tolerant rather than very strict or bossy and 'not insist on silence all the time'. S/he would not give you work that was 'too hard' for you or make you do tests and lots of writing and homework. If you found work difficult or got upset about something s/he would 'see it from the children's point of view', be understanding, 'someone good to talk to', who could 'sort things out'. S/he would give you help 'if you were stuck or not sure what to do' and explain things more than once. The work s/he planned would be 'interesting and good fun'; but s/he would be 'serious when you need to work' so some of it would be hard 'so we would learn'. The ideal teacher would not be 'too soft', rather 'firm but kind and fair'; s/he would make you do the work, be 'cross if you've done something wrong' but not angry. Instead s/he'd 'send you somewhere to think about it'. S/he would also be generous with marks and rewards like certificates and house points.

Some of these factors – being funny and prepared to have a laugh, being understanding, helping, explaining and not getting cross and shouting – became more important as children moved into the last two years of primary schooling. Providing interesting lessons was mentioned less as pupils got older. Perhaps they saw this as an unrealistic aspiration. There is, however, a strong sense of pupils who were wanting to learn and looking to their ideal teacher to 'make the hard stuff easy', 'give me work I can do, but a bit hard'. Many also aspired to be 'good' but wanted an ideal teacher to 'give second chances' and 'make me be good'. Very few children showed any sign of wanting to take responsibility for either their learning or their behaviour, and perhaps this is not surprising in the light of our discussion earlier in this chapter concerning the limited opportunities for pupil autonomy.

6.8 CONCLUSION

This chapter indicates that in general the pupils in our sample enjoyed a positive relationship with their teachers. By Year 6 some pupils, girls especially, had begun to express some ambivalence and there is evidence of boys, and some girls, already constructing a social identity based on non-conformity with teacher norms.

However, the majority appeared to accept the exercise of teacher power as 'natural' and to have some respect for the role.

As they progressed through primary school, pupils had learned to be strategic in managing their relationships with teachers, to negotiate teachers' moods and avoid the penalties of teachers' displeasure. A quotation from Max in Year 1 illustrates neatly how quickly these children, like all their counterparts, accommodated to the exercise of teacher power and worked out how to cope:

> I sit up straight. I get on well with her.
>
> (Max, Year 1, Lawnside)

It is evident, though, that this negotiation of relationships was not open, but arrived at individually with some pupils being strategically more successful and adept than others. The degree to which this operated at the personal rather than the professional level is indicated by the value pupils placed on interpersonal interaction in describing what they liked best about their teachers. This was consistent with their definitions of the ideal teacher where personal qualities of kindness, cheerfulness and a sense of humour were given greater weight than qualities related to teaching and learning. Similarly, when each pupil described their teacher's ideal pupil the emphasis was on characteristics associated with developing a positive social climate rather than attainment, ability or attitude to work.

We saw in the data related to the construct of the ideal pupil how our sample group had experienced classrooms with very different climates and teachers with different priorities. Equally in Year 6 there was a perceptible shift from the predominance of the social and interpersonal in pupils' perception of teacher relationships. The children placed more emphasis on teachers' ability to explain in ways they could comprehend, to understand pupils' learning problems, and to be helpful and willing to repeat instructions or explanations when pupils were uncertain or unclear. However, at the same time, the teacher's willingness to 'have a laugh' and 'be funny' increased in importance for them. Again, data from questions about their own and their ideal teacher are consistent.

Acceptance of teacher power and authority was emphasized by strong and increasing teacher control of classroom activity throughout the study. The pupils perceived little, if any, opportunity to exercise autonomy. The pedagogic frame was tight. There were variations across the years in pupils' preferences in choosing for themselves or being directed, but by Year 6 they were split almost equally. Many of those who wanted to choose for themselves saw it as a way of avoiding difficulty and challenge, others wanted to broaden their curriculum with more enjoyable activity or to take more control of the pace and management of their learning. The pupils who preferred teacher control did so mainly for pragmatic reasons and appeared to be exhibiting a growing instrumentality and teacher dependence as they sought to avoid the risk of doing the wrong thing or missing out on the National Curriculum.

This chapter has brought into focus some important features of the context in which our pupil sample engaged with the activity of learning. Whilst the pedagogic frame was certainly very controlled, relationships with teachers were generally good. Were children simply resigned to their role as 'pupils'? In Chapters 8 and 9 we look in more detail at pupils' perceptions of themselves and their teachers in relation to their experience of learning. But before that we consider their perspective on assessment, the final strand of the curriculum, pedagogy and assessment triad.

Chapter 7

Pupil Perspectives on Classroom Assessment

7.1   Introduction
7.2   Pupil perspectives on assessment interactions
7.3   Children's self-assessment of their personal attainment
7.4   Explanations for personal attainment
7.5   Explanations for others' attainment
7.6   Conclusion

7.1 INTRODUCTION

In previous chapters we have looked at pupils' views of the curriculum and their relationships with their teachers. We now turn our attention to their perspectives on classroom assessment, the third of Bernstein's three 'message systems'. As before, the data presented and analysed are drawn from all six years of the study and thus continue our already published accounts from the first two phases of the research. The data from PACE 3 complete the picture and enable us to look for changes and continuities across the whole period.

A central finding of PACE 1 was that teachers in the early 1990s tried to 'protect' pupils from the effects of the assessment reforms which they saw as potentially damaging to pupils and to teacher–pupil relationships. A majority of pupils in Key Stage 1 felt positive about assessment interactions. They saw classroom assessment in terms of managing the task (knowing what to do and evading the consequences of doing something wrong), the affective domain (the pleasure of being praised and the pain of being told off) and the intellectual domain (being told what educational activity to engage in next). Their responses also indicated a developing awareness of evaluative criteria and in particular of the importance attached to 'effort' in the context of school. In the second phase of the research, which covered Years 3 and 4 of the pupils' school lives, we noted slightly fewer positive and more negative responses to the question 'Do you like it when your teacher asks to look at your book?'. In addition, the children's answers indicated that they were more aware of the risks associated with teacher assessment. They aimed to produce work which was 'correct', had the required 'appearance' and would earn teacher approval. Their belief in the power of 'effort' was now well established.

Evidence from teachers and from our classroom observation in PACE 3 indicates that in the last two years of primary schooling children encountered a sharp increase in the use of routine tests and other forms of categoric assessment. In general, teachers were making less use of implicit formative approaches to assessment, and planning more explicit and focused assessment into classroom tasks. This chapter considers how the children responded in this context. We look specifically at their view of the purpose of assessment, their feelings about assessment interactions with their teacher, the assessments they made of their own and others' attainment, and the explanations they gave for these evaluations.

7.2 PUPIL PERSPECTIVES ON ASSESSMENT INTERACTIONS

Throughout the PACE study we have been interested in children's understanding of and response to situations in which various forms of assessment or evaluation were involved. In each year we asked children 'Do you like it when your teacher asks to look at your work?'. Their answers enabled us to explore two aspects of pupil perceptions. First, we were able to see whether the children saw this moment as diagnostic or formative assessment related to progressing their learning or as essentially summative, delivering a verdict on their attainment. Second, we gained access to the range of emotions they associated with assessment.

In our previously published reports of the two earlier phases of the PACE project (Pollard *et al.*, 1994; Croll, 1996) we discussed how children's positive feelings or their feelings of anxiety and vulnerability impacted on their attitudes to learning and to themselves as learners.

An analysis of six years of data enabled us to see how pupils' response to assessment episodes changed and developed. To do this we coded each response in one of four categories: positive, negative, mixed and neutral.

Table 7.1 Responses of pupils to the question 'Do you like it when your teacher asks to look at your work?' (percentages)

	Year 1	Year 2	Year 3	Year 4	Year 5	Year 6	Overall
Positive	57	52	44	43	20	13	38
Mixed	15	20	18	17	41	35	24
Neutral	6	7	6	4	15	15	9
Negative	22	21	32	36	24	37	29

Source: PACE 1, 2 and 3 child interview data
Sample: 54 children in each of Years 1–6
Date: Autumn 1990 and 1991, Summer 1993, 1994, 1995 and 1996

We have previously noted the decline in the eagerness with which children welcomed teachers' looking at their work in Years 3 and 4 and this trend continued even more strongly in Years 5 and 6. Table 7.1 shows a dramatic drop in Year 5 and the decline continued in Year 6 in the number of children who felt unequivocally positive about this assessment process. Children in the later years of Key Stage 2 had noticeably more mixed and negative feelings about having their work evaluated. Indeed, in Year 6, 72 per cent of responses were negative or mixed. The neutral 'don't mind' was as positive as most children became in their 'it depends' accounts.

The most frequently occurring word in these responses was 'worried'. In Year 1, 12 per cent of the children mentioned feeling worried. In Year 6 this had risen to a high of 42 per cent. As well as 'worried', children in Years 5 and 6 said they felt 'nervous', 'scared', 'upset', 'guilty', 'ashamed', 'embarrassed', 'shaky', 'doubtful'. One or more of these words featured in over two-thirds of the responses in these years and in all of the study schools. It is evident that the assessment moment was one that produced tension and anxiety for a majority of the children at the end of Key Stage 2.

'Looking at work' for these children almost invariably implied some kind of summative judgement. When we look more closely at the illustrative and explanatory commentary which accompanied the children's answers, we can see that their feelings about having their work looked at depended on their assessment of how acceptable it was to them or how far they anticipated it would be acceptable to their teachers. Such individually constructed self-assessment was the basis for the largest proportion of mixed and negative feelings with which they anticipated teacher evaluation. They made two kinds of judgements about the work about to be considered. First, they applied criteria of quantity, neatness and correctness that they assumed would be applied by their teachers.

> If I hadn't done that much I would be worried. If I think I have done enough I wouldn't mind.
>
> (Sam, Year 5, St Bede's)

> Sometimes I don't get much work done. Sir says we have to stay in if we didn't do much work. When I've done loads of work I'm pleased.
>
> (Shona, Year 5, Meadway)

> I feel quite nervous I might get something wrong. I don't like it when I get something wrong.
>
> (Hugh, Year 5, Lawnside)

> Depends whether me handwriting's scruffy or not. If I done neat writing I feel pleased. Nearly all the time I don't feel pleased. Sometimes she'll say 'Do it again'.
>
> (Mandy, Year 6, Audley)

> I don't like giving my book in 'cause it's a mess – I hide it at the bottom of the pile.
>
> (Frances, Year 6, St Anne's)

> Ashamed. My writing's never neat and I spell things wrong.
>
> (Kevin, Year 6, Audley)

If I've done something not quite right I feel nervous. We show each other our work. If theirs is better than mine I feel really worried.

(Esther, Year 5, Greenmantle)

I used to like it but not very much now. It worries me that I've done something wrong, especially now SATs are coming up.

(Richard, Year 6, Valley)

Second, they made a judgement of the amount of 'effort' they had put into the work. The results of this self-assessment also affected their feelings about exposing it to teacher scrutiny. As we can see from these examples, assessing 'effort' involved children's views of themselves as learners and their relationship with their teachers.

If I make mistakes I don't feel good 'cos I feel like I haven't been listening.

(Kyle, Year 5, Meadway)

If I haven't put my mind to it I think the teacher will be disappointed or angry; then I don't want to show it (to her) because she would expect more from me.

(Rosie, Year 5, Lawnside)

Sometimes I don't want her to look at it because I haven't tried. I haven't put enough effort into it.

(Jan, Year 6, Valley)

Sometimes I feel pleased if it's good but if I know I haven't bothered I get a bit worried.

(Kate, Year 6, Greenmantle)

There is little evidence here that the pupils had extended the range of criteria they had been applying in the first two years of Key Stage 2. If anything, their previous criteria had become more firmly established. However, an increase in expressions of anxiety and guilt in children's comments is evident. Associated with this, a newly prominent source of negative or mixed feelings for these pupils was a strong sense of uncertainty. They were uncertain about whether they had done what was required, about whether they had 'understood', and about how their teacher would respond. In addition, the growing preoccupation with correctness increased anxiety for some pupils who had very little idea whether what they had produced was correct or not and little awareness of the criteria by which their work would be assessed. They 'hoped' they had got it right; they felt 'lucky' when they did. This experience was reported by pupils at all levels of attainment.

When I know I've done it right I feel good. When I don't know if I've done it right I feel worried.

(Frances, Year 5, St Anne's)

Always worried at first. Sometimes you think you've done a really horrible piece of work and he says it's all right and you think 'phew'.

(Eliot, Year 5, St Bede's)

I'm actually kind of worried, nervous when I give work in at the end of the day ... I don't know what's going to happen.

(Neil, Year 6, Audley)

I don't know what she's going to say about it.

(Dawn, Year 6, Kenwood)

If you do something that you think is good and she says 'That's rubbish' then you get a bit upset 'cause you've put all your time and effort in.

(Scott, Year 6, Kenwood)

I think there's going to be something wrong all the time. I don't know why.

(Kim, Year 6, St Bede's)

I'm worried in case I did it wrong.

(Jessica, Year 6, Kenwood)

The uncertainty evident here about assessment criteria is mirrored, as we will see in Chapter 8, by an equal uncertainty about teacher intentions and the underlying rationale for much of what they were required to do.

The most negative responses to our question revealed considerable fear and apprehension about the consequences of 'getting it wrong' as the following examples show. Again, these are from pupils at all levels of attainment.

I feel guilty 'cos if you go wrong you get told off.

(Eliot, Year 1, St Bede's)

I'm worried in case she says 'Good gracious me, that's terrible!'.

(Kim, Year 3, St Bede's)

She might put you down to an easy book or cross them wrong.

(Hugh, Year 3, Lawnside)

Embarrassed in case it's not very good.

(Olivia, Year 3, Lawnside)

He might tell me to do it again if I get something wrong. I hide my book under a pile of books. I find it very worrying when I know he wants to see my book.

(Haley, Year 5, St Bede's)

I feel embarrassed if other people are around and I haven't done very well.

(Samantha, Year 5, St Bede's)

I feel not so good – just in case I've done something wrong – she might start shouting at me about quite a lot of things.

(Kevin, Year 5, Audley)

Incredibly scared. I think she will think the worst. After everything they will show your parents and I feel that my parents will find it really horrible and may ban my pocket money.

(Ben, Year 5, Greenmantle)

Worried in case she says 'That's wrong. Why did you put that?' and she says it in front of the class. It's a bit embarrassing.

(Geoffrey, Year 5, Orchard)

When I haven't done a lot or got a lot of spelling mistakes I don't like them looking at it because I know they will make me do it again or rip a page out. When I've done something good I like them to see that I can do good work.

> (Harriet, Year 6, Valley)

I think 'Oh no, I'll be in trouble now'.

> (Jeremy, Year 6, Kenwood)

Afraid I'm going to get it wrong. Frightened people will tease me – I don't like it.

> (Jane, Year 6, Meadway)

As we can see, for pupils 'getting it wrong' meant, at best, facing their teachers' disappointment that they had failed to meet expectations. At worst this would involve teacher censure, being shouted at, public humiliation and embarrassment, or having to do the work again (probably in break or dinner time). Fear of exposure was felt by both low and high attainers. We have here evidence of low attainers who tried to avoid the assessment moment by hiding books or evading attention. They also feared having their inability to understand made public by questioning or by the evidence in their books of 'getting things wrong with big red crosses'. For high achievers, reputations were at stake. To slip up meant failure to meet expectations – their own, their teachers', their families' or, worst of all, their peers'. For a few, the feeling that others were waiting with glee for them to fall off the high wire was strong. At this stage there was little evidence that children felt the need to underachieve or dissemble as a result of peer pressure. However there were two comments from high-attaining girls which indicated that for them this was a factor:

> Sometimes I have to say I don't like work or the others in my class will call me a wimp.
>
> > (Laura, Year 4, Orchard)

> Sometimes I'm worried to be called teacher's pet or 'keener' if I have done well.
>
> > (Kate, Year 6, Greenmantle)

Feelings about assessment also varied with the subject. The stakes were higher in some areas of the curriculum, usually, but not exclusively, the core subjects. Sometimes pupils felt more secure about core subject work because they had taken more care and spent more time on it.

> Depends what work it is. I don't mind her looking at my Art but I get worried when she looks at my Maths.
>
> > (Ewan, Year 6, Kenwood)

> If it's drawing then I feel good. If it's Maths I don't want her to see it and I put it in my drawer but she usually makes you show it in the end.
>
> > (Geoffrey, Year 6, Orchard)

> It depends what book she's looking at. I like it when she looks at my Science and my English because I always get them finished – and Maths. I don't like her looking at the rest.
>
> > (Eliot, Year 6, St Bede's)

In telling us about the tension produced by having their work assessed some children, in the main high achievers, went on to explain that actually it had turned out all right, that the feared or anticipated outcome had not materialized. The anxiety, nevertheless, however short-lived or misplaced, was felt and recurrent.

If I'm a bit tired or I can't be bothered to write everything that I should have, I think 'Oh no, what's she going to put?' It's all right because if I haven't understood anything she just explains it and I finish it off at playtimes.

(Kate, Year 5, Greenmantle)

I feel nervous that they will tell everyone about what I have been doing and the bad things I have done – it doesn't happen very often.

(Ben, Year 6, Greenmantle)

I feel embarrassed in case it's wrong – but it isn't wrong very much.

(Helen, Year 5, Orchard)

I'm a worried girl, I am. When she looks at my books, I think 'Oh no. My handwriting's messy.' I get so tensed up. I think she's going to tell me off for doing something wrong. She doesn't but I still get very nervous.

(Rosie, Year 5, Lawnside)

I feel very nervous at the beginning because they might not think I've done my best; but they usually say 'Well done' and that's good.

(Stella, Year 6, Valley)

When we turn to look at positive feelings about assessment interactions we find that this involved feeling pleased about work, anticipating teacher approval or perhaps some kind of reward. As Table 7.1 indicates, in Key Stage 1 most children felt unequivocally positive about their teacher looking at their work. In addition, in Years 1 to 3 the mixed, 'it depends' construction, though clearly and increasingly present, was less prevalent. In general these younger children expected that their work would be positively received and that this would please their teacher and earn them her approval.

Yes. (I like it) because she gets very pleased.

(Sharon, Year 1, Greenmantle)

I like it when she says you done it good. I feel happy.

(Dean, Year 1, Kenwood)

Yes, because I've done good work and she's pleased with me and I get a sticker like this – excellent.

(Polly, Year 1, Valley)

She just ticks it and that. I like it when she ticks it and puts a little face on it. It's all right.

(Haley, Year 2, St Bede's)

I like it. I feel I done good.

(Frances, Year 3, St Anne's)

Yes. I feel lucky 'cause she usually puts a tick and 'good'.

(Helen, Year 3, Orchard)

The pleasure in summative assessment evident in the reaction of the children in their early years survived in some measure as they progressed. However, the language chosen by the children to express positive feelings shifted interestingly over the years. Until Year 4, the most pervasive word was 'happy'. This disappeared almost completely in Years 5 and 6 when children feeling positive were more likely to use 'pleased'. Feeling 'proud' of work was also more a feature of Key Stage 2 responses. In Key Stage 2, children who felt positive some or all of the time about this form of assessment were interested in 'seeing if I get it right', 'seeing what mark I get'. They were usually optimistic about success and pleased with the work they had done. Although some mentioned rewards in the form of house points, stickers or stars, far more were concerned with getting marks and particularly ticks or comments like 'excellent'. They were also alert to the impact good work had on their teachers' moods and attitude towards them. These examples illustrate something of the range. A fuller discussion of rewards can be found in Chapter 9 where we look at their role in motivation.

> If I know some questions are right I get excited because I know I'll get house points.
>
> (Samantha, Year 4, St Bede's)

> If I've done a lot I like Mrs X to come over and say she's pleased with me, then I feel I've done something good.
>
> (Harriet, Year 4, Valley)

> I just want to know if I'll get house points.
>
> (Jacquie, Year 5, St Anne's)

> I don't really mind because if I've got some good work in there you can get stars for it.
>
> (Jeremy, Year 5, Kenwood)

> I like it. I'm going to get a good mark if I try.
>
> (Melanie, Year 6, St Anne's)

> Great because I know it's being marked, not left. You know how you've done. You get ticks and a star.
>
> (Kyle, Year 6, Meadway)

It is interesting that the pupils in Years 5 and 6 who felt most positive about having work looked at were often the lowest attainers, like Melanie and Kyle whose responses are quoted above. In a context of increased categoric assessment, their teachers were still trying to protect them, bolster their self-esteem and maintain their motivation.

In summary, across the six years of the study we found that pupils became increasingly negative about assessment. They had little, if any, concept of assessment as formative and in the later years of Key Stage 2 when assessment processes became increasingly overt and categoric, their feelings about having their work looked at became significantly more mixed and negative.

Overall, two-thirds of the sample described themselves as feeling anxious or worried about showing their work to their teacher. Many pupils were unclear about what was required of them and this uncertainty produced additional tension. In general they were not aware of the criteria by which their work would be evaluated. In assessing their own work they applied criteria of quantity, correctness, neatness and effort which they assumed their teacher would use.

7.3 CHILDREN'S SELF-ASSESSMENT OF THEIR PERSONAL ATTAINMENT

There is little evidence in any of the data collected from pupils that they were aware of being encouraged to engage in formal self-assessment as an aspect of their learning. Nevertheless they had no problem in responding each year when we asked them 'What are you like at reading?' and repeated the question for writing, Mathematics and Science. In each case they were offered a choice of 'good', 'OK' or 'not so good' as possible descriptors. We wanted to discover how confident they felt about their attainment and whether there were any changes or fluctuations in their evaluation of themselves. Table 7.2 indicates pupil responses over the six years and raises some concerns.

Table 7.2 Self-assessment by pupils of being 'good at' reading, writing, Mathematics and Science (percentages)

	Year 1	Year 2	Year 3	Year 4	Year 5	Year 6
Reading	65	63	57	41	48	39
Writing	57	50	48	54	48	37
Mathematics	61	63	56	56	50	48
Science	50	50	43	26	30	32

Source: PACE 1, 2 and 3 child interview data
Sample: 54 children in each of Years 1–6
Date: Autumn 1990 and 1991, Summer 1993, 1994, 1995 and 1996

We see here evidence of a decline in children's self-confidence which is disturbing. There is a clear downward trend in their self-assessments in Literacy and Mathematics as Key Stage 2 progressed. Year 6 was particularly striking because the children who saw themselves as 'good' at reading and writing were outnumbered by those who put themselves in the 'not so good' and 'OK' category.

What are we to make of this? Were the children losing confidence or, faced with the evidence of more 'categoric' assessment, were they offering a more 'realistic' or 'relativistic' view of their attainment? In writing in particular, a fifth of Year 6 children put themselves in the 'not so good' band. This resonates with the strong dislike of this activity which we discussed in Chapters 4 and 5 when we considered children's curricular preferences. They saw writing as a difficult and challenging activity and many children did not find it easy to maintain a motivation to succeed. Awareness of their 'performance' in spelling, punctuation and handwriting (all more specifically focused and tested as standardized assessment approached) may also have contributed to these results.

The evidence from our conversations with pupils about the writing SAT also suggests that preparation for that test required quite different skills and processes than those they were accustomed to when writing. The prescribed and limited time for producing a piece of writing, the impossibility of drafting, conferring with other readers, revising and editing meant that they 'practised for the test' as a specific and isolated form of writing. Some, especially the more able and ambitious writers, found this confusing and even annoying. It may be that this confusion affected their confidence in their ability.

In Mathematics there was a steady fall from Year 2 in the number of children prepared to assess themselves as 'good'. The figures for 'not so good' remained relatively low, as they did for reading. This may reflect the use of differentiated materials and teacher assessment designed to retain motivation and build confidence. It was often some of the lowest-attaining children who remained positive about their performance in Mathematics.

Differences between the patterns of confidence in the traditional core subjects of reading, writing and Mathematics and the 'new' core subject of Science are interesting. In Science, after a low in Year 4 there was a steady rise in the number of children who thought they were 'good' or 'OK' in this subject. This articulates with the views of teachers that they were gaining confidence in this area of the curriculum, and with the evidence of careful time planning done by the schools so that Science was clearly identified and its discrete curricular content carefully distinguished for teaching. In Year 6 too, teachers revisited areas of Science covered in the previous three years and worked on bolstering confidence (their own and their pupils') in what was still a relatively new core curriculum area. Although there was a rise in confidence, there were relatively few children who considered themselves 'good' at Science.

Overall, we see a general, in some cases a marked, decline in children's confidence in their ability to attain in core curriculum work.

7.4 EXPLANATIONS FOR PERSONAL ATTAINMENT

As the children got older, we felt they were able to explain more about the basis of the assessments they made of their attainment. Accordingly, in Year 3 we asked them about things they thought they were particularly good at and not so good at in school and then asked them to tell us why they thought they were good/not so good at those things. The range of subjects and activities mentioned in connection with being successful was very wide. Things they thought they were not good at were more frequently activities related to the core curriculum. We were, however, not so interested in the subjects nominated as the reasons the children gave for being good or not so good at something.

We coded the children's explanations for their attainment into seven categories:

- 'Home Factors' – any mention of the positive or negative impact of home: members of the family as models, skill and talent of parents, amount of help, support, teaching received.
- 'Innate Characteristics' – attainment attributed to something *within* the child that is a 'given' and can't be changed – 'just good/not good at', 'can/can't do it', may be inherited from parents.
- 'Self-assessment' – application of pupil-selected or generated criteria, references to speed of working, amount produced, making errors, not understanding, getting stuck.

- 'Effort/no effort' – references to trying hard or not bothering.
- 'Practice/no practice' – mention of being given (or not being given), taking (or not taking) opportunities to practice.
- 'Like/dislike' – reference to liking/enjoying/being interested in the area or not liking/having no interest/being bored by it.
- 'Easy/hard' – any mention of finding the work difficult or easy.

We begin by analysing the reasons children gave for being 'good' at particular types of learning.

Reasons for being 'good' at something

Table 7.3 Children's responses to the question 'Why do you think you are good at those things?' (percentages)

	Year 3	Year 4	Year 5	Year 6	Overall
Home factors	27	27	24	28	27
Innate abilities	9	10	16	17	13
Self-assessment	8	10	10	3	8
Effort	8	15	5	11	9
Practice	21	15	10	12	14
Liking	17	17	29	25	22
Easy	8	4	3	3	5
Other	2	2	3	0	2

Source: PACE 2 and 3 child interview data
Sample: 54 children in each of Years 3–6
Date: Summer 1993, 1994, 1995 and 1996

Notable here is the large group of children who consistently accounted for their success by some reference to their home and family. In addition we can see an association between liking and success becoming more prominent in Years 5 and 6, and an upward trend in the citing of innate characteristics. These personally focused explanations which, as we will see, frequently overlapped and worked in combination, outweighed the more classroom-related reasons of effort, practice and finding work easy. It is interesting how few children thought they were good at something because they found it easy. We should also comment on the children in the 'other' category who all gave the reason for their success as 'having a good teacher'.

We can gain a better understanding of the children's explanations by looking in more detail at what they said. Among the factors associated with home were the ideas, enthusiasms, talents and opinions of parents, grandparents and siblings which were all mentioned as having an effect. There is evidence, too, that the idea of inherited talent was propagated. Often the children described being drawn into the interests of those around them and 'learning' from them. They experienced a lot of encouragement to participate and be active. These factors often contributed to the development of positive attitudes and dispositions which carried over into the classroom. In this context the categories of 'liking', 'practice' and 'innate ability' overlapped and entwined with that of 'home'.

The intimate involvement of family in the construction of a positive learning identity is well illustrated by these examples:

> My mum's an artist. I come down with paper and pencil and she can help me. I practise a lot at home.
>
> > (Ben, Year 3, Greenmantle)

> I love History. My sister loves History. I think I'm good at it because she is.
>
> > (Laura, Year 4, Audley)

> My parents are accountants – it sort of runs in the family. I have lots of Maths books on my shelves at home. I do Maths in the holidays.
>
> > (Laura, Year 5, Orchard)

> I take after my dad. I go to football training with my dad every Thursday. We take other children as well.
>
> > (Geoffrey, Year 5, Orchard)

> My granny is a very good drawer and very good at making things. Ever since I was about two I learned how to put a pencil on paper.
>
> > (Olivia, Year 5, Lawnside)

> I'm quite good at Art because I take after my mum. My mum is good at it – she doesn't teach me but I watch her.
>
> > (Juliet, Year 6, Greenmantle)

> Some people say I can't sing. My nan says I can.
>
> > (Susie, Year 6, St Anne's)

The children speaking here were from homes across the whole socio-economic range of our sample. It is clear that home was a powerful influence in children's developing sense of themselves as learners and achievers and we consider this again in Chapters 9, 11 and 13.

For most children there was a clear connection between attainment and enjoyment.

> I enjoy them and what I enjoy I usually do my best.
>
> > (Polly, Year 3, Valley)

> It's a question of whether you like them or not. I really like them and enjoy them so I do them well.
>
> > (Simon, Year 5, Valley)

> I enjoy it so I do it well.
>
> > (Rosie, Year 6, Lawnside)

However, as we have noted, no children told us that they liked something because it was easy to be good at it. Rather they saw success as a *consequence of* liking. Enjoyment, their answers suggested, generated the concentration, persistence, attention and willingness to practise that they saw as underpinning success.

It's just that I like them and if you like it you put your head down and do something about it – but if not, then you really don't want to do it.

(Harriet, Year 5, Valley)

If I enjoy something I normally get into it and I usually get it right.

(Jane, Year 5, Meadway)

I enjoy learning about different countries so I think I'm good at that.

(Corinne, Year 5, Meadway)

I'm good at Drama and making up stories. I just think they are interesting.

(Jan, Year 5, Valley)

If I'm into stuff I keep trying. I like it. I know what I'm doing.

(Ian, Year 6, Meadway)

However, as we will see when we look at the reasons the children gave us for not being good at something, enjoyment disappeared quite quickly in the face of persistently 'getting stuck' and, perhaps worse, 'not knowing what to do'.

Reasons for being 'not so good' at something

Table 7.4 Children's responses to the question 'Why do you think you are not so good at those things?' (percentages)

	Year 3	Year 4	Year 5	Year 6	Overall
Home factors	5	6	2	6	4
Innate inability	11	6	24	20	16
Self-assessment	24	32	17	15	21
No effort	5	0	4	18	7
No practice	14	3	2	4	6
Disliking	5	9	19	22	15
Hard	36	44	32	15	31

Source: PACE 2 and 3 child interview data
Sample: 54 children in each of Years 3–6
Date: Summer 1993, 1994, 1995 and 1996

When we look at the reasons the children gave us for *not* succeeding we see a different pattern of explanations. The tendency in Years 3 and 4 to refer to specific weaknesses such as being a slow worker, not producing enough, and not getting things right hardened in Years 5 and 6 into an explanation based on innate characteristics, a view of self as 'not brainy' or 'no good at it'. Arguably we are seeing here the consequences of a more overt emphasis on assessment as Key Stage 2 advanced. Similarly, in the context of the classroom-based explanations for lack of success, we can contrast the shift in emphasis from not getting enough practice in Year 3 to lack of effort in Year 6. The voice of the teacher comes through clearly here along with the sense that lack of success was strongly demotivating.

The issue of motivation, in particular the relationship between liking/not liking and success/failure, requires some unpacking. On the surface the idea that success is the result of liking, conveyed by children who saw themselves as successful, appeared to be mirrored by the suggestion from those who felt they were not succeeding that failure was the result of 'not being interested'. In Year 6, for example, the children in our sample were more likely to attribute their failure to how boring a subject was rather than to how hard they found it However, if we consider the possible meanings encoded by the word 'boring' and see it as being used defensively as an explanation, an alternative reading emerges which changes the emphasis of this cause and effect formulation. The children, it could be argued, were saying that failure creates dislike, rationalized as lack of interest, which accounts for lack of effort.

With this overall picture in mind we can look at the detail of what the children said. As we have seen, some children who felt confident about 'being good' at something explained this by reference to some innate characteristic: 'I'm just good at it', 'I just have a good brain for it', 'I'm talented that way'. We noted a slightly increased tendency to use such explanations as Key Stage 2 progressed. However, the picture painted by those who see themselves as *not* achieving is much starker. After Year 4, references to innate characteristics to explain lack of success increased very sharply. The children who gave this explanation were unequivocal, as these examples demonstrate:

Spelling, I'm not brainy enough.

(Scott, Year 3, Kenwood)

You've got to be brainy for Science.

(Scott, Year 4, Kenwood)

I'm no good at reading. It's just the way I am.

(Ian, Year 5, Meadway)

Reading, I'm not as intelligent as some of the other pupils.

(Ian, Year 6, Meadway)

I'm no good at Maths.

(Juliet, Year 6, Greenmantle)

Maths, I just can't do it.

(Samantha, Year 6, St Bede's)

I can't spell.

(Susie, Year 6, St Anne's)

I'm just not any good at reading.

(Philip, Year 6, St Anne's)

These pupils attained Level 2 or 3 for the subject area they mentioned. Increasingly, as Key Stage 2 progressed they had evidence in the form of spelling, Mathematics and reading tests of their failure to measure up to the expected standard and had decided that the reason lay within themselves. With this group we can see the results of more overt and categoric assessment most sharply evident.

The shadow of assessment, however, fell over other explanations of why pupils thought they were 'not so good' at some things. From their responses it is clear that the children had inferred a number of criteria for success from their classroom experience. The reasons many gave for their low attainment simply identified the ways in which they felt they and their work fell short of these criteria. These were concerned with both processes and outcomes.

Assumed criteria for outcomes reflect those that emerged from the analysis of children's feelings about having their books looked at. They were concerned with producing an adequate amount, producing what was wanted, having a neat and tidy presentation, and getting things right:

> My work is messy.
>
> (Mandy, Year 3, Audley)

> I can't get much done – not three pages.
>
> (Haley, Year 3, St Bede's)

> I do things wrong and I feel stupid.
>
> (Amanda, Year 4, Kenwood)

> I always get spelling mistakes and I normally get things wrong.
>
> (Theresa, Year 4, Audley)

> I can't get anything right and I have to rub it out.
>
> (Sharon, Year 5, Greenmantle)

> I get half the answers wrong.
>
> (Malcolm, Year 6, St Anne's)

In relation to working processes, the dominant factor used to explain low attainment was speed of working – the inability to keep up and get finished.

> I'm always the last to finish.
>
> (Sean, Year 4, Greenmantle)

> I take longer than normal to get through it.
>
> (Brian, Year 6, Audley)

> I can't keep up because we have to write lots.
>
> (Celia, Year 6, Meadway)

This awareness of the impact of pressure of time on attainment was increasingly evident in the later years of Key Stage 2. It was also in these years that pupils' explanations for not doing well were more likely to feature a combination of factors relating to difficulty, dislike and effort. The children who had not yet got as far as defining themselves as innately destined to fail in some areas referred to the problems they were encountering with things they found difficult. Explanations here contained descriptions of problems with recall, 'not understanding', of having no ideas, being given things to do that were 'too hard', and, again, of feeling under pressure of time. They appeared across the whole range of attainment.

> I haven't got many ideas and I don't know what to write down.
>
> (Jessica, Year 4, Kenwood)

They're too hard for me. I mostly get them wrong; they confuse me.

(Mandy, Year 4, Audley)

I can't work out the sums in time and I don't understand them.

(Geoffrey, Year 5, Orchard)

It's hard to remember and there's not much time.

(Kim, Year 5, St Bede's)

It's usually a rush. I'm usually behind. There's a lot to do.

(Jessica, Year 5, Kenwood)

It seems rather boring. I find it difficult to remember things.

(Ben, Year 6, Greenmantle)

As Table 7.4 shows, pupils were particularly aware of their shortcomings in relation to effort in Year 6. The children knew that 'effort' in the form of concentrating, paying attention, working hard in class and practising were important for success and that lack of 'effort' accounted for failure. They also acknowledged that they didn't always make the required effort. The explanations they gave for this were intimately bound up with their experience of learning process. We consider these in more detail in Chapters 8 and 9.

In summary, we can see that pupils' explanations for their attainment are complex. The role attributed to home and family in successful attainment is particularly interesting and suggests learning experiences and influences on learning that were not always fully acknowledged by schools. Notable also was the low association between success and finding a subject easy; many more pupils associated success with finding a subject enjoyable. Such liking was associated with increased willingness to make an effort and to persist in the face of difficulty. The converse of this, dislike leading to lack of effort, was offered as an explanation for lack of success. However, other reasons pupils gave were not simple opposites. Finding a subject difficult was seen as a reason for low attainment, especially when the struggle to understand was exacerbated by pressure of time. Pupils also associated low attainment with having characteristics which made it difficult to meet assumed criteria of correctness, neatness and quantity. In the most extreme cases children claimed that these characteristics were innate. In this nexus of factors associated with 'being good' or 'not so good' we can discern strands which are significant in the construction of learning identity. We pursue this idea further in Chapters 9, 11 and 13. First however, we consider how the children's explanations for their own success and failure relate to their answers to the question 'Why do some children do better at school work than others?'.

7.5 EXPLANATIONS FOR OTHERS' ATTAINMENT

The question 'Why do some children do better at school work than others?' was asked in each year of the study and the children were free to respond as they wished. Interviewers used follow-up questions to encourage them to expand on their answers. As they moved up the school the children's answers were often very extended and they provided details and examples of their explanations. The data from all six years was recoded for this analysis. Frequently the children offered a number of reasons for success or failure (e.g. 'It's because some are faster and they're good writers and they try harder') and so their answers were analysed using multiple codings. We created nine categories plus 'don't know'.

- 'Effort' – used when children made reference to anything related to staying on task, getting on with work, not being distracted ('They listen to the teacher and don't muck about', 'They chat and don't finish their work but others work', 'They concentrate more') and for mention of working hard, trying hard, being persistent ('They just don't try hard enough').
- 'Ability' – general references to having (or lacking) knowledge and understanding ('They learn more', 'Some people just don't understand') and for mention of traditional ability attributes ('Because they're brainy/bright/intelligent/cleverer').
- 'Skill' – references to specific aspects of attainment were placed in this category ('They do joined writing and are very neat', 'They can colour in properly', 'Spelling comes easier and they do it better', 'They are better writers', 'Some children can't read properly').
- 'Home' – explanations of attainment related to home were categorized in this way ('Because they haven't been learning with their mums', 'They practise at home', 'Perhaps their mums and dads help them').
- 'Age' – where explanations for attainment were based on the relative ages of the children we used this category (''Cos they're older', ''Cos they've been at school longer and they've done it before', ''Cos they're little').
- 'Speed' – this category was used for explanations related to the speed at which children worked (''Cos we finish fast', ''Cos they are the quickest in the class').
- 'Individual disability/disadvantage' – references to specific factors that were said to affect attainment were coded in this category ('Some people are born with a disorder', 'He/She's got asthma/dyslexia/problems at home', 'We can't hear properly', 'Hamid doesn't understand, he talks a different language').
- 'Interest/Motivation' – used for explanations of attainment related to enjoyment/ liking/reward ('You do better if you enjoy what you are doing', 'Because they want to get a smiley face', 'When they don't like it they just don't do it').
- 'Other school' – this category was used when attainment was explained by reference to other schools that children had attended ('She was at a different school and they did different work', 'He's just come and has a lot of catching up to do').

The predominance of 'effort' and 'ability' in pupils' explanations persisted over the six years of the study. Other factors rose and fell in importance as we can see if we look at the pattern year by year.

We can see in Table 7.6 how the attributes of age, skill and speed were used much less to explain difference as the children got older; while references to the influence of home became more prominent. The significance for children of their early encounters with literacy make it perhaps not surprising that awareness of differences in skill was strongest in the first three years of school. The children's references to

Table 7.5 Rank order of categories used by the children to account for attainment (aggregated percentages)

Effort	36
Ability	18
Skill	9
Home	8
Age	7
Speed	5
Interest	5
Disability	3
Other	3
Don't know	8

Source: PACE 1, 2 and 3 child interview data
Sample: 54 children in each of Years 1–6
Date: Autumn 1990 and 1991, Summer 1993, 1994, 1995 and 1996

Table 7.6 Major categories used by children in each year to account for attainment (percentages)

	Year 1	Year 2	Year 3	Year 4	Year 5	Year 6
Effort	31	36	35	44	32	38
Ability	15	24	16	16	19	20
Skill	16	11	10	4	5	6
Home	2	2	9	10	13	9
Age	13	11	5	3	7	1
Speed	0	6	11	4	5	1
Interest	2	5	3	2	6	9
Don't know	16	5	4	10	4	10

Source: PACE 1, 2 and 3 child interview data
Sample: 54 children in each of Years 1–6
Date: Autumn 1990 and 1991, Summer 1993, 1994, 1995 and 1996

skill showed how rapidly they had assimilated criteria associated with the development of fine-motor skills and emergent literacy. Indeed, they literally saw their peers as doing better or worse on the grounds of knowing how to colour in properly, being able to hold a pencil, doing neater work, writing not scribbling, doing joined-up writing, writing a lot. A statement from one child gives a flavour of these responses:

> You can see they're doing better work by how long their sentences are. They're used to writing and they go on writing and their stories get longer and longer. The others are not so used to writing ... they only do one word in a morning.
>
> (Polly, Year 1, Valley)

In Years 2 and 3 the focus was still on literacy with a shift in emphasis to competence in spelling and being able to write quickly. It is interesting that 'speed'-related attributes – getting finished quickly, producing a lot of work in an allotted time – which featured in children's explanations of their own attainment, appeared with any prominence only in Year 2. In later years it was used as an explanation mainly by individuals who saw themselves as having particularly acute problems in this area.

The category of 'home' which appeared so strongly in children's explanations for 'being good at something' themselves was also evident when they were accounting for others' attainment. Where it was mentioned, most noticeably in Years 4 and 5, the explanations were of two kinds. One was closely related to effort in that it involved 'taking work home' and 'practising at home'. The people at home most mentioned in connection with practice were older brothers and sisters at secondary school. The second way in which home was cited as a reason for doing better at work was to do with parents as teachers.

> They get taught more at home.
>
> (Gavin, Year 4, Orchard)

> They might have grown up with a family that has done better things – good Maths or something.
>
> (Stella, Year 5, Valley)

> Their mothers are quite intelligent and might help them.
>
> (Rosie, Year 5, Lawnside)

> Allan's dad is a teacher and helps him.
>
> (Geoffrey, Year 6, Orchard)

> I think that those that do well have help from their parents at home but others don't.
>
> (Eliot, Year 6, St Bede's)

Factors related to home teaching were cited more by children in small rural schools with high socio-economic status (Orchard, Lawnside, Valley). References to practising at home were more evident in two urban schools (Kenwood and Audley). There was no mention of home factors at St Bede's and very little at St Anne's and Meadway, the two most socially disadvantaged schools, or Greenmantle where perhaps the children assumed that this was a constantly present factor for all of them.

The increasing references to home, taken alongside the rises and peaks in pupils citing 'ability' to explain difference, could be taken as an indication of increasing polarization. It was, though, rare to find a child giving 'ability' as an explanation for two years running. Most mentioned it only once during the period of the study and some not at all. However we can see that more pupils were conscious of 'ability' in Years 2 and 6 when their teachers were very concerned with their assessment, and increasingly through Key Stage 2. This articulates also with the increased emphasis on innate characteristics to explain personal attainment which we saw earlier.

When we looked for characteristics which distinguished pupils who mentioned ability we found that the attribution was made by children of all levels of attainment. However, children with higher socio-economic status used it as an explanation much more frequently – 43 per cent of the responses from SES (Socio-economic status) 1 mentioned ability as compared with 22 per cent from SES 2 and only 8 per cent of those from SES 3. This suggests that the discourse of home, rather than school, may have been a factor here.

These examples illustrate how pupils expressed ideas about ability. In Year 1 there were unequivocal statements about learners differentiated by 'ability':

'Cos they've got more clever brains.

(Robin, Year 1, Valley)

Because they are much more clever.

(Celia, Year 1, Meadway)

They might not be clever enough to do it – that's the main one.

(Samantha, Year 1, St Bede's)

Some people are better and some people are not.

(Olivia, Year 1, Lawnside)

Later, 'ability' appeared in combination with other factors in a more complex statement. The most frequent link was with 'effort' and 'home', but 'speed' and 'skill' were other associated categories. In some cases it is possible to see the impact of school and classroom organization on pupils' views. The following examples give an idea of the range of responses in Key Stage 2:

They listen more and they write neater and they're more intelligent and they think better.

(Tom, Year 3, Greenmantle)

He's in a different English and Maths group. He's intelligent.

(Esther, Year 5, Greenmantle)

The others just know it like that (clicks fingers) because they're bright. The others do try but they are not so good.

(Scott, Year 5, Kenwood)

Because they are smarter. They are like faster workers than most of us.

(Ewan, Year 6, Kenwood)

Some people are born with better brains They've been listening over the years.

(Martin, Year 6, Lawnside)

'Ability' was the second most frequently mentioned attribute. Together with 'effort' it accounted for over half of all responses in each year. As we have seen, however, there were twice as many references to 'effort'; it was the most frequently used explanation for differences in attainment in all our schools in all years. Because of this dominance we did further analysis of the responses to gain more understanding of the relative significance of the meanings we had included in this category. We developed codes related to concentration, distraction, talking, listening, trying and not trying. This analysis revealed the way in which 'behaviour' featured in the children's construction of pupils who did more or less well. In Key Stage 1, for instance, working or trying hard and being sensible was contrasted with being lazy and naughty. As the children got older and more experienced in classroom life they developed a more complex model. Most notably they began to characterize the successful pupil as one with a strategic attitude to work and learning.

Using words and phrases from the children's responses we can construct a picture of how they understood the attribution of 'effort' in relation to attainment. Those pupils who 'did better' were patient, they got on with work, put their minds to it, didn't give up, took time and trouble; they liked practising, concentrated, listened and didn't talk. By contrast, those who didn't do as well couldn't be bothered, didn't try, didn't finish. They messed about, acted daft, were silly, talked, distracted others and were distracted. The role of persistence and resilience in success is illustrated in this Year 6 response:

> They take it home and have a go at it. And if they get a mistake they have another go and try and understand it.
>
> (Jessica, Year 6, Kenwood)

It is perhaps indicative that for the highest-attaining children 'concentration' was the most mentioned characteristic, above 'trying' which headed the list for average and below average pupils. In this connection it is interesting to look at the category of 'interest/motivation' which figured most strongly in Year 6. In some cases children made a straightforward association between enjoyment of the subject matter and success, but also emerging was the idea that those who did better were motivated to get on with it or somehow enjoyed the act of working even when it wasn't immediately attractive:

> Some people are interested in work. Others are always talking and laughing.
>
> (Theresa, Year 6, Audley)

> Some people don't like to listen and don't like doing the work. I don't think anyone likes doing the work but they (the ones who do it better) do it and get it over and done with so they can get on to something else. When they (the ones who don't do well) don't like it they just don't do it and talk to their friends.
>
> (Sam, Year 6, St Bede's)

> Probably because when we're given a boring task some want to get it over and done with. Others can't be bothered and they do it badly. If you get stuck in it can be quite fun.
>
> (Ben, Year 6, Greenmantle)

We can see here the recognition of attitudes and dispositions to learning that are more likely to underpin success. Or, in other words, the acceptance or rejection of the role of pupil. The issue of motivation is central here and at least one of our respondents was very clear about where this lay as she considered her peers:

> Carol puts her head down and thinks 'At the end of the day I'm going to get something out of this – a good job.' Some of the others just think 'Oh no, another day at school.'
>
> (Harriet, Year 5, Valley)

7.6 CONCLUSION

The picture of children's experience of classroom assessment that emerges from different sections of the pupil interviews is remarkably consistent. They are aware of assessment only as a summative activity and use criteria of neatness, correctness, quantity and effort when commenting on their own and others' work. It seems reasonable to assume that in applying or inferring these criteria pupils were drawing on their experience of the assessment discourse of the classroom as evident in their teachers' spoken and written comments. Our report of the teachers' experience in the PACE study (see Osborn *et al.*, 2000) shows teachers becoming increasingly accepting of the shift to a more structured and formal approach to pupil assessment. At the same time their commitment to an intuitive diagnostic discourse remained strong. However, there is no evidence from the children that teachers were communicating anything of this formative or diagnostic assessment to their pupils. The assessment discourse that was explicit in classrooms and was shared by teachers and pupils was limited. As we will see in Chapters 8 and 9, pupils had similarly little access to metacognitive language with which to talk or think about themselves as learners, or by means of which they could penetrate teachers' intentions for them.

In general, at the end of Key Stage 2, pupils' judgements of their work were concerned with surface and structural features of written work, presentation, quantity and effort. Low attainers placed importance on correctness and the amount of work done; higher attainers were more likely to be aware of and comment on their relative effort, and living up to their teachers' and their own expectations.

The pressure of external assessment in the form of end-of-Key Stage tests appears to have had an impact on pupils' attitudes and perceptions. An agenda for learning in order to be tested (or retested), allied with an increase in overt forms of assessment, was increasingly evident as children moved through Key Stage 2. At the same time children became less confident in their self-assessments and more likely to attribute success or failure to innate characteristics. In general they were progressively less positive about assessment interactions which they had come to see as occasions which revealed their weaknesses and at worst exposed them to ridicule and humiliation. Anticipating assessment, they reported feelings of anxiety, tension and uncertainty which were sometimes acute. The anxiety was arguably a consequence of the sense that they were exposed to greater risk as their teachers raised the stakes. We see this more sharply focused in Chapter 10 when we report the pupils' experience of standardized assessment. The uncertainty was in part a result of the perceived ambiguity of many classroom tasks, something which was observed in PACE 2 and continued in Years 5 and 6. In addition, many children felt unsure and unclear about the basis of the assessments they experienced.

'Evaluation' in Bernstein's message systems is associated with power and these children certainly felt the power of their teachers as assessors, especially as the distributors of rewards and sanctions, including the giving or withholding of approval. However, it is interesting to see that other sources of evaluation began to play a significant part in their lives. The strong presence of home in children's explanations for doing well, and its association with factors of liking, enjoyment and practice, is particularly remarkable.

It seems clear that for these children assessment had more to do with pronouncing on their attainment than with progressing their learning. However, it is also clear that the assessment process was intimately associated with their developing sense of themselves as learners and as people. The children were incorporating their teachers' day-to-day evaluations of them into the construction of their identity as learners. The complexity in the construct of 'effort' as a determining attribute in attainment is evident in our analysis. Its associations with concentration/distraction and persistence/avoidance are particularly important to a consideration of learning disposition and to the notion of children developing strategic approaches to classroom tasks. There are links between these ideas and the outcomes of children's experiences of ambiguity and exposure to risk also reported in this chapter. It is to these subjects that we turn in the next two chapters which deal with children's perspectives on classroom learning and teaching.

Chapter 8

Pupil Perspectives on Teachers' Teaching

8.1   Introduction
8.2   Pupils' awareness of teachers' intentions
8.3   Pupils' understanding of teacher expectations
8.4   Pupils' views on classroom grouping
8.5   Conclusion

8.1 INTRODUCTION

In previous chapters we have examined pupils' experience of and attitude to the curriculum, their perspectives on relationships with their teachers and their experience of classroom assessment. In the next two chapters we build on this analysis as we turn our attention to the central issue of children's learning.

Our reports on phases one and two of the PACE project indicated that by 1992, when our target sample were in Year 2, the focus on categoric assessment had led to an increase in grouping by 'ability' at the expense of mixed, friendship-based groups where differentiation was by outcome. As the children completed Year 4 their teachers were preoccupied with the pressure to achieve targets within a set period and were concerned about curriculum coverage. They felt the need for product as evidence of learning and getting pupils to finish work was a priority. In addition the trend for a more explicit hierarchy of achievement and more focused 'ability'-related organization continued.

The focus in this chapter is on pupils' perception of and perspective on their teachers' teaching. In particular, drawing on data from all six years of the project, we look at pupils' understanding of teachers' instructional intentions and their perspectives on teacher expectations of them. In the third section, we consider the views of Year 6 pupils about how they were grouped for learning.

8.2 PUPILS' AWARENESS OF TEACHERS' INTENTIONS

Much of the time we spent in the project schools each year was taken up with watching teachers teaching and pupils learning. The activities we observed pupils engaged in during the systematic observation were used as a focus at the beginning of each pupil interview. Children were asked to describe the activity, say what they were doing and whether they had enjoyed it. We followed this by asking 'Do you know why your teacher wanted you to do that activity?'. The responses were coded into broad categories to produce Table 8.1.

Table 8.1 Children's awareness and understanding of teacher intentions for learning activities (percentages)

	Year 1	Year 2	Year 3	Year 4	Year 5	Year 6
Required	37	37	17	19	19	11
Don't know	25	9	10	18	16	9
Learning	17	28	44	47	53	57
Product	13	9	17	7	5	14
Assessment	3	14	9	7	7	7
Enjoyment	5	3	3	2	0	2

Source: PACE 1, 2 and 3 child interview data
Sample: 54 children in each of Years 1–6
Date: Autumn 1990 and 1991, Summer 1993, 1994, 1995 and 1996

The 'required' category was used where children could give no reason beyond the fact that the teacher said they had to do it or it was on the timetable. Responses that indicated an activity was being done because it was 'part of our topic' were also categorized as 'required' where there was no indication of awareness of any more specific learning intention. For example:

> She wanted us to do it. She chose it.
>
> (Patrick, Year 1, Orchard)

> 'Cause I'm on yellow table.
>
> (William, Year 1, Lawnside)

> She just said do it.
>
> (Malcolm, Year 1, St Anne's)

> Because it's work and we had to do it because we didn't do it yesterday.
>
> (Laura, Year 2, Orchard)

> We've been doing a lot about shapes – don't know why.
>
> (Amanda, Year 3, Kenwood)

> Because we are doing a topic about Vikings.
>
> (Trevor, Year 3, Valley)

> Because Danny brought in a woodpecker's nest and Miss said we had to write about it.
>
> (Sam, Year 3, St Bede's)

She has a list what we do every week. It's on the list.

> (Neil, Year 4, Audley)

We always do Geography on Wednesday.

> (Melanie, Year 5, St Anne's)

Because that's what I've got to do. It's on my Maths Trail. I don't know why they are there.

> (Scott, Year 5, Kenwood)

'Cause we are doing about Ancient Greeks.

> (Malcolm, Year 6, St Anne's)

Throughout Key Stage 2 there was a steady reduction in the number of pupils whose responses were coded in this way and who were unclear about why they were doing an activity. In Year 5, 45 per cent of the 'required' responses were associated with 'topic work'; in Year 6 this increased to 83 per cent indicating a lack of clarity in understanding the reasons for non-core activity beyond the fact that it was being 'done'.

The sharp fall in the percentage of pupils who said they did not know why their teacher wanted them to do an activity from a quarter of the sample in Year 1 to only 9 per cent in Year 2 suggests that children were adjusting to a classroom environment even if over a third still perceived activity as 'required'. The relatively high proportion of pupils in Years 4 and 5 who seemed puzzled by our question and could not suggest any intention behind an activity will be discussed later in this section.

Where children referred to teachers requiring a specific outcome and perceived that as the reason for an activity, the 'product' code was used. Included in this were responses relating to writing for a specific audience where pupils mentioned only the product rather than a combination of product and process:

'Cause everyone in class had to do one.

> (Jessica, Year 1, Kenwood)

(The headteacher) wanted new pictures for the corridor.

> (Kate, Year 1, Greenmantle)

'Cause she wanted everyone to make a puppet theatre like the one she made.

> (Amanda, Year 2, Kenwood)

To read out in assembly.

> (Helen, Year 3, Orchard)

'Cause the teachers in the little class wanted a story about a kangaroo.

> (Gavin, Year 4, Orchard)

Because we could put it up on display and everyone could read it.

> (Kevin, Year 5, Audley)

Few pupils expressed an awareness of teacher intentions associated with any aspect of assessment (teacher assessment, self-assessment or differentiated activity). When pupils did perceive an assessment intention it was usually related to clearly measurable aspects of Mathematics, writing and recall:

To see if we're good at Maths.

(Sean, Year 2, Greenmantle)

So she would see if we know our sounds.

(Brian, Year 2, Audley)

She wanted to see how we'd get on.

(Wesley, Year 3, Meadway)

It's called a check-up sheet. It's just to see if we can do it or not, and if you can't you might need practice.

(Simon, Year 3, Valley)

To see where we put the punctuation marks.

(Tom, Year 4, Greenmantle)

To see if we can do it in exams and work it out.

(Amanda, Year 5, Kenwood)

We did things about the way water evaporated, and wind and we did weather. He tests us to see if we can remember what we did.

(Kyle, Year 5, Meadway)

To see if we were listening.

(Esther, Year 6, Greenmantle)

It is interesting, however, that in Year 2 and Year 6, when teachers reported being very conscious of SATs in their teaching, there were fewer children who said they did not know why their teacher wanted them to do the observed activity. As such, 'enjoyment' ('Our teacher knows we like doing it/wants us to have fun') was seldom perceived as a reason for an activity. Responses that contained any perception of pedagogic intention were coded as 'learning', for instance:

'Cause she wants us to learn.

(Samantha, Year 1, St Bede's)

To help us work out 11 and stuff.

(Hugh, Year 2, Lawnside)

'Cause I'm not very good at it.

(Kim, Year 3, St Bede's)

It was the last time we were doing this and she wanted us to do some revision of what we've been doing in other weeks.

(Harriet, Year 4, Valley)

So we get more familiar with right angles.

(Brian, Year 5, Audley)

To get us used to using the dictionary.

(Jane, Year 5, Meadway)

She wanted us to get in groups to discuss what you've got to do first before you write it down.

(Stella, Year 5, Valley)

We're doing evolution – to help us learn more about it.

(Ben, Year 5, Greenmantle)

To learn to put our views across.

(Lucy, Year 6, Lawnside)

To get practice in writing letters and to thank the camp leaders for all their work.

(Gavin, Year 6, Orchard)

This category became increasingly predominant in our analysis as the children proceeded through the school, rising to 57 per cent in Year 6. As the quotations above illustrate, pupils were increasingly able to be more specific about what their teachers had in mind. In order to gain further understanding of their perceptions of learning intentions we moved to a more detailed analysis of the 'learning' category.

Table 8.2 Children's awareness and understanding of 'learning' related to teacher intentions (percentages)

	Year 1	Year 2	Year 3	Year 4	Year 5	Year 6
Progression	50	27	33	27	17	19
Information	25	7	33	35	36	20
Skill	25	53	30	23	30	25
Practice	0	13	4	15	17	36
n =	10	16	26	27	30	32

Source: PACE 1, 2 and 3 child interview data
Sample: 141 children in Years 1–6
Date: Autumn 1990 and 1991, Summer 1993, 1994, 1995 and 1996

Table 8.2 shows that the idea of learning for progression was strong in Year 1, but gradually declined through school. It was replaced, in particular, by pressure to 'practise' for assessment. On the face of it, this is clear evidence of the growth of instrumental concerns. Additionally however, such issues were also partly embedded in the particular view of progression that was adopted by many children.

The responses of some children which we coded as 'progression' revealed a generalized view of learning as ongoing and looking towards adult life. When questioned about intention, some pupils in our sample clearly felt that it was appropriate to make a connection between current learning and possible future employment:

She wants you to learn so when you get older you can write the story out and give the book to someone and the tape.

(Polly, Year 1, Valley)

So we can be a bank manager if we like when we grow up. As we get older we get nearer to being very old and ready to work.

(Finn, Year 2, Valley)

So that we know things when we go into the top class. So when you grow up you'll be able to answer your children's questions.

(Juliet, Year 3, Greenmantle)

You have to learn – when you first come to school you don't know how to do anything at all and the teachers help you to learn.

(Samantha, Year 4, St Bede's)

So when we grow up we'll know everything.

(Harry, Year 4, St Bede's)

When you get older if you want to go to study writing plays it will help you get started.
(Simon, Year 5, Valley)

Make us learn about Science to know when we're older and go for interview for a job.
(Ian, Year 6, Meadway)

More characteristically the children's views reflected a hierarchical model of learning expressed in progression through schemes and classes, and in movement from one school to the next. Learning objectives were seen as to do with getting ready for the next stage:

So when we're in a higher class we'll do it more and know how to do it.
(Samantha, Year 3, St Bede's)

Probably – 'cause I saw people trying to build a hexagram and triangles and stuff. I think that's what we're going to do next.

(Ewan, Year 3, Kenwood)

So we can get on to the next book.

(Sharon, Year 3, Greenmantle)

We have to finish them to get onto a new sum book.

(Philip, Year 4, St Anne's)

When we get in the next class she'll ask us to use much bigger numbers – like millions – so Mrs X wants us to understand them.

(Simon, Year 4, Valley)

'Cause when you go into Year 6 you're going to have to do work about that.
(Shona, Year 5, Meadway)

So when we get to the Seniors we will find it easier.

(Jessica, Year 6, Kenwood)

For the Seniors probably – because you have to do it like that and take notes in the Seniors.

(Jeremy, Year 6, Kenwood)

For our work – when we go to the Senior school – so we can get group work better.
(Rosie, Year 6, Lawnside)

Getting ready for secondary school 'cause there you get a lot of homework and personal topic work.

(Stella, Year 6, Valley)

However, although the number of pupils who mentioned progression increased in the later years, the proportion doing so steadily decreased; most notably in Year 6 where the predominant perception of learning intention was for practice.

For many of the children throughout their primary schooling, their teachers' intentions for their learning were concerned with the acquisition of skill and information:

> Because we were doing water vapour and how it evaporates. A week ago we did a thing with a kettle – an experiment. We put a plate on it and it steamed up and turned into water vapour.
>
> (Celia, Year 2, Meadway)

> To learn us how to do Viking words.
>
> (Theresa, Year 3, Audley)

> Learning about Vikings and finding out how they kept food from going bad.
>
> (Richard, Year 3, Valley)

> To find out how light goes round the world.
>
> (Olivia, Year 3, Lawnside)

> Because in Science we're learning about materials.
>
> (Martin, Year 4, Lawnside)

> Because we're learning about the nine gifts of the Holy Spirit – we do one every day now.
>
> (Eliot, Year 4, St Bede's)

> So that if someone asked us about Moslems we could tell them.
>
> (Juliet, Year 5, Greenmantle)

> To learn about then and now.
>
> (Ewan, Year 5, Kenwood)

> To teach us about animals that live underground.
>
> (Samantha, Year 5, St Bede's)

> So we could learn what's 90 degrees and what's over 90 degrees and stuff like that.
>
> (Susie, Year 5, St Anne's)

> So we will know lots of things about World War 2.
>
> (Martin, Year 5, Lawnside)

> To learn about Nigerian art.
>
> (Geoffrey, Year 5, Orchard)

> So we know it off by heart – so if someone asks us a question we just answer it straight away.
>
> (Amanda, Year 6, Kenwood)

> It learned us for our SATs.
>
> (Neil, Year 6, Audley)

> She wanted us to listen and find out 'cause really she wants to help us with our SATs.
>
> (Theresa, Year 6, Audley)

In some of these answers, from Years 5 and 6, the subtext of learning to be tested, of being required to display what you know by answering questions, is very evident. It may be that we see here some of the impact on teachers of OFSTED inspections and SATs assessment.

Where the children thought their teachers' intentions were related to skill development, the majority of responses were associated with aspects of numeracy and literacy learning:

> She wants us to learn to read and write.
>
> (Gillian, Year 1, Kenwood)

> So that we know where to put capital letters and full stops.
>
> (Sharon, Year 1, Greenmantle)

> To learn to do joined writing.
>
> (Juliet, Year 2, Greenmantle)

> To do good writing.
>
> (Jessica, Year 2, Kenwood)

> So you can learn to read really well.
>
> (Philip, Year 3, St Anne's)

> She wants us to know how to tell the time.
>
> (Haley, Year 3, St Bede's)

> To show us how it's (Maths) really set out.
>
> (Martin, Year 3, Lawnside)

> Helps you work faster.
>
> (Kyle, Year 3, Meadway)

> How to write poems.
>
> (Jenny, Year 3, St Anne's)

> Helps us to learn how to describe things.
>
> (Jan, Year 4, Valley)

> To learn my hundreds, tens and units probably.
>
> (Trevor, Year 4, Valley)

> For us to learn about capital letters and full stops and that.
>
> (Kim, Year 4, St Bede's)

> To make our stories sound more interesting.
>
> (Alice, Year 4, Lawnside)

> To learn how to spell.
>
> (Malcolm, Year 5, St Anne's)

> To learn how to measure accurately.
>
> (Eliot, Year 5, St Bede's)

> 'Cause when we are doing stories we put too many 'saids' and 'thens' in.
>
> (Haley, Year 6, St Bede's)

> To learn multiplication.
>
> (Susie, Year 6, St Anne's)

Art and Design were the only other subjects where skill learning was explicitly mentioned:

To learn the best way to draw.

>   (Harry, Year 5, St Bede's)

To learn us how to paint and design things.

>   (Carol, Year 5, Orchard)

Providing opportunities for practice was perceived clearly as a learning intention, often in relation to writing and sums:

She likes people doing it (writing) fast and she wants me to get better at it.

>   (Patrick, Year 2, Orchard)

She wanted us to do revision (Maths).

>   (Harriet, Year 4, Valley)

To give us a little practice (writing).

>   (Jessica, Year 4, Kenwood)

To practise our handwriting.

>   (Tom, Year 4, Greenmantle)

We're having a go at things we are not very good at (Maths).

>   (Laura, Year 4, Orchard)

Sometimes we get it wrong, so I just think she wants us to practise it a bit more (Maths).

>   (Rosie, Year 5, Lawnside)

She knows we are no good at maps and she wanted us to get used to it.

>   (Mandy, Year 5, Audley)

In Year 6 the percentage of explanations coded 'practice' doubled to become the perceived intention most frequently mentioned by the children, for reasons which they articulate explicitly:

To get us ready for SATs.

>   (Simon, Valley)

To get us ready for the sort of questions in SATs – to prepare us.

>   (Jan, Valley)

To revise for SATs.

>   (Guy, Valley)

Practising for SATs – could be in the test.

>   (Samantha, St Bede's)

Training for the tests in the summer.

>   (Philip, St Anne's)

To practise letter writing.

>   (Geoffrey, Orchard)

To practise for SATs.

>   (Kevin, Audley)

To get used to joining up letters for English 'cause we'll lose marks.

>   (Maura, Audley)

To remind us for our SATs.

(Neil, Audley)

In SATs you do an English test and you have to get the spelling right or lose points.

(Mandy, Audley)

In summary, we can see that the level of understanding of teachers' learning intentions began by being very poor with 56 per cent of the pupils in our sample not knowing any reason for a task or activity, or simply accepting it as a teacher requirement. On the other hand, our coding of pupil responses rises steadily to a point where 57 per cent of Year 6 pupils demonstrated some awareness of teacher intentions related to learning. More detailed analysis shows children in Key Stage 1 who have a generalized understanding of the need to 'learn' and a more explicit grasp of specific skills which they need to develop. The focus on skills is particularly marked in Year 2, which may signal greater explicitness by teachers being communicated to pupils.

Analysis of the responses coded to learning in Key Stage 2 shows a steady decline in perception of learning intentions related to progression. In Year 5 pupils saw learning as related to information and skills. In Year 6 the dominant perception was that the tasks and activities we discussed with them were designed to enable them to practise, in the majority of cases, for the end-of-Key Stage assessments. We will discuss this more fully in Chapter 10 which looks at pupils and standardized assessment.

At this point we want to make a more general observation arising from this data which relates to pupil learning. There is little evidence here of a classroom discourse which makes learning intentions explicit. Most pupils responding to our question appeared unused to thinking or talking about this topic and were driven to making inferences based on past experience. Older children were better at it, as might be expected, and higher achievers were more able to see through to and infer their teachers' intentions than their less high-achieving peers. We did observe some teachers explaining at the start of a lesson what they wanted their pupils to achieve but in general this did not mean that the children could articulate any understanding of what they were doing to themselves or to us. In short, they appeared to lack a language for talking about learning.

We will return to discuss the significance of this observation in Chapter 9 when we consider how children approach learning when they are unclear and uncertain about what they are meant to do. Here, we turn now to consider pupils' views on doing things the way their teacher wants them.

8.3 PUPILS' UNDERSTANDING OF TEACHER EXPECTATIONS

In Chapter 6 we saw how the children in our sample perceived and responded to the exercise of teacher power over curriculum activity and classroom control. With few exceptions they expected their teachers to control their behaviour and, accepting this situation, dealt with it strategically and with varying degrees of success. With regard to curriculum they saw little opportunity for any exercise of autonomy in relation to tasks, activities or time. In Year 6 half the pupils were happy to be teacher-dependent and of the other half, some saw autonomy as a way of avoiding challenge and failure, while others wanted more control over the pace and management of their learning.

With this as a background we turn to our analysis of pupils' responses to the question 'Does it matter if you don't do things the way your teacher wants them?'. We were looking here for the children's perception of how free they were to approach given tasks and activities in different ways, how much latitude they felt they had in the production of outcomes, and the degree to which they saw opportunities for negotiation. In addition we were interested in the amount of risk they perceived was inherent in their encounters with teacher expectations. Table 8.3 gives us an overall view.

Table 8.3 Pupils' responses to the question 'Does it matter if you don't do things the way your teacher wants them?' (percentages)

	Year 1	Year 2	Year 3	Year 4	Year 5	Year 6
Yes	75	66	65	60	56	38
No	21	28	24	15	13	21
It depends	4	6	11	25	31	42

Source: PACE 1, 2 and 3 child interview data
Sample: 54 children in each of Years 1–6
Date: Autumn 1990 and 1991, Summer 1993, 1994, 1995 and 1996

We see here a dominant, though steadily decreasing perception that it was important to comply with teacher requirements and expectations. Although the reference to 'things' was deliberately open to interpretation in our question, almost all the children chose to take this to mean 'doing work' and in particular they applied it to the production of written outcomes. These quotations give a flavour of their replies.

> Yes it does, because if she said do your diary first and I did Scottish Maths first she would rub it off the board and I wouldn't know what to do and she'd be quite cross about it.
>
> (Ben, Year 2, Greenmantle)

> It does because she wants the things to be right; if it's not she sends you back and you have to do it again.
>
> (Tom, Year 2, Greenmantle)

> If she says 'Don't do a line in this' and you do, you'll have to rub it out. That's why I always bring a rubber.
>
> (Neil, Year 3, Audley)

> Yes. If we do it our way she says you'll have to do it again.
>
> (Laura, Year 4, Orchard)

> Yes, 'cause Miss likes it the way she says it, and she doesn't like it the way you do it.
>
> (Jessica, Year 5, Kenwood)

> Yes. If I do it different to what she says, she'll shout at me.
>
> (Maura, Year 5, Audley)

Yes. She says 'It should be like this or like that'. She tells us off. Tells us to take it home and do it again.

(Theresa, Year 6, Audley)

On the other hand, the 'it depends' formulation starts from a low of 4 per cent in Year 1 and grows to 42 per cent in Year 6 which suggests a move away from naive 'pleasing teacher' to greater sophistication in understanding of the role of pupil and learner. In the last three years of primary school many of our sample were constructing ideas about the degrees of deviation from the norm that were acceptable, and about the fluctuating circumstances in which standards were applied. Notions of degrees of acceptable deviation clustered around three points: correctness, effort and the status of the task, as these examples illustrate:

You're allowed to do it anyway you like except for Maths. With Maths you have to do it a certain way and you're not allowed to use a calculator.

(Andrew, Year 4, Orchard)

Sometimes Miss is understanding and says 'Don't worry about it, just do it like this now'. It would matter if you didn't do the work and it was quite important, like Maths revision.

(Harriet, Year 4, Valley)

If it was all wrong you'd have to do it again, or if you rushed and it was scruffy, but not if it was a bit wrong.

(Stella, Year 4, Valley)

Sometimes it does and sometimes it doesn't. If it's not wildly what she wants, she sometimes pulls the page out and you have to do it again; but if it's just slightly wrong or if it's map reading and you've gone in the wrong place she doesn't mind, just explains it to you.

(Kate, Year 5, Greenmantle)

Sometimes. If she wants it to be on the wall. If you don't do it so well, she's not pleased.

(Mandy, Year 5, Audley)

If he knows you're not very good at it then he doesn't mind, but if he knows you're being lazy then he doesn't like it so much.

(Sharon, Year 5, Greenmantle)

If it's really, really hard he doesn't mind that much. But if it's really easy work and you haven't done it or you haven't done it properly, haven't listened to some instructions, he gets angry.

(Corrinne, Year 5, Meadway)

Sometimes – if we need to practise something it's important. But sometimes you have a choice or sometimes it's in your rough books and then she doesn't mind.

(Kate, Year 6, Greenmantle)

Sometimes. It depends on the subject and it depends on the activity.

(Ben, Year 6, Greenmantle)

If you've done the opposite she'll probably say you have to do it again. She'd say you probably haven't been listening to what I tell you. But if it's more or less what she wants, it's OK.

(Kim, Year 6, St Bede's)

If you haven't been trying she doesn't like it. But if you've been trying and it's not right she'll just say 'Go and have another think'.

> (Maura, Year 6, Audley)

It does if she told you to do it in a particular way. If she says just write it up quickly, it doesn't; in the work book you don't have to worry.

> (Kelly, Year 6, Orchard)

If it's totally, totally wrong then she's not happy. But if you've missed out a sentence or done a word wrong she just says 'Look it up' or 'Do this little bit again'.

> (Richard, Year 6, Valley)

We can see in all the examples quoted so far pupil awareness of a number of factors which impinge on teacher expectations, in particular the emphasis on effort and the variation in standard setting according to different learning tasks. There is also here the ghost of the ideal piece of work which, in the children's words, 'the teacher wants' and they struggle to achieve; and of the many idiosyncratic demands for margins, borders, lines and other features of layout with which they feel they have to comply. Additionally, these quotations point to another feature which emerged strongly from the children's responses: the risks many of them perceived of not meeting teacher expectations. These were of two kinds. First, they risked being exposed to their teacher's displeasure, anger or shouting. This might lead to losing house points or stars or exposure to public humiliation such as being sent to the headteacher. Second, they would be required to do the work again at home or in school. This might involve being kept in at playtime or missing PE. Table 8.4 summarizes this for the whole sample.

Table 8.4 Pupils' perceptions of the risks associated with not doing things the way their teacher wants (percentages)

	Year 1	Year 2	Year 3	Year 4	Year 5	Year 6
Teacher anger/ public humiliation	74	54	52	55	53	31
Do work again	16	46	48	45	47	69
$n =$	23	35	23	20	32	16

Source: PACE 1, 2 and 3 child interview data
Sample: 149 children from Years 1–6
Date: Autumn 1990 and 1991, Summer 1993, 1994, 1995 and 1996

We can see here the levelling off in perception of the risks of teachers' displeasure after Year 1. In addition there is a clear indication that the pressure to repeat work in order to do it right and get it right was more strongly felt in Year 6; a finding which echoes our analysis in previous chapters and which will be picked up in Chapter 9.

The data contain many evocative vignettes as children recalled their experience:

> I don't really know. It depends if you've done it all wrong. If you've done it just a little bit wrong you don't really get told off so it's OK. If it's all wrong you get told off and it really hurts you like someone's got really mad at you and been horrible.
>
> (Juliet, Year 3, Greenmantle)

> If it's just OK you get a tick. If it's really bad you get a message on it: 'See me'. You have to see him and you may have to write it out three times – or ten!
>
> (Eliot, Year 4, St Bede's)

> It does matter to Mrs X. She says 'You've done it wrong' and bangs her hands down.
>
> (Theresa, Year 4, Audley)

> In our topic books the page would get ripped out and thrown away.
>
> (Laura, Year 6, Orchard)

> It does. She makes you do it again and again and again. George had to do his seven times and eventually she gave up.
>
> (Geoffrey, Year 6, Orchard)

Of course understandings like these are developed interactively and socially, and we find in the data variations between classrooms and within classrooms. For instance, St Anne's had the highest number of pupils who thought doing things the way their teacher wanted did not matter, including five out of six in Year 6. However, this did not mean that they were unaware of the consequences of not meeting expectations; they were accustomed to having to do work again, but this just did not figure highly in the things that really concerned them.

> Not really. Sometimes if I've not done enough I stay in at playtime.
>
> (Jacquie, Year 6, St Anne's)

> No. I stay in at break – do it over again.
>
> (Melanie, Year 6, St Anne's)

In this school with large numbers of low-achieving, socially disadvantaged pupils, relationships with teachers were relaxed and supportive. The children expected to be shouted at and saw it as a passing and not particularly significant occurrence. They liked staying in and being with teachers. They sensed less pressure than some of their peers in other schools. These quotations from Year 5 pupils suggest something of the climate:

> No, he doesn't do nothin' really. He just says go and do something else while I'm marking your book, or something like that. So I just go and do something else whilst there's nothin' else to do.
>
> (Jacquie, Year 5, St Anne's)

> No. If you haven't done it right he just says, like, 'Go and do it again'.
>
> (Susie, Year 5, St Anne's)

In contrast, at Lawnside codings of 'No' were also frequent but, significantly, in conjunction with 'it depends'. This sequence of answers from Rosie, an average-attaining pupil, are characteristic of most responses at this small, socially advantaged, semi-rural school:

> It does matter, sometimes it doesn't. If you get upset, she says 'It's OK'.
>
> (Year 2)

> It makes her a bit annoyed and angry but she'll help you if you ask.
>
> (Year 3)

It does if it's completely wrong, not if it's a little bit.

(Year 4)

It would be nice if you did them right but she wouldn't exactly have a barney with you. She'd say 'Why haven't you done what I asked?' She wouldn't have a shout at you or anything. If you say 'Sorry, I didn't listen' she'll go, 'It's all right. Next time do it more carefully'.

(Year 5)

No not really. If it matters, she tells you.

(Year 6)

In this very different context there is evidence of dialogue and reciprocity of a different kind and a tighter focus on learning, as quotations from other pupils at Lawnside illustrate:

No. She rubs it out and she says 'I know you listened quite well, but you got it wrong'. Once the whole class got it wrong.

(Max, Year 2)

If you've done sums the wrong way round, she shows you and says 'Try it the right way next time'.

(Lucy, Year 4)

She usually tries to find the good things about the work. If she really thinks you haven't done it as well as you could, she'll ask you to start it again.

(Alice, Year 5)

Nevertheless, in this same school we find Olivia, an insecure, sensitive child under considerable pressure from home to achieve. Her responses show how very differently she found meaning in her experiences.

Yes, you get told off. She says 'If you do it like this once more you'll get sent to Mr D' (the headteacher).

(Year 2)

Well, she puts a 'See me, please' on it. (How do you feel?) Really unhappy about it.

(Year 3)

Sometimes. We have to do it over.

(Year 4)

Yes. If she expects you to be really neat, or it's a really important letter, she rips it up and asks you to do another one. It doesn't matter if you've got the answers wrong, but it matters if you haven't done it neat.

(Year 5)

Sometimes it matters – if you do it wrong and someone thinks you're stupid.

(Year 6)

Olivia's answers are more characteristic of those in schools where there was much more general agreement about the importance of doing things the way the teacher wants them. At Kenwood Amanda, like Olivia at Lawnside, was acutely aware of the risks of non-conformity:

Yes. She says 'Start all over again'.

(Year 1)

Yes. Miss rips your page out and throws it in the bin.

(Year 3)

Yes. She sometimes rips the work out of your book.

(Year 4)

In Year 5, however, in the wake of an OFSTED inspection, she seemed particularly aware of the risks her teacher is facing:

Yes. 'Cause it goes into the folders and gets passed to other teachers and they see it and Miss doesn't like it and she'll tell you off.

(Year 5)

It is not until Year 6 that she felt any sense of room for manoeuvre:

If we done it totally differently then, yes, Miss will ask you to do it again; but if it's a bit different she doesn't mind.

(Year 6)

At Kenwood pupils had the same teacher for Years 5 and 6. They all liked her very much but their responses here show them to be very aware of her likes, dislikes and characteristics, and able to develop strategies accordingly.

If she's in a good mood it's all right. But if she's not it all depends. I watch for her shouting at Simon most of the time.

(Scott, Year 5)

Yes, 'cause she likes it with one-centimetre borders and if she don't get it she gets eggy. And if you do something really scruffy she makes you do it again.

(Dawn, Year 5)

If you do it all scruffy or all horrible she'll either rip it up or say do it again. But if you add more pictures and more decoration ... I say, 'Put your heart and soul into every piece of your work', then I normally get away with it. That's what I think.

(Ewan, Year 5)

No, not really. If you have got the things down what she needs, the answers. If you set it out a lot better then you get a good thing about it.

(Scott, Year 6)

The Year 6 class at St Bede's were also generally agreed that doing things the way their teacher wanted did matter. Some recognized that there was variation but unlike their peers at Kenwood they could not discover any underlying rationale for this which would help them to cope with this ambiguity.

Yes, sometimes – but I don't know the difference.

(Samantha, Year 6)

Sometimes it does and sometimes it doesn't – but I don't know the difference.

(Harry, Year 6)

In summary, we can see that although the general trend was towards a greater awareness of relativity in teachers' expectations, the pupils in our sample exhibited very different understandings of this. Some had developed quite sophisticated understanding by the time they began Key Stage 2; others were still comparatively naive in Year 6. In addition, this sophistication was evident in two ways: skill in managing, even manipulating, the situation in order to reduce risk; and skill as learners in recognizing the possibilities of reciprocity, negotiation and taking control. The effects of classroom context and social background on pupils' understanding of and attitude to teacher expectations are also evident in the data.

8.4 PUPILS' VIEWS ON CLASSROOM GROUPING

The pupils in this project, in common with their peers in the majority of English primary school classrooms, were placed in groups in a variety of ways and for different purposes. In 1996 we asked the target pupils, then in Year 6, to explain to us how they were grouped and what they felt about that. To contextualize our analysis of this data we indicate in broad terms the kinds of classroom organization our sample group experienced in this final year of Key Stage 2.

A visitor entering a primary school classroom in England in 1996 would be most likely to see children seated in groups around tables. During the course of the day, as they engaged in different tasks and activities, these children might move, more or less often, to other locations (in or out of the classroom) and be working with different pupils. The members of a group might work collaboratively, in pairs or individually. In addition there would be periods when the children were working with their teacher as a whole class. The teachers of the pupils in the PACE research described to us how, within this generally common pattern, they used groups to manage teaching and learning and in particular how they decided on the composition of groups. To a greater or lesser extent they applied criteria related to attainment (usually referred to as 'ability') and behaviour or social relationships to decide which children should be placed together. However, other factors such as the number of pupils (our target pupils were in classes of between 23 and 31, with an average class size of 28), mixed-age classes, size of classroom, availability of resources, and school policy on teaching and learning all played a part.

There was some difference in teachers' approach to where children sat when they came into the classroom each morning. In most cases this was decided by the teacher because pupils would stay in these groups for much of their working day. At inner-city Meadway the two Year 6 teachers were agreed:

> It's about combinations that work.
>
> (Mr Forest)

> You decide groups so as to cause as little social and behavioural problems as possible, who works best with whom.
>
> (Mrs Johnson)

In Valley, a village school with a class consisting of Years 4, 5 and 6, the approach was the same:

> While we try to sit them with their friends, we also try to sit them in a situation where they're not going to spend the whole day talking and not being on task. They understand they will be moved so the onus is on them if they want to sit with their mate.
>
> (Mrs Lamb, Headteacher)

In contrast at Lawnside, another village school with a mixture of Years 5 and 6 in the same class, the teacher allowed the children to decide where and with whom they sat.

> It's really friendship groups. They group themselves. They normally sit in the same place each day but they can move if they want to and they can arrange it between them.
>
> (Mrs Wright)

In two classes the teachers had modified or abandoned the traditional model of children in groups.

> Because of their atrocious behaviour and the fighting that was going on after Christmas, I separated them, boy/girl, with the tables in pairs and not blocked together.
>
> (Mrs Jones, Year 6, Audley)

> They've got their own seats in a row – four rows facing the front – and the rows rotate every Monday. So the back row becomes the front and they all move back one except for the two at the front in the hot seats. They sit there for as long as it's necessary. In September they're told they may choose by whom they sit, but I tell them it won't last long and it never does, for one reason and another.
>
> (Mrs Thomas, Year 6, St Bede's)

With these different starting points as a base, our target pupils and their classmates were then reorganized for different purposes. All were placed in 'ability groups' for Mathematics and some for English. In some cases this meant being placed in a 'set' drawn from more than one class. For example, in Meadway 50 Year 6 pupils were set for both subjects; in Greenmantle the same approach was used for 88 Year 5 and 6 pupils. In contrast, at St Bede's pupils worked individually on differentiated tasks and schemes but 'ability-based groups' moved from their rows to work with their teacher 'around the Art table' on Mathematics and sometimes English. This strategy was used with a different emphasis in Meadway where, when the whole class was working individually or in groups on, for instance, History or Geography, the teacher would 'take all the special educational needs, low ability and those with English as a second language to work with me at a big table in the middle'. The most 'ability-based' organization was at Kenwood where, following school policy, children were placed and did most of their work in one of four groups as a result of reading and Mathematics tests. There was movement up, down and between groups as a result of various assessments.

Groups that did not take 'ability' into account were also created. At Audley Junior the tables were moved from their behaviour-controlling pairs for Science.

> I bring the tables together, not in ability groups, because they tend to share and talk in Science; it's not necessarily the bright ones who read well or who can do Maths who get Science work into their heads.
>
> (Mrs Jones, Year 6, Audley)

At Lawnside for one session a week pupils were taught as a year group and for some Art, Music and Dance they were 'family grouped' across Key Stage 2. At Valley they were 'mixed up in different ways for different activities, so they do more'. In non-attainment-based groups low achievers were frequently placed with 'bright' or 'more able' pupils on the assumption that they would be 'helped'.

This then, in broad terms and with some illustrative examples, was the context from which Year 6 pupils responded to our questions about grouping. Grouping in the main was a device for managing the allocation of individual tasks or targeting teaching. Pupils in groups worked for the most part on individual outcomes and less frequently on tasks which required extensive collaboration.

Pupil perceptions of how they were grouped

Although their teachers consistently used the shorthand term 'ability', we included both 'ability' and 'attainment' in our coding of pupil responses to the question 'How does your teacher put you into groups?'. We were interested to see how far children's usage mirrored or departed from their teachers'. The full range of codes used, with examples, is set out below.

- 'Ability' – used when children expressed their understanding in terms of some fixed notion of 'ability'.

  For English and Maths it's ability groups.

  (Sean, Greenmantle)

  Group 1, you have to be brainy; Group 2, you got to be a little less; Group 3, you got to be not very brainy; but Group 4, you got to be pretty dumb.

  (Scott, Kenwood)

  In Maths and English it's split into about four groups of who's cleverer at it and who's not so clever.

  (Kim, St Bede's)

  Green, all the brainy ones; purple, all the not so brainy (Maths).

  (Martin, Lawnside)

- 'Attainment' – used for children's formulations which carried more fluid attainment-based meanings.

  In Group 1 we just do it and if we need help we go and ask Miss. In Group 4 they need help and Miss gives them help.

  (Jessica, Kenwood)

  She looks at our work and compares it with other people and puts us in groups with people who are at the same level.

  (Samantha, St Bede's)

  Because of the different levels and standards people are at.

  (Jan, Valley)

- 'Behaviour' – used where children suggested that a reason for grouping was for discipline and control.

It used to be who you wanted then because of the silly ones we got split up. Now she puts you boy and girl on each table.

(Brian, Audley)

He puts people off our table with people off another so we can work good.

(Malcolm, St Anne's)

She splits me and Gavin up all the time. She thinks we don't work but we do. We talk a lot but we always finish on time.

(Geoffrey, Orchard)

- 'Other' – for example, random grouping, age, letting us choose, the school 'house' or 'team' system.

It's randomly, or according to age or where you are in class.

(Kate, Greenmantle)

In Maths I think it's ability. Sometimes it's age.

(Kelly, Orchard)

She tells us who to go with for different reasons. In Spellings it's some who can do it a bit harder.

(Lucy, Lawnside)

Some are lower in Maths than others and we sit on different tables. When we're not doing Maths we have another place, we choose.

(Stella, Valley)

In Maths and English it's who's clever and not so clever. For Science we're in any group and there's house groups.

(Kim, St Bede's)

- 'Doesn't/Don't Know' – used when children could not explain the basis for grouping or claimed that they didn't work in groups.

I don't know how different groups are sorted out. I'm happy with different groups.

(Juliet, Greenmantle)

We have groups for Science, English, Maths and reading. I don't know how we are divided.

(Haley, St Bede's)

She never puts us in groups.

(Maura, Audley)

We have to work on our own. She tells us where to sit but there aren't groups.

(Helen, Orchard)

Table 8.5 was compiled using multiple codings.

We can see from this table and from the quoted examples that the children have a good grasp of the complexities of classroom organization. They are very aware of

Table 8.5 Pupils' understanding of the basis for classroom groupings (percentages)

Attainment	30
Other	28
Ability	20
Doesn't/Don't Know	14
Behaviour	8

Source: PACE 3 child interview data
Sample: 54 children from Year 6
Date: Summer 1996

those areas of the curriculum where they are grouped by 'attainment' or 'ability', categories which were mentioned in seven of the nine schools by two-thirds or more of pupils. In St Anne's and Audley Junior pupils were more aware of their teacher's behavioural concerns or thought they experienced little or no group work. At Lawnside and Valley pupils produced the most varied and multiple explanations. There is a clear connection between the classroom as described by their teachers and pupil perceptions. However within classes, not unexpectedly, pupils are more aware of some factors as they impinge on them personally. In this connection the 'ability/attainment' formulation is interesting, as is the focus on behaviour. We develop these ideas further in this and subsequent chapters. For the moment we consider how children felt about the ways they were grouped.

Pupils' feelings about the way they were grouped

As shown in Table 8.6, the majority of pupils were happy with the ways they were grouped.

Table 8.6 Pupils' feelings about the way their teachers grouped them (percentages)

Like it	58
Neutral	17
Dislike it	15
Mixed feelings	9

Source: PACE 3 child interview data
Sample: 54 children from Year 6
Date: Summer 1996

At a second level of analysis we coded the children's responses to reveal the reasons that lay behind their preference. These fell into four broad categories within which there were both positive and negative feelings.

- 'Peers' – reasons related to the other members of groups:

Sometimes I don't like it if it's people who mess around and don't work. Some people want to do everything and won't let you have a go.

(Kate, Greenmantle)

It's a good idea because you can't act daft and play up with your mates.

(Neil, Audley)

I prefer it when we can choose ourselves because otherwise you end up with being with people you don't want to be with.

(Mandy, Audley)

I feel annoyed. I don't like being split up from my friends.

(Gavin, Orchard)

I don't mind as long as I've got at least one friend.

(Olivia, Lawnside)

If you were in a group of brainy people you would feel left out. It's better to be in a group with people who can do just as much as you.

(Eliot, St Bede's)

- 'Work' – reasons related to opinions of the work perceived to be connected with groups:

For English I'm in Group 2. I preferred Group 3 because you got more work but it wasn't that hard.

(Amanda, Kenwood)

I don't like it in the first group much. I do like it, but not doing the work. Groups 3 and 4 get all the easy stuff. They are lucky.

(Jeremy, Kenwood)

I wish I wasn't so clever really. Like for Maths I'm in the top group, and English, but I can't keep up sometimes. Other groups get less work and more time.

(Kim, St Bede's)

- 'Variety' – reasons related to the variety of experiences made possible by groups:

I like it because it gets you used to secondary school.

(Juliet, Greenmantle)

I think it's better than staying with the same teacher all the time. Some teachers are friendlier than others, some let you sit by your friends and some have more fun activities than others.

(Ben, Greenmantle)

I like it. If you're with the same people every day you would get a bit bored, so I like the groups.

(Haley, St Bede's)

I think it's OK because you work with different people and you get to know people a bit better.

(Harriet, Valley)

- 'Competition' – references to the group hierarchy which related to ideas of competition:

> I'm just happy where I am in every group. I'm not ready for Group 1 yet. Too hard. I don't want to be in, like, the lowest group.
>
> (Ewan, Kenwood)

> I think it's good because it makes you work hard to get into the next group and if you're in the top you have to make sure you don't drop.
>
> (Tom, Greenmantle)

> I feel really dull. If Year 5s are in a higher group, that makes you feel really dumb.
>
> (Martin, Lawnside)

> It's all right but Elroy and Fran – they lose team points. We all lose some but they lose lots.
>
> (Ian, Meadway)

Table 8.7 Reasons behind pupils' feelings about how they are grouped (percentages)

	Peers	Work	Variety	Competition
Like it	27	17	10	8
Mixed feelings	10	4	2	2
Dislike	10	2	0	2
Neutral	3	4	0	0
Total	50	27	12	12

Source: PACE 3 child interview data
Sample: 54 children from Year 6
Date: Summer 1996

We see here that half the children in our target group evaluated grouping in terms that in some way involved their peers. For most, the important criterion was being with or separated from friends. However there are also negative and mixed feelings about having to work with uncongenial people and the problems involved in group process. We will see more of both these points when we look in more detail at pupils' views on learning in the next chapter. Next in importance were factors related to level of work. Pupils were concerned to be where the level of work demand was both satisfying and comfortable; differences in desire and taste for challenge were discernible. Overlapping with this (and with feelings about their peers) was the idea of competition associated with groups. There is no really strong evidence of competitive pressure or of the threat to the preservation of dignity and self-esteem. Only 12 per cent of the criteria deployed referred to this as a factor. This might seem encouraging but for some of our lower achievers there was considerable anxiety associated with their positioning in groups. Scott provides an example of some of the very powerful feelings they experienced.

> I'm in Group 3. That means I'm not very brainy. I want to go up to Group 2 because I know I can handle that ... I work hard. There's one girl, she's in Group 1 and I don't

reckon she works hard at all. She knows lots of things but she doesn't deserve to be in that group. I was in Group 2 and then I went to Group 3 and then I went into Group 4. And I thought 'I ain't going in Group 4'. And I worked really hard and me and James got up to Group 3. And then he went back to Group 4.

(Scott, Kenwood)

Equally, different kinds of groups provoked strong responses in some high achievers, as Jane demonstrates. She was in the top set for Mathematics and English at inner-city Meadway. For other class work she was in a very 'mixed ability' setting.

For Maths and English there's a smart group and a not-so-smart group. I don't care about that really. But working with not-so-bright people – I hate that. Because they don't understand. They always get on my nerves. They're like 'How do you do this? How do you do that?' And, like, you try to get on with your work and they're interfering. If I've got nothing to do it's OK, but it gets so frustrating when you've got something to do. You just want to get on with your work.

(Jane, Meadway)

8.5 CONCLUSION

We have been concerned in this chapter to penetrate pupils' understandings of their teachers' actions in relation to their learning. The evidence from the children in our target group indicates that as they moved up the school they were increasingly able to explain what they saw as their teachers' intentions. However, they had a relatively limited conception of these intentions, based on inference rather than confident knowledge. Pupils appeared to be surprised to be asked why their teacher wanted them to undertake a specific task or activity and, in the same way that we have noted their limited access to assessment discourse, they had little or no language that helped them to discuss learning processes.

Their perception of teacher expectations ('Does it matter whether you do things the way your teacher wants them?') was focused on written outcomes. They were increasingly aware that teacher expectations varied according to a range of factors. These included the status or stage of the work, the teacher's view of what a pupil or group was capable of in terms of effort or achievement, and, they suggested, the teacher's mood. A concern for the children was to find out as precisely as possible 'what she wants' and to respond to well-known idiosyncrasies. Some were more concerned than others about the risks of failing to meet expectations. These risks were mainly seen as teacher anger or displeasure. This might involve having to suffer being shouted at, publicly humiliated or required to do work again. The variation in anxiety was found within classes but more often could be accounted for by differences in classroom climate between schools. It was notable that pupils associated teacher expectations with performance outcomes, with product rather than processes. As with teacher intentions, their view was largely instrumental, concerned with 'getting through' the task rather than with learning *per se*.

Our enquiry into pupils' understanding of their teachers' organization of groups in Year 6 showed that they were aware of 'ability' and 'attainment' as factors used to define groups, especially in Mathematics where the majority of pupils were aware of being divided up in this way. In general, pupil perceptions were in line with teacher approaches. For instance, where grouping was a prominent feature of a classroom, pupils were more conscious of and concerned about work as 'hard' or 'easy' and their position relative to others. However, a majority of pupils in the sample were happy with the way they were grouped, or at least accepted it. They liked having friends in their group, felt comfortable about the work demands made of them, and were positive about the variety and competition that groups introduced. Those who were less enthusiastic about their experience of groups disliked being separated from friends, having to work with people they found uncongenial and uncooperative, and felt that they were misplaced either by having too much or too little demanded of them. Evidence of competitive pressure was not strong in relation to grouping. However, included in the data are examples of individuals (both low and high achievers) who expressed anxiety and dissatisfaction about their experience.

With these findings in mind we expand the picture of pupil learning that emerges from the PACE project by turning from children's understandings of what their teachers do to their accounts and exposition of their own learning.

Chapter 9

Pupil Perspectives on Learning

9.1   Introduction
9.2   What makes pupils worry about school work?
9.3   What makes pupils feel pleased about school work?
9.4   Pupils' views of working with others in the classroom
9.5   Issues in pupils' feelings about school learning
9.6   Pupils' explanations for being distracted
9.7   Conclusion

9.1 INTRODUCTION

> We were drawing our masks, then we have to design a pattern to put on it. I like that. It's educational. (What does educational mean?) When something's interesting and you're learning as well.
>
> (Corrinne, Year 3, Meadway)

The succinct definition of 'educational' that Corrinne provided so confidently when she was 8 years old is a good starting point for our discussion of what the children in our target sample told us about learning. The association that she makes between interest, enjoyment, activity and learning is one which many of the children made explicitly or by implication, as we have seen in previous chapters. However, although Corrinne has identified an aspect of learning which we all recognize, our experience as adult teachers and learners tells us that there is more to this complex and mysterious process. The question of what factors combine to help children become successful learners is of perennial interest to teachers, parents and anyone involved in education. In this chapter we continue our attempt to address this question from the perspective of the PACE pupils.

It is generally accepted that for learners of all ages the idea of motivation is central both in the initial stages of learning and later when things may become more difficult and challenging, when effort and persistence are required. In this context indicators of time spent engaged in or managing learning tasks, as opposed to time distracted from the task, are significant. There is also much discussion about the merits, individually and in combination, of extrinsic and intrinsic motivation. In addition we might consider ideas of learning style; the acquisition of good and bad attitudes to, and understandings of, learning including, as we have seen in the previous chapter, the development of a range of strategies for coping with the learning situation. It is to these themes that we now turn.

9.2 WHAT MAKES PUPILS WORRY ABOUT SCHOOL WORK?

We begin by looking at what makes pupils worry about their work on the grounds that anxiety can be demotivating and create a context and attitude that militates against learning. In addition we want to consider what pupils told us they did when they were worried. A question, 'What sorts of things make you worried about your work?', was added to the interview schedule and continued to be asked throughout Key Stage 2. Responses were coded into seven categories:

- 'Appearance' – references to neatness, for example: 'looks scruffy', 'untidy', 'bad handwriting', 'rubbing out you make a hole', 'all smudged and horrible'.
- 'Correctness' – references to getting things right, for example: 'when I know I've done something wrong', 'doing mistakes and it's in "best" ', 'if there were loads of corrections', 'lots of red crosses'.
- 'Quantity' – references to producing enough, getting finished, working to time limits, for example: 'if I do half a page', 'if I've done only a few lines, or only the date', ' 'cause I haven't finished', 'when I don't do as much as Miss wants'.
- 'Quality' – references to personal dissatisfaction with quality of work, for example: 'if I'm not pleased, if the story isn't interesting', 'if it didn't have good ideas in it'.
- 'Understanding' – references to finding work 'difficult', 'getting stuck', being 'confused', 'struggling', 'didn't understand it'.
- 'Distraction/interference' – references to worry about own behaviour having influenced work produced, for example: 'if I've been chatting'; worry about interference by other children, for example: 'when I turn my back and someone's drawn all over it', 'people keep talking and I can't concentrate'.
- 'Fear of exposure' – references to concern about public humiliation, peer awareness of failure via teacher marks or comments, being seen to be not keeping up, for example: 'because everyone was ahead of me', 'someone saying it's not good. Making fun of it', 'if I got a D'.

We can see in Table 9.1 the strength of children's concern in Years 3 and 4 about superficial features of their work and with overt evaluation in the form of ticks and crosses. They were worried about what could be seen and measured, an emphasis which is illustrated by frequent references to Maths, spelling, punctuation and

Table 9.1 Factors that made pupils worried about their work (percentages)

	Year 3	Year 4	Year 5	Year 6	Average
Appearance	34	36	12	0	22
Correctness	33	37	10	4	22
Quantity	17	9	15	2	11
Quality	3	4	7	0	4
Understanding	5	3	26	84	27
Distraction	6	3	8	3	5
Fear	2	8	22	7	5

Source: PACE 2 and 3 child interview data
Sample: 54 children in each of Years 3–6
Date: Summer 1993, 1994, 1995 and 1996

handwriting. However, in Year 5 and even more dramatically in Year 6 the focus of their concerns moved to not being able to understand things, how to do something and get it right. In Year 6 this predominated over all other factors. The criteria of 'quality' which was gaining ground in Year 5, albeit applied mainly by high achievers, disappeared completely; fewer children mentioned 'quantity' or (though they may still have felt it) fear of being publicly humiliated. They were clearly much more conscious of the need to 'understand' which was mostly expressed as 'knowing *how* to do it' in order to 'get it right'. In this they were not far removed from their younger selves who were concerned about correctness. The focus was still on outcomes rather than thinking processes.

If we look more closely at their accounts of not understanding we get an indication of some of the strategies they used to deal with their worries:

> Last year I was struggling with my work and parents can come in and they give them time to talk about it. My parents came to talk to my teachers, it was to do with Maths and I wasn't getting it. My mum went in and then explained it to me and I could do it.
>
> (Harriet, Year 6, Valley)

> I was worried about Maths. I was having trouble with decimals. Then it was discussion day with parents and Miss told them I wasn't doing very well with my Maths and Mum and Dad had a chat with me and now I can do them.
>
> (Eliot, Year 6, St Bede's)

> In Maths group. It was finding two middle numbers – it was dead hard. Miss just told me to leave it. I was stuck for ten minutes. I just told my mum about it – she taught me how to do it and I went back and did it in school. She taught our Chris how to do the same thing. He's 13. Then Cherie had a problem in the same book. I told her.
>
> (Jacquie, Year 6, St Anne's)

The strategy of getting help from home was quite frequently employed, sometimes as a collaboration with school, sometimes initiated by parents who enquired about problems, sometimes by children. Parental involvement was not always welcomed or successful, but in answering this question pupils were very satisfied with the outcomes and even, like Jacquie, happy to share their newly acquired expertise.

Home, as we will see later, figured very large in many children's learning. Here the impact of parental intervention was not so much to secure a high level of achievement as to build the confidence to go on.

A second strategy was to turn to other pupils in the classroom for support.

> Sometimes if we have to describe ourselves or write about home I don't have anything interesting to say. I usually ask another pupil or copy somebody's then I get the hang of it after, once they've started me off.
>
> (Kate, Year 6, Greenmantle)

> Decimal points. When we had the teacher it was confusing but when someone else like Jess showed me I understood a bit, but not much.
>
> (Dawn, Year 6, Kenwood)

Here we have just two of the many examples in the data of pupils looking to their peers for help. We see Kate using other pupils to get her going when she is stuck for ideas. Her reference to copying is unembarrassed because she knows that the writing she eventually produces will be her own. Dawn's struggle with decimals is of a different order. She is confused by her teacher and not sure quite how much this has been helped by her friend. Jess's help, though, has made her feel that she has made a start. The theme of peer teaching is one we return to in Section 9.4.

The final strategy we consider in this section is asking teacher. The Year 6 pupils in the study showed a much greater willingness to 'ask teacher' than those in Year 5. This may be a mark of their greater confidence, a comment on positive relationships, or an indication of a pressure to perform which drove them to seek help. As individuals all pupils have different attitudes to asking for help and we can see evidence of this in these examples:

> If I don't quite know I go and ask the teacher. I don't feel embarrassed, I just feel I need some help.
>
> (Stella, Year 6, Valley)

> I just go and ask him. He helps. Our Sir helps. Put your hand up and he comes and helps. I don't feel ashamed or ought like that.
>
> (Melanie, Year 6, St Anne's)

> Sometimes in my Maths I get stuck on sums and I don't know whether to ask. I think I won't get finished if I don't ask so I'd better. I don't like asking.
>
> (Kim, Year 6, St Bede's)

> Once or twice in Maths ... with not understanding. I get angry. I just sit down and close the book, especially if I find it boring. I chat to me friends. It's a habit. Sometimes I go to the teacher; most of the time I work with friends.
>
> (Mandy, Year 5, Audley)

The reluctance of Kim and Mandy (both high achievers) to ask for help contrasts with Stella and Melanie's relaxed confidence. Esther, in this next example, disliked Maths and found it hard. Her teacher was convinced she was underachieving. In Year 5 Esther took refuge in avoidance and chatting, though she worried about the consequences. In Year 6 she delayed but finally accepted the strategy of asking.

When I haven't done much work in Maths because I've been talking too much.

(Esther, Year 5, Greenmantle)

In Maths when I get stuck. I sit there for a little while ... If I'm not sure I go up to the teacher.

(Esther, Year 6, Greenmantle)

When faced with questions, teachers have to make decisions about whether to repeat explanation or demonstration or require pupils to 'work it out'. Responses to the challenge to think experienced by our sample were very varied.

Just before Christmas I didn't understand it at all and the teacher was trying to get us to work it out for ourselves and she wouldn't explain it to me. But there were several of us who didn't understand and we spent ages just trying to work it out and then when we did eventually work it out we did it quite well, but some of us nearly ended up crying. It was just so hard.

(Richard, Year 6, Valley)

If I get stuck I go and ask Miss and see if she can help me. Sometimes it helps. Sometimes she says you have to figure it out for yourself. Then I go back and think what I can do. Usually I ask Jason if I'm sitting next to him.

(Haley, Year 6, St Bede's)

On one piece of Maths I was there for ages trying to do it and when I did them it was all wrong. Mrs B asked me to do them again. Some people were helping me but I still didn't understand. (How did you feel?) Worried.

(Amanda, Year 6, Kenwood)

In my Maths last term I kept getting stuck on the same thing. I did it about ten times and I kept getting stuck. And Miss told me to do it again and finally I got it right. She told me how to do it.

(Harry, Year 6, St Bede's)

Richard and his group had the resilience to survive the struggle, even though it nearly reduced some of them to tears. Haley is typical of those pupils who avoided the challenge by asking their peers. However, as Amanda's response illustrates, this strategy does not always work – understanding did not dawn and the worry remained. Harry's teacher at St Bede's eventually gave in and told him how to do it. She was quite aware that she was 'being worn down' and that he was resisting her challenge. In the press of classroom activity it is not surprising that pupil attempts to reduce the level of challenge to something they found more comfortable were often successful.

I wrote a poem and it was supposed to rhyme but I couldn't get it to rhyme. So I went to see Sir. (What happened?) Sir said I could do one that didn't rhyme.

(Samantha, Year 5, St Bede's)

As these examples demonstrate, whether the pupils looked to home, peers or teachers for help when they were worried, their approaches and experiences were varied. We end this section by contrasting the strategic confidence of Kate and the resilience of Richard and his group with the response of low-achieving Malcolm who had nothing to deploy but helplessness.

When I haven't done enough. I had to stay in until I done a bit more. I still got to stay in and try to get the answer. I don't get no help. I still got to stay in.

(Malcolm, Year 6, St Anne's)

9.3 WHAT MAKES PUPILS FEEL PLEASED ABOUT SCHOOL WORK?

In parallel with the question about feeling worried, when the children were in Year 3 we added the question 'What makes you feel pleased about your work?'. We retained this question in Year 4. In the final two years of the study we adapted this question and invited pupils to tell us about 'a time when you felt very pleased because you'd done some difficult work'. In each year of the study we also asked them 'What happens when someone does their work really well?'. The data from these questions form the basis for the analysis in this section.

We were not surprised to find the pupils in Years 3 and 4 generating categories which, as we have already seen, they consistently used when discussing their work. As before, they were pleased by the neatness and correctness of their work, by the quantity they produced, by their speed of working and their ability to finish.

Nice writing, no rubbing out, no smudging, no words wrong.

(Samantha, Year 4, St Bede's)

If I finished. I don't usually finish.

(Andrew, Year 3, Orchard)

If it gets a tick and if it's really neat.

(Helen, Year 3, Orchard)

In addition, a third of the sample were pleased by being praised and rewarded, while a smaller group expressed intrinsic pleasure in work they perceived to have quality. These responses are quantified in Table 9.2.

Table 9.2 What pupils were pleased with about their work (percentages)

	Year 3	Year 4
Rewards/Praise	32	33
Appearance	29	28
Correctness	15	16
Quality	12	10
Speed/Quantity	10	8
No Answer	2	5

Source: PACE 2 child interview data
Sample: 54 children in each of Years 3 and 4
Date: Summer 1993 and 1994

Reward systems

Rewards appeared in the form of stickers, team points, certificates, lollipops and special privileges They accounted for 20 per cent of the responses in Year 3 and 17 per cent in Year 4. Praise was categorized to include references to assessment-related comments, things people said and other forms of recognition such as showing the work to the headteacher. Pupils frequently linked the two categories and for this reason we show them together in the analysis. Some examples illustrate children's responses:

'Cause I finished it all and I got an excellent.

(Malcolm, Year 3, St Anne's)

When I get team points or good comments or when I can choose. When I can read what I've written to another class or show another teacher.

(Kate, Year 3, Greenmantle)

When I get a certificate.

(Jenny, Year 4, St Anne's)

If somebody said 'That work's very good'.

(Tom, Year 4, Greenmantle)

We can contrast this pleasure in extrinsic reward and recognition with that which seems to derive more from an intrinsic satisfaction with the work:

If I read it and think I've written a good story. If it's good I'm quite pleased.

(Sam, Year 3, St Bede's)

The teacher didn't say anything but I was proud of it because it was better than the others. I wasn't rushing on like the others.

(Theresa, Year 3, Audley)

If it's good. If I've tried my best.

(Lucy, Year 3, Lawnside)

If it looks good and I really like what I've done.

(Alice, Year 3, Lawnside)

If I've took my time and worked hard and got on with it.

(Rosie, Year 3, Lawnside)

When I feel I've done very well. If I've enjoyed it I think I've done well.

(Polly, Year 3, Valley)

If I've done it really neatly and it's something I know I'm good at, then I think, 'That's brilliant'.

(Ben, Year 4, Greenmantle)

You look at the folder (portfolio) – you see how you've changed through the years and how you've joined up writing.

(Laura, Year 4, Orchard)

These children, as well as valuing products, were aware of the significance to *them* of the time and effort they had put in and of their intrinsic enjoyment of the process.

Laura, uniquely, took pleasure in seeing how much progress she had made. These emphases were not frequent features of the reception of work in the children's schools and classrooms. However, the children were well aware of the many systems designed by their teachers to recognize their effort and achievement. When we asked the pupils 'What happens when someone does their work really well?' they described a variety of symbolic rewards (stickers, stars, points, certificates) sometimes arranged in hierarchical structures ('there's gold silver and blue stars', 'two smiley faces means you get a star', 'if you get enough stars you might be Star of the Week', 'if you get five stickers you go to the headteacher and you might get a certificate', 'the team with the most points gets a prize'). Such systems were mentioned more by pupils in Key Stage 2 than other categories such as assessment (marks or comments), praise and public recognition (showing work or having it displayed), and privileges, as Table 9.3 shows.

Table 9.3 Pupils' explanations of what happens when someone does their work really well (percentages)

	Year 1	Year 2	Year 3	Year 4	Year 5	Year 6
Praise	35	36	13	14	25	24
Assessment	31	35	25	29	25	24
Symbolic reward	20	21	40	54	49	52
Privilege	14	8	2	3	1	0

Source: PACE 1, 2 and 3 child interview data
Sample: 54 children in each of Years 1–6
Date: Spring 1991 and 1992, Summer 1993, 1994, 1995 and 1996

The decline in awareness of privileges (choosing, using the computer, extra play) is mirrored by the rise of symbolic reward systems which in all schools carried some school-wide dimension and involved presentations at assemblies. In four of the project schools children were members of 'houses' or 'teams' so that their winning or losing of points carried significance beyond their classroom. In their explanations pupils were most aware of symbolic systems but many accounts combined most or all categories and made clear their understanding of the overlap in operation between reward for effort and for attainment.

> Sir tells them when he hands back their book. He puts 'Very good' or gives two house points if you've tried really hard. There is a house cup for the most points at the end of the year. You can get house points for trying really hard even if you haven't been able to do that much.
>
> (Samantha, Year 6, St Bede's)

> It's just a bit of fun where you win the cup every year if you have the most points. I felt good when I got some house points.
>
> (Harry, Year 5, St Bede's)

Some pupils were acutely aware of how many (or few) such symbolic awards they had received. Some even admitted to feeling 'a bit jealous'. However they were also clear about the way teachers manipulated the system: 'Mrs X does it very equally.

She's very fair'. The focus as they saw it was often less on the learning evident in their work than on general approbation of positive attitudes such as effort.

When children described praise and public recognition of their work, mentioned less in Years 3 and 4, they were more expressive, as these examples illustrate:

> She shows it to us and she goes 'Look at this, it's wonderful'.
>
> (Corrinne, Year 1, Meadway)

> She says it's excellent. If it's writing, she chooses your words that describes and reads the stories out.
>
> (Kelly, Year 3, Orchard)

> They get an A. You show your work in assembly if it's really, really good.
>
> (Corrinne, Year 5, Meadway)

> Sometimes she says 'Right, you've done a really good piece of work and I'm going to display it'. She puts it in the class or the hall so everyone can see it. Sometimes it goes to Mr Henderson (headteacher).
>
> (Carol, Year 5, Orchard)

> She puts 'Good, excellent work' at the bottom and says 'Good work'.
>
> (Geoffrey, Year 5, Orchard)

> Well they sometimes give team points or they put 'Very good work' and a big tick.
>
> (Juliet, Year 5, Greenmantle)

> Usually get team points and sometimes it's read out in class, or if it's art work it goes on the board. If it's a project people clap.
>
> (Kate, Year 6, Greenmantle)

The specific attention to and celebration of individual pieces of work, rather than the distribution of symbolic rewards, appears to have been of particular significance to many of the children.

It is interesting that children very rarely referred to being pleased with or rewarded for work in Maths. Maths, as we saw in the previous section, was the cause of many of pupils' worries. 'Getting stuck' was more quickly evident in Maths than in other subjects. Equally, writing and Art were more likely to be given public recognition. However, as we turn to pupils' accounts of the pleasure they derived from 'doing a difficult piece of work', we see Maths once again playing a dominant role, making up 36 per cent of the stories in Year 5 and 40 per cent in Year 6.

Overcoming difficulty

The sources of pleasure in overcoming difficulty predictably varied with individuals. For some it was pleasing to find they could do something others found hard.

> I finished it and got it all right. Some of the other people found it really difficult.
>
> (Harriet, Year 6, Valley)

> I was the only one who finished. No-one else could do it. It was really difficult.
>
> (Laura, Year 6, Orchard)

Others found personal satisfaction with the pleasing outcome of a task on which time, care and ingenuity had been expended.

I was really pleased with my tree (a picture) because it took me a long time and it was really good.

(Juliet, Year 6, Greenmantle)

We were making clay models. I used a ruler to make all the sides straight. People made fun of me for that but I didn't care because it was the best I could do. And I liked it.

(Eliot, Year 5, St Bede's)

A different kind of satisfaction resulted from a challenge met and overcome, with or without help.

It's this quite hard Science. I'm getting the gist of it and I'm doing it now. It's really quite hard actually. I'm taking it home tonight and I'm going to finish it off. I'll work it out myself probably.

(Jeremy, Year 5, Kenwood)

Our teacher told us a lot of things. There was nothing to read; we just had to listen, summarize it and keep it in our minds. That was really hard but I did quite well.

(Alice, Year 5, Lawnside)

There was this map what I drawed. We wanted to trace it but you couldn't. We put it up against the window to let light through it and that was really good. We got a good report about that. I was pleased. I worked with Jeremy. It was his idea. We done it really good. That was one of the best work I done.

(Scott, Year 6, Kenwood)

Me and Guy had to work together with a trundle wheel to find the distance round the playgrounds. We did it in a really short time and I was pleased with myself. The teacher was pleased too.

(Richard, Year 5, Valley)

I figured out how to do square roots by listening to Sir teaching other people. I wanted to figure it out myself.

(Wesley, Year 5, Meadway)

Then there was the pleasure of the 'penny dropping' or of finding that something feared was within their capability.

I got 24 for a Maths test on multiplication. Most people only got 20. I'd been practising by accident – now I always do them at home 'cause she says there will be a test every day.

(Tom, Year 6, Greenmantle)

I didn't really understand it and I got really confused. But I looked at the paper and I read it. I had a go and then it was really easy. It was rectangles and right angles. Jess showed us how to do it on the board and Jess said 'If you put it properly you will get the right answer'.

(Dawn, Year 6, Kenwood)

Sir gave us this dead hard work (in Science) and I was like this (mimes biting her nails) thinking I won't be able to do it. But when I finished it, it was just completely right. I just felt good.

(Jacquie, Year 5, St Anne's)

I've always had problems with Science. I get muddled up in the conclusions, the method ... yeah ... and the results. All the writing. But, you know in cookery books, they have about the method? I found out about that. (How did that happen?) I was just ... Mum was making a meal and she had recipes ... I was looking through and I found methods ... and that's how I knew. (How did that help?) Well the teacher been telling us about, you know, the methods and conclusions and stuff. It reminded me. It was the same.

(Martin, Year 6, Lawnside)

We were doing multiplication. I turned over the page. I saw this page full of sums and I thought, 'Oh no. This is going to take me forever'. About half an hour later I'd done it. I thought, 'Yes! I've done it'. The good thing was when I looked in my book next day, I got them all right.

(Rupert, Year 5, Lawnside)

I was struggling. Hugh was sitting next to me. He helped and I got it right. He told me how to work it out.

(Martin, Year 5, Lawnside)

It was Maths. I got through it. Concentration did it.

(Kelly, Year 6, Orchard)

In percentages I was really muddled and then someone said something to me about how to work it out and then I could do it really easily.

(Jan, Year 6, Valley)

In some cases what the children recalled was not the content of the learning but how they experienced the event. For example Gavin who, as we noted in the last chapter, objected strongly to being put in a different group from his friend Geoffrey because they liked to chat, remembered with some satisfaction 'I got them all right. I was sitting on my own. Not talking. I just got on with it' (Gavin, Year 6, Orchard).

What can we make of all these tiny memories of difficulty overcome? What can they tell us about children learning? We can see here pupils who have been surprised by success. 'I thought I'd never get through it', 'It looked really hard'. In Year 6, in particular, our data suggest teachers were raising expectations and challenging pupils to meet them. The success stories included here were the result of accurate teachers' judgements about what pupils were capable of and pupils with the disposition and the confidence to 'have a go'. These are also pupils who are articulating their personal experience of things that they 'know' theoretically are important factors in learning, in particular concentration, effort and working to time. In some of the accounts, moreover, there are indications of other learning-related skills less obviously promoted in classrooms such as lateral thinking and improvisation.

Most children did not (and when prompted could not) recall the details of the 'difficult work' they had engaged with. Once they knew 'how to do it' they could not explain what it was like not to know, nor could they pinpoint how they came to 'understand', or exactly what it was that 'someone said' or did that helped them. Their accounts do however provide yet more evidence for the role of interaction in learning. In the next section we consider what pupils told us about working with their peers.

9.4 PUPILS' VIEWS OF WORKING WITH OTHERS IN THE CLASSROOM

Whether working as a whole class, individually, in pairs or in groups pupils in the PACE study were in frequent interaction with each other for a variety of purposes, not always of course productively associated with their learning. As we saw in Chapter 3 pupils in the study spent two-thirds of their time working individually or interacting with others. Even when notionally in a group they were working individually. In these conditions, who pupils said they liked to work with assumed a particular significance. For the PACE pupils and their classmates their peer relationships were a vital factor in accomplishing each day.

For these reasons we were particularly interested in gaining pupils' perspectives on working with others. The analysis in the previous section indicates the role that both planned and informal interaction with their peers played in some children's learning. Classroom organization in groups or pairs is designed to facilitate such interaction. These examples illustrate pupils' experience of how things can go:

(Preparing a puppet show) No, I didn't like it because Caroline was getting on our nerves. She wasn't getting on with her writing.

(Amanda, Year 2, Kenwood)

We were weighing the things (plastic cubes) and then adding them up. Then we put them in the book. I liked some of it. Vicky and Peter were messing about. They wouldn't do it properly ... We didn't do it all.

(Mandy, Year 2, Audley)

(History – listening to a tape, answering question and writing the answers) It gave me a headache and an earache ... it was too loud ... Tony was playing with the controls.

(Jessica, Year 3, Kenwood)

(Writing an acrostic poem) She told us to do a poem about Vikings. We got into partners and me and Vanessa made up a poem together. Sometimes it was a bit hard. I liked it because it was good fun and I had time to find out about Vikings.

(Jan, Year 3, Valley)

(History) She puts us in groups with people I don't like, so we argue.

(Ben, Year 4, Greenmantle)

Me and Ned and George had to work together. We had cards and we had to put them all flat face with the numbers at the bottom and we had to pick them up and, say I had 11 and 2, I had to pick another and make that number out of them, like 20. And we had to use add, subtract, divide and multiplication. It was fun. I like playing games where you turn over. I like doing investigations.

(Rosie, Year 5, Lawnside)

Last week we did a play while the others were at the gala and they gave us a demonstration on a sheet of how to do it, and then we had to carry on from that sheet and today we are writing a full play. I like it when we are working together. We get more ideas to turn into the actual play.

(Simon, Year 5, Valley)

I like Art. It's just good fun because of everybody's ideas. Usually we're not allowed to use other people's ideas. You get a bit stuck and you're thinking 'Oh what shall I do now?'.

(Hugh, Year 5, Lawnside)

We've been asked to get into groups of two or three and there are some titles on the board and you choose one of those, or you can make your own play up and you've got to re-enact the play and you've got to discuss what happens next with your partners. You get to work with some of your friends and you can choose who you are and everyone gets along really well.

(Stella, Year 5, Valley)

Some groupings work well, others do not. What from the pupils' point of view makes the difference? In Chapter 8 we saw what pupils in Years 5 and 6 of our sample thought of their teachers' approach to grouping. We also asked them to tell us which of their peers they liked to work with and why. An analysis of their responses throws some light on this question.

Table 9.4 Pupils' criteria for choosing people to work with (percentages)

	Year 5	Year 6
Good at working in groups	32	42
Can give help	28	19
Is my friend	20	17
Has expertise	14	14
Is on the same level	5	5
Don't know	1	3

Source: PACE 3 child interviews
Sample: 54 children from each of Years 5 and 6
Date: Summer 1995 and 1996

We see here a strong and increasing emphasis on wanting to work with people who were 'good in groups' with over 40 per cent of the sample in Year 6 including this as a criterion. They were in considerable agreement about the qualities that were needed. Good people to work with are those who 'work hard', 'don't argue', 'don't boss you about' or 'think they should be in charge'. They 'don't talk too much', 'don't laugh and joke and act daft' because that 'stops you doing your work' and 'getting on with it'. They 'let you have your views', 'listen to everyone's ideas', then they 'get down to the work, don't take hours to do it' and 'get things done'.

There was a distinct overlap for some children between nominating people with these qualities and their friends. This was particularly so for girls who felt that the understandings built up socially in the playground and out of school were very helpful in the classroom.

We are all quite close friends. We get on pretty well. We don't argue.

(Kate, Year 5, Greenmantle)

We all put our ideas in and everybody listens to everybody else. We've got to be better friends over the year.

(Dawn, Year 6, Kenwood)

When I work with other people (than her friends) it's different. I don't know what they know, what they can do. Someone I know I can tell them anything. I work hard with them.

(Lucy, Year 6, Lawnside)

They are my friends. I can get on with them. It's quite easy to work with them. We can talk, discuss things. If I was working with someone else it's not so easy. If I don't get on with them it just makes it harder to work. You understand it when your friends say something that maybe others don't understand.

(Alice, Year 5, Lawnside)

Although a few boys shared this view, they were more likely to choose people to work with who were not their friends, including girls. Only 13 per cent of the sample selected both boys and girls to work with. Of these the majority (9 per cent) were boys. Girls, as we have seen, were more likely to restrict their choices to like-minded friends. In Year 6, when learning was getting serious, some boys were quite consciously avoiding their friends, as these examples illustrate:

Sometimes Gavin (his friend), but sometimes not because he messes around and gets silly some of the time.

(Geoffrey, Appleton)

Diane and Roy (not his friends) because they don't laugh and joke about and stop you doing your work.

(Eliot, St Bede's)

Some, boys and girls, were noticeably strategic in their selections, putting together combinations which covered all the attributes they felt were needed.

Zoe is brainy, Cathy is jolly, Sue is nice to work with.

(Esther, Year 6, Greenmantle)

Caroline for Maths and on things like Science and that. Probably Meg or one of the boys for the hard stuff. Meg is so smart and she helps me with everything I don't know on the sheet.

(Ewan, Year 5, Kenwood)

Felix knows a lot and can help you understand. I sometimes like working with girls because they are quieter and gentle, and you feel really clever if you have to give them a spelling.

(Eliot, Year 5, St Bede's)

I like to work with brainy people like Sasha. Louise is the same as me in Maths. I like outdoor activities with Bridget, like measuring the playground.

(Kim, Year 6, St Bede's)

If you're working they don't disturb you. If you want to lend something they'll lend it you.

(Mandy, Year 5, Audley)

Sarah and Emma are my best friends. Stella gets down to the work and it makes me do it as well.

(Harriet, Year 6, Valley)

George is good at English. Ned's good at drawing, a bit. Will I like working with in Maths. If there's a few questions, sums and things I don't get, they help me.

(Martin, Year 5, Lawnside)

Mike always does something really funny. Rupert's quite serious, he gets on with things. We can get on and do the work quickly.

(Hugh, Year 5, Lawnside)

We can see in these extracts the way in which some pupils are invested with useful expertise. There are links between this and the idea of looking to others for help. In many cases the notion of help was reciprocal.

We usually work together. If we don't know what something is we explain it to each other.

(Amanda, Year 6, Kenwood)

If the teacher's out of the room or she's busy, sometimes I ask a friend and they give me an example and I go away and work on it.

(Dawn, Year 6, Kenwood)

However, for low achievers in particular having another pupil to turn to when they were struggling was very important.

They always help me if I do something wrong or, if I can't do something, they would help.

(Sharon, Year 5, Greenmantle)

They just help me a lot. They are a bit brainier than me.

(Scott, Year 6, Kenwood)

Sometimes they help me when I am stuck. Other people, when you ask them a question, they just get on with their work.

(Harry, Year 5, St Bede's)

When you're stuck on a word and you ask them, they'll tell you. Other people don't tell you.

(Philip, Year 5, St Anne's)

They give you some of the answers.

(Malcolm, Year 5, St Anne's)

Bashir helps you when you're stuck. He spells a word. Wesley, he helps me more. He wouldn't tell me straight away. He tells me how to do it but that takes longer.

(Ian, Year 5, Meadway)

They help me. They're really good with their work. They help me with my answers.

(Shona, Year 5, Meadway)

He don't rush ahead. He just waits for you if you are being slow.

(Scott, Year 5, Kenwood)

They help me if I get stuck . . . they help me work my way to the answer. They don't tell me.

(Emma, Year 6, Audley)

There is a clear sense in the data of some pupils who were seen as 'kind' and generous with their help. Others like Jane, whose views on people who kept pestering her and stopped her 'getting on' we saw in the last chapter, gave help more reluctantly. The small percentage of pupils who mentioned liking to work with people who were at the same level were, in the main, high achievers.

> They are the same sort of standard as me. They know the same as me.
>
> (Ben, Year 6, Greenmantle)

> We all like the same things and we all have good imaginations. We all work hard.
>
> (Kate, Year 6, Greenmantle)

> 'Cause we're all like on the same sort of standard, so it's quite easy.
>
> (Brian, Year 5, Audley)

> They are the same – how can I put it? – intelligence. If we are stuck we can help each other sort it out rather than disturb the teacher.
>
> (Brian, Year 6, Audley)

> 'Cause we are all on the same book, about the same stage.
>
> (Maura, Year 6, Audley)

There is arguably a tension for pupils as well as for teachers between the values of 'mixed-ability' groups and grouping by attainment. All these pupils were used to being grouped by attainment, as we indicated in Chapter 8, and were presumably drawing on that experience as well as of undertaking tasks and activities in other curriculum areas. Although some pupils clearly had collaborative activity in mind when making their choices, many perceived 'working with' someone as sitting with them while working individually. In this connection there are signs of peer-dependence as an alternative or addition to teacher-dependence among low achievers. Many of these pupils experienced some anxiety when any of their peers to whom they looked for support were not available.

> In Maths we do it all together. We help one another. I'm worried that my friends aren't there. They might be away.
>
> (Jessica, Year 6, Kenwood)

> I'm more comfortable asking help from my friends.
>
> (Kevin, Year 6, Audley)

> 'Cause you do the first page, right, and then you got to do the second page on your own. Some people that's good, like Jenny and Martin, are fast workers and they help me.
>
> (Malcolm, Year 6, St Anne's)

> It's dead hard to make decisions what to do on your own.
>
> (Philip, Year 6, St Anne's)

Overall the responses suggest a learning-oriented attitude to working with peers. From the whole sample only four pupils in Year 5 and two in Year 6 (all girls) offered 'having a laugh' and 'having a chat' as the sole reason for choosing people to work with. As we have seen explanations were generally complex and where 'fun' was a criterion it was usually modified by more work-related factors. The example of Jeremy illustrates that many pupils seemed also to be accepting of their teachers' attempts to help them to work by removing them from distracting friends. In Year 5 his teacher moved him away from Steve onto a different table. When we interviewed him he was happy to nominate Ingrid as someone to work with:

> I was chatting a lot 'cause I used to sit next to Steve. Miss moved me onto Ingrid's table. We work together on our Maths, English and topic and all that. We help each other. When I work with Ingrid I get on with work a bit better.

A year later he chose Ingrid again.

> We've always been good at working. She doesn't talk too much and we can get on with work. (But she's a girl) She acts like a boy. Fits in well. Plays football and the same games as us. I like Ingrid as a friend and working with her.
>
> (Jeremy, Year 6, Kenwood)

Analysis of the responses by school reveals patterns which also suggest a similar teacher impact on the children's explanations. At Valley, Lawnside and Orchard, three small schools which had retained a more integrated and learner-centred approach to the curriculum, pupils offered more complex and sophisticated reasons related to group process. They were much more aware of qualities needed to be successful in collaborative work. At Audley and St Bede's the emphasis was more on being sensible and getting on with it. A third emphasis was discernible at Kenwood where we had the most references to pupils looking to give and receive help. In inner-city Meadway, by contrast, pupils were more concerned to get help than expecting to give it. There was also a tension between the urge to 'get the answers' and the desirability of 'working it out'. In this school there was also a reflection of the volatility of relationships in the classroom, of the need to stay away from people you got angry with, and of the flashpoint potential of borrowing equipment.

The evidence presented in this chapter so far confirms the importance of the social dimension of learning. In the next section we look more generally at pupils' positive and negative feelings about their experiences of classroom learning and discuss some of the attendant issues.

9.5 ISSUES IN PUPILS' FEELINGS ABOUT SCHOOL LEARNING

In Chapters 4 and 5 which dealt with pupils' perspectives on the curriculum we saw that fun and interest were the criteria most used to determine what activities and subjects they liked. Almost as frequently mentioned were activity and being able to succeed without too much difficulty. Interest was something the children in our sample felt but found hard to explain. Sometimes it was something they brought to school with them, but more frequently it was something they looked to their teachers to provide. The various meanings encoded in the word 'fun' are equally difficult to unpack. Pupils in the study used it to identify what they saw as opportunities for social activity, especially 'having a laugh'. They also linked it with activity and autonomy, and applied it to experiences which they enjoyed and where they were deeply engaged and evidently learning. Certainly as they grew older they were more aware of themselves as both learners and achievers. Our database of pupils' responses from Key Stage 2 provides a range of examples which we use to develop a picture of the classroom experiences children felt positive about.

> Topics are hard, but I like doing hard things.
>
> (Scott, Year 4, Kenwood)

> I enjoy imagining stories and writing them down so everyone can see.
>
> (Lucy, Year 4, Lawnside)

> I'm brilliant at Art. I just enjoy it and Mr X doesn't mind if we get it wrong, as long as we try.
>
> (Melanie, Year 5, St Anne's)

> I like finding out about things. I think it's fun when we do research.
>
> (Hugh, Year 5, Lawnside)

> I like using my imagination and with drama and dance workshop you've got plenty of space to move around in, and nobody cares what you do because everybody is doing their own thing.
>
> (Kate, Year 5, Greenmantle)

> I like copying it out and making it presentable (Handwriting).
>
> (Stella, Year 6, Valley)

> You can make things up, use your imagination (Writing stories). You don't get bored.
>
> (Celia, Year 6, Meadway)

> We're good because we put our ideas together from what we read – we don't argue (Reading comprehension).
>
> (Maura, Year 6, Audley)

> I like finding out about the History and what people do in other countries.
>
> (Richard, Year 6, Valley)

> I like sports like skittle ball. I don't think I'm particularly good at them; I just enjoy it, get excited.
>
> (Maura, Year 6, Audley)

From this representative selection we can construct a picture of the kind of learning these children found motivating. They responded to opportunities to be active and creative and to find things out, they liked to be challenged and to collaborate, they enjoyed feeling that they could get things wrong and it wouldn't matter, and they got satisfaction from a job well done, even if this involved routine and repetition, and from public acknowledgement of that.

There are in this description strong parallels with our findings reported in other chapters about the *demotivating* consequences of an overcrowded curriculum and of the pressure of high-stakes categoric assessment which led to a tighter, teacher-centred frame. Pupils frequently experienced very different learning situations from those described above. In particular, the pressure of time and the weight of curriculum content militated against autonomous, pupil-centred approaches and an emphasis on attainment created anxiety and a disinclination to take risks especially in relation to learning in the core curriculum.

To develop and exemplify this analysis we identify a number of issues: time pressure, ambiguity, uncertainty and risk, noise, talk and boredom which were consistently cited by pupils. As we examine what they said, we will see how these factors interacted to produce a context which for many pupils was unsympathetic to positive learning.

Time

After 1990, for teachers and pupils in primary schools, time assumed a significance far in excess of that in pre-National Curriculum classrooms. As the companion book to this demonstrates, teachers developed detailed plans for teaching the content of the new curriculum and felt constrained not to depart from these and risk failing to achieve complete coverage of what had been prescribed. The fact that this curriculum was accompanied by standardized assessments of the core subjects in Years 2 and 6 intensified this concern, especially when results began to be publicly reported. What was the effect of this on the pupils who were engaged in this curriculum?

We saw in Chapters 4, 5 and 6 evidence of children in Years 5 and 6 losing enthusiasm for core curriculum subjects and experiencing few, if any, opportunities for autonomy in their learning. We have also seen how often pupils generated criteria of speed and quantity when evaluating their work or their attainment. There is little question that for them, as for their teachers, the pressure of time was a very present feature of their learning experience. The requirement to 'get work done', 'get it finished' was strongly perceived, as were the risks associated with not keeping up.

> If I'm behind I have to catch up.
>
> (Tom, Year 3, Greenmantle)

> I'm dead slow.
>
> (Philip, Year 3, St Anne's)

> We only have half an hour. I can't get much done. Not three pages.
>
> (Haley, Year 4, St Bede's)

> It's hard to remember the story and there's not much time to finish it.
>
> (Kim, Year 5, St Bede's)

> I'm OK at it. It's just that it takes me a long time.
>
> (Mandy, Year 6, Audley)

They also felt they had little control over their learning even though there were clear expectations about what they would complete. As we will see in the next section, many pupils worried about what they had not done to the point of being distracted by thinking about unfinished work when they were supposed to be engaging with new learning. For others the pressure of time impacted on their view of ways of working.

> I got behind with Maths 'cause I was going out of class for lots of things. I was still on Week 1 in Week 7. Then one day I got a lot done 'cause the lady what we read to wa'n't in. So I caught up five weeks and I took it home for the rest.
>
> (Dawn, Year 5, Kenwood)

Sometimes you have loads of pieces of topic work and you get fifteen minutes to do them. Then you go straight to Maths for about an hour.

(Ewan, Year 6, Kenwood)

I don't like topic. We have to go in groups and people mess around and we don't have enough time.

(Kate, Year 6, Greenmantle)

One consequence of this was some pupils whose main concern with work was to get it over and done with as quickly as possible.

I wanted to finish my Science as quick as possible and do my Scottish Maths. I don't like Scottish Maths. I wanted to get it out of the way.

(Olivia, Year 3, Lawnside)

If it's not something I enjoy, then I'll rush on it.

(Sam, Year 5, St Bede's)

I like language because I do that quickly. And I normally get them all right as well. I'm really fast. I've finished most of the time.

(Jane, Year 6, Meadway)

My friends show me the correct answers. (Does that help you learn?) No, not really. It helps me get more work done, and it's quicker.

(Martin, Year 6, Lawnside)

This perception of the need for getting things finished and out of the way is an indicator of the growing instrumentality of these learners to which we pointed in Chapter 6. There is little evidence in the data of any deep engagement with learning. On the contrary, we find pupils who felt the tension between what had to be done and the amount of time they had to do it. They were in effect being prevented from thinking about what they had experienced, or were deliberately selecting only tasks and activities that could be accomplished in the time available. Two examples illustrate this.

Theresa in Year 6 described work in Science where they had in turn heated bread, banana, cheese and chocolate in a spoon over a candle. She had much enjoyed this. In fact, the investigation had so intrigued her that she tried it out again at home with her mother, using chocolate. When she was asked about it she said she thought it was to find out 'how many minutes it takes to toast things'. When prompted, however, she recalled that it was about 'temporary and permanent changes'. She thought they had done it because 'our teacher wanted us to listen. She wants it to help with our SATs. It might come up in the SATs – what temporary and permanent change means, what happened'. Even with this instrumental rationale, Theresa couldn't stop thinking about this experience, partly because it fascinated her and partly because she knew she had to write about it. She described what was in her mind as the teacher was talking to the whole class in another lesson. 'I was trying to keep it all in my memory – then I can write about it. But then she was doing something else, so it all got muddled.' Then later she was listening to a story and 'fiddling with plasticene'. As it went from hard to soft in the warmth of her hand she was 'thinking about changes' and lost the story.

Theresa attained Level 4 in Science and could probably have answered a question on temporary and permanent changes if one had come up. But her account suggests someone who was not given enough time to think about and really get control of this concept. The investigation was done, written up and the class moved on. An indication of her own sense that she had no more than a tenuous grasp of this learning is found in her own assessment of her achievement in Science. 'I don't know what I'm like in Science. I've had a few marks in my book saying "good", "excellent". I don't know what I'm like.'

The dilemmas created when time presses on curriculum and pedagogy are also illustrated by Sean, a high achiever at Greenmantle School, who explained in Year 5 why he had *not* taken advantage of the opportunity to choose an activity in Art, a subject he liked.

> I didn't choose a card in Art because they all looked really hard; because they were all done by proper artists and they were all done in like a year or something; but when we do it we have to do it in a term or less and we have less time to do it because we're in school and we have only an hour a week.

Sean's perception of the task his teacher had set as unrealistic and unachievable in any terms to which he might aspire raises questions about motivation and the nature of the learning experiences available where the curriculum is crowded and time is at a premium.

Ambiguity, uncertainty and risk

In contrast to Sean, Geoffrey was a low achiever. He attained Level 3 in all subjects. Comments he made over three years illustrate how awareness of time pressing made him all the more aware of what he couldn't do.

> I'm not quick enough. I never know what to write. I just sit there and I don't know what to do.
>
> (Geoffrey, Year 4, Orchard)

> I can't work out the sums in time. I don't understand them. Everyone else is getting on with their Maths and saying that it's easy.
>
> (Geoffrey, Year 5)

> I couldn't do it and I was really stuck. Everyone else had finished.
>
> (Geoffrey, Year 6)

The theme 'I don't know what to do' is a noticeable motif in the pupils' responses. For Geoffrey and other low achievers it signified a dreadful paralysis where all they could do was worry about the consequences. The risks in terms of failure and exposure were very present.

> I was doing this work in English. I didn't know what to do. I was worried if I got the questions wrong.
>
> (Ian, Year 5, Meadway)

Dawn, an average achiever, summed up the situation very neatly:

Some people are really good and they know what they are doing. Other people get really confused and they don't really know what they are doing. Some people can work hard but they still get confused and they don't really know what they are doing. Sometimes I listen but I don't always understand.

(Dawn, Year 6, Kenwood)

As Dawn suggested and other pupils confirmed, ambiguity and uncertainty can be experienced by any learner.

I only like Science when we're doing the activity. The writing up afterwards gets boring. Sometimes I don't know what to write. Nobody will help you. The teacher is doing something with another person. You're asking your friends and they're busy or they don't know either ...

(Rupert, Year 5, Lawnside)

In Maths I find it easy; I've just got on to the highest level. In Science I don't always understand what I have to do.

(Richard, Year 6, Valley)

I do work hard when I know what I'm meant to be doing. But I sometimes get stuck on knowing what I have to do.

(Lucy, Year 6, Lawnside)

I can never get into it. I can't understand what the teacher's saying properly.

(Kate, Year 6, Greenmantle)

Here is evidence of a failure of communication between teachers and learners, and between learners and tasks. The following illustrations show how some pupils, successful and less successful, had considerable understanding of themselves as learners.

I know things like how to do things in the book. But I get stuck on things and it takes me quite a bit, even after Mrs W has explained it to me, to understand them. I always judge my work on how I understand it. And how many I get right. When I've finished I think well, I've worked really hard at it and it looks really good. But you can like your work but not understand something very well. It's really just the way you understand things.

(Lucy, Year 6, Lawnside)

I just don't concentrate enough. I don't listen. I just feel I don't know how to do it. I try my hardest and every time it's like I ... it adds up to a billion or it's full totally wrong. (What do you do?) I start again. My friends help. I don't ask the teacher 'cause I feel I can do it. I keep on trying. I feel I can do it and I just leave it sometimes. And I mark it and I know I've just got to do it again.

(Hugh, Year 6, Lawnside)

I enjoy hard work. It's just that I didn't understand this English. I'm on Level 7, Book 3 and the higher the book the harder it gets. If I understand it I can do it. If you don't understand it you don't know what to do. If I stuck at it and took it home and practised, I think I could get a go of it. In class I was miles away. I go miles away and then I just can't remember where I was or anything. I can't remember the daydream ... It takes me a long time to get through English, longer than normal. Say I had a 20-card sheet for Maths, I'd get through that in ten minutes. In English I'd get through that in about an hour. See what I mean? ... I really enjoy Maths. I don't daydream in Maths ... On the computer Miss said 'I want to see you make any shape tessellate'. To start off I did squares, which is pretty straightforward. (Why do that?) To get used to it I think, rather than jumping in the deep end. (Were you worried you might not manage it?) No. I always like a good lot of venture into different things.

(Brian, Year 6, Audley)

Sometimes there's easy parts. Sometimes when it's a bit harder I'm not sure what to do. In reading there's big words and I'm not sure what to do, and I ask Sir and he says 'You can work it out. You know what to do' ... I know what I'm doing in Art ... Reading, I'm not as good as the others. They go reading to the small kids. We do reading in class. They work hard and don't give up. They keep going until they can do what they can do and what they can't – if they like it. I like copying, you don't have to use your brain so much but I prefer writing out of my head – what I really think. Mr F wants us to get on without fussing. (Do you fuss?) When it's a bit too hard, like History when there's questions and he don't help you. Sometimes it'd be pretty hard and you need some help if you're not sure what to do.

(Ian, Year 6, Meadway)

These extracts are not chosen to demonstrate a typology but rather to show how *individual* these pupils were. Although some of them exhibit similar characteristics, the combination for each is unique. Lucy's statement negotiates between performance and understanding; Hugh, having identified his faults, still maintained a faith in trying and a reluctance to seek help; Brian, faced with a challenge in English slipped into daydream and looked to home as the place where, with practice, he might 'get it'. In Maths, though, he was by no means averse to risk-taking. Ian, very teacher-dependent when things got hard, comparing himself unfavourably with others in reading and looking for the easy way out in writing, nevertheless asserted that he knew what he was doing in Art.

Noise

Noise, or more specifically, other pupils shouting, arguing, laughing or just chatting, was an issue for a large number of children. It was an issue which revolved around 'concentration' and concerned, in the main, pupils' ability or otherwise to ignore other people's conversations or to avoid being drawn into them. The overlap with conditions of uncertainty and risk were evident in the data in that many pupils mentioned noise and chatting in association with moments when they felt unsure about their work. At this point they became more aware of the noise around them and more prone to joining in the chat. Pupils from all levels of achievement mentioned this sort of noise but it appeared more frequently in the responses of low achievers as an explanation for their 'problems' with the work. We discuss distraction more fully in the next section, but some examples here illustrate the analysis so far and open up the area.

People keep talking and I can't concentrate. I hardly do anything.

(Geoffrey, Year 4, Orchard)

Sometimes I get distracted if someone's shouting or there's noise in the class or people talking on other tables. My friend opposite shouts quite a lot. It happens quite a lot of times.

> (Haley, Year 5, St Bede's)

The boys on my table were talking about films they saw last night. It just makes me lose concentration ... It's mostly when I'm doing Maths ... I love Maths to bits but I really lose concentration 'cause it's really hard and I start to worry and I work fast and get in a muddle.

> (Rosie, Year 5, Lawnside)

This morning my mind never wandered because it was silent and I could concentrate on what I'm doing. Sometimes when you're doing cutting out or sticking it gets a bit noisy. You start talking to the person next to you, your mind goes off the work and you get it wrong. When it's quiet you can focus on what you're doing.

> (Wesley, Year 5, Meadway)

I'm thinking about all my other work I'm behind on. I try to concentrate and get it done but sometimes people talk to me and I get distracted. I don't normally have trouble concentrating.

> (Kim, Year 6, St Bede's)

I get aerated about people talking and bugging me. I get distracted. Whenever someone comes to my table my mind makes me do it and I wish they would be quiet. Like Felix and Dean come up to you and ask you things and Felix shouts out when Mr X asks a question.

> (Eliot, Year 6, St Bede's)

Noise distracts me.

> (Harry, Year 6, St Bede's)

Kim's contribution indicates that again pressure of time is associated with anxiety and distraction.

Boredom

In previous analyses we have indicated the challenge to the researcher in decoding the various meanings that pupils appear to have invested in this word. Pupils in this study made a consistent association between effort and enjoyment. Conversely they explained lack of effort by invoking boredom. Some pupils who claimed to be 'bored' were using the term to identify moments of uncertainty when they felt at risk. Others, in particular high achievers, used it to describe moments when they felt distinctly understimulated. For example, Ben mentioned feeling bored from Year 4 onwards.

> I try to think of something else as much as I can. Otherwise it's pretty boring.
> > (Ben, Year 4, Greenmantle)

> When it's so boring I don't think of anything. I just stare out of the window, forgetting everything.
> > (Ben, Year 5, Greenmantle)

> I fiddle with something because things are harder and then you get distracted. But also if things are too easy.
>
> (Ben, Year 6, Greenmantle)

Kate, another high achiever, also described retreating into daydreaming when things got uninteresting or ambiguous and noisy.

> Sometimes when I don't try it's boredom. Sometimes we have a whole load of worksheets and I don't understand what they are trying to get me to do and because there are a whole load of people asking I just sit there and daydream and play with bits of paper.
>
> (Kate, Year 5, Greenmantle)

The pressure on curriculum content and assessment also affected the kind of tasks pupils were given. We have already noted pupils' perception in Year 6 that a large proportion of their teachers' intentions for activity were to do with practice. In addition the shift from more open-ended tasks to exercises from schemes seems to have been demotivating for some or accepted with weary resignation.

> (A Maths test sheet) You had a graph and you had the information and you had to find out the cost of something ... Then you had to draw a parallelogram. Well, it gives you practice so you know what's coming. I don't really enjoy it though, but you know you have to do it to help you understand it.
>
> (Harriet, Year 6, Valley)

> We were working from a book and we had to write sentences and there was missing words and we had to find the right ones. Sometimes it's a bit boring. Sometimes it's dead hard and you're sitting there and you can't do it.
>
> (Jacquie, Year 5, St Anne's)

Kim's changing attitude to literacy activity over the period of the project focuses this issue.

> I did the picture then I have to do the writing. I liked doing the picture. I don't like the writing very much. It's difficult to write the letters.
>
> (Kim, Year 1, St Bede's)

> I made up a story with Alistair and Jason. I liked it a little bit because it was a funny story when they read it out.
>
> (Kim, Year 2, St Bede's)

> (Letter-writing related to story read aloud in class) We had to write to a lady – I forgot her name – about how Sophie got up to the Highlands. I liked it. It was fun.
>
> (Kim, Year 3, St Bede's)

> (Junior English Book 3) They asked you questions and you had to finish the sentences. Put in the missing words. I didn't like that much. It was a bit boring.
>
> (Kim, Year 4, St Bede's)

> We had to write sentences and change the word 'said' in every sentence to a different word. It was OK. There was a part where you had to write the whole thing out. I didn't like that. I didn't mind changing the words.
>
> (Kim, Year 6, St Bede's)

In the negative nexus created by pressure of time, feelings of uncertainty and risk, and reaction to activity perceived as uninteresting, pupils developed defensive responses. These, as we have seen, included daydreaming, having a chat or, our observations record, 'making trouble'. We pursue these ideas further in the conclusion to this chapter and in Chapters 11 and 13. However, first we consider what pupils' accounts of positive learning experiences in the core curriculum can tell us about motivation. We start with learning in the classroom and then look at the role home plays in learning.

Enjoyment

In opposition to the overall trend, the database does provide examples of very positive enjoyment of learning in Maths, English and Science. It should be noted, though, that as some of the quotations make clear, such enjoyment was seen in relation to unusual rather than routine activities.

> There was shapes and we had to say if it was a hexagon or a pentagon or one of them. Write it out and colour it in, two hexagons the same colour, two squares the same colour. That was all right. It wasn't boring like it usually is. Sometimes we have pages of long division. Sometimes it's like 10.45 to 12.30 just doing long division. Today it was testing to see what I'd learned so far ... I remember when I didn't know any of these shapes.
>
> (Wesley, Year 5, Meadway)

> We had to find out about woodpeckers ... I liked it, it's not one of my favourite pieces of work, but I like finding out about them.
>
> (Sam, Year 5, St Bede's)

> It was doing 90 degrees and circles and things like that. We done two circles, one big and one little one, and slit it down and just turned it to see if all these angles were 90 degrees. There was like a triangle and if it fit in, it was 90 degrees. I likes doing it. It was unusual like. Usually you just sit there doing Maths.
>
> (Susie, Year 5, St Anne's)

> We had a body and took the insides out and we had to put it back together and talk about it. It was fun and it was better than just being told about it.
>
> (Juliet, Year 6, Greenmantle)

> We were going though the mud and different insects and we chose one and looked at it through a magnifying glass and wrote about it in our Science book. It was good because we were allowed to go out to find insects.
>
> (Sam, Year 6, St Bede's)

> A personal topic. We have to find out information from home and from school and then we make a book out of it and draw pictures and diagrams of what we have found. I like finding out information and writing it down.
>
> (Stella, Year 6, Valley)

> (Maths activity with shape) We had to cut all three shapes out and then make a repeating pattern. On the last one I used a mirror image. I liked using the mirror, it was fun. Mrs X set me a challenge and I tried to do it.
>
> (Richard, Year 6, Valley)

We have here yet more support for the analysis presented earlier in this section and in previous chapters of the motivational effect of investigative and practical activities. There is also in some of these short extracts a sense of learners appropriating new knowledge with a feeling of pleasure and some surprise. Furthermore, there is a sense of an earlier point in learning where progress is good and achievement and understanding are accumulating. Pupils perceived that investigative and practical activities, which most liked, occurred less frequently than those that required sitting, listening, writing and recording, which most of them disliked. However, in talking of learning at home, children mentioned both being active and engaging in routine 'bookwork'. The emotional temperature of their accounts is very different from their references to classroom learning.

Learning at home

Although we did not specifically enquire about the degree of learning support offered by parents or other family members, children regularly volunteered such information. As we saw in Chapter 7 families were intimately involved in the way many pupils assessed their abilities. The examples with which we start this section are from homes across the whole socio-economic range of our sample and communicate a sense of families who were directly supporting and encouraging children's learning:

> My dad teaches me at night and he gives me 200 sums to do in half an hour.
>
> > (Melanie, Year 3, St Anne's)

> My dad's a steward on an aeroplane and we go on lots of vacations.
>
> > (Simon, Year 4, Valley)

> 'Cause when I was about five my dad told me all about History – about Henry VIII and Elizabeth I.
>
> > (Jacquie, Year 4, St Anne's)

> My mum does sums with me.
>
> > (Dawn, Year 4, Kenwood)

> It's things I've heard about before from my family or on TV.
>
> > (Sharon, Year 5, Greenmantle)

> My dad teaches me things. He's quite clever. I'm a fast learner, same as my dad.
>
> > (Eliot, Year 5, St Bede's)

> My dad does Art with me at home. He helped me do a picture and it was displayed.
>
> > (Kelly, Year 5, Orchard)

> I've got books at home. My mum got them for me. I brought some in.
>
> > (Brian, Year 6, Audley)

> I'm probably learning it from my parents. Mum's quite good at Art. Dad helps me out with wood and making things.
>
> > (Hugh, Year 6, Lawnside)

I do a lot of reading at home. My mum gets me all these books.

(Jane, Year 6, Meadway)

We learn about forces in Science and I repeat it to my mum and dad and they say it's right. Mum says I'm good at Maths.

(Tom, Year 6, Greenmantle)

We have included here no more than one illustrative response from any child. However, for many of the children references to home and family featured prominently as they talked about learning. In particular, what they learned at home about subjects and about themselves had an effect on their attitude to the curriculum as well as their view of themselves as learners and achievers. Their comments reflect the encouragement of individual or shared interests which promoted liking. Indeed, when children connected being good at something with liking it, their explanations frequently included references to doing it at home; divisions between home and school, and work and play dissolved, as in these examples:

At home I've got loads of modelling things and I make stuff out of them like islands and boats – out of papier-mâché and pipe cleaners.

(Tom, Year 3, Greenmantle)

I normally make up stories at home. I wrote some for my baby sister to read.

(Dawn, Year 3, Kenwood)

I spend a lot of time at home thinking about that sort of work.

(Ben, Year 4, Greenmantle)

I go down the park to play football and practise every night. I do drawing at home when I'm getting bored.

(Hugh, Year 5, Lawnside)

I had lots of books when I was little and I used to write them out. Now I just keep on writing.

(Haley, Year 6, St Bede's)

I go to a tutor for Maths and English – it's not because of that, though; I do it all the time and I like it.

(Olivia, Year 5, Lawnside 5)

There is a genuine sense of motivation and engagement here. However, we cannot find any clear association between this and the outcomes of the core curriculum assessment at the end of Key Stage 2. The children we have quoted attained across the range of Levels 3–5.

Of course the connections children were making between home activity and school attainment were not always in the core curriculum subjects. Attainment aside, there is here a sense of two kinds of learning, different in quality and not always accorded equal status in school. There is also, of course, the issue that all children did not have equal access to this kind of support and interest from home. Our study in general found little evidence of polarization in children's attitude to each other. However, where it did appear to some extent was in some children's explanations of why some people do better at school than others, where the perceived advantages that some children had at home were mentioned.

In summary, this section has looked at what children said they liked and disliked about the processes of learning and identified significant factors and issues. In general they were motivated by interest, activity, challenge, success and the feeling that they were free to fail, by satisfaction in what they had produced and the acknowledgement of their achievement. Many also reported a variety of learning experiences at home. We have argued that the effect of the National Curriculum and its assessment on teachers and pupils was to focus a number of issues in relation to learning. The pressure on time resulted in many pupils placing more emphasis on performance in the form of work completed than on understanding. In addition 'getting things done' was perceived as more important than producing work that was personally satisfying. As we have seen in previous chapters, time pressure also had the effect of placing learning firmly in the domain of the teachers, who were perceived to be in possession of what had to be learned. Hence, in particular, low achievers became more teacher-dependent and most children felt that it was wise to let teachers control learning or 'we won't know what to do' and 'if you did it yourself you'd go wrong'. Boredom with routine and repetitive tasks of little intrinsic interest, and with lack of challenge, was felt by some pupils. However, when they were unable to cope with challenge, pupils' feelings of uncertainty and exposure to risk produced paralysis or evasion in the form of daydreaming or other distracting activity. Distraction is a significant feature of any learning situation and was a factor which we included in our systematic observation. We probed and developed the issue by asking pupils about when and why they were distracted and what they were thinking about. It is these data which we consider in the next section.

9.6 PUPILS' EXPLANATIONS FOR BEING DISTRACTED

One strand of the PACE research involved systematic observation of teachers and pupils in the classroom. Among other things, we monitored when the children were task-engaged and when they were distracted. The analysis of these data is contained in Chapter 3 where we show that levels of distraction remained relatively stable over the six years of the study with a low of just less than 18 per cent in Year 6 (Table 3.8). Girls, pupils with high peer status, high achievers and those from non-manual backgrounds were less likely to be distracted than other categories of children. The factor most strongly related to levels of distraction was attainment, but even here there was considerable variation, accounted for in the main by gender. For example, for pupils who attained Level 5 at the end of Key Stage 2, the range of average task engagement was from 44 per cent to 77 per cent and for distraction from 8 per cent to 30 per cent. Our analysis also shows low attaining pupils with average levels of task engagement of over 70 per cent. These were the ones who kept their heads down and avoided notice by appearing to be engaged in the task.

As this last comment illustrates, measuring distraction has its problems. For observers it is a category with high inference. Frequently judgements had to be made about whether a pupil apparently gazing into space was listening and thinking about the lesson or mentally miles away. So in the third year of the study we decided to explore more fully with the children their experience of being distracted from a task.

With reference to an observed activity we asked 'When you are working at something like that, and you seem to be concentrating, are you really thinking about other things?'. Wherever possible we discussed with the children specific times when in our observation we had judged they were 'distracted'. We probed the children's responses by asking them to give us other examples of when they were distracted from the task and what sorts of things they were thinking about. The children's answers were open, honest and reflective and provided interesting insights into their sense of themselves as learners. The question was retained each year for the rest of the study.

Overwhelmingly the children admitted to being distracted at least some of the time, as shown in Table 9.5.

Table 9.5 When you seem to be concentrating are you sometimes really thinking about other things? (percentages)

	Year 3	Year 4	Year 5	Year 6
Yes	85	91	91	81
No	13	9	7	13
No answer	2	0	2	6

Source: PACE 2 and 3 child interviews
Sample: 54 pupils in each of Years 3–6
Date: Summer 1993, 1994, 1995 and 1996

We were also interested in what they were thinking about and when and why they became distracted.

Table 9.6 What the children said they were thinking about when they were distracted (percentages)

	Year 3	Year 4	Year 5	Year 6
After school/family	38	44	47	36
Other work/work	19	13	6	20
Daydreaming	10	7	10	5
Playtime/friends	8	16	5	7
'Other things'	5	5	8	7
No answer	20	15	24	25

Source: PACE 2 and 3 child interviews
Sample: 54 pupils in each of Years 3–6
Date: Summer 1993, 1994, 1995 and 1996

Clearly there is a consistent proportion of children, some two-fifths, acknowledging being regularly distracted by thoughts about after-school activities or family issues. There is also steady reference to 'daydreaming' and thinking about playtime and friends. However, we can also see here further and more concrete evidence of an interesting trend we identified in the previous section; that is, the relatively high proportion of pupils who reported being distracted because they were thinking about other work. Sometimes it was about things they would rather be doing:

> I want to play on the computer.
>
> (Philip, Year 3, St Anne's)

> I was thinking about the story of Thor and the giants. Sometimes when I do Maths I think about the Vikings.
>
> (Polly, Year 3, Valley)

> I'm thinking about playing with the Technology trolley. You make things.
>
> (Malcolm, Year 4, St Anne's)

> Sometimes in the Maths group I think about swimming. I'm in the top group.
>
> (Jacquie, Year 5, St Anne's)

> I wish I was doing Maths or something I enjoy. If I'm doing things I enjoy I don't think of other things.
>
> (Haley, Year 6, St Bede's)

In this case we have a group of low achievers all escaping from uncertainty by thinking about more congenial and less demanding learning activities. Sometimes it was about things that had interested, puzzled or intrigued them in work they had done earlier, or even things that had occurred in the task they were engaged on, which they were thinking about rather than keeping up with the teacher's plan for the lesson. Neil, like Theresa whose experience we recounted in the previous section, was also fascinated by the Science investigation involving heating substances in a spoon over a candle.

> I was thinking about what was going to happen next with the investigation and thinking about the stuff we'd had in the spoon.
>
> (Neil, Year 6, Audley)

> When I'm doing my Maths I'm thinking about my weather vane. I wanted to get on with it.
>
> (Harriet, Year 3, Valley)

> I was thinking about History – about the plague.
>
> (Kevin, Year 4, Audley)

More frequently their distraction was associated with anxiety or a kind of panic that militates against concentration.

> I think about what we'll do next. I might not be able to do it and I might get told off.
> (Dawn, Year 3, Kenwood)

> I'm worrying what I'm going to do on Geography next, or Science, or Longman. I worry that people are getting past me.
>
> (Neil, Year 4, Audley)

> I'm doing my topic and I think about Science. I do my Science and I think about Maths.
> (Dawn, Year 5, Kenwood)

> I think about all my other work that I'm behind on.
>
> (Kim, Year 6, St Bede's)

I'm thinking about other work that I have to finish by next day.

(Samantha, Year 6, St Bede's)

There is a connection to be made between children's accounts of thinking about other work and what they told us about when and why they get distracted from the task in hand.

Table 9.7 Children's reasons for being distracted (percentages)

	Year 3	Year 4	Year 5	Year 6
Boring/hard	13	8	23	26
Other children	4	2	17	9
Chatting	4	7	8	10
Time of day	9	7	8	2
No answer	70	76	44	53

Source: PACE 2 and 3 child interviews
Sample: 54 pupils in each of Years 3–6
Date: Summer 1993, 1994 1995 and 1996

The most frequently mentioned reason for 'thinking of other things', as we saw in the previous section, was when work was too hard or there was a high risk of failing.

When I'm stuck I want to go onto something else.

(Juliet, Year 3, Greenmantle)

When there's something really, really hard and I think Miss will rip it out, sometimes I think of other things when I'm working.

(Amanda, Year 3, Kenwood)

When you are thinking you have lots of good ideas, but they disappear when you try to write them down and so you start thinking of other things. But eventually I come back to it some way or another.

(Harriet, Year 5, Valley)

Sometimes when I'm doing Maths, if I don't want to do it I just think about Manchester United.

(Scott, Year 6, Kenwood)

If I concentrate on what I'm doing I usually end up going wrong so I think about other things.

(Eliot, Year 6, St Bede's)

Again, these are all low achievers except Harriet who, as her comment shows, is experiencing only a temporary distraction and is quite in control.

As we saw in Chapter 7 (Table 7.6), pupils were particularly aware of their shortcomings in relation to effort in Year 6. Their explanations for lack of effort pick up on the issues of boredom raised in the last section and show how this leads to distraction and lack of concentration.

I get mixed up in things. I can't concentrate in Science 'cause I'm not very good at experimenting and writing results and things.

(Rosie, Year 5, Lawnside)

When something is boring I don't pay attention and I get things wrong.

(Jane, Year 5, Meadway)

I can't work it out and my mind wanders.

(Juliet, Year 6, Greenmantle)

Sometimes I find it really boring and I start playing with things.

(Theresa, Year 6, St Anne's)

Because of all the copying – when I copy I get bored and my work gets untidy.

(Kyle, Year 6, Meadway)

I can't keep up – you have to write lots. You don't have to work anything out – just copy things. I can't stop chatting.

(Celia, Year 6, Meadway)

Sometimes you just don't listen to instructions and then you are worried. Sometimes he tells you and then he goes over it again but you're still not listening and the teacher says 'Why aren't you listening?' and you've got to say 'I was talking to someone'. And you get told off.

(Sam, Year 5, St Bede's)

It is clear that distraction is closely bound up with the issues we raised in the previous section – time pressure; ambiguity, uncertainty and risk in relation to tasks; noise and talk that undermines concentration; and boredom caused by activities that were deemed uninteresting. However, it also has links with the first section of this chapter where we looked at what made pupils worried about work. In particular, we can see that distraction is sometimes the result of worry about falling behind or having to hurry. In this sense, it is again a product of the pressure of time. Ironically, distraction also often arises when pupils are worried about their personal lack of motivation (not listening because they are bored, chatting or dreaming). Worrying about work products which might not meet teacher expectations is itself distracting.

9.7 CONCLUSION

In the examples quoted in this chapter, and through similar responses elsewhere in our data, the pupils identified a range of factors which contribute to their feelings about how they learn. For all learners, the *pressure of time* had a significant impact and this is notable in relation to this recognized period of 'curriculum overload' (Dearing, 1993). Other key motivational issues were the perceived boredom or interest of content and task; the degree of clarity or ambiguity of the task (not understanding what they had to do or why they were doing it); having insufficient skills to tackle the task assigned; and having insufficient conceptual grasp of the subject so that it was deemed 'too hard'. Many pupils described the interaction of difficulty, lack of interest, low motivation and variable effort which produced a downward spiral of morale and attainment. In this, the impact of time pressure, uncertainty and risk played a large part.

Many children in discussing their learning accepted responsibility for not doing well in some things. There were, however, some children who offered defensive explanations for their lack of success. In the following examples the children convey a sense of how exposed they felt when they were faced with something they found difficult and which they feared they could not cope with. To protect themselves they placed responsibility elsewhere – with their teachers, their families or their genes.

> I'm not good at writing journals when things are on my mind or sometimes I have a headache 'cause I can't sleep at night. I think I'm going to get them wrong.
>
> (Ewan, Year 3, Kenwood)

> If you have to read something hard, sometimes people are too busy to help. Mrs X helps with the bit you are really stuck on and not the rest.
>
> (Stella, Year 3, Valley)

> Mrs G writes on the board. I don't understand it. In lots of different subjects that happens. She writes all funny. It's all joined-up writing and I can't read it.
>
> (Carol, Year 5, Orchard)

> Science – I don't learn a lot outside school. Some people do.
>
> (Gavin, Year 5, Orchard)

> I'm no good at Geography because me dad didn't tell me nothing about it.
>
> (Jacquie, Year 5, St Anne's)

> We had this teacher, I didn't know her. She was quite strict and I didn't know her at all and we had a (mental) Maths test and she rushed through and in the end I didn't get many right at all. I was really worried and she shouted at us. I was really, really worried about what she was going to say to me. It was my most worried ever. She was a very strict woman. I thought she might have sent me to the headmaster.
>
> (Rosie, Year 5, Lawnside)

> I don't know much about it because I haven't been taught much. I hold my pen funny, that's why my writing is a problem.
>
> (Tom, Year 6, Greenmantle)

> English, I hate English. Last time I did a mock SAT I got all worked up.
>
> (Jeremy, Year 6, Kenwood)

> Spelling – when I try hard enough I can do it, but sometimes I can't even when I try.
>
> (Melanie, Year 6, St Anne's)

Such answers were at the extreme end of a continuum from 'confidence' to 'anxiety' but they suggest that pupils who saw themselves as 'not doing well' experienced a good deal of uncertainty, frustration and tension.

What is interesting in this context is the very different ways pupils in the study coped with uncertainty, ambiguity and risk, the strategies they adopted, the dispositions they developed and the identities they were constructing of themselves as learners. The case-studies in Chapter 11 provide examples of pupils engaged in this process and Chapter 13 looks in some detail at more theoretical issues in the development of identity and disposition in connection with learning. However, we will first examine one more area of pupil experience – pupils' responses to the experience of standardized assessment.

Chapter 10

Pupil Perspectives on Standardized Assessment

10.1 Introduction
10.2 Pupil perceptions of the significance of SATs
10.3 Taking the tests
10.4 The experiences of high and low attainers
10.5 Conclusion

10.1 INTRODUCTION

In 1992, at the end of our cohort's Key Stage 1, teachers had gone to great lengths to protect the children from the knowledge that they were being assessed. Testing was presented as normal curriculum activity and kept as low-key as possible (Pollard *et al.*, 1994). However, by the end of their Key Stage 2, our data show that testing was entirely overt and explicit. Moreover, it was so high-profile that other features of the assessment process such as Teacher Assessment had come to assume secondary significance. In this chapter, we focus on the pupils' experience of the Key Stage 2 SATs.

Our investigation revealed many structuring effects of this high-stakes form of assessment particularly, but not exclusively, in relation to Year 6. Teachers reported their growing awareness of the SATs throughout Year 5 and 6, but by the Easter of Year 6 all schools in the study reported careful revision activities, particularly in relation to Science content, and most schools gave pupils experience of previous SATs tests. As well as checking that they had covered the curriculum, teachers wanted to familiarize children with test conditions and techniques: working in silence and with time limits, leaving time for checking, moving on if you get stuck, showing your working, etc. The degree to which the children were aware of advance preparation for the week of Key Stage 2 tests varied from school to school. In some they felt they had been practising a lot and were very conscious of revisiting work they had done in Years 4 and 5; elsewhere they had done a few tests in the weeks immediately before SATs week.

To gain some insight into the experience of the tests themselves, in each of our nine study schools we observed a Year 6 class taking Key Stage 2 tests. Additionally, in each school we interviewed our six target children and six others, including where possible those who had taken part in the previous Key Stage 1 SATs study. The aim was to achieve a range of attainment and an equal mix of boys and girls. In all we carried out 103 of these interviews. Every Year 6 child within our study schools was invited to fill in 'speech' and 'thinks' bubbles in a SATs story comic strip (see Appendix 2 for an example). A total of 223 completed comic strips were collected and analysed. We hoped by this combination of data-gathering to gain access to the children's perceptions of and feelings about their experiences during this period.

In this chapter we begin by reporting children's understanding of what the SATs were for. We then move on to the process and experiences of actually taking the tests. As at Key Stage 1, the Year 6 teachers sought to mediate the external requirements and to make them more palatable for their class, but we particularly focus on differences in the experiences of high and low attainers.

The SAT performance of children in English, Mathematics and Science is cited in this chapter in terms of 'level', e.g. Sally, 3, 4, 4. 'A' denotes absence from the test, and 'N' indicates that taking the test was not judged appropriate, usually because the pupil had some form of special educational need. The target for our Year 6 11-year-olds in each subject was Level 4. Level 2 was a target for 7-year-olds. Level 6 is a projection for 14-year-olds.

10.2 PUPIL PERCEPTIONS OF THE SIGNIFICANCE OF SATs

What views did pupils have on the purposes of the tests? How did they make sense of them? At different points in the interviews in the week of the tests we asked the children 'Does it matter what results you get?' and 'Do you know why your teacher asked you to take the tests?'.

By far the most common answers concerned the use of SATs to inform secondary schools about the children before they 'went up' the following year, and national evidence of performance by pupils and teachers for 'the government'. However, another major theme was the consequence of the assessments in terms of social identity. Children were aware that the 'results' were categoric and public. They were concerned that they should not feel humiliated by them, and were aware of the 'high-stakes' meaning of the assessments for significant others such as parents and peers.

Secondary school transfer

Many children thought the tests mattered because the results controlled access to another school, and thus to their futures. In Meadway this anxiety was particularly intensified by the presence in their class of a girl who, unusually, was repeating Year 6. For Wayne and Kyle this signalled a possibility that they found very worrying.

> Yes, it matters 'cause if you fail in all of them you have to stay back a year.
>
> (Wayne, Meadway, N, 3, 3)

> Yes. I want to do well so I can get good marks to go to high school so I won't stay behind a year – sometimes you have to.
>
> (Kyle, Meadway, 2, 2, 3)

Shona, at the same school, also saw the tests as a hurdle:

> People that marked the tests say if you can go to your next school. I don't know who they are. They take them away and mark them. They tell the score. If you got no marks you can't go where you want to.
>
> (Shona, Meadway, 3, 3, 3)

Low attainers at other schools had much the same concerns:

> You might not get into the seniors to get as good education.
>
> (Barry, St Anne's 3, 2, 3)

> I was worried. I thought I wasn't going to pass or I'd get told off and that they wouldn't take me at another school.
>
> (John, Kenwood, 2, 2, A)

Having older siblings in secondary school or parents informed about education gave some other children a more relaxed and confident attitude. This was much more evident in schools serving a high socio-economic status catchment area such as Greenmantle.

> No. It doesn't matter. I'm going to Rodney High School anyway. It doesn't determine a place.
>
> (Esther, Greenmantle, 4, 3, 4)

> Well Rodney's already done and we'll be judged on what we do next year – so I'm not sure if it matters really.
>
> (Roy, Greenmantle, 3, 4, 4)

A majority of children, however, believed the tests mattered because the schools they were going to would use the results to make decisions about which groups or sets they would be placed in. For instance, many high attainers took the SATs seriously because they wanted their new schools to get an accurate impression of them:

> If you say I can't be bothered and just write any old thing and you're, like, clever, your school will think 'Oh, I'll just put him in the bottom group' and you think 'Why am I in this group with all the … ?'.
>
> (George, Lawnside, 5, 4, 5)

> If you don't do well the next school won't think you are good at some things when you really are.
>
> (Bianca, Orchard, 5, 5, 5)

> You can't do really bad so they put you in a lower group and the work might be too easy.
>
> (Angela, Orchard, 5, 5, 5)

There was a general expectation that there would be 'setting' in secondary school, and children were already seeing possible future identities:

I'd prefer to be in the top class than in the dunces' class.

(Julian, St Anne's, 4, 4, 4)

I'd be sad because with the bottom they'll treat me differently to the middle and high – some might say you're rubbish at everything and that would make you upset.

(Ned, Lawnside, 4, 4, 3)

Others just wanted to be in the 'right class'. Most notable, though, was the number of children who had inferred a logic for the testing process that was based firmly on ideas of progression in learning. Tests mattered because it would enable secondary schools to:

... find out how good we are ... see if we need to learn more in some subjects.

(Jeff, Orchard, 4, 4, 3)

... see what you've learned, how much you've learned, know what to teach you.

(Adrian, St Bede's, 3, 3, 4)

... see what standards we're at in our work so ... they know what work we could do and what we're not so good at.

(Jane, Meadway, 5, 5, 4)

... have an idea of what you can cope with, what they can expect from you to show your teachers, people in charge of teaching and stuff. What you can do and what you can't so they know where to put you. We did SATs in the first school 'cos we were going to a new school. They was simple.

(Corrinne, Meadway, 4, 4, 3)

Those with insider knowledge, however, had a sceptical, and arguably more realistic, view of progression:

It matters a bit in the high school but my brother says in the first year they give everyone Level 3 work anyway.

(Brian, Audley, 4, 5, 5)

It gives the secondary school an idea but they don't use it to put you in sets, they wait and see.

(Josephine, Lawnside, 4, 5, 4)

Accountability to government

Coming across almost as strongly as the link with secondary transfer was the sense that the children associated the tests with measurement, accountability and the provision of 'national' evidence.

They are to judge what we have done ... and to prove that we have done everything.

(Sean, Greenmantle, 4, 5, 5)

It's not our teachers it's the government. Everyone in England does them.

(Corrinne, Meadway, 4, 4, 3)

The teachers didn't decide – the government or someone did. To see how much we've learned in years gone by, taken into our brains.

(Rosie, Lawnside, 3, 4, 3)

Some children were very aware of the role of the government in the testing system and suggested that teachers were being tested along with, or even rather than, pupils.

To show the government or someone like that that the teachers have been teaching us well.

(Amanda, Kenwood, 4, 3, 4)

This view that SATs were also assessing teaching appeared to have been made explicit by some teachers such as Mrs Wright at Lawnside.

She said it was to show how well they'd been teaching us. Lots of people think it will go off to senior school. I think it's to show how we've progressed.

(Sandra, Lawnside, 3, 4, 4)

Everyone has to do them – everyone who goes to school. The National Curriculum and the government make you do them. It doesn't matter to me, but it definitely matters to the teachers 'cos it shows how much she's taught us. It's more important for her.

(William, Lawnside, 4, 4, 3)

Just like an assessment. To see how well Mrs W has taught us.

(Josephine, Lawnside, 4, 5, 4)

They have to know how much you've learned since you've been at this school and they want to know what your teachers taught you.

(Lucy, Lawnside, 4, 4, 4)

Sometimes understanding was the result of individual curiosity.

It's so the government could see if the teachers are teaching right. I asked my mum what they were for.

(Barry, St Bede's, 3, 3, 2)

I asked Mrs N (headteacher), she said the government made them up.

(Ibrahim, Meadway, 3, 3, 3)

Even when not expressed as explicitly as in the examples above, the themes of accountability and national measurement were present in data from over 80 per cent of pupils. All the children at Orchard, for instance, mentioned that the tests were national, that all schools had to do them, and that everyone was doing the same – although they could not explain why.

Categoric assessment and differentiation

Two-thirds of the children interviewed were explicitly aware that the SAT results constituted some sort of 'official' judgement of them. Even the third who claimed that the tests did not really matter qualified that opinion in some way, usually by referring to marks. For instance:

I'm not bothered, but it would be good to get a top mark.

(Miriam, St Anne's, 3, 3, 4)

It doesn't really matter, as long as I'm not a Level 3.

(Ben, Greenmantle 5, 5, 5)

Not really, as long as I don't get loads of poor ones. If I do I might get a bit worried.

(Tom, Greenmantle, 4, 4, 5)

I wanted to do my best but I wasn't bothered. If I got low scores, then I would be bothered 'cos I'd think I could have done better and I'd think I'd be a bit upset.

(Glenn, Lawnside, 4, 5, 4)

The sense that Key Stage 2 SATs were a high-stakes activity, and could threaten self-esteem, social status or even lead to some form of stigma, was evident in many responses.

The teachers will mind, and I will too.

(Roger, Greenmantle, 3, 4, 3)

Mum would like me to get a high level.

(Louise, Audley, 5, 5, 5)

It might to my mum and dad and my family. My family wouldn't like it (if he was at the bottom). My mum would be nagging at me: 'Why didn't you do really well, when you know so much?'.

(Ned, Lawnside, 4, 4, 3)

My brother wants me to do as well as he did.

(Theresa, Audley, 4, 3, 4)

We've had a lot of practice so I'm not going to let my parents down.

(Hugh, Lawnside 3, 4, 3)

I think I'll do terribly and get a Level 3.
(Olivia, Lawnside, who had been having extra coaching from a tutor after school, 4, 4, 4)

I'm worried about what class I'll be in at secondary school. Mum wants me to do well so I'm worried about that as well.

(Zoe, St Bede's, 5, 4, 4)

Indeed, the hierarchical and categoric nature of the assessment and the power of the tests to differentiate had been internalized by most of the children.

It would prove how intelligent you are.

(Graham, Kenwood, 3, 3, 4)

All tests are important 'cause you get scores, marks. It shows your ability.

(Corrinne, Meadway, 4, 4, 3)

To see what level you are ... If you are Level 1, 2, 3 or something like that.

(Rupert, Lawnside, 4, 4, 4)

Some low attainers even saw the tests themselves as something that you had to be qualified to do. For instance, Scott at Kenwood knew that not everyone in his class did the tests and construed this as a lack of eligibility:

'Cause you're good at doing tests or qualified enough to do them; one person never did them. He's not exactly brainy. He's pretty thick but he can't help that.

(Scott, Kenwood, 3, 3, 3)

In that school, as elsewhere, some pupils did the 'tasks' provided by the testing authorities for lower-attaining children as a safety net before the tests. The Year 6 teacher described one girl's response to doing a task:

She came to me in tears and she said, 'I'm stupid and I'm thick'. I said, 'What do you mean?' and she said, 'Well, they've put me in for a Level 2 and the others say "If you're only a Level 2 at your age, then it's time you grew up" '.

(Mrs Green, Kenwood)

Only three of the nine schools decided to use 'extension tests' for high-attaining children, and none of the children who took these tests was awarded Level 6. Extension tests sometimes became a somewhat stressful experience, as the case of Laura at Orchard demonstrates.

Laura took the Maths extension test. She was generally acknowledged by her class to be the best at Maths and doing better than Laura in a class test was considered to be quite remarkable. Clyde, an average attainer, showed himself in his comic strip thinking before the Maths SAT: 'The Maths marks now. Laura 100, Clyde 000. This is going to be hard', and in the cell which invited him to imagine what others in the class might be thinking he wrote, 'Laura you're a genius'. Laura's teacher thought that Laura would not reach Level 6 because the class had not covered a number of areas assessed in the test, in particular algebra. However, Laura's parents were keen for her to do the test. They had been giving her extra work and teaching her at home. On books of tests that they had bought for her they said she was achieving Level 6 or 7. Our field notes record the teacher explaining that she allowed Laura to take the test as a 'public relations' exercise. Observation of the test showed Laura frequently stuck and not able to understand what to do. She attempted nine of the fifteen questions and at the end looked both unhappy and relieved. In her interview Laura talked about the Maths tests and revealed something of the pressure she was under from home:

I was very nervous. After each of the ordinary Maths papers I went though the questions with Dad on the phone at work and he told me whether they were right. They were all right except one on each paper. I'm good at Maths. I practise a lot. But the Maths extension test was really horrible; I didn't have enough time.

(Laura, Orchard, 4, 5, 4)

The comic strip text she created after the extension test shows even more clearly how upset and angry she felt about it (Figure 10.1 below). Before the test she tells herself, 'I must be calm'. When she looks at the test she thinks, 'This is hard', and her recreated stream of consciousness during the test repeats this refrain: 'I can't do this', 'Not another hard one', 'I can't do this one', 'Oh no, I haven't finished'.

She knew she had not done well in the test and that her parents would be disappointed. In contrast to her eager conversations with her father about the standard test, she imagined herself saying, 'I don't want to talk about it', and she expected her family at home to ask, 'Why? Why? Why?'. The thoughts she gave other children in the class showed her feelings about other social costs to her of this differentiation: 'She's a show-off', 'She's a teacher's pet'.

At Meadway and Audley decisions about who was to take the extension tests were delayed until after informal marking of the standard tests. Pupils were aware of this and at Audley, as we will see later, considerable tension, competition and excitement was generated among some of the children: 'I bet I got an extension test'. Others, in their cartoon texts, wrote statements such as: 'I hope I don't have to do the extension'.

Our analysis suggests that the categoric nature of the SAT procedures made differentiation much more overt for the children. For instance, Celia at Meadway showed her understanding of the inherent tensions:

> While you're at junior school I don't think it matters. When you go to high school it does. If you get Level 6 or 5 you go in a higher group. If you get 1 or 2 you go in a lower group. They can't put you in a group where you find it really hard. They put the ones that like it, the ones that are good at it, in a higher group; the ones in between in the middle group; and the ones that aren't very good – well, they go in the smallest group. They don't like saying it, but it's true. They don't like to admit it, but we know it's true. They don't want to upset the other children.
>
> (Celia, Meadway, 3, 3, 3)

Celia placed herself with those that are 'in between' and not as one of the 'other children'. It is clear from earlier quotations and from the sample as a whole that, particularly for average and low attainers, the consequences of being at the bottom for self and family were far-reaching and unwelcome. Celia's analysis acknowledges the pedagogic argument but also the social consequences ('they don't want to upset the other children') and school's awareness of them ('they don't like to admit it, but we know it's true').

The discourse of 'levels' and of ordering of achievement was apparent in both interviews and SAT stories, and it appears that the SAT assessment was already positioning and polarizing children as they moved into the secondary phase. In 'speech' and 'thinks' bubbles, pupils positioned both themselves and each other.

> 'You'll do good'. 'I'm not that good'. 'I'll do average'.
>
> (Jane, Meadway, 5, 5, 4)

> 'I think I'll do average'. 'I'm gonna fail'. 'About a three – nothing over that'.
>
> (Corrinne, Meadway, 4, 4, 3)

> 'You'll probably get a 5'. 'I'm only going to get a 3'. 'I have to get a five'. 'I did rubbish'.
>
> (Roland, Greenmantle, 3, 3, 4)

> 'That was average'. 'Think I got most of them right'. 'Bet Sam knew the answers to all of them'.
>
> (Dennis, Greenmantle, 4, 4, 5)

> 'Think I'll get a 4'. 'Think I'll get a 3'. 'I've done bad, very bad'.
>
> (Neil, Audley, 4, 5, 4)

Figure 10.1 An extract from Laura's SAT story for her extension test in Mathematics

'I'm shaking'. 'What if I only get a low level'. 'You'll do all right'.

(Annette, Audley, 4, 4, 4)

'I can't spell. I'll only get Level 2'. 'I've done bad. I'll only get Level 3'.

(Annie, Audley, 4, 3, 4)

'She must be thick. I did that one easy'.

(Sasha, St Bede's, 5, 5, 5)

'That was easy'. 'You're a keener'. 'I found it hard'. 'He probably got them all wrong'.

(Harry, St Bede's, 5, 5, 4)

'I'll bet Felix answered every one'.

(Glenn, St Bede's, 3, 4, 4)

'I'm scared'. 'It's not going to be hard'. 'I know it all'. 'It's easy for you'. 'I know my score is going to be bad'.

(Aidan, St Bede's, 3, 3, 4)

'I'm going to be sick'. 'I'm brainy and I'm not going to get any wrong'.

(Gareth, St Anne's, 3, 3, 3)

Teachers confirmed this perception. For instance, in Kenwood the class teacher told us 'The children were already categorizing themselves before they started: "Are you a Level 3 or are you a Level 2, or are you thick enough to be a Level 1?"' (Mrs Green, Kenwood). In considering the issues raised by these and other data from this stage of the study, factors associated with attainment and socio-economic issues became more sharply focused. The children who exhibited the most anxiety when taking SATs were low attainers, often from schools serving less well-off families. The most relaxed children were those who consistently achieved Levels 4 and 5. In general, these came from higher-achieving schools in more affluent areas. Indeed, it was only from these better-off children that we had any indication of the assessment being for the learner, rather than for some outside agency – though even in this group such a rationale was rare.

So we could see what we know and see if we still know what we done in past years.

(Alistair, St Bede's, 4, 4, 4)

So you know how you are getting on, not just the teachers.

(Ben, Greenmantle, 5, 5, 5)

Such higher achievers were also more likely to tell us that the tests did not really matter that much.

It's just one thing that happened on one day.

(Keiron, Valley, 5, 4, 4)

Doesn't matter if you can't do some questions and other people can.

(Harriet, Valley, 5, 4, 4)

If someone else isn't pleased with them but I am, it doesn't matter. I know I've tried my best.

(Jan, Valley, 5, 5, 4)

Matter? Yes and no. I can do better in secondary school.

(Alistair, St Bede's, 4, 4, 4)

One or two really could not see why, if information about attainment was required, their teachers could not just provide it.

It doesn't tell you really how good you are, 'cos some of 'em you've hardly done before and some you've done years ago. Why do they need to know all this? All they need is the teachers to tell them. I said that to Mrs T. Why do we have to do this? Why can't you just tell them? She said (that) they need proof of how well we've done.

(Ned, Lawnside, 4, 4, 3)

It's to see how we're getting on. I don't know why they don't just ask the teachers.

(Ben, Greenmantle, 5, 5, 5)

10.3 TAKING THE TESTS

During May 1996 everyone in our study schools was aware that something significant was happening. The Year 6 children had been prepared through the previous term and parents had been advised of the SAT dates well in advance to ensure attendance. Other teachers and pupils were 'helping' and sympathetic to the Year 6 pupils and their class teachers. Many parents were evidently ready at home to calm their children as necessary. The children themselves knew that they were approaching a major educational hurdle.

For test week pupils were issued with timetables, furniture was moved, children were regrouped, silence reigned for long periods, and treats were planned to mark the end of the ordeal. The physical arrangements for taking the tests varied from school to school. In three of our schools the children stayed in their own classroom for the tests, in five others they were in the school hall, and in one school the two Year 6 classes were regrouped and located in different rooms around the school.

However, the circumstances and priorities of each school created quite particular climates in which testing took place, and these had a considerable impact on their interpretation and on pupils. We can convey something of this variation by looking in more detail at testing in Meadway and Lawnside – schools serving an inner-city area and a leafy suburb respectively.

SATs at Meadway

Meadway was an inner-city school with an ethnically mixed population. A very high proportion qualified for free school meals, many children did not have English as a first language and in 1996 several Year 6 children had severe behavioural problems. Thirty of the 46 children taking the tests had special arrangements for teacher support and time extensions, and on most days ten staff were involved in administering the tests.

The school had a tradition of caring for pupils and there was an awareness of problematic backgrounds and the challenges that the SATs posed for many of the children. The thought and attention given to the physical arrangements in which the children were to take the tests is an illustration of this. The children were divided into groups and located in rooms around the school rather than being all together in the hall. A Year 6 teacher commented:

> I'm sure there are some schools in this authority where they would bring them into the hall – maybe they think it gives them the right atmosphere for a test. I find that very cold, that idea. This school is different. I think we get the best out of our children in the way we've done it. Keep them close, keep them as a unit. They feel happier in small groups. They get very close to teachers.
>
> (Mr Forrest, Meadway)

For the tests some children stayed with their class teacher, others moved to different rooms where they were supervised by special needs and support teachers.

> They often react very badly to change, so we practised this with them the week before – this idea of going off in groups. To begin with some were saying, 'Why am I going here?' 'Why am I going there?'. Some didn't want to be separated. But I think they got confident with the routine; appreciated being in their own room with their special teacher.
>
> (Mr Forrest, Meadway)

Our field notes record one teacher collecting her group from the classroom and giving them all a reassuring hug before the Writing SAT. Notwithstanding all this teacher support, many of the Meadway children were extremely preoccupied with the question of the 'marks they might get' as their SAT stories showed:

> I hope I get good marks. I tried really hard. I hope my mum will be very happy with the marks I get.
>
> (Amelia, 4, 4, 4)

> What if I don't get any marks? People will laugh at me.
>
> (Shona, 3, 3, 3)

> I hope I passed. I hope I passed. I hope I passed. I hope I passed. Oh, I hope I got high marks.
>
> (Jamila, 4, 4, 3)

> I thought I would fial (sic).
>
> (Elroy, 2, 3, 2)

> I don't know what I'll get.
>
> (Yasmeen, N, 3, N)

> How did I do? Did I get them right or wrong?
>
> (Duncan, 3, 3, 3)

Why was performance so prominent in the minds of so many children? Following the pilot SATs of the previous year Meadway had become much more achievement-orientated. As Mr Forrest explained:

> It was a surprise to be told that the average child is Level 4 when our average is between 2 and 3. Last year a couple of children got 5s; some didn't make 3 when we hoped they

might, and they had to be caught by the tasks. They were happier working in a small group. They didn't manage the test.

(Mr Forrest, Year 6 teacher, Meadway)

In facing this situation a number of factors played a part. Head and staff were all committed to the children and were concerned that they might not be doing as well for them as they should. In addition, they were very aware of the policy rhetoric of attainment and qualifications, of an imminent OFSTED inspection, and of comparison with other schools.

There are pressures because we don't want to be seen to be doing badly, which is a great shame – the issue of competition between schools. There's definitely pressure for us to have some decent results. And at the same time you want the children to do the best they can.

(Mrs Sanger, headteacher, Meadway)

Meadway teachers were also aware of the pitfalls on the path to raising achievement and there was some ambivalence about the testing agenda. However, they felt that there was little alternative. The staff thus reappraised their approach to planning and teaching. In particular, to challenge potential high achievers, they created two top sets for Maths and English drawn from the two Year 6 classes. These were taught by the head and deputy head. Additionally and inexorably, SATs became a more prominent feature in their thinking.

We told ourselves 18 months ago that we wouldn't teach to the tests, but I think that has actually happened. We practise ... like little mini-tests, leading up. There's a lot more of those than we ever had before. We're becoming more test-orientated.

(Mr Forrest, Year 6 teacher, Meadway)

A 'pecking order' (a Year 6 teacher's phrase) that all children understood was becoming much more overt and significant both in and out of school. Amelia's awareness that 'good marks would make (her) mum happy' indicates her understanding that her performance was now overt and public. The consequences of this shift appeared to be a reinforcement of the concept of failure for many children and, for low attainers, to create particular concern about marks. For instance, the original of Elroy's 'I thought I would fial' (sic) is written in extremely tiny letters, a contrast to his large Afro-Caribbean frame and loud personality. His teacher was aware of potential consequences:

At the moment they feel quite happy with the differences. If it was constantly reinforced with numbers and they were made to feel that they were 'lesser', then I think you could have problems. I suppose that's the danger of it: they get stuck with a number and that's all they think of themselves as.

(Mr Forrest, Year 6 teacher, Meadway)

At the time of our study categoric assessment had increased differentiation and was having a powerful effect on the construction of learner identity. As they moved into secondary school many of these children had internalized evaluative processes and had, in their own terms, already identified themselves as 'school failures'. The circumstances of some schools made it easier to manage the SATs in educationally constructive ways, and to minimize such adverse feelings among the children.

SATs at Lawnside

In 1995 Lawnside moved from a varied collection of buildings, including the original wooden school of 1931, into a new purpose-built school with a nursery. Pupil numbers grew steadily over the six years of our study and in our final year the school population was 186, including the first nursery intake. The school was located in a semi-rural situation on the edge of a large Midlands conurbation. Most pupils were from relatively affluent homes; some lived in the immediate neighbourhood, some in adjacent authorities. Children eligible for free school meals or with special educational needs were in single figures. All children had English as a first language. The school worked hard to retain a village school identity and its caring ethos.

The fifteen Year 6 pupils of 1996 were in a mixed-age class with Year 5s. During SATs week whenever a test was timetabled, Year 5 pupils moved to other locations in the spacious new school enabling Year 6 pupils to have the room to themselves. They sat two or three to a table, stayed in the same seats for each test and were supervised by their class teacher. The atmosphere appeared quite relaxed: children arrived, gathered in groups to discuss the latest television episode of *The X Files*, their cycling proficiency tests, or the class newspaper they were working on. Some made a point of checking the SATs timetable and reminding each other of what they had to do and how many tests were left. Our field notes describe the atmosphere before the Writing SAT as 'bubbly and happy'. These observations were very accurately reflected in the cartoon strips where most of the speech bubbles in the classroom before the test were filled with non-test related chat.

Their teacher though had detected that they were a bit worried and frightened, and she tried to put them at their ease. Indeed, on the evidence of our interviews and the cartoon strips, the children were experiencing some nervousness at the start of the tests. However, for most this declined as the week went on. Some even began to enjoy it. Hugh decided, 'It's just part of education to have tests', and Martin announced calmly to the class, 'SATs are just like exams', suggesting that for these children tests had been normalized. William, a low/average achiever, told us: 'In the past I'd go wobbly with fear. The word test killed me. Now I think, "It's a test – what else is it?"'. Lucy agreed: 'When I was in Year 5, I was more afraid of tests. Now you're not afraid 'cos you're growing up and you've got to think – well, you're not meant to be scared – just have to get on with it'. However, this class probably had less explicit preparation for these tests than any other in the study. According to their teacher: 'We did some test runs a few week beforehand, but not last year's SATs'. Sally confirmed this: 'We've done practices: Science sheets, stories, comprehension – like test papers'.

The overall impression was of confident, articulate children in a school with an explicitly non-competitive ethos. Although there was general (and accurate) agreement about which of them would do best in the tests, they were quick and keen to identify other positive factors and specific difficulties in other children, for instance Jack's expertise on the computer and his dyslexia. During the tests they were mutually supportive, aware of each other's feelings, exchanging encouraging smiles and nods, and mouthing 'Are you all right?'.

Reconstructing the tests in the cartoon strips, the children recalled their teacher's advice about finishing in time, reading through, showing your working, etc., and her words of encouragement. They also noticed the silence and how others seemed to be feeling. In interview some commented how, especially in writing, they were working in a different way from usual. The approach to procedure was conformist but quite low-key. For instance, in the Writing SAT Alice and Lucy, having stated that they had finished and were happy with their work, were allowed to leave ten minutes before the end to conduct an interview for the class newspaper with a school visitor. Before the second Maths test their teacher suggested 'Put a reading book on your table. A few finished early yesterday – you weren't a disturbance but it will give you something to do'. Later, the children did not recall any detailed post mortems with their teacher after the tests beyond a general enquiry about how they were feeling.

For most of the children the school's low-key approach meant that it was simply a case of getting through the week. In their cartoon strips all of them completed 'When all the tests were over I thought . . .' with some expression of relief. In these cartoons only one child made any explicit reference to outcomes or performance. This was Olivia who showed herself walking to school and thinking, 'I'll do terribly and get Level 3'. In interview Olivia told us that it was important for her to do well and that her parents had arranged coaching for the tests. Her friend Sandra was also being coached. Unlike the rest of the class (including Olivia), Sandra's initial nervousness did not disappear. In contrast to her calm appearance, she talked in interview of feeling increasing pressure as the week progressed:

> On the first day I thought it would be all right, but as it went through the week I got more and more stressed. At the end I was like shaking all over. It might have been 'cos I was quite sure of myself doing well and then I thought I was too sure and doing worse. But I think I did OK.
>
> (Sandra, Lawnside, 4, 4, 3)

Sandra told us that 'Everyone at home was asking, "Do you think you'll pass?" I think that made me get nervous. I don't think they meant to but they have this habit of asking a lot of questions, especially Dad'. Their teacher was aware of such home pressure on some children and worked to create a climate which would diminish its impact. This seemed to have been successful for William who told us that every time he got home after a test his father asked how he had done:

> He wanted to know the results, but we have to wait. He wants me to be clever – become really bright and know lots of things.
>
> (William, Lawnside, 4, 4, 3)

William's account indicated that he understood his father's ambition but saw it as unrealistic. He knew what he could do and was happy with himself:

> I'm just normal. I try to be cleverer, but . . . (shrugs).

Consistent with this approach was the attitude of the Year 6 teacher to enquiries from the parents of two high-achieving children about extension tests which they had heard were being done at other schools. As she explained:

> We have decided not to do extension tests. I will not put them through something they may not do well at. I'll explain to the parents. I think those who might have done them

will get a good Level 5 which is fantastic. But that is as far as we will go.

(Mrs Wright, Lawnside)

Despite the fact that the testing was far more overt at the end of Key Stage 2 than it had been for Key Stage 1, the examples of SATs at Meadway and Lawnside show continuities with our findings about teacher concerns and actions. As they had four years earlier, teachers sought to 'shield' and 'protect' their pupils from what they judged to be the worst effects of the SATs. This was particularly successful in the relatively high-achieving environment of Lawnside. The teachers of inner-city Meadway, however, felt under rather more pressure. They knew that the performance of their pupils fell below national norms and that they were due for inspection very soon. Despite their espoused commitments, they therefore moved to introduce setting and more explicit testing. Their pupils became more aware of differentiated achievements and this began to impact on pupils' sense of identity as learners. To develop this idea further we look specifically at the ways in which higher and lower-attaining pupils responded to and felt about their SAT experiences.

10.4 THE EXPERIENCES OF LOW AND HIGH ATTAINERS

As we have seen in the preceding section a good deal of tension and ambivalence surrounded the testing experience. Analysis of the full range of 103 interviews and 223 comic strips by Year 6 pupils suggests that for many of the children in our study the results they sought to achieve in the SATs were closely associated with their sense of themselves as people and as pupils. Teachers were well aware of this. Indeed, where they felt it possible, they tried to reassure their pupils and somehow diminish the power of the tests to create anxiety and pressure. However, at the same time they felt the need to urge the children to perform well and meet high expectations.

Studies of two schools set a context for a consideration of how teachers attempted to mitigate the effects of the SATs, and of the consequent effect on both higher and lower achievers.

Kenwood and lower achievers

Kenwood was a large urban junior school with a mainly white population and largely low to middle socio-economic status. In 1996 the school had just emerged from a very turbulent period with a poor OFSTED report and a change of head. Mrs Green, an experienced Year 6 teacher who had just been given responsibility for assessment, saw the tests as 'a terrible pressure for 11-year-olds'. Some, she felt, would 'rise to the occasion', but she reported that others had experienced 'sleepless nights, been sick, wet the bed, haven't wanted to come to school'. The adverse OFSTED report had enhanced pressure on the school to demonstrate the standards of its Year 6 pupils and Mrs Green felt there were considerable parental expectations. In particular 'they want to be able to say it was the school or the teacher's fault that their child hadn't reached the standard'. The governors and headteacher were also concerned. As the year group leader, Mrs Green thus felt considerable responsibility for the children's results. Nevertheless, she was keen to reduce the pressure she felt the children were experiencing.

> I really do try and get over to them that it's a piece of paper, it's not a life and death situation, because I really do think it affects them.
>
> (Mrs Green, Kenwood)

This message was clearly received by a third of her class, all of whom put some version of 'Don't worry. It's only a piece of paper' in the speech bubble for their teacher talking to them before the test. For one, Dawn, it had also become part of her own discourse. She completed the 'thinks' bubble of herself on the way to school with, 'Oh well, it's only a piece of paper'.

However, alongside this echoing of a comforting rhetoric, there was evidence of children's awareness of other pressures to 'do well' for the school, Mrs Green and themselves. They felt themselves in a state of some paradox and tension. Parental discussions on the personal significance of the test seemed to be apparent in the life narratives some of the children were projecting for themselves. For instance, three children in interview drew an association between this 'piece of paper' and their future educational and job prospects.

> It matters a lot I reckon, 'cause it mainly does your future for you – getting you into a school you want to go to and colleges and all that.
>
> (Ewan, Kenwood, 4, 4, 4)

> It probably affects your job – when you go to get a job. 'Cos like when you do your SATs at the senior school, that goes to what job you can do.
>
> (Ingrid, Kenwood, 4, 4, 4)

> My mum said if you get good results you get a good job. But I don't really care about that. I just wouldn't get paid and then I wouldn't be able to own my own house and things like that and I wouldn't have no money to go out and buy new clothes. I'd just stay in the house with my mum and dad and my brother and sister.
>
> (Keith, Kenwood, 3, 3, 3)

Field notes of the SATs being taken at Kenwood show how the tensions inherent in the situation were enacted. Mrs Green was warm and encouraging both before and after the test, but enacted the more formal requirements of invigilation during it. Whilst she tried to reassure the children, at the same time they were very aware that the school had been criticized in the recent OFSTED report and that Mrs Green herself was anxious that they perform well. It was a high-stakes experience quite unlike any other within their primary schooling.

For some low achievers, such as Joy (3, 3, 3), the pressure was considerable, as she described in interview:

> Before they started I wasn't that keen 'cos I didn't know what I had to do. I thought it was going to be like really, really hard. To start with I felt sort of all right inside of me but after I'd begun I didn't know what to do. I panicked a lot 'cos I felt I didn't know what to do. I didn't know what to do. I asked Miss to read out the question but she couldn't tell me the answer. In the Writing I didn't know what to write about and I was just losing my mind. I didn't know what to write about. It was just like going through my head and I

didn't know how to do it. I was thinking like I was going to do this and I was going to do that ... and I just lost the words and I didn't know like what to do. I didn't know what to write. In the end I just wrote something that I could do ... I just put in full stops and things where I thought they would be.

(Joy, Kenwood)

Joy had been 'doing tests at home, Mum got papers from the school and she's been helping me'. There was a lot riding on these tests for Joy's sense of herself and her hopes for her new school:

If I get on really well, I won't have to go to a special needs teacher. I've had enough of it ... I don't want to do it any more.

(Joy, Kenwood)

However, the benignly created pressure induced a panic of 'not knowing what to do' which was sadly dysfunctional.

Another child, Sally (3, 3, 3), was particularly concerned to avoid 'being shown up' because of her poor performance. She talked about the Reading SAT:

I never had a good night and I just felt lousy and I wanted to go back to sleep and I just didn't want to do it. I was shaking. I never got all the way through it. Some of it I just didn't know, some I just didn't do. I don't think I told my friends about what I did in case it wasn't very good. I didn't want to get shown up about it.

(Sally, Kenwood)

Sally, like Joy, felt ambivalent about support from home. Her mother had also obtained practice tests from school and had been coaching Sally in test technique:

She told me 'If you don't get one, go on to another one'. She was getting me right into it so I knew what I was doing. She really wanted me to get on with SATs – she really wanted me to do it. She was going on about it. Before she was saying, 'Don't worry about it', and every day she always gave me 'Good luck' on what I was doing.

(Sally, Kenwood)

For Sally though, there was an additional self-imposed pressure. She knew her school had had a poor OFSTED report and been subject to 'naming and shaming' in the local and national media and she felt a responsibility here too:

I thought, like, I had to do really good results ... some goes to the school to make out how it's doing. I thought I should do good on that one, help the school to get good marks; last year it didn't do very well.

(Sally, Kenwood)

The theme of not showing yourself up in front of your friends, of losing face or risking ridicule frequently recurs in the data from lower achievers in other schools. Above all, they didn't want to talk about the tests. They didn't want to be reminded of how painful and uncomfortable it was, or be reminded of the things they had found hard, or of the fact that they didn't know what to do.

We didn't like to remember it so we didn't talk about it.

(Eliot, St Bede's, 4, 3, 3)

I just said it was easy.

> (Douglas, St Anne's, 3, N, 3)

I didn't talk to my friends – I didn't want to because if I said an answer and it was wrong they would laugh.

> (Barry, St Bede's, N, 3, 2)

Few low-attaining children felt in control of the test. They were aware of the techniques and knowledge that they should have mastered, but they felt unable to recall and apply them. For instance, when checking for spelling and punctuation errors they were more likely to make changes in optimistic desperation, rather than to use knowledge or understanding systematically. If urged by a teacher to 'keep trying', they often simply made a guess. Although they usually finished what they could do before the end of the test, sometimes, for instance in the Writing SAT, they felt constrained by the reminders about time. They were also frequently confused by the wording of questions, specialized vocabulary, layout and instructions. Many just did not understand what they were expected to do.

Valley and higher achievers

Our data from higher achievers reveal that whilst the SAT period was not without its anxieties, the children had far more fulfilling experiences. In particular they show children who were more aware of and in control of the technique of taking the test.

I was always nervous that I might not get finished. So I always kept my eye on the clock. ... Luckily I had time to check through.

> (Jan, Valley, 5, 5, 4)

I didn't want to rush and make silly mistakes; I wanted to finish on time. I missed out a bit I had on the planning sheet because it was too long.

> (Kate, Greenmantle, 5, 5, 5)

I had previously planned the story but I had to choose which title it would fit.

> (Ben, Greenmantle, 5, 5, 5)

Higher attainers were also more likely to conduct post mortems with friends and teachers. They did not mind admitting to 'getting stuck' because this happened only on some questions.

I talked to my friends about what I got stuck on.

> (Pauline, St Bede's, 5, 4, 4)

They were aware of high expectations from home and school but in the main this was not a disabling pressure because they felt confident of success. The reassurance that their performance would be acceptable as long as they 'did their best' provided a comfortable fallback position – which most did not, in fact, expect to need.

As we saw in the case of Lawnside, schools serving relatively well-off communities found it easier to generate a calm, non-threatening atmosphere over the test period. The case of Valley illustrates this further. Valley is a small, two-class village school in the south-west of England. The children live in the village or neighbouring villages and are mainly from professional middle-class families. At the time of the study there were only nine Year 6 pupils. Interviewed in test week, the very experienced teaching headteacher (who shared the Year 6 class) said she thought the children did not feel any pressure from the school in relation to SATs. In the event 85 per cent of the results at Valley were at Level 4 or 5. None of the children did tasks and the school made a conscious decision not to use the extension tests because:

> It was yet another hour and I didn't think they'd get anything out of it. It was not a learning experience for them, even if they'd come out with a Level 6, which was doubtful. Even if they had the Teacher Assessment wouldn't be Level 6 because we haven't covered the work.
>
> (Mrs Lamb, headteacher, Valley)

The headteacher administered almost all the tests herself, whilst the children stayed in the familiar surroundings of their own classroom. She explained how she had offered 'extra jollying along . . . loads of patting on the back, even when they haven't done very well, because they need to know that I'm on their side. We're going into it together and we will do our best and we will come out the other side and that will be it'.

In writing the text for their cartoon strips, four of the children put variations on the 'do your best' mantra into the mouths of their teacher, into the speech of children encouraging other children, and into their own 'thoughts'. In the context of this class the value attached to 'trying hard' and 'doing your best' was underpinned for most children by the probability of success. Most, however, self-confidently asserted it as the criterion by which they would measure their own efforts whatever the outcome.

> You just have to do the best you can. It doesn't matter if you can't answer some questions that other people can.
>
> (Harriet, Valley, 5, 4, 4)

> As long as I'm pleased with them I don't think it matters. If someone else isn't pleased but I am, it doesn't matter. I know I've tried my hardest.
>
> (Jan, Valley, 5, 5, 4)

> It does matter a bit, but in the end I'll know I tried my best.
>
> (Heather, Valley, 5, 3, 4)

> It shows teachers how good we are but I don't think it matters too much. I know I have to try my best.
>
> (Richard, Valley, 4, 4, 4)

Analysis across each of the nine schools studied suggests that the construction of an identity as someone who 'tried their best' or 'did as well as they could' was very important for a large number of the children. Indeed, the development of such an identity and attitude was, on the evidence of the children's comments, encouraged by many parents as well as teachers. At Valley the emphasis on effort appeared successful in providing reassurance of what was expected in a class where most children were already confident of success. However, at other schools the meaning and viability of 'doing your best' varied significantly depending on the academic capabilities of the children. We illustrate this in the case of Audley where it had quite different implications for higher and lower attainers.

'Doing your best' at Audley Junior

The 22 Year 6 pupils at Audley included a high proportion of pupils, almost all boys, who were described as 'from disturbed backgrounds'. These children had been presenting a considerable behavioural challenge to their teacher, Mrs Jones, and relationships between the children also required careful management. Mrs Jones was also very aware of the headteacher's hopes 'that we have better SATs results this year'. Indeed, the tests had been high on her agenda for much of the year, as she explained:

> I've been using past papers and they did a sort of mock SATs in January to show where their strengths and weaknesses were. I marked it as for the requirements of last year's SATs. Then I took each child individually and went though the papers with them and showed them where they were coming short. Most of them acknowledged that they would need to speed up especially with the English paper. The last half term I did the 1994 papers with them. A lot of them said they were working faster and getting through more of the paper.
>
> (Mrs Jones, Audley)

On the morning of the first test of 1996 she told us:

> I'm more nervous than the children. My husband said he thought SATs were meant to be low-key. They are until you realize they are going to be reported, used by secondary schools, used in league tables – then it's every man for himself.
>
> (Mrs Jones, Audley)

She recalled the previous Friday at the end of school: 'I told the children, "Take your books home, take your files, read anything"'. Similarly, in the classroom before the children went to do their first test, Mrs Jones asked them:

> What's required of you today? (No answer) What do you have to do? Yes, your best. If you can't do them, don't get upset or worried; just do your best, that's all we expect.
>
> (Mrs Jones, Audley)

In the hall everything was set out with a pencil, protractor and ruler at each chair. On the side were extra pencils and other equipment and a box of large tissues. Two teachers were assigned to invigilate. One of the Year 6 pupils, while helping earlier to organize the chairs and tables, remarked on looking round 'There's still one problem – our heads!'. This was Brian, an able child but receiving weekly support sessions to help him manage his emotional and troublesome behaviour. He had identified the all-important factor on which so much depended. He also knew that both he and his teacher had high expectations of his SAT achievement. His mother had been working on revision with him at the weekend, he had been in bed at eight o'clock the previous night ('I've never been so early'), and he had his lucky coin in his pocket.

The range of attainment in the class was wide and in the following account we contrast the experience of SATs as reported by those children who were expected by their teacher to attain the highest and lowest scores. Seven pupils were described as the 'bright' group from whom it was hoped and expected the Level 5s would come. Another six were assessed as unlikely to get above Level 3 in any core subject. There had been much discussion of extension papers and the 'bright' group were very aware of their significance. Six of them had been allowed to attempt the Maths extension paper from the previous year. Throughout SATs week, discussion and speculation about who would be doing extension papers occurred several times amongst staff and pupils.

The experiences which the 'bright' group recalled in their interviews and cartoon constructions are all very similar – they approached the tests with a mix of nervousness and excitement. Distinctively however, they felt in control of both content and process: 'Good, I know what to do because we did this the other day', 'I've done this before. I can do it, it's easy', 'We've been practising long division for ages', 'It got harder in the middle of each test but I didn't get more worried', 'I had lots of time to check', 'I finished in time and read it though', 'Have to read it, time yourself, pace yourself'. They were also confident about their achievement: 'I didn't miss a single answer. I've done it!', 'I think I've done well'. They all thought they had done a lot of revising and practising of fractions, spellings, Science topics, punctuation and grammar, story planning and setting tests for each other at home and at school. They had discussed 'what might come up' with their teacher: 'In Science we'd talked about all the questions. Mrs Jones couldn't believe it. She'd revised it all with us'. This last utterance gives us a sense of how powerfully their teacher was present in this testing process. In several of the cartoons children filled a teacher speech bubble with comments that suggest they sensed that their performance was being closely monitored: 'Some people were making silly mistakes. Some gave me a brilliant surprise', 'I saw a few people making stupid mistakes – you weren't reading the instructions'. This chimed exactly with our field note observations: 'The teachers invigilating are obviously upset by some of the "silly mistakes" they have seen', and with Mrs Jones's own comment: 'I cringed at what some of them had written. If only I could say "What do you mean?" "Think again"'. She was strongly present also as someone who gave feedback on performance:

> Mrs Jones told me I'd done well. She thinks I'll be a Level 5
>
> (Louise, Audley, na)

> Mrs Jones told me I'd got all my spellings right – some people made silly mistakes
>
> (Nadine, Audley, na 5, 5, 4)

> I know what I did on the Maths. Mrs Jones said I got 32 out of 40 on them both and I did the best in the class, which excited me. When she looked at my Reading test she smiled at me – that was a give-away
>
> (Brian, Audley, 4, 4, 5)

After each test, Mrs Jones conducted some kind of post mortem. After the Writing SAT she asked 'When I said "Go back and see if you can put anything in", how many did? What did you like about it? How did you cope?' Getting no answer, she continued:

> I was dead impressed. I saw paragraphs and speech marks. I don't know if the examiners will be impressed but I was. This afternoon I'll look at your spelling tests from yesterday and try to work our how well you've done. I'll then see if some of you will do the extension.
>
> (Mrs Jones, Audley)

Mrs Jones then went on to explain that doing the extension would not mean that you got any more marks for the standard test. At which point, we noted, one of the children asked 'Why are we doing it, then?'. Guy, one of the 'bright' group, told us:

> After the tests Mrs Jones went over the answers. It made some people feel good and some bad. I made eight mistakes in Science.
>
> (Guy, Audley, 5, 4, 4)

Among those 'feeling bad' were the lower-achieving six. They approached the tests with no excitement and lots of nervousness.

> I was nervous as soon as I got to school and went to the hall. As the week went on I was still nervous in the tests
>
> (Gerald, Audley, 3, 3, 3)

> I was a bit scared at the weekend – then I didn't want to think about them
>
> (Peter, Audley, 3, 3, 3)

> I was nervous for each one
>
> (Karen, 3, 3, 3)

They didn't want to talk to each other about what or how they had done, nor did they like their teacher going though the paper. They were either sure they had 'done bad' or did not know how they had done. They simply wanted the whole thing to be over and done with. Extracts from two SAT story cartoon strips encapsulate an experience most of this group shared.

> I woke up and thought: 'Oh no, the Maths test. I'm not good at doing Maths' ... Our teacher said: 'Well you know how to do this. You only did it last week'. I looked at the paper to see what I had to do. I thought: 'Oh no. There's loads of hard ones' ... I put down my pen and thought: 'Oh dear, this is too hard for me'. At the end of the week I thought: 'Yes, no more SATs and no more being nervous'.
>
> (Gary, Audley, 3, 3, 3)

> I woke up and thought: 'Oh no, I don't really want to go to school today because it's the SATs'. In our classroom people were talking: 'Are you nervous, Gary?' 'A bit' 'I'm worried. Are you?' 'Yes, bad style'. Our teacher said: 'Don't worry. Good luck'. I looked round the room and noticed: 'nervous people, people flicking through pages'. I looked at the paper to see what I had to do. I thought: 'Oh no'. While I was doing the test I thought: 'Oh my ... Oh bad ...'. I put down my pen and thought: 'I wonder if I have done good or bad'. After it was over I talked to my friends: 'Wasn't it hard?' 'Yes'. I imagined what some of the others might be thinking: 'I don't want to do them' 'I'm worried'.
>
> (Neil, Audley, 3, 3, 3)

Previous Teacher Assessments for half of this group included several Level 2s. Kevin was one of these and he had a very negative view of his capability. At the beginning of the Writing SAT he refused to sit down. He said 'I can't sit still for an hour. I don't want to do it'. Eventually he was persuaded to try and agreed to sit opposite Brian. At his interview he said he found English hard, but he 'just did it'; he wasn't used to doing the planning so he 'didn't know what to do'; he thought he'd written 'about 25 lines'. At the end of the Writing SAT, our field note observation noted him going with Brian to join a group of children gathered round Mrs Jones. She explained, 'He left as soon as he discovered they were talking about who was going to take the extension test'. In the event, Kevin was assessed at Level 3 for all three SATs.

The data from all the children in this class show them very conscious of 'levels'. They talked about their own performance and, in the cartoon strips, they expressed their perception of what others might think about them.

> In the mock tests I got Level 5 in Maths and Science and Level 6 in English. I hope at least to get this.
>
> > (Nadine, Audley, 5, 5, 4, Ext N)

> Mum says I got Level 2/3 before (Key Stage 1) so I've doubled in the years. I wanted to see how good I really was. Now I can see for myself.
>
> > (Brian, Audley, 4, 5, 5, Ext N)

> I probably got a 4 at least.
>
> > (Guy, Audley, 5, 4, 4)

> I think I'll get Level 3. I think I'll get Level 4 (cartoon bubble).
>
> > (Neil, Audley, 4, 5, 4)

> What if I get Level 3 but the teacher thought I'd get 5 or 6? (cartoon bubble). You'd better get Level 6 (parent speech bubble).
>
> > (Molly, Audley, 4, 4, 4)

> Hope I get Level 5.
>
> > (Rory, Audley, 4, 4, 4)

> I think I've got Level 3.
>
> > (Timothy, Audley, 3, 3, 3)

> I have done bad. I only got Level 3.
>
> > (Karen, Audley, 4, 3, 4)

From the lowest-achieving group this foregrounding of levelling and its categoric nature produced anxiety, lack of motivation and avoidance tactics. They did not see assessment as progressive: lower grades were 'bad'; if you got one you had 'failed'. Asked if he thought he had done OK, Peter replied, 'No. I think I done rubbish' (Peter, Audley, 3, 3, 3).

The group differentiated themselves from the 'bright' group quite explicitly:

> Louise, Nadine and Brian will do well 'cos they're clever – got a brain.
>
> > (Kevin, Audley, 3, 3, 3)

> Louise, Nadine and Brian will do well. It's just natural for them, they're good at everything.
>
> > (Gary, Audley, 3, 3, 3)

We see here the clear signs of feelings of helplessness from the lower achievers in contrast to the confidence of the more successful children. For some, stress and anxiety were associated with a challenge that could be met; for others, it was simply too much and too humiliating.

10.5 CONCLUSION

In reviewing and concluding this chapter it is worth referring back to Chapter 7 on routine classroom assessment. There we saw that pupils were increasingly thinking of assessment in summative ways, and there was little awareness of formative assessment providing constructive feedback on their learning. The amount of overt testing had increased in classrooms throughout Key Stage 2, and it appeared that teachers were increasingly focusing on performance outcomes rather than learning processes. This was particularly marked by Year 6 and the preparations for the SATs.

Within the present chapter we have noted some continuities from Year 2 to Year 6 in teacher attempts to reassure pupils at the time of SAT testing. However, the pressure at Key Stage 2 was far greater and the assessment process was much more overt. Of course, the stakes were higher for some teachers than for others. The effects of OFSTED inspections, league table positions and pressure from parents all created pressures and expectations to which some schools were more exposed than others. Nevertheless, many teachers attempted to preserve pupil self-esteem by promoting a 'do your best' ethic, and offered considerable support in terms of practice and test-taking techniques. However, the risk of mixed messages was considerable and the comments of many children reflected both the reassurance of teachers and parents and the pressures of their expectations. Overall, the children seemed only too aware that whilst 'trying' was worthy, 'achieving' was actually the required outcome.

Some pupils, particularly high attainers and the resilient, appeared to enjoy aspects of this. Some were fortunate in attending schools that had created secure, non-threatening climates and enjoyed peer cultures that were conducive to learning. In such circumstances high attainers began to feel more confident and even exhilarated during the test period. However, we have also seen how other pupils, particularly lower achievers, found it hard or could not cope. Under pressure they became demotivated and dysfunctional as the difficulty of the SAT challenges overwhelmed them. In such circumstances they tended to deny the tests – not wanting to talk about them, desiring not to be seen as 'getting it wrong', or asserting that 'tests are boring'. A few low achievers also become disruptive and uncooperative.

The consequence of the increased amount of overt testing, its categoric nature and the considerable significance attributed to it was a considerable increase in pupil differentiation. By the end of the SATs, children seemed more sure than they had ever previously been of who was 'bright' and who was 'thick'.

Of course pupils were active in confirming, contesting or trying to reconstruct their learning identities – which they were aware would carry forward into secondary school. In this the role of 'significant others' in the family and amongst peers was very evident from their responses to our SAT cartoon strips. Parents and siblings, peers and teachers were clearly expected to play a role in mediating the 'official' result and in giving it personal meaning. In this way the SAT event was interpreted and made sense of. In some schools, such as Lawnside, there was a broad congruence between the perceptions of home and school. Elsewhere, such as Kenwood Junior where a recent inspection had led to a reduction in confidence in the school, this was more problematic. Indeed, those children expected to have to manage some mixed messages.

Clearly the Year 6 SATs were the symbolic culmination of the children's primary education, the 'acid test' of their achievement. As we will see from the case-studies that we consider in Chapter 11 and from the discussion of learning disposition in Chapter 13, the potential significance of SATs in 'officially defining' the children as learners was considerable.

Chapter 11

Case-Studies in Learning Disposition and Identity

11.1   Introduction
11.2   Sean – learning Mathematics
11.3   Haley, Kevin, Richard and Amanda – developing learner identities
11.4   Neil – the influence of others
11.5   Jessica and Scott – responding to the SAT challenge
11.6   Laura, Alice, Kim and Kate – girls' confidence and dependence in Mathematics
11.7   Philip – saving face with a 'tough' identity
11.8   Conclusion

11.1 INTRODUCTION

In the preceding chapters in Part 2 of this book we have reported our analysis of data related to pupils' experiences of school learning over the six years of the PACE research. Because of the extent of the data from this longitudinal study we organized it under separate headings to reflect aspects of curriculum, relationships, pedagogy and assessment which have been the focus of previous reports from PACE. However, we recognize that, in reality, there is interaction between the various issues that we have dealt with separately. This interaction creates holistic contexts for learning and for learners. In this chapter we integrate the data into a number of case-study accounts of pupils, and thus exemplify and illustrate themes we have identified in earlier chapters. In telling the stories of some of the children in this way, we aim to return the focus of our research to where we feel it rightly belongs – in the unique experience of individual pupils.

This chapter thus has an integrative and holistic purpose, representing the cumulative impact on individual children of the full range educational factors that we have reviewed. Additionally we aim to sow the seed for a second order and rather different form of analysis. In demonstrating how individual children deal with complex classroom contexts, we will draw out the ways in which their experiences influence the development of pupils' identities and dispositions as learners. In Chapter 13 we will build on this, and consider whether the development of learner identity deserves greater recognition in educational provision.

11.2 SEAN – LEARNING MATHEMATICS

This case-study tells the story of Sean, a high attainer, and how he came to hate Mathematics. Sean is the youngest of five children and has lived all his life in the same house with his parents. The house and the school, Greenmantle, which he attended for all his primary years are situated in a small market town in the English Midlands with a mix of traditional farming and light industry. The area also attracts commuters to nearby cities and, increasingly, self-employed consultants like Sean's father who set up his own business when he was made redundant. The school has a high proportion of affluent, professional families. It has a long history and enjoys a good reputation as a fairly 'traditional' school.

During Sean's time in Greenmantle children's progress was organized in two-year blocks and classes were age-mixed on this basis. Teachers in each block worked together to plan the curriculum for their classes. In the last two years of Key Stage 2 this extended to the teachers of the three classes involved spending several hours each week working with each other's children. The most marked example of this was the creation of sets for English, Maths and PE across the three classes. Maths and English took up a large part of the morning session. The groups, which varied in size, were described informally by the teachers as 'top, middle and less able'. The Year 5 teacher explained how the sets were created:

> In the summer the Year 4s and 5s will be tested in English and Maths with a view to streaming them for the autumn. In about October they're tested again. We know them then as teachers and then we can shuffle these streamed groups around.

In addition there was regular testing at the end of each unit of work in core subjects, a verbal reasoning quotient test encouraged by the local education authority, and pupils were given pilot/mock SATs in the spring. Each pupil also had an individual portfolio of moderated work assessed to National Curriculum levels in the core subjects. In Maths this included an element of self-assessment where pupils discussed with the teacher whether they felt they had attained a particular target. One Year 6 teacher reflected on this increase of formal over informal assessment: 'It's almost a secondary school model; but we need to have records of achievement for parents and OFSTED. If a parent comes in we need proof'.

The school monitored test results, especially mock SATs. In Year 6 (1995–6) there was concern in the school about the lack of pupils who had attained Level 5 in English the previous year: 'At the moment we are pushing paragraphing and spelling and punctuation and higher reading skills'. The rest of the curriculum was taught in 'mixed-ability' groups but in some areas the three teachers divided National Curriculum topics and children moved between them. The teachers saw this as a strength but expressed some concern that the arrangement left them less opportunity to get to know the children in their registration group and to deal with pastoral matters.

Asked if the Key Stage 2 curriculum requirements had affected his teaching and the children's learning, a (male) Year 6 teacher said:

> From the children's point of view I don't think it has made any difference. They see schools as places where they're given tasks to do. They're not too bothered. I think they have been delivered a greater range of knowledge. It may be that it hasn't been delivered with as much flair or excitement. Perhaps there's less inspirational stuff there. But I certainly feel I've given them more in terms of quantity.

This then was the context in which Sean spent six years as a learner. In Year 5 he was described by his teacher as 'very able. He's a very bright lad but unless you test him, unless you actually push him to the limit, you wouldn't know it looking at his work. He's very laid back and he's really quite lazy'. However, 'he does listen. It goes in. He scores tremendously high results in any tests we give him'. True to form Sean attained Level 5 in the Maths SAT at the end of Key Stage 2. What he had not developed was any enthusiasm for Mathematics. However, it was not always so. In Year 1 we observed him engaged in a practical Maths activity involving shapes and colours. The task for his group was to create a picture of a house using different shapes for walls, roof, windows, etc. and to make each shape a different colour. The notes at the start of our systematic observation show Sean involved in discussion about the task with the group and then working with apparent concentration. Later on in the activity the observer noted 'Children discussing what they should and shouldn't do. Sean takes the lead here'. At the end of the lesson: 'Sean continues with his task even when asked to tidy up – clearly keen to finish'. In Year 2 he described to us with considerable pleasure making a Maths monster, an activity involving addition, cutting, colouring and sticking: 'We had to put in a box how much it made, colour it in, cut it out and stick it on a piece of paper'. He liked the end product because it 'looked like a tortoise'. He liked it even more because 'Mrs P said mine was excellent. She gave me one of the hardest'.

In the context of an 'infant' classroom and a relatively relaxed integrated curriculum (maintained in the face of the National Curriculum) Sean seems to have relished the challenge of the hardest task. However, in Key Stage 2, as we will see, the classroom climate changed and with it Sean's feelings about Maths.

In Year 3 the school signalled the passage to Key Stage 2 in quite specific ways: 'They have spelling tests for the first time, tables tests. Some children find it a little bit daunting' (Year 3 teacher). Weekly plans for the Year 3 class indicated a much more subject-based approach and emphasis on the Maths scheme (daily) over other Maths activities – weighing, measuring, ordering – which were done in ability groups. In this year Sean chose Maths as his most liked subject: it was 'quite good, a bit easy'. In Year 4 he liked Maths 'sometimes, but not always'. He did not like it 'when it's hard and I'm the last to finish'. He knew that there was an expectation about an amount to be done and told us about an incident when he was really worried.

> In Maths, I had only done two sums in a quarter of an hour and we had to show our books to Mrs X . She didn't see that I had only done two sums 'cause lucky for me I had forgot the date.

He was beginning to have a sense of the pressure of time, the need to complete work and to get on. With the emphasis on these as criteria Sean's slowness in working, his liking for having a chat about the work, and being relaxed and sociable became problematic.

As Key Stage 2 advanced Sean continued to be seen as 'able' and 'bright'. His teachers could only explain his apparent lack of motivation and application by referring to his 'laziness'. What had happened to the 7-year-old who relished being challenged by 'the hardest'? Why did a child who attained Level 5 at the end of the Key Stage constantly refer to Maths as 'hard' and develop a powerful dislike of the subject? Sean's own commentary on the situation suggests some of the factors that contributed to this change. In Year 5 he chose Maths as the subject he liked least and explained his reasons for this at some length:

> Maths, I just don't really like it. I think it's because most sums are hard. If you are on a blue book you go on to an orange book. I had just started the first page of the blue book on the last day of term and I was moved to the orange book. The first pages were easy and then it got harder and harder.

Just a few moments later in the same interview, however, he embarked on a relaxed and thoughtful anecdote about a sum he had just encountered:

> It was about chocolate bars. It said how much a pack of three is – 39p – and how much one is – 15p ... I saw that as 2p cheaper. I was saying to the person who sits next to me, 'That's a rip-off – for the one bar that was 15p'. And then I saw the question: how much cheaper is one bar in a pack of three? Just thinking about real sweets, I've realized they are cheaper in a pack of three. It's like that for Opal Fruits.

It did not occur to Sean that his discovery of a 'chocolate bar rip-off' and a conjunction between Mathematics and the reality of his world was worth mentioning to his teacher as well as his friend. The task he perceived in Maths was to work through the pages and the books getting sums right, not talking about them. Any intrinsic enjoyment he experienced was not seen as connected to the goals set by the teacher which were clearly evident in the overt hierarchical structures of the Maths scheme. Sean was not particularly competitive and it is also entirely possible that the ever-present assessment inherent in the scheme undermined his confidence in his capability. There was considerable pressure to 'perform' in the very public assessment arena of Greenmantle classrooms and Sean's 'laziness', his apparent reluctance to 'deliver', may well have been the consequence of an anxiety which he dealt with by engaging in sociable chat, withholding effort as a form of self-protection.

In Year 6 Maths was still his least liked subject and he was defining himself, perhaps again defensively, as someone who disliked using his brain.

> Maths is the first subject in the morning and your brain has to work really hard. With PE it's more physical and you don't have to use your brain so much.

Sean's self-assessments are also revealing. He told us in Year 5 that he was in between good and OK at Maths on the basis of two criteria: test results and getting finished – 'When I do exams I'm near the top but when I do normal Maths I'm one of the last'. In Year 6 he said he was 'good but very slow'. Getting finished became important for him as he accepted and tried to meet classroom criteria. How he felt about his teacher looking at his work depended on how much he had done: 'If I've done a lot, yes. If I haven't then, no'. He thought he was good at things where he was one of the first to finish. However, finishing first was not his preferred way of learning and there were costs when he tried to meet this criterion. His Year 6 teacher mentioned him as a fast finisher but suggested that sometimes the speed was secured at the expense of quality.

We see Sean in a situation which contained considerable tension for him. There was a mismatch between what he enjoyed about learning, the conditions under which he could thrive (and which were present in his early years) and the dominant criteria for success operative in his Years 5 and 6 classrooms. In these circumstances, although he tried to conform, his motivation was low.

We can see further evidence of the contradictions and uncertainties he was dealing with if we look at his explanations of why some people did better at school work than others. In Year 5 he suggested that chatterboxes don't do well; but he loved to chat and he knew he could do well:

> I think some people are natural chatterboxes, like me; but I work while I'm chatting. Those that do well put extra effort in. Some people don't listen and so that means they don't know so much.

The next year he had decided it was all about effort:

> Suppose some people are just made for it – born workers – mostly hard work.

In neither of these examples is it clear whether he included himself amongst the pupils he was describing.

Sean's choice of things he liked is also revealing. In Years 5 and 6 he chose as his favourite subjects things he enjoyed but was not good at, Technology and Art:

> I like making things. I'm always slow. We had to do a little book. I hadn't got very far.

> I like doing Art but I'm not very good. We were painting with acrylics. I did a vase with a few flowers and in the background was a tree with red apples and a distant hill and some sun and some shadows. I liked doing it because you can experiment with painting different colours and creating different effects.

Did he find these subjects more intrinsically interesting? Was he responding to a teaching/learning style that gave him a little more autonomy? As a 'slow worker' did he feel less pressure and less risk in these non-core areas? Behind his relaxed, charming, laid back surface and the knowledge that he was good at core subjects, was he worried by all the overt assessment? His construction of the ideal teacher suggests that the answer to all these questions is 'Yes'. In Year 5 his focus was on teaching and learning. He wanted a teacher 'who would let us have free choice all the time and help us with everything'. In Year 6 the concern was with assessment; he wanted a teacher who was 'not strict at all, funny, will tick every question – they would tell you the answers and wouldn't give you hard tests'.

In this context though, Sean was able to reflect on learning processes and act strategically. He could 'read' his teachers. He knew in Year 5 that when he was answering questions for two of his teachers it mattered that he did things the way they wanted them done; for the other two teachers he felt he could change things and use his own judgement about how to do it. In Year 6 he knew he could depart from doing things the way his class teacher wanted them when they were given a choice. He recounted at some length a discussion with his teacher about a radio programme she had heard where it was said that when children are given a choice they work better. He thought that he agreed with this. However, the opportunities he had to exercise choice and use his own judgement in these years were few.

The classroom culture he inhabited at the end of Key Stage 2 was not ideal for Sean's development as a learner. His experience suggests that, contrary to what his teacher believed, he had noticed and reacted to the lack of 'flair or excitement' in the teaching which a focus on quantity and the pressure for results had produced. However, with the tensions and contradictions we have suggested, in Year 6 Sean was still able to say in answer to our question about whether he liked the teacher to look at his work, 'It depends if I'm happy with my work myself'. This assertion of the validity of self-assessment in the midst of such a barrage of categoric assessment is strangely heartening. However, it seems sad that although he attained Level 5 his experience of Mathematics did not make it possible for Sean to develop the enthusiasm of Key Stage 1 into an intrinsically motivated interest in the subject.

11.3 HALEY, KEVIN, RICHARD AND AMANDA – DEVELOPING LEARNER IDENTITIES

Taking as a starting point their beliefs about why some people do better at school work than others, we develop the stories of four pupils and their changing view of themselves as learners.

Haley at St Bede's (SATs Level 3, 3, 3)

I don't know but when they gets tired they gets lazy. My sister gets lazy as well, and my dad – he doesn't get up in the morning.

(Year 1)

Because they get on well with their work and they don't mess about or nothing. They don't say, 'Miss, Miss', they just get on.

(Year 2)

It's because some are faster and they're good writers and they try harder.

(Year 3)

They learn a lot and they don't muck about and don't want to do other things.

(Year 4)

They just are really. Get it in on time and do the right things. Just ... I don't know.

(Year 5)

They're just brainy. They're born like that.

(Year 6)

In her first two years at school Haley explained success in terms of effort, getting on with it, and not messing about. She enjoyed school and her easy acceptance of its routines is summed up in her response when asked how she felt about having her work looked at: 'They does a tick and then we doos (sic) our Maths. I feel happy'. In Year 3 she continued to mention effort but added speed and skill in writing. Her growing awareness of the importance of these additional factors in her own experience is evidenced by her concern about her teacher's evaluation of her work:

> When I started work I'd only done the date and Miss came to look. I hurried and did two lines and she said 'Not bad' and I thought 'Oh, thank God'.

(Year 3)

She already seems to be positioning herself with those who do not have the characteristics she associates with doing well.

Effort in the form of 'not mucking about' was still very evident in her reasoning in Year 4 but this time she added a reference to interest and motivation – those who do well in school work 'don't want to do other things'. She seemed to be suggesting that being able to work at things you do not particularly like is a factor in success. Evidence from her teacher this year suggests that this was not something Haley found easy to do:

> She's in the bottom ten of the class. I used to teach her mum – she was in the bottom ten too. Haley would like a very pleasant time with no hassle whatsoever. She doesn't push herself. She's quite a sweet girl and no trouble behaviourwise. She just doesn't listen. Switches off very easily.

In the last two years of Key Stage 2 Haley's reasoning about success was moving away from 'effort' towards 'ability'. She saw others 'doing the right things' but she couldn't explain why it happened – 'They just are'. In Year 6 her teacher described her attainment: 'Quite poor. She tries hard but doesn't produce the goods. She struggles'. Her approach to her work was characterized as 'positive; she is polite, asks questions, is not shy'. But 'she doesn't always get it right'.

The evidence of Haley's own commentary on her experiences is far from positive. The feelings she reported about the activities we observed her engaged in showed decreasing enjoyment and increasing ambivalence. Assessment or evaluation of her work made her tense and very worried. She cared very much about getting things right.

> I feel nervous. He may say, 'No, that's wrong'.

(Year 4)

> I mind a lot. He might tell me to do it again if I get something wrong. I hide my book under piles of books. I find it very worrying when I know he wants to see my book.

(Year 5)

I don't like giving in my book because it's a mess. I hide it at the bottom of the pile. She doesn't normally say it's good on my English. On my Maths she said I was getting better. But I just don't like handing in my book.

(Year 6)

For Haley there was a lot at stake in these moments and this anxiety was carried over into her learning where her response to being encouraged to 'figure it out' was to 'try to think, but usually I ask Kyle'. It was important to Haley to work with people who could help her because that reduced the risk of not knowing what to do. In a climate so focused on 'producing the goods' and getting things right, Haley had little resilience when faced with difficulty and compared her work unfavourably with what others produced. By Year 6 she had developed a self-fulfilling prophecy view of her capability: 'If I say I can't do things, I'm not good'.

For Haley, 'effort' was no longer an adequate explanation for 'doing better' and she moved to a much bleaker and more explicit statement of the idea she had been circling around the previous year: 'They're just brainy. They're born like that'.

Kevin at Audley Junior (SATs Level 3, 3, 3)

Girls don't know much.

(Year 1)

Don't know.

(Year 2)

'Cos they've been trying harder at home.

(Year 3)

I don't know.

(Year 4)

'Cos they've got brains.

(Year 5)

They got a brain what works.

(Year 6)

'Cos they're clever – got a brain.

(Year 6 – SATs interview)

In Year 3 when Kevin was attributing success to effort at home his teacher wrote on his end of year report: 'He's got ability but he does not apply himself. He needs constant supervision to ensure that he is gainfully employed. He will not realize his true potential until he accepts responsibility for his own learning'. In conversation she characterized him as having 'poor ability and poor attainment, but also underachieving. I don't really think he sees it as his job to put effort in in order to get results out. He spends a long time on work-avoidance tactics'. In class Kevin was being urged to stay in his seat, not wander about talking to people, and to concentrate and make an effort. None of these featured in his explanations of success.

Although he attained Level 3 in the Key Stage 2 SATs, Kevin was consistently rated by his teachers as attaining at Level 1 or 2. In Year 5 he was 'in the poorer group for most things'; in Year 6 his teacher told us he was 'low ability'. Most teaching was in 'ability groups' so Kevin was continually presented with the evidence of his place in the scheme of things. Over this period, too, he was in trouble in the playground for 'being a bit of a bully and picking on others'. At home his parents were splitting up and because of the associated violence he was being cared for by his grandmother.

Not surprising perhaps that by Year 5 he had decided that what mattered for success was having 'brains'. In class in Year 6 his behaviour was causing problems and the work-avoidance commented on in Year 3 was still evident. His average level of distraction this year was 25 per cent and he was observed engaged with a task only 42 per cent of the time on average. But his teachers liked him and had not quite given up.

> I don't think he really sees the point of it. He gives up very easily with the slightest of tasks. Sometimes I've spent dinner times with him, and come the next lesson he'll sit there and he'll say 'I don't know what to do'. And I'll say 'Well, Kevin, I spent yesterday with you doing it'. And he just pushes things away. 'Oh well, I don't know'. He gives up.
>
> (Mrs Jones, Year 6 teacher)

He thought his teacher was 'kind' but complained about her availability to help him.

> Normally she's with all the girls but she helps you if you are stuck very bad. The worst is she says, 'I'll not be five minutes' and then a couple of minutes later she goes off with someone else.
>
> (Year 6)

Given the circumstances Kevin was not likely to 'take responsibility for his own learning' in order to 'realize his true potential' as his Year 3 teacher required. Instead he consistently exhibited the characteristics of teacher-dependence and 'learned helplessness'. He attributed his failure, by implication, to the fact that he was not one of those who had 'a brain what works'.

Richard at Valley (SATs Level 4, 4, 4)

> Some people concentrate more.
>
> (Year 3)

> Maybe they have more patience and they concentrate and some of the others rush and only do a bit. The patient ones write two pages and they look things up in dictionaries.
>
> (Year 4)

> Some people understand better than others. I don't know why.
>
> (Year 5)

> People are always better at some things than others. They understand it more.
>
> (Year 6)

In Years 3 and 4 Richard's explanations for success reflected very strongly his teacher's comments about him in Year 3:

> I'm trying to slow him down . . . he's always there, finished. 'Have you checked it?' 'No'. He's always really keen to be the first to finish and I'm trying to get him to see that first is not always best – if you slow down a bit . . .

In Year 5 his school report said 'must check work carefully and not forget to check spellings', but his teacher's view in interview was that he had

> learned this year to take care with what he does . . . and (that he) doesn't have to gallop through at all costs. He's learned the value of taking time, thinking, checking, talking about what he's doing, thinking it through beforehand.

In Years 5 and 6 Richard's answers suggest that he had moved beyond instrumental explanations of success and failure (which he seems to have dealt with in his own learning) to grappling with the idea that doing better at work is about understanding, that some people 'understand better' than others, and that this can vary depending on what 'things' they are doing. The sense that Richard is reflecting on learning processes is endorsed by his teacher's remarks:

> He's definitely a thinker . . . He takes on board what you say and has a little think about it. He often asks questions about things and sometimes he will sort of agonize about it quietly but he's begun now to realize that it's worth querying something if you are not sure, if you perhaps don't agree. So I think he looks on learning as a sort of challenge – part of life and an important part.
>
> (Mrs Lamb, head and Year 6 teacher)

As a significant other in the development of Richard's learning disposition his teacher appears to have helped him to this focus on understanding (rather than effort or cruder notions of 'ability' such as 'got a brain') by her encouragement of thoughtful and interactive learning processes.

Richard's comments on learning activities were consistently connected with enjoyment. He thought he was good at things because he 'concentrated' (Year 3), 'I know what to do and how to do them and I don't get stuck so much' (Year 5), and because he liked 'finding out about things' (Year 6). In his work he was concerned with quality and willing to have a go when his teacher set him a challenge. In Chapter 9 we have already cited Richard and his group as showing persistence when required to work something out by themselves. Our systematic observation shows Richard with a very low average for distraction (9 per cent) and a high level of task engagement (72.7 per cent). When we asked him about being distracted he said, 'It doesn't happen when I'm doing something hard because I'm concentrating too much'.

During his time at primary school Richard appeared to have developed very positive learning dispositions. However, in Year 6 there were signs that circumstances were posing a threat to his sense of himself as a successful learner. In the summer of Year 6 he told us,

> I used to like it (when my teacher looked at my work) but not much now. It worries me that I've done something wrong, especially now that SATs are coming up. I'm a bit worried about them.

The emphasis on assessment that Valley, like all the others schools, felt they had to make created for Richard a sense of risk that he had so far not experienced in his learning. It is to be hoped that this was a passing phase and that his previous liking for open-endedness and challenge reasserted itself.

Amanda at Kenwood (SATs Level 4, 3, 4)

They think in their minds and the others don't.

(Year 1)

They learn more and work harder.

(Year 2)

Some might be faster ... only get one page done when others do five.

(Year 3)

Some people practise at home more.

(Year 4)

I think it's just because they take their work home and they get it done quicker because they are quick writers.

(Year 5)

People that do better practise more and they are more determined to learn and get higher marks.

(Year 6)

Amanda's analysis reflects much of her own experience over the six years of the project. Practising at home in particular became a very significant factor for Amanda as in Year 6 she became more work-oriented and determined to get higher marks herself. Her teacher, commenting on her change of attitude, connected this with the closer links between the school and Amanda's mother and the amount of support she was getting at home. Amanda had always liked homework but it was not until Year 6 that any parent took an active interest. Amanda's disposition was evidently benefiting now from a close congruence between home and school values in relation to learning. In addition, we can see in Amanda's nominations the emphasis on speed which, we noted in Chapter 9, preoccupied so many pupils. This is very much a reflection of classroom emphases. In Year 5, for instance, our field note observations recorded the teacher's reception of a Maths worksheet: 'Oh that's very fast for you isn't it? That's the fastest you've ever done it'.

Before Year 6 Amanda's attitude had been characterized as 'could try harder' (Year 1), 'lacks confidence' (Year 3), 'immature, needs attention' (Year 4). Maths in particular presented her with a learning challenge, and one which she was reluctant to face:

She doesn't like Maths ... she tends to try ... if I say, not to do it. Well, it takes a long time to encourage her, to motivate her to do Maths ... For Amanda the easiest way of dealing with the whole subject is to avoid it.

(Mrs Green, Year 5 teacher)

In other areas she was described as: 'Strong-willed. She works well if she enjoys it – if she doesn't work can be "lost", or she'll sit and talk to somebody else and look as though she's working hard. She'll even volunteer to do something for me'. This sophisticated strategy of evasion ran parallel with Amanda's anxiety about performance. 'If I do things wrong I feel stupid' (Year 4), 'I'm worried she is going to say, "Do that again"' (Year 4), 'I'm nervous. Worried 'cause I'm afraid I might do something wrong' (Year 5). She was very dependent on her group to help her out.

In Year 6, when her teacher saw such a change in her Amanda still claimed 'If I don't enjoy it I don't put as much effort in'. Maths was still a challenge but her own account of one example of this does not suggest evasion:

> On one piece of Maths I had, I was there for ages trying to do it. And when I did do it I got them all wrong so Mrs G asked me to do them again and then I got them all wrong again. And I did them again and I got a few wrong, and I asked. I was there for ages doing it. About three days. They were about 'time' but it was a weird one because it didn't explain that much. Some people were working with me but I still didn't understand it when they were telling me. In the end Mrs G said 'You don't have to do it again', so I just left it.

In the end Amanda was let off the hook but the account does not suggest a strategy of deliberate failure or of attrition with the aim of being told. Rather there is a sense of the struggle to understand and some disappointment at being told to stop in such an unsatisfactory way. This interpretation fits well with Amanda's teacher's view of her more purposeful disposition. In her comments on group work too she stresses reciprocity though she is happy to depend on others' expertise: 'I'm not that good at spelling. If I have to write something I usually have to ask someone', rather than develop independent strategies.

Amanda's comment in Year 6 about having her work looked at, 'Worried, but pleased if she puts excellent', suggests a more positive (even optimistic) view of assessment. It is not possible to tell from the data whether the imminence of standardized assessment brought about this greater degree of focus and resilience. About her experience of the mock SATs, Amanda managed only a non-committal 'It was OK', but she appeared unworried.

It is fairly certain though that a combination of teacher, parent and friends (the 'group of strong girls she liked to work with') sustained her in developing a more positive disposition and a more confident sense of herself as a learner.

11.4 NEIL – THE INFLUENCE OF OTHERS

Neil's story examines the role of significant others in the development of learner identity.

Neil attended Audley Junior School. A child of a second marriage, he had an older half brother. Neil and his father bred budgerigars. 'I've got about 200, in a big shed. Me and Dad, we go to shows and show 'em.' Throughout the PACE study Maths was Neil's favourite subject. In Year 6 he recalled work he had done in the Year 5 class, a year in which his teacher had attended a course for Maths coordinators. She had set him a problem: 'It was a Maths puzzle. Miss told me I done some very hard work and done it good'. He recalled that she had 'taken it to college'. His teacher did not remember this. That year, Year 5, she assessed Neil as 'middle ability – operating to the best of his ability'. She thought his Maths had improved. 'He was on quite a low book but I moved him on because I felt that he was capable of more'. In Year 4, when he was 'on a low book', Neil chose Maths as his most liked subject: 'It's more exciting because you get to do a lot more things like measure water, weigh things and sums'. The next year, when his teacher identified him as 'middle ability', he chose Maths again ''Cos I like adding up sums. I'm one of the best in the class I think. Last time I got 20 out of 20 and 10 out of 10'. His teacher in Year 6, however, described him as 'reasonably able ... might be a Level 5' but assessed him eventually as Level 4.

In the same Year 6 class of 23, Brian ('mathematically far advanced'), Helen and Michelle were identified as the 'most able' at Maths. Their teacher described how they and three others (not including Neil) had been allowed to 'have a go' at the previous year's end-of-Key Stage extension paper. 'Those were the ones that I felt, if they were going to be borderline, let's bring them in and let's let them see it.' She had been allocated some of the special needs teacher's time and asked her to 'give my bright ones a couple of hours' boost forward ... It was quite a luxury ... I feel very guilty always catching up with the ones who can't ... who get stuck ... and perhaps not seeing some of the middle ones, or not pushing on with the better ones'. When they had done the test their teacher sent them back to the special educational needs teacher: 'She'll go through all the answers and you'll see and you'll say, "Oh yes, I could have done that"'.

Why was Neil, also a borderline Level 5, not included? Had his teacher not noticed Neil's ongoing enthusiasm for Maths? In class he was described as 'quiet, cooperative, no trouble'. 'If you put comments on his work, then he'll respond and he'll come and say, "Am I doing this better? Is this what you wanted?"' But perhaps Neil was too quiet and cooperative, except when he was in trouble in the playground. This teacher had already identified behavioural problems with certain combinations of children as one of the influences on her planning and teaching. He got on well with most children in the class but there had been one or two fighting incidents at lunchtime involving Brian who had a long troubled history of challenging behaviour. The two had to be kept apart or there would be 'fireworks'. In interview his teacher talked of her relationship with the children: chatting at lunchtime in class and in the playground, finding time to sit and talk; she illustrated her answers with anecdotes and recollections of the children but Neil's name did not come up. Talking about him she mentioned his lack of social skills, noticed at school camp. At a mealtime he had been 'ill-mannered to the point of vulgarity' and was sent to his room. He had also been in trouble in school when another pupil had, without his permission, read the 'private diary' pupils were encouraged to keep and told Miss about the 'bad language' in it. The attitude of another pupil, Julian, whose father was a doctor and who had been bullied earlier in the year by Brian, who saw him as an academic rival, impressed her more. At an individual post-trial SAT review with Julian she pointed out what in his work was 'bringing him down'. As she explained, 'He's a sensible boy and he immediately said, "All right then what have I got to do for the next level?"' Neil, eager for Maths, but anxious and socially inexperienced seems unlikely to have exhibited this kind of response.

There are also issues here of cultural capital. Brian, adopted into a professional family, was perceived as 'a problem' but 'a charmer'. 'He can go off the rails but he knows when he's gone too far. He'll say "I'm sorry. I'm sorry."' Neil, kept apart from Brian, also felt ill at ease with Julian, the doctor's son, with whom he had been paired for work:

> He lives in that old school house at the top. And he don't, like, come down to where we live so we can't play with him most of the time. Dan and Liam and Scott live all near me so we just play all the time. I like to work with them. We work together proper and we don't act daft.

Unlike the confident Brian, Neil felt ambivalent about showing his work to his teacher. He could not predict her response:

> I'm actually kind of worried because if she don't like it, or if she likes it. Like I'm nervous.

Lacking confidence that he had his teacher's endorsement for his self-assessment that he was good in Maths, he cited his father as evidence:

> He used to learn at school, do lots of sums, every three seconds he did a multiplication. He teaches me how to do long multiplications. I don't know what he's saying really because I can't explain.

Neil's confusion reflects a lack of congruence between school and home. The family were viewed as 'trouble'. His father, a manual worker, 'came into school in dirty overalls to complain about something that wasn't anything to do with the school'. There is no evidence in the data of any encouragement of Neil's capability in Maths. He seemed constantly unsure about this. Asked to identify pupils who were good at school work he nominated Helen, Michelle and Brian and added 'I'm good. I'm OK'. Interviewed before the end-of-Key Stage 2 assessment, Brian said, 'Actually I want to do them. To see how good I am'. Neil said he was 'OK. But I don't really like doing it in case it don't work out right'. In the event Neil, like Brian, attained Level 5 in Maths. He told us he 'got on quite good' with his teacher. In the context of an interview and a direct question he said he would like her to 'give me hard sums to do when I want and feel a need for them' but he hadn't asked.

What is remarkable about this example is that Neil managed to maintain his enthusiasm and, to an extent, his confidence when he appeared to be getting comparatively little endorsement from his teacher. Kept out of the elite Maths group in order to preserve harmony, Neil seems to have got his main emotional support for his view of himself as 'good at Maths' from his father. His model of the ideal teacher was 'a man who likes football and helps you if you are in trouble', which suggests a degree of mismatch with the teachers he actually had. As a significant other, his teacher in Year 6 did little to reinforce his sense of his capability in Maths. His social inadequacy may have made him less likely to be viewed as a pupil with 'potential'. What is clear is that a disposition to persist and be self-reliant, evident but not accountable for in the data, enabled him to be successful.

11.5 JESSICA AND SCOTT – RESPONDING TO THE SAT CHALLENGE

This case-study tells the story of Jessica and Scott as they took the end-of-Key Stage 2 tests in Writing at Kenwood School. In Chapter 10 we saw how the pupils at Kenwood were dealing with conflicting messages from their teacher. While telling them that the tests were not important, she was also demonstrating her acute anxiety that they should all do well. This was made more problematic for them by the strong relationship between class and teacher. This was the children's second year with Mrs Green and they all liked and respected her, and felt secure in her class.

> The others are always too nice or too miserable. She's all in between. If she's in a bad mood she'll walk about and check on your work so you do better work. She's kind, she's nice and she's very thoughtful. She helps you a lot.
>
> (Scott, Year 6, Kenwood)

> She's funny. She makes us laugh and we make her laugh.
>
> (Jessica, Year 6)

We can see the tensions inherent in SATs week played out in this account of the Writing SAT constructed from field notes during which observation was focused on those two pupils, Jessica (4, 4, 4) and Scott (3, 3, 3).

> At 8.55 the children came into the classroom. It was the fourth day of tests and they seemed resigned and accepting; there were no overt signs of anxiety. A group gathered around Mrs Green and one girl was heard to say that she would like it like this all the time: 'We get more work done'. Soon after 9.00 the children were at their tables, reorganized so that each child could sit separately, in alphabetical order, pencil cases at the ready. Scott and Luke had set up rows of plastic models of footballers on their tables as mascots. Mrs Green called the dinner register and asked if anyone wanted to go to the toilet. Half the class went out.
>
> At 9.10 Mrs Green called for attention: 'Right let's have you sitting down and listening please'. Scott, anticipating problems and already wanting reassurance, asked 'Miss are you allowed to use your dictionary?'. Before she could respond she had to deal with questions about who was doing the extension tests. In the subsequent discussion no names were mentioned and there was no indication of whether anyone would be taking these tests. It is interesting that in a class where there were no Teacher Assessments above Level 4 for English this was still on the children's agenda. After this diversion Mrs Green moved to the instructions for the Writing test. 'Right now, you need to listen carefully.' She explained about the planning sheet and the writing book, asked questions to check understanding of the difference between a story and 'information writing'. During this Scott tidied his mascots and fiddled with his pencil sharpener. Was he following these instructions? Jessica appeared more attentive.
>
> Mrs Green conducted a quick interactive session about story writing, emphasizing the need for a title, beginning, middle, end and sentences. Looking directly at Scott she emphasized 'Right, sentences Mr Carpenter'. Finally she gave out the planning sheet.
>
> At 9.15 Scott began straight away without stopping to tick a 'starting point'. Lips pursed and with great concentration he wrote, in sentences, across both pages. When he had in essence written a story, he listed the names of his characters. Jessica, having read the booklet, made notes using and ticking the points to remember: setting, characters, how the story begins, what happens. She then looked around and waited. Eventually she

went back to her planning sheet and added 'How it ends' and 'Middle'. She stopped and waited again.

At 9.30 Mrs Green: 'You may start now writing your story. Remember, every story has a start and middle and an end. (The assumption is that everyone is writing a story.) If you need another sheet of paper you must say so. Don't forget what a sentence is.'

At this signal Scott moved immediately to the writing booklet. His story was about a boy called Luke and a talking teddy bear (see Figure 11.2). He wrote with great care, his chin on the table. He was elaborating on and developing the story he had already written on his planning sheet. The developments included an argument about age between Mum and the bear, a violent death – the bear's in a fight with the dog – Luke's grief, a funeral, resurrection in the form of the son of the bear, and a final earthquake which wipes out all the characters. The observer recalled Scott a few months earlier saying: 'I was worried about the SATs and stuff and I had just sat a practice one and my grandad died. He lived with me. It was quite a shock.'

While writing Scott put his hand up to ask if he could alter a word he thought he had spelt wrong. Mrs Green: 'Yes, and you can use a dictionary'. She then moved around the class and put a dictionary on each table. Scott worked on. He accidentally kicked the leg of his table and his footballers crashed to the floor where he left them. There was little response from the other children to this diversion. After ten minutes Scott had produced eight lines. He used his feet to scoop up his mascots and began writing again, occasionally looking at his 'notes'.

Jessica wrote steadily from the start (see Figure 11.1). Throughout she managed to effect the exchange of an error-removing pen with Clare who was sitting in front of her.

When Mrs Green informed the class that they had 30 minutes left (no evidence that they were watching the clock) Jessica had written a page and a half and was reading through her story carefully. Scott was now on his second page, pausing to look up a word in the dictionary.

Mrs Green: 'You have another twenty minutes. If you think you have finished will you please check your work again. Check everything again. You should all be doing at least, at least two to three sides. You should all fill up the paper. At least.'

At this point Jessica had written a page and a half and finished the story she planned about talking toys.

Mrs Green to Jessica: 'How many sides have you done?'

Jessica: 'I'm on my second.'

Mrs Green: 'Well do some more.'

Jessica started writing again – she changed her final full stop to a comma, wrote 'then …' and launched into another story, this time about a talking hamster.

Mrs Green circulated, encouraging the children: 'Good boy, well done', 'Well done', 'Good'. She was reading what they had written. The children worked on quietly.

Mrs Green: 'You have fifteen minutes to go.'

Scott had now covered a page and a half. He wrote 'The end'.

Mrs Green: 'You've got ten minutes left so you should be thinking about how you are going to finish.' She moved to Scott. 'Are you sure you've done everything? You are going to check?' Scott asked whether he should put a capital letter on Billy. She smiled and asked 'What do you think?' He corrected all his lower case bs. He read his story through again, but very quickly, his eyes flickering across the page.

Mrs Green: 'Five minutes left. If you think you have finished, check capital letter, full stops, everything you have been taught, everything. Check that your name is on the front of the paper.' Her final comment produced a flutter of activity – here was something they *could* do.

Look Who's Talking!

"One night I was in my bedroom fast asleep when I heard a noise". It sounded like talking but when I got out of my bed I found all my toys were alive. With that I ran down stairs and woke up my mum and Dad and said "my toys are alive, quick come and see". When they got up there they were all back to normal. The next day my cousin came round to stay for the week. When I went to sleep I heard the noise again, but this time I woke up my cousin because she was sleeping in the same room as me.

When I woke her up she said "whats the noise... I said "look"!

The toys were tidying up my bedroom, my cousin said "excellent"!. Then I said "hello" why are you doing this for us". The toys said "we are you friend but not your cousin.".

The next day I woke up and
found it was all a dream. I
rushed down stairs to tell my
mum and dad, then they said
"your cousin is coming round
for the week. Oh no not again!"
It was really fun with my cousin
she was really funny, it did not
happen again thank goodness "But
the next day some thing else
happened my hamster had died
then all of a sudden it came
back to live and started to
talk. I was so happy, I could
even ask her if she was
alright or if she wanted any
more food. Then one day my
uncle came round and he was
a vet and he made my hamster
back to normal. It wasn't that
fun because when she had
gone back to normal, I couldn't
ask her weather she was

alright. But that was ok because
on the weekend we brought a
male hamster and my hamster
was a she and when she had
babies, my hamster must of had
some talking powder left in
her. So when they mated it
must of passed through her to
the male and the babies. So all
of them could speak to each
other. It was so fun because I
could ask them their real names.
and they were chrunchie, Rebecca,
Hannah, Sara and the Dad name
was tom. So they all lived happily
ever after.

THE
END!

If you need more paper, ask your teacher.

SCAA, Statutory Assessment Team, Newcombe House, 45 Notting Hill Gate, London W11 3JB
ACAC, Primary Team, Castle Buildings, Womanby Street, Cardiff CF1 9SX
© Crown copyright 1996

Figure 11.1 Jessica's Key Stage 2 Writing SAT story

Scott had finished. He looked around and waited, fiddling with his pencil sharpener.

Jessica was checking her work. She seemed to be watching Mrs Green for cues as to when and what she should be doing.

Mrs Green: 'Well done. You've done really well. You have three minutes left.' Scott was putting his pen and pencils away in his pencil case, packing up, folding his paper. Jessica was reading the front sheet of her booklet.

Mrs Green, stood up, watching: 'You have one minute left.' Most children had finished. Some were reading their work, a few made corrections. Scott was playing with his mascots.

Mrs Green who had appeared tired, resigned, anxious, impotent throughout, then said: 'You should be finishing off your final sentence. All right. Now stop.' The papers were collected. The children, somewhat subdued, lined up for assembly.

The tensions for this very committed teacher arose from her concern for the children's feelings and her anxiety that they perform well. The consequences of that tension for the children are well-illustrated here The observer's notes comment on the atmosphere created during the test as 'a combination of support and threat, open to being enabling or constraining'. At the end of the test Liam (Level 3) was in tears and being comforted by Mrs Green. She told us that he was upset because 'he didn't think he had done as best as he could'. A sense that the children felt they were somehow expected to outperform themselves in the tests is difficult to avoid. The teacher interview about the SATs is full of references to 'being disappointed' in what the children had produced, and to their 'performances which weren't what any of us expected'. Yet the teacher assessment and SAT levels were the same for all, including Liam, except six children – for four their SAT score was higher, only two were lower. The external pressures on the teacher for good results may have prompted unrealistic hopes.

Mrs Green's well-intentioned encouragement and standard setting during the test certainly had an adverse effect on Jessica. The whole week, Jessica told us, she was 'worried 'cos I wanted to do my best'. She said she found Maths easier 'because I know what to do'. The Writing SAT was the hardest: 'I didn't explain it that well – I wasn't sure what I was doing. I found it too long, 'cos you had to write three pages; some people had to do three but some had to do less than three.' Since the end of the test she seemed to have rationalized her teacher's comments and now believed that the test was differentiated in its demands. Her response when she deduced that the story she had written was inadequate also suggests a lack of clarity about the criteria on which her work would be assessed. It was only during the test that she discovered a criterion of length (invented by her teacher) which appeared to be important and she immediately did her best to respond, thus unbalancing her planned story. Her behaviour during the Writing SAT, the way she watched her teacher for cues, made it an unsettling experience for her, even if it did not affect the assessment.

Scott thought the tests were 'pretty hard really. They just made you scared. I didn't want to do 'em'. He thought the writing test was the hardest because 'you had to write a lot, your hand started to get tiring; you had to think a lot; it took all the energy out of your brain'. However he wasn't scared of the Writing test ''cos we'd done one already and I got a Level 2/3 or 3/4, so I thought it's not that bad'. He thought the story was 'quite easy ... it just came to me all at once'. For Scott the previous test had reassured him that he was somewhere around Level 3 and that was

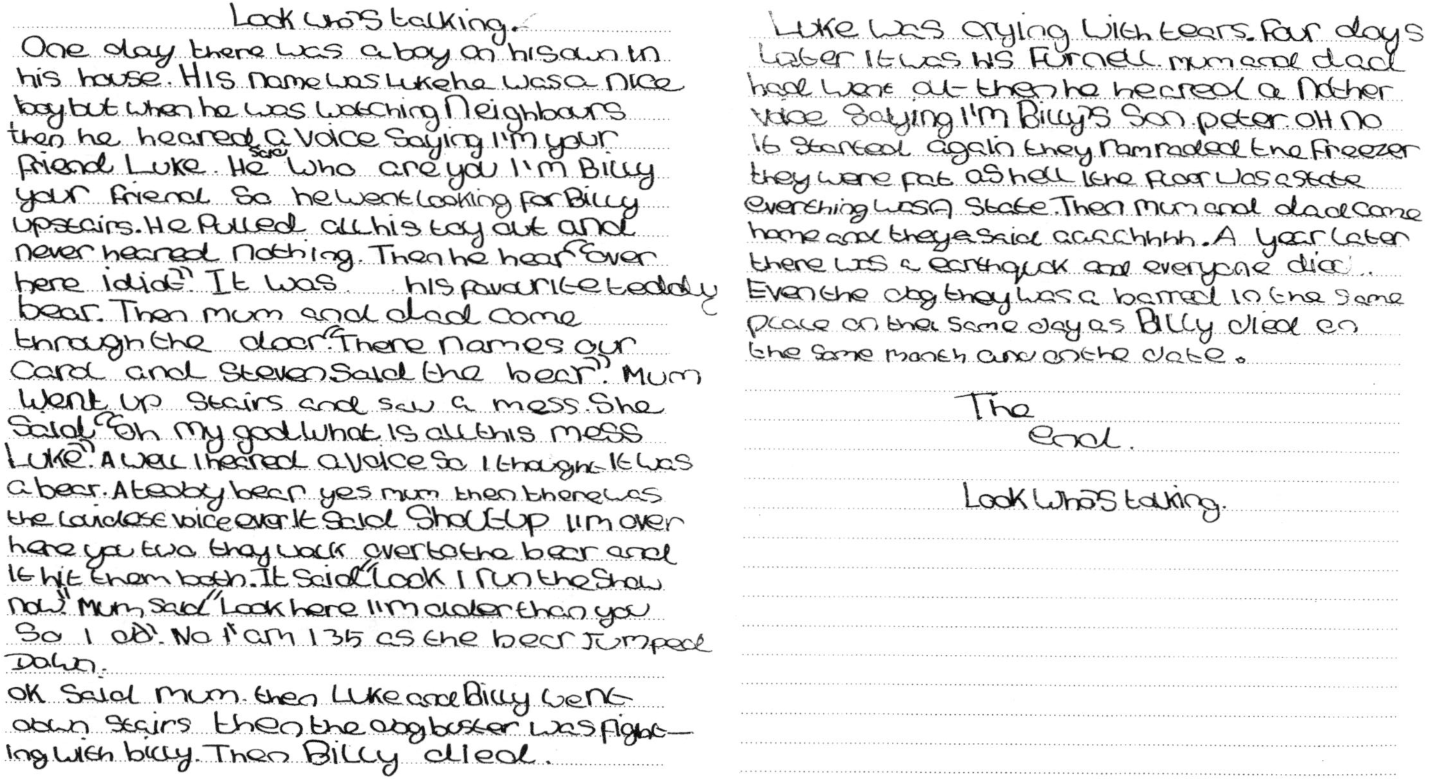

Look who's talking.

One day there was a boy on his own in his house. His name was Luke he was a nice boy but when he was watching Neighbours then he heared a voice saying I'm your friend. Luke he go. Who are you. I'm Billy your friend. So he went looking for Billy upstairs. He pulled all his toy out and never heared nothing. Then he heard over here I did? It was _____ his favourite teddy bear. Then mum and dad come through the door "There names are Carol and Steven Said the bear? Mum went up stairs and saw a mess. She Said "oh my god what is all this mess Luke? A voice I heard a voice so I thought it was

a bear. A teddy bear. yes mum then phone was the loudest voice ever. It Said Shut-up. I'm over here you two they look over to the bear and It hit them both. It said "Look I run the show now? Mum Said "look here I'm older than you So I did? No I am 135 as the bear jumped down.

ok Said mum then Luke and Billy went down stairs then the bag boxer was fighting with billy. Then Billy died...

Luke was crying with tears for days Later it was his Funrel. mum and dad had Luke out then he heared a nother vioce Saying I'm Billy's Son peter oH No. It Started again they hammaled the Freezer they were ras as hell like Ron was a skete everything was a State. Then mum and dad come home and they said aaachhh. A year later there was a earthquck and everyone died... Everyone day they had a burrel to the same place on the same day as Billy died on the same month and on the date.

The
end.

Look who's talking.

Figure 11.2 Scott's Key Stage 2 Writing SAT story

sufficient for him. This left him free to attack the story he wanted to tell as he thought best and not be worried that his planning (unlike Jessica's, which is a model of the suggested approach) was unorthodox, or that he might not have written enough. He wrote 'The end' when he still had fifteen minutes left, but his teacher, apparently expecting less of him than of Jessica, did not comment.

As a significant other Mrs Green had worked with Scott to develop his self-confidence. In Years 3 and 4 he had, in the main, a model of his attainment as being fixed: 'I'm not brainy enough', 'You've got to be brainy for Science'. But in Year 6 he had decided that 'the ones who don't do very good take time to think about it. Put more time and effort in'. He placed himself in this category and added 'If you do something you think is good and she says, "That's rubbish" then you get a bit upset'. Although he still believed that 'the others just know it like that (clicks fingers) because they're bright' he also believed in the power of effort. However it seems clear that less was expected of him than Jessica and this meant that he exhibited less anxiety about the writing and thus felt free to disregard the instructions and do it his way.

Jessica, on the other hand, was perceived as a higher achiever. She too believed in the power of effort and of persistence. She saw herself as one of those who do better at school work and explained they were successful 'because they have a go at it and if they get a mistake they have another go and try and understand it'. This very well describes her approach to the test. Unfortunately, although she had persistence she was also teacher-dependent, or at least dependent enough to assume that utterances during a test should not be ignored. As a consequence she became confused and lost confidence in herself.

11.6 LAURA, ALICE, KIM AND KATE – GIRLS' CONFIDENCE AND DEPENDENCE IN MATHEMATICS

Of the children in our sample who attained Level 5 in the end-of-Key Stage tests the girls were less confident of claiming that they were good at Maths and Science than the boys. In English, girls who were high achievers were much more likely to say they were good. Of the equal number of boys and girls who scored Level 5 in Maths only one of the boys did not consider himself good at Maths. Of the girls, only two told us they thought they were good at Maths, the other three claimed to be 'OK' or even 'not so good'. This case-study looks at the attitudes, dispositions and learning identities of four of these girls.

Laura

Laura at Orchard, like Alice, thought she was good at Maths. These two both had a long-standing confidence in their mathematical ability. In Year 2 when she joined the study Laura told us 'I'm really good at Maths. I do Maths at home every day. I love work and I'm very good'. The next year she still thought she was 'very good – I'm in the top Maths group. I've been practising'. By Year 5 she assessed herself as 'excellent' and added 'Maths is my best subject. I want to be a Maths teacher when I grow up. I've always wanted that. Both my parents are accountants. It runs in the family'. In Year 6 she confined herself simply to a succinct 'VERY good' but the capital letters were clear.

Laura's references to home and family were a regular feature of her interviews and always with reference to Maths:

> Mum buys me Maths books at home.
>
> (Year 3)

> I'm good at Maths. My parents are part of it. They are accountants. It runs in the family. I have lots of Maths books at home. I sometimes do Maths in the holidays.
>
> (Year 5)

> I'm good at Maths. My mum and dad are both accountants.
>
> (Year 6)

At home Laura's identity as successful, even exceptional, at Maths was constantly reinforced and even perceived by her as inevitable destiny. At school she saw her teachers as not dissenting from this view and supporting her progress:

> I like her. She's kind – and it's the way she sets hard Maths. She gives me Year 6 Maths. When I'm in Year 6 I don't know what she'll do.
>
> (Year 5)

> If I have problems in Maths I ask for help. She comes straight away to see me if I put my hand up.
>
> (Year 6)

Her ideal teacher was one who 'gives you hard Maths and hard work and lots of homework', and she was happy to acknowledge a match between herself and her perception of the ideal pupil as someone who 'gets on and doesn't talk'.

She saw herself as someone who enjoyed work: 'I just go and I never stop', 'I just think about what I'm doing and I want to finish it', 'I always think about work'. She was pragmatic in her approach to learning, preferring the teacher to choose as this ensured more order and efficiency. She was pleased to be 'the only one that finished' in Maths, to be 'top of the class' and to have the teacher put 'Fantastic. Well done' on her work. Only once, in Year 4, was there any sense that being successful in Maths was not something to be celebrated. In that year she told us 'Sometimes I have to say I don't like the work or the others in the class call me a wimp'.

It is interesting that in Years 5 and 6 she said she did not know why some people did better than others at school work, whereas previously she had nominated characteristics which matched her own: 'they work harder, they know better' (Year 2), 'they don't talk; I never talk until I've finished', 'they've had more practice'. It may be that we see here the beginnings of a strategic dissembling with a peer group which appears ambivalent about or antagonistic to achievement.

Nevertheless Laura's confidence in herself remained intact. Approaching the SATs she said 'I felt worried, but I calmed down. I knew I could do it'. Her experience of attempting the extension test, however, was not happy, as we saw in section 10.2 above.

Alice

Alice's story at Lawnside is in some ways very similar to Laura's, showing a similar sense of mastery of Mathematics. In Year 2 she told us 'I like Maths; it's my favourite subject. My dad does me divides at home. I'm highest in the class at Maths as well'. Her self-assessment as 'good' was consistent each year. In class she was openly acknowledged by her teachers as outstanding in Maths. Efforts were made to find her more interesting and extending work and she was regularly called on to help other pupils who were finding it hard to understand – a task which she undertook with good will, skill and some pleasure. The children in her class consistently named her as particularly good at Maths and spoke of her as someone they went to for help, confident that she would be able to explain things effectively.

Throughout the six years of the project Alice was consistently regarded by her teachers as 'mature', 'confident', 'self-reliant'. Alice herself thought correctly that other people saw her as 'a hard worker'. She was also resilient and persistent in her approach:

> I keep trying to see if I can do it in the end. I don't like to give up.
>
> (Year 6)

She saw herself as like the ideal pupil in Year 5, 'a nice person, caring, helps people, someone who supports us and cheers us on at football' and in Year 6, 'someone who's kind of quite good at the work'. Similarly she matched her descriptions of people who do well in school work: 'they're cleverer' (Year 2), 'they don't talk all the time' (Year 3), 'they concentrate more' (Year 4), 'they listen more and take it all in' (Year 5), 'they listen and understand; they want to learn' (Year 6).

So Alice in Year 6 was aware of the role of motivation in learning. However, when we asked her if she wanted to learn she replied, 'Yes, so I can get a career and a job when I'm older'. Her motivation, it appeared, was extrinsic and instrumental. That year she was involved in a Maths activity her teacher hoped she would find challenging. When we asked her how she felt about Maths generally, she replied, 'I don't like Maths really. It's probably what I'm doing at the moment . . . It's doing the same thing all the time'.

In addition to an apparent decline in the enjoyment of Maths, Alice in her answers in Years 5 and 6 seemed less confident than in earlier years. Her attitude to having her work examined in previous years had been very positive: 'If she says do some more, I like it because I like doing work' (Year 2), 'It helps me if I do something wrong' (Year 3), 'I'm proud' (Year 4). In Year 5 she was anxious that she might not have done as well as she could:

> I think she'll probably like it. But if I don't feel I've done so well, I'll feel a bit nervous if I'm handing it in because I know I could have done better.

In Year 6 she somewhat surprisingly nominated as her ideal teacher 'one who won't compare you with other people in the class; make you feel upset', but she then asserted that this didn't happen in her class.

There is a sense here of the tension involved in consistently living up to your own and others' expectations. Her teachers sensed this. In Year 5 her teacher thought that

Alice sometimes 'felt vulnerable ... she's never failed ... I think she wonders what it's like elsewhere, how she'll measure up'. In Year 6 her teacher worried that she was bored but also noticed that she was afraid to participate in a swimming gala, although she had volunteered, and that she did not want her story read in a school assembly. It seemed that she was confident only in known, secure contexts. Was she perhaps thinking of the imminent move to secondary school? Whatever the reason, like Laura she was confident about her ability to cope with the SATs:

I think I'll find they're not very difficult ... it's just to find out how much you know. If I did find them difficult I'd feel disappointed in myself.

Kim

Kim at Kenwood experienced a loss of confidence in Maths in Key Stage 2. In Year 2 she thought she was 'very good' but was reluctant from then on to commit to more than 'OK'. Her self-assessments were accompanied by qualifying remarks: 'I get a lot right but if I get them wrong I get really stuck', 'It takes me a long time'.

The speed at which Kim worked was a central issue in the construction of her identity both for her and her teachers. She thought she did not match her own definition of the ideal pupil in Year 6 because 'I'm a bit slow'.

In Year 5 her teacher described her:

Not a high flier, a real plodder, solid, steady, no wildly brilliant ideas, meticulous, competent, nothing will shift her speed.

The next year her slowness was again a defining issue.

If she moved herself she could be really good. It's just the speed at which she works which holds her back really.

Kim told us in Year 6 'I don't usually finish first but if I do I'm pleased', 'I don't normally have trouble concentrating but I think about all the other work I'm behind on', 'If I get stuck on a sum I don't know whether to ask. I don't like asking but I think I won't get finished if I don't ask so I'd better', 'The teacher thinks I'm a bit slow. She makes comments'.

In contrast to Kim's ambivalence about asking questions, her teachers saw her as a pupil who 'asks for clarification and once she's happy will explore and extend' (Year 5) and who 'if she doesn't understand something she asks' (Year 6).

Asking appears to have been a risky strategy for Kim. In fact her replies over the years in relation to having her work examined were full of apprehension. She worried that she had 'done it wrong' (Year 2), that the 'teacher would say, "That's terrible"' (Year 3), 'in case I've done lots of mistakes' (Year 4), 'if I've not done much' (Year 5), because 'I think that there's going to be something wrong all the time'.

Kim faced an acute dilemma: she felt insecure but did not want to be seen as dependent, so did not seek as much help as she really wanted. In this context it is hardly surprising that she lacked confidence in her ability to attain in Maths.

Kate

Kate at Greenmantle who with Level 5 in all subjects was one of the highest attainers in our sample, was consistently perceived by her teachers as 'very bright', 'very able'. She was also seen as difficult, unusual, challenging, independent and outspoken. Comments from teachers suggest that her achievement at the end of Key Stage 2 was not unexpected. Why then was Kate's self-assessment of 'average' in Maths so muted?

The interview data show that she consistently used external evidence from the classroom to make her self-assessment. In Year 3 she told us she was 'very good. I'm on the highest book in the class'. The next year she thought she was good because 'I was the first on Stage 3 in my class. Miss T says I'm quite far ahead'. Towards the end of the key stage, however, the evidence in her judgement meant that she was only 'OK'. 'I'm average. Not really near the bottom but not fabulously near the top'. Kate was not unique in her approach to self-assessment. All the children at Greenmantle regularly referred to the Level, Stage or Book they were 'on' and to where they were in the hierarchy of attainment; they fell easily into naming who they were ahead of or behind.

In Year 3 Kate's sense of herself as a learner was more secure:

> The teachers choose me because they think I'm quite clever and I enjoy doing things.
>
> (Year 3)

In these years also she enjoyed Maths:

> I like sums and it keeps me occupied, otherwise I might get bored.
>
> (Year 2)

> I like hard sums and working with a calculator.
>
> (Year 4)

However, as Key Stage 2 progressed she was less secure:

> When we do something new I get worried. I wonder if I am getting them right.
>
> (Year 4)

> In Maths I couldn't do something. I felt ashamed because everyone else could do it.
>
> (Year 5)

> Sometimes I don't think I'm doing very well.
>
> (Year 6)

She also frequently found herself bored by repetitive and intrinsically uninteresting tasks in Maths and other subjects to which her response was to daydream and 'not really bother'. But the part of her which was driven to achieve (and she came from a high-achieving family) was concerned when it came to having her work looked at:

> Sometimes if I'm a bit tired or can't be bothered to write everything I should have, I think, 'Oh no, what's she going to put?'.
>
> (Year 5)

I'm pleased if it's good, but if I know I haven't bothered I get a bit worried. Sometimes I'm worried to be called 'teacher's pet' or 'keener' if I have done well.

(Year 6)

Like Laura, Kate was concerned about how her achievement would affect her relationship with her peers.

Kate had a well developed view of what characteristics were associated with success. In Year 1 she told us that people who don't do so well 'don't look back, don't check their work'. She also cited the importance of concentration and working quickly. In Year 5 she thought that those who did well 'concentrated more' and some who didn't were 'silly and mess around'. But she also observed that for some people 'it comes in one ear and out the other. They sort of understand what is going to happen but they don't understand what to do'. Kim had noticed this too: 'Some talk a lot; some just don't know how to do it as well. I talk to Chloe at playtime – she doesn't really understand'.

Recognizing the needs of these learners as well as her own, Kate saw the ideal teacher as one that 'let us do things slowly', 'will explain', 'helps you if you're stuck or not sure', 'tells you off if you do something stupid'. She did not see herself as the ideal pupil: 'I don't do as I'm told. Sometimes I don't listen', but she was happy to accept the teacher's control and do what she says.

Although she was not prepared to assess herself as more than 'average' in Maths she was quite confident about the SATs:

I'm a bit nervous. But I think I will do all right. Some people panic.

(Year 6)

Here we have an essentially capable, confident child whose sense of engagement and mastery at Mathematics was threatened by both the boredom of the curriculum and the cultural risks of being seen to be too successful. Nevertheless, she had a reflexive knowledge of herself and her own learning strategies.

What can we say about disposition and identity on the basis of these four cases? The influence of home, peers and teachers on the development of identities and dispositions is well illustrated. In addition to the powerful shaping evident in Laura's case, we also saw how she and Kate were concerned to avoid having the identity of 'keener', 'wimp' or 'teacher's pet' foisted on them by their peers.

As the girls each negotiated their identities and sought to accomplish their learning of school Mathematics, they encountered various tensions between boredom and challenge, teacher control and autonomy, and risk and security. In the prevailing classroom culture Laura was probably right to surrender control to her teacher, but this did not make it conducive to providing the open-ended challenge which she also wanted. She settled for structure and security which would bring results. Also strongly present in Kate and Alice's stories are anxieties about constantly meeting high expectations, and of both achievement and effort, set by themselves and others. These are difficult to sustain but the risks in terms of self are high. Even a pupil like Kate who has the confidence and individuality to resist the system feels this pressure. With Kate and Kim we see also the impact of powerfully articulated criteria – working quickly, hierarchies evident in schemes – on pupils' views of themselves.

11.7 PHILIP – SAVING FACE WITH A 'TOUGH' IDENTITY

This case-study tells the story of Philip and what happened to his sense of himself as a learner in Year 4. Philip is the youngest of three children in a stable, supportive family. His father was long-term unemployed but his mother worked. His teachers described him as 'always well-turned out, never scruffy or untidy, always well-mannered'. Philip's brother and sister, seven and two years older respectively, preceded him through St Anne's, a large Catholic primary school. His parents communicated with the school and were considered cooperative and responsive. His sister was described as 'protective but not over-protective'. When he was in Year 2 she was a library helper and regularly asked his teacher how he was getting on.

St Anne's was situated in an area of extreme social disadvantage. At the time of our study the school had the highest take-up of free school meals in what was one of the poorest councils in the north-west. It served a large overspill housing estate where there was a high level of unemployment and many broken families (often supported by an extended network of relations and friends); social services were involved with many of the children, some of whom were on the 'at risk' register. Coincidentally with the start of the research a new two-storey wing had been added to the pre-war buildings, originally separate infant and junior schools; beyond the tarmac playground were the playing fields of the adjacent secondary school and there were plenty of trees.

After Year 1 all Philip's class teachers were male and for two of these years he was taught by the same person. Classes were mixed-ability but the children were set for Maths and English across Years 3 to 6. In addition Philip was in mixed-age classes where decisions about their composition also involved assessments of attainment; for instance in Year 4 Philip's class included five high-attaining Year 3 pupils and in Year 6 he was one of 14 'lower attainers' grouped with 16 Year 5 children. Throughout Key Stage 2 Philip was in classes where his year group was consistently assessed by their teacher as 'not as good' as the younger pupils.

Teaching at St Anne's was highly structured and formal with heavy use of work books especially in Maths and English. Any semblance of subject integration rapidly disappeared in Key Stage 2 under the pressure of National Curriculum requirements. In general children experienced a combination of whole-class teaching and individual work with everyone doing the same activity at the same time and little evidence of opportunities for pupils to take any control of their own learning. Choice was available only when all set work was finished so many children never got it. In Years 5 and 6, however, work in Technology provided an exception in the form of cooperative group work and the encouragement of collaboration.

The emphasis through the whole school was on extrinsic motivation in the form of points awarded for behaviour, attitude and effort or for 'excellent' or 'very good' work. Competition between individuals resulted in merit certificates given each week to two pupils in each class and presented in assembly. Continued achievement could earn bronze, silver and gold certificates and a headteacher's award for outstanding work. In each class teams competed in a house point system for a half-termly reward or privilege. In class, lollipops were a popular feature of the reward system. The children appeared to enjoy the excitement and the rewards. Whole-class teaching also frequently incorporated a competition or a game and we saw the reward of a lollipop or the sanction of a squirt from a water pistol used in one class as a good-humoured control mechanism, especially to defuse tense situations. Children responded positively to this; there was a lot of humour and warm relationships between pupils and teachers. The Catholic ethos of the school had a strong influence; there was an emphasis on politeness and caring for others, pursued consistently by teachers in response to what one of them described as 'the chaotic homes these children come from'.

This was the context in which we followed Philip through six years of primary education. At the end of Key Stage 2 he achieved Level 2 in the Maths SAT. In English and Science he was ungraded in the tests but awarded Level 2 for both on the basis of the tasks. He was one of the lowest attainers in a year of low attainers. Of the 44 children in the year less than half were assessed at Level 4 by test or Teacher Assessment. In English, where they performed best, 41 per cent attained Level 4; the figure for Maths was 18 per cent and for Science 14 per cent. Girls generally outperformed boys. There were two boys who attained Level 4 in all three tested subjects but they were not in Philip's class.

In the story of Philip's progress as a learner Year 4 emerges as a particularly significant time. Before then he had been a low achiever, lacking in confidence but keen to do well and making progress especially in reading with help and support at home and the discovery that he had poor eyesight and needed to wear glasses. In Year 3 his teacher described him as enjoying the work, being responsive, 'very much a Mr Middle-of-the-Road. When he remembers to wear his glasses his written work is very neat, very tidy, very careful. His work rate's picking up . . . he doesn't seem to have many problems with work'. His end-of-year report recorded him as 'a very good and sensible boy who never gives less than 100 per cent effort'. However, less than a year later in the summer of Year 4 his class teacher was describing him as 'extremely disruptive . . . poor ability level . . . confrontational . . . difficult to handle . . . a very tough little boy'. During Year 5 he appeared to have controlled his aggression towards other children. However his attitude to learning was deteriorating. His Year 5 teacher commented:

> He has a very low opinion of his own ability in terms of education. If you tell him that he's to finish five sentences he just says, 'There's no way I'm going to be able to do that'. . . . He's a pleasure to have as long as you accept the fact that he isn't going to do any work for you. If you press him, he just doesn't do it.

This did not change in Year 6 where his teacher despaired of Philip's poor motivation and the lack of effort which he believed was limiting Philip's attainment.

> Most of the time he'll sit and do very little . . . and when you tackle him about it he begins to sulk and won't do any more . . . depending on what kind of mood he is in, he'll shut up shop and he won't do a thing.

In the Spring Term too the aggressive, rude, surly behaviour to staff and other pupils returned, culminating in a direct challenge to authority in the swimming baths. Philip's parents were consulted. They could not offer any reasons for this but said they would 'have words with him'. They cooperated in keeping him away from school for a day and suggested that the teachers might use, as his mother had, the fact that he was 'mad keen' to go to the local secondary school as a bargaining chip. She had been telling him that the teachers from that school were going to come to St Anne's to decide if he was the sort they wanted. When his teacher tried it Philip replied 'I'm not bothered, don't care'.

What happened to Philip around Year 4 that might account for this change? Attempts to explain human behaviour are fraught with problems and it is rash to over-simplify. However, we want to suggest that at least a contributory factor was Philip's response to the more overt assessment practices of Key Stage 2. Evidence from his interviews and classroom observations suggests that in about Year 4 he became more sharply aware of his position as a low attainer. We want to argue that he began to develop a range of strategies in response to this and used other aspects of himself to construct an alternative identity.

For the first three years of his primary education, when we asked Philip how good he thought he was at Reading, Writing, Maths and Science he replied 'good', 'very good' or 'excellent'. At the end of Key Stage 1 he was assessed as Level 1 in the core subjects but his teacher's account of how the testing was handled suggests that Philip had little if any awareness of the process or the outcomes. The assessment was spread out over a six-week period and the time frame was kept vague for parents who were informed only that during that half term 'we'll be doing some assessment tasks, not every day; don't worry because it's nothing over and beyond what children normally do'. For the children it was presented as part of the prevailing competitive system: 'I just treated it like an ordinary piece of work ... I tried to make it fun for them and they were greedy to get points for doing well'. The children wanted to know how they had fared and how many points they had scored but this was deliberately fudged by making it a team effort and telling them 'This group did very well and got x number of points for their team' or 'You got a lot of answers right; you didn't get them all right'. The intention throughout was to keep from the children's minds any idea that they were being tested. (As we saw in Chapter 10 this contrasted very strongly with the approach to Key Stage 2 testing.) The outcome of this for Philip was that he associated himself with other children in his class whom he identified as 'good at work'. Asked why they were successful he replied ''Cos they're good like me and they are quick at work'.

In Year 3 Philip had the same teacher again. This was a conscious move by the school 'to try to keep the ethos of the infant department going in the lower juniors ... we're trying to keep the mood and the approach to work less cynical ... they grow up too quickly when they get to the junior department'. Philip had encountered some 'grouping by ability' in previous years and in Key Stage 1 he had received special needs support for his reading. However, this 'infant ethos' and the approach of his class teacher seem to have largely mitigated a developing awareness of his low attainment. In Year 5 Philip recalled his Year 3 teacher Mr Matthews, an experienced, popular and committed teacher, as the 'best teacher in this world. He'd shout at yer and then like he'd shake hands and everything with yer, saying he's sorry'. At that time, Philip told us, he was having difficulty with spelling and was afraid of getting it wrong and getting shouted at. 'I always used to get shaky and I couldn't use to spell them ... I always used to cry and say to Mr Matthews I can't do them.' The experience of failure here was somehow tempered for Philip by the nature of his relationship with his teacher and at the time he still saw himself positively as 'very good' at writing and spelling. There is evidence though in his interview that year that he was beginning to be aware that he was not meeting his own criterion for success – being quick at work. About his writing he said, 'Sometimes I'm dead slow. It's just difficult'. Children who did well at work became 'them' rather than 'like me' and he explained that they were successful because 'they're the quickest in the class'.

In Year 4 this awareness became sharper and more intense. The whole class (mixed Year 3 and 4) was now grouped for 'ability' and Philip was in red group identified by the teacher as consisting of those in need of 'learning support'. For Philip this meant being withdrawn from English once a week to work with a support teacher. In addition all the pupils in Key Stage 2 continued to be set for Maths and English across four years. Philip was in the bottom set for both. He worried 'when I know I've done something wrong'. For the next three years his self-assessments in core subjects were characteristically expressed as 'all right', 'OK', 'not so good'. 'Getting stuck' was a frequent feature of the accounts he gave of his experience. In Maths: 'Sometimes I'm all right but when I get stuck it's dead hard'. In reading: 'I just think I'm not any good – I always get stuck on some words'. He also continued to use the criterion of speed in his judgements of success: 'They can work faster and like finish faster – sometimes I finish last'. Unable to sustain a sense of himself as 'good at work' he began to construct another identity.

It could be argued at this point that a combination of nature and culture was influential. During Year 4 Philip had a growth spurt and became the tallest and heaviest child in the class. The way his class teacher described him conveys a powerful sense of a boy defining a new role for himself in the face of impending 'failure'.

> He likes to be seen as tough ... likes to mix with the tough ones in Year 5 ... He's a volcano ... can't cope with the suggestion that he's in the wrong; tries to avoid it ... he wants his own way ... sulks ... sometimes walks out of class.

In this year too Philip told us that when he was distracted in class he was 'thinking about my girlfriend and me mates ... She's older than me, in another class'. At the beginning the toughness was expressed in part in aggression towards other children. Our field notes provide evidence of fights in the playground and reported bullying particularly of one younger, high-attaining, attention-seeking boy in his class whom he found particularly irritating. However, Philip was consistently described by most teachers as 'likeable' and in Year 5 our sociograms showed him as the most popular boy in the class, part of a tight-knit group of boys (including his best friend Malcolm, another low attainer and the smallest boy in the class) and with three girls vying for his attention. He and Malcolm were having boxing lessons at a club where his grandfather, father and uncle were all involved. The school too seemed to be colluding, if jokingly, with Philip in this tough guy role: 'Philip gets the lunch boxes. We have trouble with people pinching stuff – Philip doesn't let them pinch stuff'. There was also evidence that the challenge of managing him had made him a special case: 'I have to tolerate certain behaviour off him I wouldn't tolerate off anyone else – grabbing people round the neck and pretending to threaten them'.

'He knows his own limitations and doesn't want others to see,' was one teacher's summing up of Philip in Year 6 and this provides a persuasive motivation for a number of strategies Philip developed for dealing with learning tasks in the classroom. He generally attempted even less than the minimum required. If pressed he copied from others, a move which with his tough reputation carried connotations of 'smart' rather than 'cheat'. This strategy, again only half-jokingly, was noted by his teacher. 'He sits next to Amanda, the girl he "sees". We all think this is quite good because he can copy off her.' Amanda was a relatively high attainer and Philip seemed to stay more on task when placed with this sort of pupil. We observed him in Year 6 working with two more able Year 5 boys. The task was to write a playscript based on some History work. Philip seemed motivated but very unconfident. He frequently asked for help from the boys: 'What next?', 'Wait for me', and needed constant reinforcement and support. This he got as they showed him where to look for spellings and pointed out the need to put in speech marks. He told us he liked to choose who to sit next to: 'If you ask them when you're stuck then they'll help you'. Philip's insecurity and reluctance to expose himself to 'getting it wrong' made him very teacher-dependent in a classroom context which in any case did little to encourage learner autonomy. When required to work individually in lessons he was task-focused only when the teacher was working with him one-to-one. Our observations of him show long periods of distraction often involving other pupils. In a Year 5 Maths set (Philip's least favourite subject that year) he sat on a table with Malcolm and two girls from another class. They were supposed to be working individually from the Maths scheme. Philip started by having a long discussion about his new very short haircut with Malcolm. He then turned to the girls who were counting out plastic cubes, took some cubes away and threw some from the box onto their counted pile. As one of the girls went to complain to their teacher Philip was suddenly on task. Later in the same lesson another six-minute observation is all distraction with Philip picking his nose, stuffing cubes into his mouth and chatting about birthdays.

The strategy of attempting very little work left Philip, increasingly aware of assessment, with the need to explain his attainment. Classically he identified factors outside himself to account for not doing well. He had problems with reading because he forgot his glasses, or they were bent and he was getting new ones. He didn't get much done because he was distracted by the people who 'worked fast and wrote loads' and then came to talk to him. In common with all the other children in his classes he looked to teacher assessment in the form of comments to tell him how good he was: 'Sir tells you if you're right, excellent and that'. In Year 4 he thought he was good at drawing and painting because 'Mr Chance gives me a tick and sometimes writes "excellent, good"'. In Year 5 he would choose always to draw rather than write and preferred Technology where they worked in groups to Maths where he was always getting stuck. He didn't like showing his teacher his work: 'I get a bit shaky in case it's wrong and I have to do it again'. Similarly in Year 6 he was feeling 'a bit shaky' about the SATs because 'they're dead hard'.

Philip's behaviour and comments in this year suggest his considerable ambivalence about the end-of-Key Stage 2 assessment. He said that he liked Maths and writing and doing all the SATs practice. He enjoyed 'being on Maths for ages' and 'sitting near Mr Bridges and getting loads of work done'. He was proud of getting 'excellent' for a story writing test. 'I thought it would be difficult at first. When I got into the middle of the story it wasn't so hard.' But he was also acutely aware of the hierarchy of attainment in his class; he correctly identified the high attainers and explained their success by stating 'they can just work better'. His friends – characterized by their teacher as 'the rabble rousers' – were all low attainers. We observed a spelling test where the pupils marked each other's work and then read out the scores. This was a very public demonstration of relative success and contrasted sharply with the motivational grades and comments given on individual work. There was laughter at the pupils (including Philip) who scored only two, which was not much mitigated by the teacher's comment 'There's nothing to laugh at. It was a difficult test that'. In the same week the class was doing a Maths practice test. Philip was sitting at the front near the teacher but was getting no help and reacting badly to the situation. He described it later:

> I turned over and tried to do the next page. Couldn't do that either so I turned over . . . 'Sir, I can't do it'. Mr Bridges got cross. 'Well go on to the next one'. He wasn't like telling me off. I just felt dead annoyed. 'Sir, can't I have any help on this page?'.

His teacher told him not to sulk. 'There are plenty of others in the class who can't do it but they're not sulking.'

Such assessment moments brought Philip up sharply against the reality of his attainment. In such situations he could not reassure himself with 'excellent' comments or the comfortable sense that doing lots of practice would make it come out all right. His teacher offered another slant on this when he talked about the problem of engineering a top place for Philip's team in the house points competition. 'I keep throwing points at them but they don't put them on the chart – they've never won.' As assessment became palpably more real and earnest, winning lollipops in a contrived competition may have lost its appeal. It seems unsurprising that it was at this point in the year that Philip's aggression towards other pupils returned and his rudeness and lack of cooperation with teachers became much worse. The supportive relationship he had enjoyed with previous teachers and his very noticeable success in the school football team ('I went to football training last night and Sir said that I was good') were not enough. At this point he wasn't sure that he liked his Year 6 teacher who was desperate for Philip to do something so that he could be helped to improve. 'Sometimes he's dead nice to yer, sometimes he's not.' Philip's reaction to Mr Bridges' attempts to get him to produce some work and to confront his learning problems was extreme: he got his parents to come to school and complain about what Mr Bridges had done and said.

The extent and nature of Philip's anxiety was confirmed during the week of the SATs. We observed Philip and interviewed him. The thoughts he gave himself in the bubbles of our 'SAT Story' strip cartoon provide a sharp indication of his state of mind. Waking up and walking to school he is thinking 'about the test'. During and after the test his thoughts are all variations on 'I have got it wrong'. For what he will say when he gets home he puts a face-saving 'Mum, I think I have got the test right'.

This account suggests a number of factors interacting in the formation of Philip's identity in these years. Within the increasingly overt assessment framework of Key

Stage 2 of the National Curriculum, Philip was unable to address or deal with his learning problems. After a relatively protected three years he went into a class (taught by a busy deputy head with less time for demanding individuals) where his low attainment became more clearly apparent to him. He seems to have decided at this point to refuse to join a race in which he could not succeed and began to characterize himself as someone who didn't meet his own criteria for success – doing a lot, finishing fast, getting it right. Instead he discovered another kind of success. His tough reputation meant that lots of people admired him and wanted to be like him. His humour and likeability meant that long-standing friends were amazingly tolerant of his aggression to them and others. Teachers too, with other pupils to teach, had to cope with the challenge he presented and, at least in part, accommodated this emerging identity. Philip told us that he enjoyed his time at primary school; it was a sociable experience. While there we saw him develop a repertoire of strategies and survive attempts to make him learn or modify his behaviour. In Year 6 he was looking forward to going to secondary school. We may ponder how the identity he was taking with him would serve in this new context.

Philip's response to a culture so imbued with assessment was at the extreme end of a continuum of reaction. However, as we have seen in the preceding chapters, many pupils shared his feelings about assessment and experienced a similar loss of self-esteem. Elements of Philip's strategic response to this, which positioned him in opposition to work and learning and required him to withdraw effort and cooperation, can be seen in other low-achieving pupils in the study. In such situations teachers had little chance of encouraging persistence and could at best achieve only containment.

11.8 CONCLUSION

In this chapter we have offered accounts of the development of the learning disposition and identities of thirteen children. This analysis augments the more thematic treatment of Chapters 4 to 10, and represents a different way of making sense of the PACE data-set. In particular, rather than offering descriptions of annual patterns of perspectives across the whole pupil sample, we have harnessed available resources to focus on individuals, often drawing on a full six-year data-set. We have thus tried to convey something of the integrated and holistic 'lived experience' of pupils during their primary school careers.

Did Sean lose interest in Maths, or did school Mathematics actually lose touch with Sean as he developed? Our brief vignettes on Haley, Kevin, Richard and Amanda indicate some of the major influences on their development and sense of themselves as learners over the six years. For Neil we highlighted in more depth the influence of parents, peers and teachers, whilst Jessica and Scott illustrated different personal responses to SATs and the ways in which these were rooted in the children's sense of learner identity. Laura, Alice, Kim and Kate showed girls managing both mastery and dependence, whilst the sad story of Philip causes us to reflect on the strategic choices that are open to lower-achieving boys in an increasingly categoric assessment environment.

Comparing the six boys and seven girls in these case-studies, there are many similarities in the issues and concerns that they faced but also significant gendered differences in the cultural resources and opportunities available to them. For all children, we saw how learning disposition was affected by their successes or difficulties in learning and by the social influences and significant others that give meaning to such events and feelings. We saw too how national education policy, albeit mediated by LEAs, schools and teachers, impacted directly on children's classroom experience. In general, the tightening of curriculum subject specification, pedagogic frame and assessment categorization, and the accompanying pressure on time made classrooms more challenging places where children often felt vulnerable.

Perhaps this is entirely satisfactory, for there is little doubt that children were being challenged to learn more and to perform at higher standards. However, it is also clear that the experience of primary schooling was also affecting children's self-beliefs, their understanding of themselves as learners and their identities as people. This raises much more serious and significant issues.

In the rest of this book we revisit our three major research questions and take this discussion much further. We will argue that primary education is not and cannot be just about 'performance'. It will also inevitably embrace the development of personality, self-confidence and identity. We can then ask: Will present systems for the delivery of standards and performance actually enhance or undermine commitment to lifelong learning? Indeed, in preparing our children for the challenges of the next century, is the balance of recent education policies appropriate?

Part 3

Research Questions Revisited

Chapter 12

Major PACE Findings on Teacher and Pupil Experience

12.1   Introduction
12.2   PACE findings regarding teacher experience
12.3   PACE findings regarding pupil experience
12.4   Conclusion

12.1 INTRODUCTION

In the final part of this book we take stock of all of the PACE project's substantive findings on both teacher and pupil experience in English primary schools during the early and mid-1990s, and analyse their significance.

We begin with the report of teachers and schools that is provided in our companion volume (Osborn *et al.*, 2000), and also referred to in Chapter 3 of the present volume. We then summarize our answer to our first major research question: How did pupils perceive and experience the introduction of the National Curriculum and assessment?

Figure 3.1 and Table 3.1 set out the contrastive theoretical framework which we developed to highlight some key issues in the discourse and practices of schools and classrooms in changing circumstances (Pollard *et al.*, 1997a). This development was heavily influenced by Bernstein's work (1996), though he is not responsible for our application of his ideas.

On the one hand, Bernstein suggested that during the 1960s there had been a 'remarkable convergence' (p. 54) in various fields of social science around the concept of 'competence'. He argued that competence had its own 'social logic' – an implicit model concerning communication, interaction and the agency of individuals, presenting them in terms of the 'active and creative construction of a valid world of meanings and practice' (p. 56). Bernstein argued that the assumptions of this social logic had influenced the authors of the Plowden Report (CACE, 1967) and we elaborated on his insights to provide a summary of the ideals of this 'liberal progressive' education.

On the other hand, Bernstein also drew attention to the alternative social logic of a more recent 'performance model'. As he put it, this emphasizes 'the specific output of the acquirer, the particular text the acquirer is expected to construct, and the specialised skills necessary to the production of this specific output, text or product' (p. 57). The pedagogic discourse of the performance model is thus much more categoric, assertive and directive than that of the competence, or 'liberal progressive' model.

Of course we know from sociological analyses that a school curriculum, or indeed an education system, is likely to be a site of struggle between competing interests (Apple, 1993; Ball, 1990, 1994; Bentley, 1998; Elliott, 1998; Goodson, 1987, 1994; Quicke, 1999; Richards and Taylor, 1998; Young, 1971, 1998). Perhaps this is inevitable, since education is essentially concerned with the shaping of the young towards some imagined future. But, amongst all those that are available, *whose* imagined future should prevail? There is plenty to debate.

In the first PACE volume (Pollard *et al.*, 1994), we described one contest across this disputed terrain when successive Thatcher and Major governments in the 1980s and 1990s challenged the established assumptions, practices and ideologies of the teaching profession. We represented this as a 'struggle for values, understanding and power'. We revisit some of these themes below in our review of the major findings of the full six years of the PACE data on teachers' perspectives, experiences and classroom practice.

12.2 PACE FINDINGS REGARDING TEACHER EXPERIENCE

The consequences of the differences in the fundamental assumptions of the 'liberal progressive' and 'performance' models can be traced in terms of the organization of schools, the conditions of teachers' work, and practices in classrooms. This has of course been a major aspect of our analysis of teacher experience following the introduction of the National Curriculum (Osborn *et al.*, 2000). For the purposes of the present book, we introduce our major findings on teachers under three headings:

- Challenges to professionalism, work and values
- Teachers' strategic responses
- Classroom practice.

The issue of school change, and of variations between and within schools, will be considered later in this chapter.

Challenges to professionalism, work and values

In our summative PACE book on primary school teachers (Osborn *et al.*, 2000) we described their experience of the 'avalanche' of policy initiatives of the late 1980s and

1990s. We documented how they had felt increasingly besieged by critics and demands for accountablility from outsiders, especially parents, whilst losing little of their deeply-held sense of moral accountability to pupils. We described many teachers' experience of increasing stress as the growing proliferation of external requirements left them less and less space for personal professional discretion. For many, the effects of this increase in pressure and constraint were exacerbated by their belief that what they were being asked to do was not educationally desirable or in the best interest of their pupils. The increasingly high-profile and externally-controlled national assessments provided one of the most widespread causes of such conflict. However for some teachers, particularly those working with pupils from difficult social and economic backgrounds, the National Curriculum itself caused stress and frustration since teachers felt it could not meet such children's particular needs.

Significant changes also characterized teachers' work and values (Acker, 1999; Campbell, 1998; Troman, 1996; Webb and Vulliamy, 1996a; Woods *et al.*, 1997). In PACE we reported the growing sense of resignation and instrumentalism of many as they found themselves constrained in terms of curriculum content and teaching methods. As sensationalist and politicized debates rolled around in the media, the shift from professional autonomy to contractual responsibility as the basis for accountability was associated for many teachers with increased stress, value conflict and reduced job satisfaction. They began to feel bound by the demand for 'delivery of performance' beyond all other considerations. Further, they felt that the more affective side of teaching – the sense of vocation and investment of self – was being undermined by pressure to become 'expert technicians' in transmitting predefined knowledge and skills to their pupils (Hargreaves, 1999; Jeffrey, 1999; Nias, 1989). The policy emphasis of successive Conservative governments on education as a 'commodity' to be delivered and measured was at odds with many teachers' views of education as being fundamentally concerned with personal development (Proctor, 1990).

Teachers' strategic responses

For a considerable number of teachers, the worst effects of the changes described above were mediated by a growth in collegiality. This had often been a strength within primary schools (Nias *et al.*, 1989), and in the circumstances of the early 1990s teachers increasingly felt the need to work together to cope with the new challenges and its effects. Thus curriculum planning, whole-school coordination, preparation for inspection and external communication, as well as teaching itself, were increasingly likely to be characterized by teachers pooling their different knowledge and skills in complementary ways. At their best, these developments were highly creative and empowering, resulting in some or all teachers in the school feeling a new sense of professional achievement.

Examples of such developments have also been documented by other related studies such as Richards (1998) who refers to the 'confident domestication' of the National Curriculum in small rural primary schools, with a pragmatic adaption of policy directives to their own particular circumstances. Assessment understanding and expertise have grown (Craft, 1996; Gipps *et al.*, 1995; Torrance and Pryor, 1998). Reception class teachers have developed ways of promoting high quality play (Bennett *et al.*, 1997). Nixon *et al.* (1997) also refer to the emergence of a 'new professional' whose values and practices represent a creative incorporation of new requirements into core professional values. Hargreaves (1994) links this to organizational development. On the other hand, other research such as Woods (1995) and Woods and Jeffrey (1996) has documented the skill and creativity of teachers in protecting their values, imagination and engagement with pupils *despite* the National Curriculum and other requirements.

Many headteachers developed and deployed considerable skills in managing these developments whilst others, perhaps finding the new challenges overwhelming, resorted to more autocratic methods. The latter were found to inhibit the development of collegiality and the incorporation of the National Curriculum into new forms of professional practice. Thus our data reveal many teachers whose experience of school management produced 'contrived collegiality' (Hargreaves, 1991) and a contractual, rather than a professional, engagement. Other studies such as that of Menter *et al.* (1996) and Hatcher (1994) have taken this idea much further and related the erosion of primary school teachers' commitment to their repositioning and commodification within a more managerial labour process.

Overall we found that where the individual teacher, or the school as a whole, lacked the confidence to engage in the 'creative mediation' of external policy directives, or where individual or personal circumstances made this difficult, the picture was likely to be one of conflict, stress and disillusion. Thus, whilst some teachers were able to generate a creative response to the new, very challenging educational environment, others, often for reasons to do with personal biographies or the challenges posed by particular pupil intakes, were depressed and disheartened by it. These tended to be older, more experienced teachers who objected to new requirements on principle, or found it difficult to revise their professional values and educational practices. However, a key variable in the capacity to cope with change was found to be confidence, both in terms of each individual teacher's professional skills and knowledge and more generally as a person. Some just could not cope, for instance, with greater subject knowledge requirements. Others, skilful, knowledge-able, committed and confident, simply became tired of the struggle or were unwilling to compromise. Many experienced teachers and headteachers took early retirement or left the profession under sickness schemes. Whilst the reconfiguration of the profession has continued through new training, appraisal and pay structures, our evidence showed that younger or more recently trained teachers accommodated to the new structures and requirements and began to take them for granted as 'the way things are'.

Classroom practice

The powerful combination of National Curriculum directives and public rhetoric on the one hand, and national assessment and OFSTED inspection requirements on the other (Jeffrey and Woods, 1998) left little room for individual teachers or schools to redefine what was to be learned, when and to what standard. Discretion concerning time, space and control over the content of learning was increasingly denied to both teachers and pupils. Indeed, the progressive reduction of both teacher and learner autonomy is arguably the most pervasive and significant result of the policy agenda that was launched by the Education Reform Act 1988.

The findings from our companion volume reveal a clear shift away from teacher commitment to 'constructivist' models of learning towards new understandings framed by a perception of teaching and learning in terms of the delivery and incorporation of an established body of knowledge (Leach and Moon, 1999). Whilst important continuities with the past should be acknowledged (Alexander *et al.*, 1996; Swann and Brown, 1997) our evidence suggests that there were also significant changes in classroom practice.

We summarize our analysis at classroom level in terms of the three key 'message systems' of curriculum, pedagogy and assessment which our core sample of pupils experienced in the nine schools we studied throughout the project. We found a situation in which the curriculum was increasingly strongly 'classified', in Bernstein's sense of an explicit division between subjects. Classrooms were also increasingly strongly 'framed', in that teachers' discretion over how to teach was progressively diminishing and this structuring was being relayed on to pupils. Finally, assessment was becoming increasingly categoric, regular and high-stakes as requirements for accountability and performance measures became more prominent and explicit. These findings are a direct echo of those reported in Chapter 3 and a detailed summary of that chapter is offered below.

The potential effects of the trend towards whole-class teaching, teacher instruction, subject timetabling and ability grouping were thus reinforced by an assessment system which increasingly commodified achievement, shifting the educational balance in favour of cognition rather than affect, and emphasized product rather than process. The result, Osborn *et al.* (2000) report, is an increasingly pressured classroom life, permeated by an instrumental focus on pupil performance.

It would be wrong to assume, however, that the picture of change has simply been one of teachers accommodating to the requirements placed upon them. Policy initiatives are not translated wholesale into school and classroom practice, but rather are subject to a series of mediations which are the product of successive interpretations and reinterpretations of them by actors at various levels of the system (Ball, 1994). Osborn *et al.* (2000) also highlight the way in which teachers had become 'policy-makers in practice' striving in particular to protect their pupils from what they perceived to be the worst effects of recent policy changes. They also document a range of changes and strategies at school level (see also Chapter 3 of the present book).

In seeking to understand teachers' different responses to recent policy initiatives and the significance of these differences, the issue of professional motivation is crucial. In our companion volume we documented the gradual movement from a covenant-based professionalism, linked to *intrinsic* satisfaction, to a contractual, performance-based motivation, driven by the demands of external accountability and assessment. We hypothesized that this is likely to lead to a decline in teachers' sense of moral, self-imposed accountability and commitment (see also Campbell, 1998). Although largely indefinable, such facets of professionalism are nevertheless fundamentally important and have a significant effect on the quality of the classroom experience of *pupils*.

From this base of knowledge of changing professional and classroom circumstances, we can again review how they impacted on pupil experience. We do this in a little more detail by revisiting chapter by chapter the key findings within the present book, and by relating them to other relevant research.

12.3 PACE FINDINGS REGARDING PUPIL EXPERIENCE

Observed changes in classroom practice (Chapter 3)

In Chapter 3, explicitly using data from observations of *pupils*, we recorded a tightening of each of the three major 'message systems' of the classroom – curriculum, pedagogy and assessment. Despite the Education Reform Act's intention that a 'broad and balanced' curriculum should be provided, the initial decision to set up a ten-subject curriculum was defeated by complexity, subject-based overprescription, lack of time and priority given to the 'basics'. However, integrated topic work did wane, and single-subject teaching grew. There was a considerable increase in whole-school curriculum planning, particularly for subject progression. Pedagogically, whole-class interaction in the 1990s was double that of the 1970s, though individual task work remained in its predominant position (see also Galton *et al.*, 1999), Nevertheless, teacher time spent on instruction rose dramatically, as did the proportion of closed questions used. Setting and new forms of attainment-based group work developed. Teachers struggled to develop and sustain formative assessment as a direct link to learning processes, and initially protested at the demands imposed by SATs. However, adaptions to the tests and the passage of time produced more accommodation to the new requirements. The washback effect of assessment began to be felt well beyond Years 2 and 6. In the later years of our study inspection requirements started to have a similar influence.

The net result of these developments was a tightening and greater specification in curriculum classification, pedagogic frame and assessment categorization. The struggle between the teaching profession and the government reached a new accommodation after the 1995 implementation of the Dearing Report (Dearing, 1993), but this did not affect the basic reality that a transition from a competence-based, liberal progressive discourse to a performance model of education had been accomplished. Of course, this was taken further after the election of New Labour in 1997, particularly in relation to focus and pedagogic prescription on literacy and numeracy.

Pupil perspectives on curriculum subjects (Chapter 4)

Our findings on pupil perspectives again show the failure, this time in children's minds, of the aim of the Education Reform Act to establish a 'broad and balanced curriculum' (see also Campbell *et al.*, 1993). For our pupils schooling remained focused on the basics of reading, writing and Mathematics. English and Maths remained dominant in all six years of their experience, with the balance tilting from concerns with reading in the early years to greater emphasis on Maths in Key Stage 2. Writing was a major pupil concern throughout and was generally disliked. There was little evidence of pupil awareness of activities such as speaking and listening in English or problem solving in Maths.

Science established itself only slowly and, again, evidence of the prominence of practical investigational work was weak in what the children told us. Pupil accounts of subjects in the arts and humanities reinforce those of teachers in documenting a squeeze on available time.

In 1996 two-thirds of Year 6 pupils reported that there was 'not much' or 'no' choice of curriculum activity, and the evidence suggests that teachers' curriculum control strengthened over the period of study as they strove to comply with external requirements. We found that pupils became increasingly aware of the weight of subject content and the pressure to perform. Their comments in the later years of Key Stage 2 convey this awareness, but, as we commented in Chapter 4, it was passively experienced 'though sitting, listening and writing rather than through activity'.

Pupil judgements on the curriculum (Chapter 5)

We looked carefully at how children evaluated the curriculum and at the criteria that they used. Our annual league table of pupils' favoured curriculum activities showed the relative unpopularity of structured, routine and time-consuming activities of the core curriculum at Key Stage 1, but they crept back into favour in Years 3 and 4 as basic capabilities were consolidated and extended. However, at the end of Key Stage 2 there was a dramatic resurgence in the popularity of Art and PE, and the surprise of finding only five activities (out of the sixteen about which we enquired) for which children felt more positively than negatively (PE, Art, Technology, TV watching, listening to stories). Overall curriculum dissatisfaction was clear, and pupils appeared to favour those subjects associated with physical and expressive activity, entertainment, little demand for writing and reduced assessment pressure. However, both Mathematics and writing (to some extent) reflected a polarization of views.

In terms of the criteria used to make these assessments, we looked at six constructs: success/ease – fail/hard, interesting – boring, activity – constraint, autonomy – constraint, educational – non-educational, and fun – not fun (see also West *et al.*, 1997). Subjects deemed difficult were generally disliked. On the other hand, the criteria used for positive choices consistently reiterated 'fun', 'activity' and 'autonomy'. Interestingly, the negatively viewed criteria all relate to what we have called a 'teacher zone of influence' (Pollard *et al.*, 1994) and to 'official' adult concerns, whilst the positive criteria clearly articulate with pupil culture.

An interesting and worrying finding was that their success in a subject did not necessarily mean that pupils liked it. Children would work at a subject despite their lack of motivation, knowing that a good result was expected of them, but many were anxious to minimize effort when they could. Even where a subject was deemed to be 'interesting', the way it was taught and experienced could undermine motivation. Low achievers felt particularly exposed by some subjects which they found confusing, hard to understand, or in which performance was categoric and public such as Mathematics. They often preferred the fun, activity and less exposing nature of PE or the relative security of drawing.

We concluded Chapter 5 by stating: 'it is difficult to avoid a sense of children in flight from an experience of learning that they found unsatisfying, unmotivating and uncomfortable' (see also Cullingford, 1991; Pollard *et al.*, 1997b).

Pupil perspectives on teacher–pupil relationships (Chapter 6)

The story here is a much more positive one. Pupils felt that their relationships with teachers were generally good, indeed many enjoyed their interaction – particularly when occasional joking, sparring and 'having fun' formed a part. Almost all the children were accepting of teacher authority through most of the primary school years though, towards the end, girls became more ambivalent and some boys began to explore more 'anti-school' identities. Our annual interviews and observations showed how children learned to strategically manage their relationships with teachers. By Year 6 many were able to skilfully detect teacher mood and intention and negotiate accordingly. Some, however, continued to lack such insights or skills.

Pupils had clear ideas about the personal qualities they liked in a teacher – the 'ideal teacher'. Kindness, fairness, cheerfulness and a sense of humour were particularly important, and such criteria consistently came before more instructional capabilities. Ideas about teacher perception of the 'ideal pupil' echoed this, with an expectation that teachers would favour obedient, quiet, helpful, polite and sensible children. Criteria such as intelligence or speed at learning were not major factors. Both these findings are interesting because they suggest that pupils prioritize the affective and social dimensions of their relationships with teachers, rather than the intellectual or cognitive. The first concern of children in the confines of school is to ensure that they are not vulnerable to teacher power – being told off, embarrassed, bored or having to do work again. Only then did intrinsic qualities as a 'teacher' *per se* start to feature. In Year 6 however, with SATs looming, there was a surge in concern that teachers should be good at 'explaining' and in 'helping children to understand'.

The perspectives of the children indicate that classroom frame gradually tightened over the period of study. Teacher control was consistently strong and pupils reported very few opportunities in which they could exercise autonomy. Indeed, although many children liked the idea in principle of being able to choose things for themselves, the evaluative context of classroom life led most to accept and prefer high levels of teacher guidance and control. The reasoning seemed to be that: 'you've got to do something, but you might do it wrong and get told off or have to start again. So, you might as well just do what she says from the start'.

Our pupils conveyed a type of passive acceptance of teacher authority. They were generally happy and felt enlivened by occasional humour in relationships with their teachers. Most gradually developed their skills at negotiating with teachers. However, their thoughts were almost entirely directed towards social relationships. They spoke very little about intellectual interaction or about learning, stimulus or challenge. The overall impression is that the children's prime concern was to get on with their teachers well enough to 'get by', to accomplish the routines of the classrooms and to avoid risk. They were certainly not seeking a guide at the cutting edge of their learning.

Pupil perspectives on classroom assessment (Chapter 7)

Classroom assessment has been a powerful element of professional discourse and is seen as having positive formative potential in providing feedback and enhancing children's learning. Sadly this process is not apparent from the accounts provided by pupils at any point during our study. Rather they consistently perceived assessment as a summative activity and applied associated criteria of neatness, correctness, quantity and effort. Low attainers were particularly concerned with correctness and with the amount of work completed, whilst high attainers tended to focus on the effort they had made. However, in both cases the criteria used failed to attend to the inherent qualities of the work produced. Routine classroom assessment drew attention to surface features of tasks and of learning.

SAT testing at the end of Year 2 and Year 6 appeared to have had a significant effect on perceptions, with children increasingly feeling the salience and significance of such testing. Worryingly we found evidence that children became less positive in self-assessments of their own capabilities, and became more likely to displace responsibility by attributing success or failure to innate characteristics (see also Reay and William 1999). As Key Stage 2 progressed the children's feelings of anxiety developed further as teachers increased the amount of routine testing. Additionally, they often felt uncertain and vulnerable when ambiguous classroom tasks were combined with a high-stakes, categoric assessment climate.

The children communicated their awareness of classroom assessment as an exercise of power, making it clear that they appreciated the need to monitor and adjust to the perspectives of their teacher, and also revealing their attempts to construct a viable classroom identity for themselves. Nevertheless, as we concluded in Chapter 7, 'it seems clear that, for these children, assessment had more to do with pronouncing on their attainment than with progressing their learning'.

Pupil perspectives on teachers' teaching (Chapter 8)

In Chapter 8 we reported on what our target pupils understood about their teacher's educational objectives as they moved through primary school. To begin with, their understanding was very poor, with most declaring that they 'didn't know' or simply explaining that they 'have to do' whatever was required of them. Children regularly seemed surprised to be asked for their opinion on teacher intentions, adopting the relatively passive stance that decisions on the sequence of things to be learned are decided *for* them. Where pupils did express a view, it was often vague and seemed based on general inference rather than on explicit knowledge. They seemed to lack a language for expressing or discussing such issues. Having said that, a general awareness that schooling is for 'learning' was increasingly expressed over the six years of data-gathering, starting at 17 per cent in Year 1 and rising to 57 per cent of pupils in Year 6. Within the latter figure 36 per cent of replies were concerned with 'practice' and were associated with preparation for SATs. There was a steady decline in awareness of progression, but acquiring information and skill development remained prominent issues throughout.

Our slightly naive enquiry concerning whether 'it matters if you don't do things the way your teacher wants them' was intended to tap children's perception of classroom autonomy, independence and risk. Predictably, most children declared that teacher expectations mattered considerably, though there was a steady increase in the proportion whose answers were coded 'it depends' (from 4 per cent in Year 1 to 42 per cent in Year 6). This suggests the gradual development of a more sophisticated understanding of the possibilities for variation, particularly regarding expected degrees of correctness and effort in relation to the importance of the task. Some children became particularly skilled at negotiating with their teachers, whilst others remained dependent on them. Two main consequential risks of failing to comply with teacher expectations were identified. First, teacher anger or public humiliation might be incurred, with a risk to self-esteem; second, children might be asked to 'do work again', almost inevitably involving 'more writing'. By Year 6, the latter was a concern for 69 per cent of pupils interviewed.

The pupils in our study experienced a wide range of group-based forms of classroom organization and management. They were aware of the bases of such grouping, and we coded attainment, ability and behaviour as particular criteria. Generally, they liked being in such groups and four main reasons for this were identified. Being with peers was the main one, with group activity providing a source of diversion, sociability and fun. Groups were also appreciated for enabling pupils to 'get on with work', though they could also sometimes result in work being 'too hard'. Other children liked being grouped because of the variety it could provide, whilst some were particularly aware of the hierarchy and competitive edge which grouping structures often began to formalize. For some, particularly low achievers, group position was a source of some anxiety if they felt their dignity was undermined by their placement.

In this chapter we found that children were unclear about teachers' specific intentions and were unable to discuss them coherently. Whilst some increased their negotiating skills as they grew older, many more simply aimed to comply with teacher expectations for fear of being told off or made to do work again. Most children were very aware of teachers' group organization strategies and generally found them helpful, either socially or to accomplish work. For others, they denoted status. Overall however, they were accepted as facts of classroom life. Again, there is little evidence of pupils' active engagement with the learning implications of teachers' pedagogic intentions, expectations or strategies.

Pupil perspectives on learning (Chapter 9)

This chapter revisited and extended our understanding of pupil perspectives on classrooms as a place to learn. Initially, in asking what 'worries' children when they do their work, we again found the relatively superficial criteria of appearance, correctness and quantity arising. Later, in Year 5 and particularly Year 6, there was a considerable swing towards wanting 'to understand' albeit with the relatively pragmatic intention of satisfying assessment requirements. We got the impression that the challenge of tasks was raised in Year 6, and children took pleasure from their successes. 'Good work', we found, was progressively encouraged during Key Stage 2 through symbolic reward systems such as stars, stickers or certificates. Pupils were aware of these public forms of evaluation and for some they were a source of affirmation, for others of anxiety. Most children liked working with others in groups. They were seen primarily as a source of help with work and of friendship.

We looked across our data-set at some of the key issues that children identified in relation to their learning. Unfortunately, for most of the time these factors seemed to work against the generation of positive engagement and intrinsic motivation. Pressure of time was regularly identified, particularly in Key Stage 2, in relation to maintaining pace in completing tasks and moving on to the next. The ambiguity and uncertainty of many classroom tasks also generated a sense of risk for pupils. This was a common feeling in relation to new challenges that were perceived as difficult. Classroom noise was identified as a source of distraction, and the classic contrast between 'boredom' and 'enjoyment' again emerged. Where school learning became difficult, specific guidance from home was clearly important to many children. Not only was this a means of taking learning forward but it was also a tangible form of personal support for each child as a learner.

Children's explanations for classroom distraction suggested that the pressures of time, ambiguity, uncertainty, risk, noise and boredom accumulated to produce conditions in which distraction was used as an 'escape'. Despite, or because of, the pressures of the classroom, pupils felt the need to break off from their work from time to time. Whilst such distraction seemed embedded in routine expectations and rarely produced problems for teachers, it signalled instrumentality and 'getting through the day' rather than high levels of learner engagement.

Pupil perspectives on standardized assessment (Chapter 10)

Having previously addressed testing at Key Stage 1 in some detail (Pollard *et al.*, 1994), we focused on the tests at the end of Key Stage 2. The children in our study were in no doubt that these SAT tests were of great significance. They believed that they had particular importance for their imminent transfer to secondary school and their likely forthcoming placement into classes and sets. Many children were aware of the categoric and differentiating nature of the SATs, and regarded them as a form of 'official' judgement on their learning. Some, particularly lower attainers, found this very stressful and the discourse of 'levels' was strong.

When the tests were taken in the summer of 1996 there were special arrangements in all of the schools, and there was a significant variation in the classroom climates that were created. Some were more calming, others reinforced the 'high-stakes' nature of the SATs. We illustrated this with the cases of inner-city Meadway and suburban Lawnside. Meadway was highly pressurized, with teachers feeling exposed to public scrutiny and conveying their anxieties to the children. Lawnside's confidence and ethos mitigated against such anxiety, and children were put at their ease in low-key ways. As with our previous findings at Key Stage 1 (Abbott *et al.*, 1994; Pollard *et al.*, 1994), there was thus considerable variation between schools.

We particularly drew attention to the differences in the assessment experiences of lower and higher-attaining children. Low attainers such as those at Kenwood felt exposed by the tests. Normal sources of support, teachers and peers, had been withdrawn there and left to their own devices, many struggled. They were then particularly concerned to avoid being humiliated by their peers by being labelled a 'failure'. Many such children simply wanted to forget about the tests, whilst others began to generate explanatory or face-saving accounts. Higher achievers such as those at Valley were more positive. Many benefitted from support both at home and school, and they were more likely to have their efforts reinforced by their peers. Teachers often tried to offset the risk of personal hurt by encouraging children to 'simply do your best'. However, we saw in the case of Audley how this was not enough to mask the very different experiences of high and low-attaining pupils. Whilst the teacher's rhetoric was one of equal valuing of each child's personal effort, the children were in no doubt at all about who was successful and who was likely to 'fail'. Low achievers felt helpless in the face of the tests. The process was socially and academically differentiating.

Case-studies in learning disposition and identity (Chapter 11)

We offered case-study accounts of thirteen children to illustrate the overall, experienced effect of classroom circumstances. Having reviewed pupil behaviour and perspectives in relation to curriculum, relationships, pedagogy, assessment and learning, we wanted to represent it more holistically. In so doing, we began to highlight the ways in which classroom experiences had a cumulative effect on the development of pupils' identities and dispositions as learners. Indeed, it can be seen that national education policy impacts on individual children in extremely fundamental ways.

12.4 CONCLUSION

So what have we got here overall? In one sense the PACE project has documented the great *success* of the educational policies of successive governments. In the 1980s teachers were deemed to have too much control over educational policy, practice and provision. Sir Keith Joseph (Secretary of State for Education 1981–6) followed the presumption of Prime Minister Callaghan (Callaghan, 1976) and declared that there had been 'producer capture' by the professionals. The Conservative government resolved to wrest such control away. The result was the Education Reform Act 1988, annual rounds of supplementary legislation (on inspection, opting out, funding, training, etc.), a seemingly endless output of a series of educational quangos (NCC, SEAC, SCAA, QCA, TTA, etc.) and repeated campaigns by media and politicians that appear to have been designed to humiliate and undermine teachers. It is not surprising that many committed primary school teachers felt hurt and bewildered. The result however, developed further by the Labour government after 1997, was that a new, national *system* for educational provision had been created. This system is extremely coherent and embraces curriculum, pedagogy, assessment, teacher training, teacher supply, inspection, school development, funding, pay, target-setting, publication of results, the role of governors, parents, LEAs, consultants, and so on. Thus we are now a very long way from the uneven quality and patchy provision of entitlements that characterized English primary schools in earlier decades – some really excellent, some dreadful (HMI, 1978). Further, by 1999 there were signs that standards of pupil performance were rising, at least for those subjects measured by SATs at age 7 and 11 (OFSTED, 1999). Could we say then that the disruption has been worthwhile? That progress is being made? It all depends of course, on what we regard as progress. Consider some descriptions of schooling from the past.

Here is Willard Waller writing in 1932:

> The teacher–pupil relationship is a form of institutionalised dominance and subordination. Teacher and pupil confront each other in the school with an original conflict of desires, and however much that conflict may be reduced in amount, or however much it may be hidden, it still remains. The teacher represents the adult group, ever the enemy of the spontaneous life of groups of children. The teacher represents the formal curriculum, and his interest is in imposing that curriculum on the children in the form of tasks; but pupils are much more interested in life in their own world than in the desiccated bits of adult life which teachers have to offer. The teacher represents the established social order in the school, and his interest is in maintaining that order, whereas pupils have only a negative interest in that feudal superstructure. Pupils are the material in which teachers are supposed to produce results. Pupils are human beings striving to realise themselves in their own spontaneous manner, striving to produce their results in their own way. Each of these hostile parties stands in the way of the other; in so far as the aims of either are realised, it is at the sacrifice of the aims of the other.
>
> (p. 195)

This quotation was used in Pollard (1985), a book which analysed the ways in which primary school teachers of the 1970s negotiated good relationships with the children in the classes and thus avoided conflict. Of course, such relationships are still achieved today, but Waller makes some very telling points and teachers today now have far less scope to act responsively, to reach out to pupils, and to engender engagement.

Now consider this excerpt from Philip Jackson's *Life in Classrooms* (1968):

School is a place where tests are failed and passed, where amusing things happen, where new insights are stumbled upon, and skills acquired. But it is also a place in which people sit, and listen, and wait, and raise their hands, and pass out paper, and stand in line, and sharpen pencils. School is where we encounter both friends and foes, where imagination is unleashed and misunderstanding brought to ground. But it is also a place where yawns are stifled and initials scratched on desktops, where milk money is collected and recess lines are formed ... There is an important fact about a student's life that teachers and parents often prefer not to talk about. This is the fact that young people have to be in school, whether they want to be or not. In this regard, students have something in common with the members of two of our other social institutions that have involuntary attendance: prisons and mental hospitals. The analogy, though dramatic, is not intended to be shocking, yet the school child, like the incarcerated adult, is in a sense a prisoner. He too must come to grips with the inevitability of his experience. He too must develop strategies for dealing with the conflict that frequently arises between his natural desires and interests and institutional expectations. The thousands of hours spent in the elementary school classroom are not, in an ultimate sense, a matter of choice.

(Jackson, 1968, pp. 5, 9)

Waller and Jackson were commenting on schooling in the USA and did not have in mind the characteristics of English primary education of the 1990s but their claims, insights and images are certainly arresting and, in some respects, ring true of the English situation. Indeed a broad overview of the PACE data on pupils suggests that many *were* playing the system, *were* reserved, *were* bored, *were* risk-averse, and *were* shy of full engagement in learning. Our pupils, supported by their peer culture, appeared to have learned to hold back. They thus avoided being portrayed as a 'keener', 'swot' or 'teacher's pet', but they also failed to maximize their learning opportunities. Ironically, they were often supported in this reservation by teachers whose practices, professional judgement and strategies for survival also reflected external requirements and who felt constrained by the critiques, expectations and inspections that now framed their work. Is it possible, one might speculate, that a new meshing of teacher and pupil strategies could become institutionalized around a new, mutual instrumentality?

The systemic reforms of recent years may thus have succeeded in controlling teachers, making them accountable, standardizing educational provision, increasing subject knowledge and teaching skills, and focusing attention on 'the basics'. Further, they may also be beginning to produce results in terms of a narrow range of performance measures. But it is doubtful on the basis of our evidence that they have overcome the seemingly endemic problem of pupil motivation and engagement in learning within schools. The children we interviewed over the six-year period of data-gathering were consistently pragmatic and instrumental about their schooling, and poorly informed and non-reflexive about their learning. They could be taught to perform in terms of the increasingly narrow echo of the elementary school curriculum of English and Mathematics, but what of curiosity, imagination and creativity? We are certainly now a long way from the learning experiences provided and described by people such as Isaacs (1930, 1932), Armstrong (1980) or Paley (1981, 1990) in which learning engagement and the appropriation of knowledge by children are key themes. Perhaps it was ever so within institutions of mass schooling.

However, it is necessary to ask if this situation is good enough. Is this all that we should expect a modern education system to deliver?

In the next chapter we focus on the issue of learning disposition more directly, and offer an analysis of some of the issues that would need to be considered if we wanted to construct a more educationally balanced and effective education system.

Chapter 13

Developing Learning Disposition

13.1 Introduction
13.2 Learning disposition
13.3 Learning through life
13.4 Conclusion

13.1 INTRODUCTION

In this chapter we reflect on the major patterns of evidence that we have collected and consider them in relation to our second research question: Did the introduction of the National Curriculum and assessment facilitate or undermine the development of positive pupil learning dispositions?

This was not one of our original research questions when PACE was first conceptualized, but we focus on it now because of the significance of the topic for the future of education policy, and because we believe that the evidence of the PACE project highlights some issues of potential concern.

Since the Education Reform Act 1988 both Conservative and Labour administrations have pursued broadly similar education policies. Indeed, although the Conservative pressure for privatization of schooling was dropped by Labour, successive governments since the 1980s have sustained a continuous process of systemic change. The driving logic of this programme of change has been to enhance 'standards of attainment' and the 'educational performance' of pupils, teachers and schools. Thus at the millennium, curriculum, pedagogy, assessment, appraisal, training, pay, inspection, target-setting, resourcing, praising and condemning are now all in the service of this goal, within an increasingly integrated system from pre-school to higher education and beyond.

However, there are some particular priorities, the most important of which is undoubtedly the sustained determination to increase performance and standards of pupil attainment. Closely following are aspirations to develop social cohesion and a commitment to lifelong learning. For instance, the New Labour election manifesto of 1997, *Because Britain Deserves Better*, declared:

> Education is not just good for the individual. It is an economic necessity for the nation. We will compete successfully on the basis of quality or not at all. And quality comes from developing the potential of all our people ... Primary schools are the key to mastering the basics and developing in every child an eagerness to learn ... We must learn throughout life, to retain employment through new and improved skills.
>
> (pp. 7–9)

Excellence in Schools (DfEE, 1997), the White Paper which followed the election, similarly stated:

> We are talking about human capital in the age of knowledge ... We must overcome the spiral of disadvantage, in which alienation from, or failure within, the education system is passed on from one generation to the next ... Our goal is a society in which everyone is well educated and able to learn throughout life. Britain's economic prosperity and social cohesion both depend on achieving that goal.
>
> (Foreword and p. 9)

This ambition that all children should be educated to be both knowledgeable and competent in the present, and flexible, problem-solving learners for the future has been a long-standing ambition of governments. Perhaps it is essential in our rapidly changing world of cultural, technological, economic and political interdependence, diversity and innovation. However, we believe that the potential tension between these goals has been barely recognized and deserves further consideration.

For instance, is it possible despite undoubted progress in 'raising standards' that the sustained, systemic pressure to enhance short-term performance could actually start to inhibit long-term commitment to lifelong learning and thus increase social differentiation? The PACE data reported in this book and summarized in Chapter 12 seem to suggest that this could be a serious issue. In this context it is interesting to reflect on the fact that a closely related project comparing the learning of primary school pupils in England and France (Broadfoot *et al.*, 2000) offers evidence that English children have been more flexible and independent in their thinking and problem solving than the relatively 'rule-bound' French. However, it is suggested that this capacity, which has been a strength of English primary education, could be undermined by the new, more formal structures and requirements.

In this chapter, we offer some possible explanations of how the problem may arise. We begin by considering what is known about learning disposition. We then review an explanatory model which has been developed within one of the PACE federated projects – the *Identity and Learning Programme* (ILP) (Filer and Pollard, 2000; Pollard, 1990; Pollard and Filer, 1999; Pollard with Filer, 1996). This offers a wide-ranging interpretation of how children learn from a range of experiences and social influences. Relating PACE data to this model casts light on the effects which national education policy has had, and may be having. In conclusion, the PACE analytic model is extended in relation to learning and the overall analysis of this chapter is discussed in terms of the challenges that it poses for government policy.

13.2 LEARNING DISPOSITION

A great deal of research has been conducted by social psychologists on motivation and the importance of positive dispositions to learn. For example, 'locus of control' (Rotter, 1954) refers to a person's *generalized* expectation of the source of control over events. People with an 'internal' locus of control usually believe that they are responsible for what occurs in their lives. They tend to think that success comes about through their own efforts. Others with an 'external' locus of control tend to be less confident in their own abilities and feel unable to control their lives. Working within a behaviourist social learning theory, Rotter suggested that an expectation of internal control develops when a person's behaviour is positively reinforced, so that they come to believe in their own capabilities. However, this wanes if there is no reinforcement. Indeed, if there is sustained experience of powerful external forces or individuals, people tend to adopt an external locus of control. Empirical studies have documented the ways in which people with an internal locus of control tend to engage more actively and spontaneously in learning. They select more challenging tasks, are able to sustain their efforts and are better disposed towards lifelong learning. They also reveal better interpersonal relationships, emotional adjustment and life satisfaction. In large scale correlational studies, it is notable that locus of control is more strongly associated with achievement than any other factor, including measured IQ (Kalechstein and Nowicki, 1987).

Can we say then, that children's 'eagerness to learn' derives from environmental reinforcements and their previous experiences? There is certainly some truth in that argument, but the behaviourist position has a major limitation in that it does not take full account of the interpretations which may be made of experience. Of course, all human beings constantly seek to explain and make sense of events taking place in the world around them. This happens so routinely that it is almost 'without thinking', and yet thinking is certainly involved. In particular, we *attribute* events and outcomes to particular causes.

One of the first psychologists to focus on the process of attribution in everyday life was Heider (1958) who aimed to uncover the 'naive psychology ... hidden in our thinking about interpersonal relations' (p. 14). Attribution theory has been developed in many areas, but one of the most important concerns the ways in which children attribute causes of their academic performance. Weiner (1986) constructed a model of this based on the assumption that beliefs about the causes of success and failure mediate the relationship between feedback and future performance. He suggested that children are likely to attribute success or failure to one of four main causes: ability, effort, task difficulty and luck. These causes can be categorized in terms of internal or external causes, and their stability or instability over time (see Figure 13.1).

This conceptual framework can be used to highlight how affective and cognitive factors interact together. Thus, if a primary school pupil such as Haley (see the case-study in Chapter 11) attributes her perceived poor performance to low effort, as she did in her early primary school career, she may feel some shame (an affective reaction) but at least she knows that she can do something about the problem (a cognitive reaction), and there is therefore no fundamental damage to her self-esteem.

	Internal causes	External causes
Stable causes	Ability	Task difficulty
Unstable causes	Effort	Luck

Figure 13.1 Attributions of academic performance

However, if the cause is seen as a basic lack of 'ability' (seen as a stable, internal cause), as Haley did towards the end of her primary school career, then there is a much bigger problem. Affectively, she may develop a sense of personal shame which may be compounded by a belief that there is little that she can do about it. Her self-esteem and commitment to lifelong learning are therefore likely to be undermined. As Haley put it: 'They're just brainy. They're born like that. If I say I can't do things, I'm no good'. Chapters 7 and 9 of this book provide many similar examples of children's understanding and attributions in relation to the learning attainment of themselves and of others (see also complementary accounts by Gipps and Tunstall, 1997; Reay and Wiliam, 1999).

Dweck (1986, 1999) has elaborated this thinking by analysing children's tacit theories of intelligence. Where intelligence is believed to be a *fixed entity*, children tend to adopt performance goals and seek to maximize positive judgements of their competence. If they believe their ability to be high, they are likely to have a form of 'mastery orientation'. However, those who think that their ability is low are susceptible to 'learned helplessness'. The attributions of such children focus on a belief in their low intelligence as a stable and internal factor in performance, with self-confidence and esteem being drawn into a negative spiral. Within our case-studies in Chapter 11, both Kevin and Philip provide clear illustrations of this process. Sadly, in the case of Philip, his way of coping with his growing sense of educational failure was to present himself as 'tough', indicating the prospect of a difficult trajectory for the future if he engages with anti-educational peer cultures. On the other hand, where children perceive intelligence as malleable and open to *incremental development*, they will tend to have a more positive disposition. Irrespective of their belief in their inherent ability, they are likely to adopt a mastery orientation towards their learning. Again Chapter 11 offers examples, such as Amanda, Laura and Alice, of pupils who had just such a strong sense of personal capability and also received strong external support from their parents and the particular culture of their female peers. They were normally able to maintain resilience as learners, even when they felt bored or challenged.

Dweck recognizes, as do we, the legitimacy of the drive for school pupils to achieve appropriate educational standards. However, she is concerned that *too much* emphasis on performance could become counter-productive. She writes:

> But aren't performance goals necessary in our society? Of course they are ... when students need to display and validate the skills they have. (However,) the problem with performance goals arises when proving ability becomes so important to students that it drives out learning goals. Problems arise when the ability students are measuring is their fixed intelligence. Then performance-goal failures can catapult them into a helpless response.

These problems don't arise as readily with an incremental-theory framework. The ability that incremental students are proving when they pursue a performance goal is not their fixed intelligence, but rather the skills and knowledge they have at the time. If they do poorly on a test, this simply means that their present skills and knowledge need to be augmented, not that a permanent deficiency has been revealed. They are thus spurred to constructive effort and prompted to seek new learning opportunities.

(Dweck, 1999, p. 152)

One major problem which we have concerns the perception of 'intelligence' which is dominant in common-sense thinking. Drawing on Muscovici's theory of social representations, Mugny and Carugati (1989) found that generalized conceptions of intelligence are 'based essentially on the theory of natural inequality and giftedness'. Their synthesis suggests the major social representation of intelligence in Western societies as:

a gift which is divided unequally among the population; in need of protection through policies of discrimination, particularly in schools; the sum total of mental and social aptitudes which develop within the family; but still largely a question of biology.

(p. 50)

Broadfoot *et al.* (2000) suggest that such assumptions are particularly deeply embedded in English culture. They contrast England and France:

(In France) positive attitudes (to school) are related to the nationally-driven assumption that educational success is based on effort, rather than ability; (and) on a separation of the 'self' as a whole from the business of learning ... In England, where the emphasis on innate ability is so deeply ingrained in the individualist educational discourse, lack of progress is more likely to be perceived by pupils as their being 'thick' or 'dummies'.

(p. 197)

Thus despite what is known about the complexity of influences on affective behaviour (Howe, 1990) and even the suggestion of multiple forms of intelligence (Gardner, 1985) and influence of emotion (Goleman, 1996), belief in generalized intellectual capacity is still very strong. It even penetrates the discourse of politicians and senior educationalists. For instance the Chief Inspector of Schools, Chris Woodhead has regularly encouraged teachers to 'organise pupils according to their ability' (HMCI, 1998; OFSTED, 1999). Of course this could just be a colloquial use of terms with reference to 'attainment' being intended, but such usage is commonplace in official publications and speeches. However, the potential motivational consequence of official and cultural reproduction of the belief in a fixed entity rather than a variable position is enormous.

More recently, Claxton (1999) has attempted to distil the key features of 'learning power' – the capacity to learn and adapt in flexible ways. He argues that learning is a pressing necessity for modern societies, but that attempts to develop it are badly distorted by outdated ideas. He writes:

As the world moves into the age of uncertainty, nations, communities and individuals need all the learning power they can get. Our institutions of business and education, even our styles of parenting have to change so that the development and the expression of learning power become real possibilities. But this will not happen if they remain founded on a narrow conceptualisation of learning: one which focuses on content over process, comprehension over competence, 'ability' over engagement, teaching over self-discovery. Many of the current attempts to create a learning society are hamstrung by a tacit acceptance of this outmoded viewpoint.

(p. 331)

Such a 'narrow conceptualisation' is again revealed in the thinking of the chief inspector who tends to reach for a simple transmission model. Thus, when asked near the millennial turn to clarify the purposes of teaching, Mr Woodhead replied: 'To me, it means that teachers transmit those aspects of our culture that we think worth preserving' (*Newsnight*, 22 October 1999). This is a long way from the forward-looking emphasis on competencies and 'learning how to learn' now being advocated by organizations such as the Royal Society of Arts (Bayliss, 1999) and The Industrial Society (Kell, 1999).

Thus, whilst the importance of pupil motivation and commitment to lifelong learning is officially recognized in many public policy statements with reference to 'the habits of mind on which learning depends' (Barber, 1997, p. 6), 'eagerness to learn' (Labour Party, 1997, p. 7), or even the minimalist goal that pupils should 'concentrate on their work' (DfEE, 1997, p. 15), there are many contrary pressures in the requirements and accountability systems that schools and teachers now face. Further, the substantive findings of the PACE projects that we reviewed in Chapter 12 of this book appear to warn that over-emphasis on the basics in modern education policy could unwittingly lead to a *reduction* in pupil motivation, and could thus threaten what has previously been perceived by many countries as a particular strength of English primary education. Indeed, a significant proportion of pupils seem to have became instrumentally concerned with 'playing the system', with superficial learning and trying to avoid boredom. Whilst many children may 'perform' despite their lack of intrinsic engagement, our research suggests that we should be particularly concerned about the attitudes and lifelong learning skills of pupils.

Frank Coffield, director of ESRC's *The Learning Society* research programme, has reviewed a different range of data in relation to post-16 education, and reached similar conclusions. He argues that a new conceptualization of learning is needed:

A new *social* theory of learning is required. (This) argues that learning is located in social participation and dialogue as well as in the heads of individuals; and it shifts the focus from a concentration on individual cognitive processes to the social relationships and arrangements which shape, for instance, positive and negative 'learner identities' which may differ over time and from place to place.

(Coffield, 1999, p. 493)

With such ideas in mind, we illustrate the approach to such a social theory of learning with which one of us has been closely associated. As with the case-study accounts contained in Chapter 11, the purpose of this is to illustrate the complexity and interconnectedness of the factors associated with learning. However, the approach is more analytical, and using the 'designatory' potential of ethnography (Hargreaves, 1978) offers a way of conceptualizing the major issues.

13.3 LEARNING THROUGH LIFE

The Identity and Learning Programme (ILP) is a longitudinal ethnography – a very detailed study of the lives of eighteen children through each of the thirteen years of their compulsory schooling. It began in 1987 and lasted until 2001. Whilst initially drawn from two contrastive primary schools, the children attended ten different secondaries and the research focused on how they learned and made their way through a succession of new situations and experiences during their schooling. Whilst parents and teachers may hope to provide security and opportunity within the social settings which are created in homes, classrooms and playgrounds, such contexts also often contain challenges and threats which children have to negotiate. As children develop, perfect or struggle with their strategies for coping with such situations, so they learn about other people, about themselves and about life. Of course, as we have seen in our companion volume (Osborn *et al.*, 1997) and in Chapters 3 and 12 of the present book, the introduction of the National Curriculum with its associated changes in pedagogy and assessment generated a particular set of new challenges for English primary schools during the 1990s.

A major outcome of the ethnographic study has been to develop theoretically informed models of social factors involved in learning. For example, Figure 13.2 derives from Pollard with Filer (1996).

In Figure 13.2, the question of where and when learning is taking place raises socio-historical issues at the levels of country, region, community, school, home, etc. For instance, the context of government and policy-making in England during the 1980s and 1990s was extremely significant to the children studied as part of the PACE project. Regional and LEA differences in economic, political and cultural factors also affected each child's experiences, even if they may not have been aware of such influences. Although these were not a particular focus of the PACE project, our national sampling in four different regions and eight LEAs, and across urban–rural and varied socio-economic settings, made us acutely aware of these significant structural contrasts in circumstances. At the school level too, our 48 schools revealed major variations in the nature of headteacher management practices and teacher culture, and consequential contrasts in the school climate as a learning environment (see Osborn *et al.*, 2000, Chapter 11). At more detailed levels, the specific contexts within which children interact with others – the home, the classroom and the playground – each have unique characteristics with socially constructed rules and expectations guiding behaviour within them (Pollard, 1985). Those of the classroom tend to be more constraining than those of home or the playground but each is important in structuring children's experiences. Teachers, parents and children live *through* the particular circumstances of time, place, culture and experience. They thus contributed to the biography and identity of each individual. For instance, the classroom vignette of Jessica and Scott taking their Writing SAT in Kenwood Junior (see Chapter 11) provides an example of a specific, high-stakes, classroom episode in which the interplay on the pupils of circumstance, task and identity is extremely clear. Whilst the children struggle, their teacher is shown to be torn between her culturally embedded commitment to individual children whom she knows so well and the new, impersonal and procedural requirements of the national testing system.

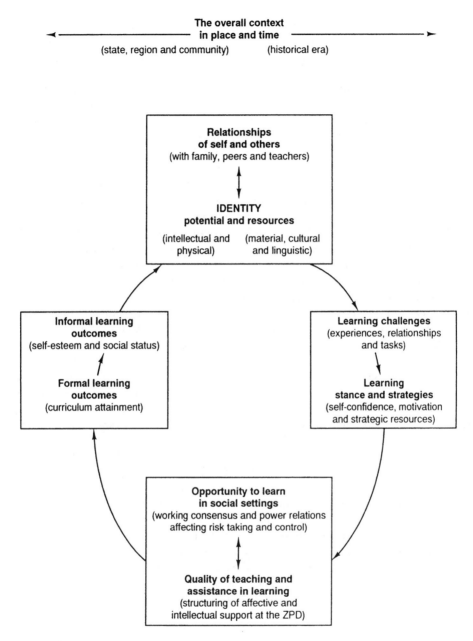

Figure 13.2 A model of learning, identity and social setting

To understand children's *identities* we must pay particular attention to the 'significant others' in each child's life; to those who interact with them and influence the ways in which they see themselves. Beyond interview and observations such as those conducted by the PACE team, we thus need to understand each child's relationships with parents, siblings, peers and teachers, and the ways in which these relationships may enhance or diminish their self-confidence in themselves as learners, and their views of how learning occurs. For instance, are children encouraged to believe that they have a fixed intelligence, or that they can progressively develop from new learning experiences? The case of Neil in Chapter 11 illustrates how a father's support for Mathematics can contribute to pupil resilience even when a teacher is less supportive. The cases of Laura and Kate reinforce the importance of parental expectations, but also draw attention to pupils' need to manage their identities in the evaluative context of peer culture. For instance, Laura felt extremely exposed by her parents' and teacher's decision that she should take the Maths extension test (Chapter 10).

Every child also has both physical and intellectual potential which, over the primary school years, continue the formative and developmental stages which began at birth. The gradual realization of physical and intellectual potential rolls forward to influence self-confidence. Physical and intellectual capability are areas in which psychologists and biologists have made extensive contributions to studies of child development and learning (e.g. Meadows, 1993). Understanding is still developing rapidly, particularly in neurological studies of the brain and mind (Greenfield, 1997).

Identity is also very much influenced by factors such as gender, social class and ethnicity, each of which is associated with particular cultural and material resources and with particular patterns of social expectation which impinge on children through their relationships with others. For instance, the influence of gender is very apparent in the cases reviewed in Chapter 11. Philip reached towards the male youth identity of 'toughness' to salvage his dignity as he became increasingly exposed by more differentiated pedagogy and categoric assessment. On the other hand, girls such as Alice, though active with friends in private spaces, tended to present themselves more cautiously to teachers and sought to satisfy teacher expectations despite their feelings of unease. Age, status, and position within the family, classroom and playground are also important for the developing sense of identity of young children because of associated patterns of experience and cultural forms of interpretation.

The model contained in Figure 13.2 focuses on the learning challenges which children face as they grow up. These are very wide-ranging and occur in home, playground and many other settings as well as in the classroom. However, once at primary school, each child has to learn the pupil role – for instance, to cope with classroom rules and conventions, to answer his or her name at registration, to sit cross-legged on the carpet and to listen to the teacher. Then they must respond to the curricular tasks which they are set. As Chapter 3 demonstrates, in English primary schools at Key Stage 1 during the early 1990s this included large amounts of work on the core curriculum, perhaps 35 per cent of time spent on English, 15 per cent on Mathematics and 8 per cent on Science, and at Key Stage 2 the amount of English fell whilst Maths increased and testing and individual work also grew in significance.

In close association with these issues concerning the *content* of new learning challenges, we need to consider the *perspectives* of children about their curriculum and schooling and this has been the key task of Chapters 4 to 11. We have seen that the issue of motivation when facing a new learning challenge is particularly important. Whilst studies such as those of Rotter, Bandura, Weider, Dweck and Claxton have shown the enormous significance of self-efficacy and learning disposition, implicit theories of capability, and qualities of resilience, the ILP has analysed and illustrated in detail how such factors connect to formative social processes of identity-construction and to available cultural resources and social expectations throughout school careers. The longitudinal nature of the PACE project enabled us to mirror this analysis.

Whatever the initial stance of a learner, he or she must then deploy specific *strategies* in new learning situations. The range of strategies available to individual children will vary, with some being confident to make judgements and vary their approach to tasks whilst others need guidance and encouragement to move from tried and tested routines. Jessica and Scott provide an example of this, when confronted by their Writing SAT (Chapter 11). Jessica's persistence and strategic resolve contrast considerably with Scott's almost fatalistic resignation and dependence on his mascots and any teacher advice he could glean during the test.

Another key set of issues are concerned with the risks and opportunities associated with learning. In particular, how supportive is the specific learning context? One might consider a full range of settings in home, playground, classroom, etc. In the context of traditional White English middle-class families, for example, social expectations are perhaps at their most structured where set meals occur, such as Sunday lunch; but the same social phenomenon crops up in playgrounds when children confidently assert the rules of games, such as 'tig' or 'What's the time Mr Wolf?'. There are also many times when actions are far less constrained, when family or peer expectations take a more relaxed form, allowing more scope for individual action and playfulness. The same phenomenon occurs in classroom life. Indeed, Pollard (1985) used the concept of 'rule frame' to describe the nature of the rules-in-play in any particular situation or phase of a teaching session. Rules-in-play derive from the gradual negotiation of understandings about behaviour which routinely takes place between the teacher and pupils. Thus a teacher's introduction to a lesson is usually more tightly framed and controlled than the mid-phase of a session in which children may disperse to engage in various tasks or activities. Such contextual variation is inevitable, but the PACE study suggests that the framing of classroom life has steadily increased during the 1990s (this volume, Chapter 6; Osborn *et al.*, 2000, Chapter 8). This is an incremental pattern, and the PACE data raises questions concerning its consequences for pupil engagement in learning. We saw in the cases of Sean, Philip and others that the combination of pedagogic frame, curriculum prescription and categoric assessment had a demotivating effect because the children could not find a means of expressing themselves and affirming their identities within school.

Of course, the nature of negotiation between children and others has always varied in different settings and there is always an element of this which is concerned with the exercise of power. In general, adults have the power to initiate, assert, maintain and change rules, whilst children must comply, adapt, mediate or resist. Most teachers and most parents, for most of the time and in most settings, act sensitively towards young children so that there is an element of negotiation and legitimacy in the social expectations and rules which are applied in particular situations. Sometimes this is not the case, there is less legitimacy and the children may well become unhappy or believe that they have been treated 'unfairly'. Following the introduction of the

Education Reform Act 1988, many teachers reported a concern that, because of curriculum overloading, assessment and other requirements, they were unable to maintain the 'good relationships' with children which they felt to be so important (see Osborn *et al.*, 2000, Chapter 3). This teacher concern was not affirmed by the children in our study. As we saw in Chapter 6, they felt that their relationships with teachers were generally good. However, it is interesting that the criteria that they apply to the curriculum so clearly reflect the priorities of child culture rather than those of the formal school agenda. School pupils may get on reasonably well with their teachers, but they still occupy the structural position of children and develop associated perspectives.

The question of teacher–pupil relationships is important because within the relatively individualized and competitive context of English culture (Broadfoot *et al.*, 2000), only a child with a confident learning stance is likely to take chances within a context in which risks and costs of failure are high. In some classrooms, children may thus keep their heads down and the same may be true in some families or playground situations, perhaps where sibling or peer rivalry creates a risk to status or dignity. In focusing on learning processes, we thus need to consider the *opportunities and risks* which exist for each child to learn within different social settings – the context of power relations and social expectations within which he or she must act and adapt. In Chapters 6 and 9 we saw how pupils prioritized their concern to avoid embarrassment and the risks of being told off. Some situations may be low-key and feel safer, in which case the child can feel secure to give it a try. In the case of others, the stakes may be higher and a child's self-esteem may be vulnerable to social pressure or public critique from siblings, parents, peers or their teacher. As has been well established through media incidents in the last decade, the publication of league tables and high-profile media critiques of teachers and schools in England has a regulative and differentiating effect on the cultural context in which education takes place. PACE findings regarding Years 5 and 6 suggest that avoidance of risk through instrumentalist conformity may have begun to drive out the playfulness and emotional engagement which is associated with deeper and more creative personal learning (Claxton, 1999, forthcoming; Goleman, 1998).

The *quality of the teaching and assistance* which a child receives in different settings is also clearly vital to his or her success as a learner, and this has been a priority area for initial and in-service teacher development programmes focusing on subject-knowledge and instructional techniques. Social constructivist psychology offers a clear analysis of the importance for learning of the guidance and instruction of more skilled or knowledgeable others (Mercer, 1995; Wood, 1988). Whether support is provided by parents, teachers, siblings or peers, the principle is the same: that children's learning benefits from the 'scaffolding' of their understanding so that it can be extended across the next step in their development. Unfortunately, the PACE findings that we reported in Chapters 8, 9 and elsewhere indicate that the classroom process is far more mundane from the pupil perspective. Firstly, we found that children had only vague conceptions of teachers' instructional objectives. Rather than engaging in some synergetic process between teacher and pupil to extend existing understanding, most children were simply concerned to do what they needed to do to avoid being embarrassed or told off or having to do work again. We found that children felt pressured by classroom time constraints and struggled to develop task engagement. There was little evidence of meta-cognitive, learning-focused awareness.

However, the *ways* in which a child's understanding is challenged through teaching are recognized to be of great importance, and Pollard with Filer (1996) suggests that it is necessary to facilitate emotional engagement as well as intellectual challenge. Goleman's work on emotional intelligence (1996) assembles a wide range of evidence on this point. Additionally he argues (1998) that new patterns of life in modern developed societies are threatening emotional stability. Indeed, in the case of modern schooling, both parents and teachers have been found to be worried that children can feel 'overpressured' and we should note the continuing emphasis which is placed on children being 'happy and settled' (Hughes *et al.*, 1994; Osborn *et al.*, 2000, Chapter 4). However, PACE pupil data suggest that children's perception is more practical and prosaic. Accepting their lot, they simply want to find things 'interesting', have a little 'fun' and be treated fairly at school (Chapters 5 and 6). However, given the opportunity to imagine freely, they seem likely to opt for more physical activity, imaginative play and choice over how they spend time. That of course, would not necessarily provide experiences from which pupils would satisfy government basic skill targets, but a new priority of creating positive levels of learning disposition, intellectual engagement, and self-awareness as learners might require more learner-aware forms of provision.

What are the outcomes? is the final question posed by the model (Figure 13.2). The first and most obvious outcome concerns the *achievement* of intended learning goals. These may range from the official curricular aims which are set by teachers as a result of school or National Curriculum policy, through to the challenges which are presented as part of peer activities in the playground and the new learning experiences which confront each child as he or she grows up within the family at home. Learning thus produces relatively overt yardsticks of attainment whether the child is learning letter formation in handwriting or about number bonds, how to skip, swim or play a new game, or how to hold their own in family conversation. So what has been achieved? What is the new level of attainment? What can the child now do and understand? Such questions are of particular importance because, beyond issues of explicit achievement and the new forms of action which become possible, lie associated consequences for the ways in which young learners perceive themselves and are perceived by others. We saw the process and pressures of assessment in Chapters 7 and 10 and noted in both cases how pupils perceived assessment in summative terms. This has a direct affect on their self-perception, albeit after mediation by parents, peers and teachers (Filer and Pollard, 2000; Reay and Wiliam, 1999).

Social differentiation occurs when children become distinguished one from another. In school children may have little control over this – for instance, they may be organized by age-group, 'ability-group', or gender. Ability-grouping or setting has come to be of particular significance following the introduction of categoric assessment, formal reports, target-setting and inspection. Pupil performance has become more high-stakes and more overt – a classic form of differentiation. The consequence of this is likely to be a growth in polarization. Thus those who succeed choose to socialize with each other, and those who do less well seek to preserve their dignity by discarding any learning ambitions they may have once held and join forces with others in the same position. In Chapter 11 we saw the beginning of this in the case of Philip. The social consequences of such patterns are a progressive divergence in children's sense of identity and capability leading ultimately to different life-chances and the risk of social exclusion (Banks *et al.*, 1992; Connell *et al.*, 1982; Gillborn and Youdell, 1999).

Children's self-esteem is likely to rise as achievements are made. Maturational 'achievements' such as having birthdays, losing teeth or just becoming taller are often marked with particular pleasure by younger pupils as they see themselves 'growing up', but many more attainments are accomplished in the home, playground and classroom as children face new experiences and challenges. The classroom setting is, of course, particularly important because it is the source of official educational judgements, whilst the home setting offers the support, or otherwise, of parents – the crucial 'significant others'. We saw this in the cases of Neil, Laura and other children in Chapter 11.

Regarding social status, it is arguably relationships within peer groups which are of most significance to children. For many children peer group membership is both a source of great enjoyment in play and a source of solidarity in facing the challenges which are presented by adults. In such circumstances some children lead whilst others follow and high status may well be associated with popularity, style and achievement in facilitating 'good fun'. On the other hand, peer group cultures can also be exclusive and reject children from membership if they are unable to conform to group norms. We saw how Laura and Kate, whilst trying to attain highly, had to manage this aspect of their identities. However, if a child's learning and performance regarding peer expectations are deficient, their social status is likely to be low with a consequent roll-forward effect on their sense of self-esteem and of personal identity and the risk of a negative spiral.

The process is thus brought full circle and we return to the first question posed by Figure 13.2 – to identity – *who is learning*. This cyclical conceptualization represents the process of learning in a social context, with the effects of social relationships and learning achievements accumulating over time to contribute to the formation of identity. In the case of young children, as we saw from our case-studies of Haley, Kevin, Richard and Amanda, it is particularly necessary to monitor the ways in which patterns of adaption and achievement evolve or stabilize in response to changing social circumstances.

13.4 CONCLUSION

We noted in Chapter 1 that human learning has been a continuous process for millions of years. We develop our biological inheritance by interacting with our physical and social environment. Thus development and experience interact together, producing learning and change (Blyth, 1984). Modern educational innovations such as schooling and planned curricula represent a socially constructed intervention into this fundamental process.

At the start of a new century, as new literacy and numeracy campaigns become institutionalized together with a renewed emphasis on targeted instruction, homework and assessment, we would do well to really think through the implications of how to maximize pupil motivation and belief in personal learning capacity. Successive phases of the PACE project have shown how pupil motivation and engagement in school is vulnerable to erosion at a time when national requirements are imposed and when teachers' scope for curricular and pedagogic responsiveness to children becomes limited.

The comprehensive findings of PACE on pupil perspectives have been linked to the *Identity and Learning Programme*. Together they highlight and substantiate the major intervening variables concerned with children's personal self-confidence as learners as they negotiate their pupil careers. It is clear that parents have a significant mediating role in learning, as do relationships with siblings and peers. There is also a continuous need for skilful, sensitive and socially-aware management of pupil motivation by teachers. A simple way of expressing key complementary factors in the educational process is shown in Figure 13.3.

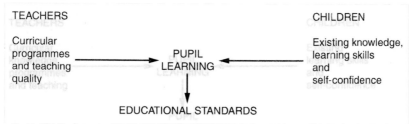

Figure 13.3 Complementary factors in pupil learning

It is important to note the differences in the nature of these elements. An instructional programme can be organized in sequence or at any particular point in time (a holiday literacy programme, for instance) and can be specifically targeted to yield measurable outcomes. It is relatively discrete and precise, and is readily amenable to policy prescription, school development plans, teacher training, assessments and the new technologies of 'performativity'. However, the development of the knowledge, learning skills and self-confidence of a learner is built on the entire accumulation of a child's previous experiences. It is subtle and multifaceted, requiring empathy, understanding and judgement from teachers as well as subject knowledge. The child in the classroom is working through a pupil career, is developing physically as well as personally, is engaged in a process of becoming. Whilst this is much less tangible than the 'raising of standards', it is no less important. Indeed, the reality is that these two major sets of factors interact together to produce both educational and personal outcomes. This suggests a need for *balance*. Sustained attention to curricular instruction should be complemented by provision for the development of pupils' learning skills and self-confidence. An over-emphasis on focused, basic instruction risks undermining curriculum engagement and the self-belief of children as learners.

Primary education may well be, as Richards (1998, 1999) has suggested, poised 'at a hinge of history' between the hegemony of the performance model and an emergent set of new ideas influenced by Vygotskian and socio-cultural theory (see, for instance, Pollard, 1999; Silcock, 1999) and cumulative evidence on effective teaching (e.g., Croll and Hastings, 1996; Galton *et al.*, 1999; Gipps, 1994; Hastings, 1998).

Chapter 14

Childhood and Education: Past, Present and Future

14.1   Introduction
14.2   A recent history of childhood
14.3   Structural change and education policy
14.4   A challenge for the future

14.1 INTRODUCTION

In this final chapter, we conclude by returning to the third of the key questions that we posed in Chapter 1: What is the significance of recent education policy in terms of how children and childhood are understood in modern English society?

In addressing this question, we begin by briefly tracing the ways in which conceptions of 'children' and 'childhood' have changed historically in relation to structural developments in English economy and society. We then consider some of the social factors which influence English childhoods in modern times. Finally, we highlight some key policy contradictions and ask: How should we educate our children for the future?

This concluding focus on historical and macro-structural issues affecting children reflects the influence of Qvortrup (1993, 1997). Whilst recognizing the importance of studying child perspectives and discourse about children, he argued for the overriding significance of structural analysis. As he put it: 'childhood is constructed by a number of social forces, economic interests, technological determinants, cultural phenomena, etc. ... (including) the discourse about it' (Qvortrup, 1997, p. 2). In other words, 'childhood' is a cultural form which responds to and is shaped by more fundamental underlying forces. Thus the ways in which childhood has been conceptualized has varied in relation to social and economic circumstances, material interests and cultural interpretations. The opportunities and constraints which children experience in the present therefore have to be understood in the context of both historic and modern structures, processes and material interests.

The significance of this is to show that modern education policies associated with the National Curriculum, assessment, school inspection, teacher training requirements, and so on, reflect the social circumstances, material interests and cultural interpretations of 'childhood' of our own time and place. Education policy, like any other, is a social and political construction. Despite the daily intensity of teaching and learning for those working within the present education system, it is possible to stand back and problematize it. In particular, we would argue, we need to consider whether the conceptions of children and childhood which are implied by the present National Curriculum and its associated systems are well-founded. In so doing, we will be exploring what Prout (1999) argues is an 'unresolved tension' in late-modern societies around the construction of childhood. He writes:

> On the one hand, there is an increasing tendency to see children as individuals with a capacity for self-realisation and autonomous action; on the other, there are practices directed at greater surveillance, control and regulation of children's everyday lives.
>
> (p. 1)

One of the overarching aims of the present book has been to trace how this unresolved tension is played out in terms of modern English primary education.

14.2 A RECENT HISTORY OF CHILDHOOD

We begin our account by briefly reviewing and contrasting three periods in English history as they affected the mass of working people – those associated with nineteenth-century agricultural society and the industrial revolution, with the gradual growth of social welfare provision in the late nineteenth and early twentieth century, and with recent decades prior to the millennium. For each of these periods, we argue that it is possible to distinguish a particular manifestation of childhood as a reflection of underlying structural factors.

Childhood in the nineteenth century

At the start of the industrial revolution, most of the population of England lived in rural locations. Almost 90 per cent of men worked in agriculture and family life for the majority of working people was focused on the farm, smallholding or village. Family networks were often large and mobility was poor, so that most young children grew up within a relatively stable web of extended family relationships. There were high levels of fertility and infant mortality, and women spent large proportions of their adult lives in childbirth, childcare and in agricultural and domestic work. Life could be extremely hard and children of working families were expected to become relatively independent and make a contribution from a young age. They were inducted to labour in the fields, to assume childcare duties, or to help with other practical family needs as deemed appropriate to their gender. In most communities there was very little organized provision for health or education. In consequence, serious illnesses or accidents were often disabling or fatal and most of the population was illiterate. However, the church was much respected as the moral cornerstone of the rural community and children were inducted into its beliefs and seasonal rituals from a young age. Roads were poor, travel depended on walking or riding, and there were few means of information and communication available to working people about the world beyond their communities. Although broadsheets gradually became available in market towns, news was still largely conveyed by word of mouth among the mass of the rural poor as a complement to the stories and songs of the oral tradition.

Thus both boys and girls were expected to work and to contribute to satisfying the needs of family and community. There was very little sentimentalization of childhood as an age of innocence, rather the church emphasized the fall from grace, the deficiencies of humankind and need for discipline in work, family and religious devotion. The industrial revolution began a gradual process of urban migration but children's labour in the countryside remained very significant right up to the middle of the twentieth century.

The industrial revolution saw a gradual growth in the population of new towns and cities and a decrease in the rural population as families migrated to find work. In the urban setting, children continued to make an economic contribution from a relatively young age and were a significant element in the workforce of textile mills, coal mines and other industrial settings. It is well known that their labour was considerably abused, for production technologies and working conditions were extremely demanding and safety was often compromised. High levels of fertility and mortality were sustained, particularly amongst the poor, and the average family size was still over six children in the 1860s.

However, the expanding urbanization and industrialization gradually brought the development of a social and economic infrastructure. Roads, canals, railways and postal communications were improved immeasurably so that different towns and regions began to be interconnected economically, socially, culturally and politically. New manufacturing and other technologies produced considerable increases in productivity, making the reliance on child labour less necessary. Religious and charitable bodies began the provision of schools and hospitals, until these roles were taken up by the state. Slowly the previously dominant vision of children as deficient or flawed, requiring the discipline of family, work or schooling, began to be challenged by a new conception of children as capable of moral and intellectual growth, but corrupted by the social and economic pressures of the time.

Childhood and the development of social welfare

In the last decades of the nineteenth century and early decades of the twentieth, there were profound changes in the ways in which children were perceived. In the first place, the development of new public health and education provision began to be thought of in terms of human resource and social control. Thus more skilful and reliable workers were required by the rapidly growing domestic economy and to exploit the opportunities offered by imperial expansion around the world.

'Standards' in the educational 'basics' had to be raised, and the system of payment by results ensured that costs were kept under control. In addition, particularly following the extension of the franchise in 1867, it was considered essential to ensure the provision of an appropriately 'civilizing' education. The new scientific under-standings of medicine, child development, education and social welfare provided an additional impetus in the identification of children's distinct needs as a social group. Indeed, the major influence of the modernist social project began at this time with the gradual institutionalization of provision for children and the progressive establishment of new, specialist, child-focused professions.

Through such processes the status of children was transformed. The newly identified social and personal needs of children were now to be met by the new institutions and professionals of the education, health and welfare services. Compulsory schooling replaced wage-earning work as the accepted occupation of children from the ages of 5 to 12 or 13, and such 'pupils' were to be separated off and protected from the harsher realities of the adult world until they had matured and become educationally prepared to enter it. Thus, whilst exploitation of children's labour had been culturally acceptable in both agricultural and early industrial societies, a new, sentimentalized ideal of the 'natural' and 'dependent' child emerged. This conception was particularly promoted through the development of the middle-class, the rise in significance of the nuclear family, increases in living standards and a steady fall in the birth rate. In such circumstances children gradually came to be seen more in terms of their emotional and affective value. Feminist historians have linked this transformation to similar processes which affected women at the same time. Thus Firestone argues that:

> The rise of the modern nuclear family ... reinforced the development of an ideology of childhood, with its special indigenous life style, language, dress, mannerisms, etc. ... And with the increase and exaggeration of children's dependence, women's bondage to motherhood was also extended to its limits. Women and children were in the same lousy boat.
>
> (Firestone, 1979, p. 39)

This 'lousy ideological boat' carried women and children on the same basic course for most of the twentieth century. Education, health and welfare systems developed to support them, and the ideal of motherhood and conception of childhood as an age of dependence and innocence grew. Perhaps this conjunction of ideas reached its apotheosis in the post-war 1950s when women were encouraged to return to the home after World War Two. By then, labour-saving domestic equipment had become more affordable and mothers were thus able to invest more time in childcare and the family. There were strong norms and expectations surrounding this. For instance, Bowlby's book, *Maternal Care and Mental Health* (1951), helped to establish the idea of 'maternal deprivation' as a explanation for poor social adjustment and educational progress. Most children were born within marriage and divorce was unusual, carrying considerable social stigma. The ideal, projected now by advertising, the growing mass media and even the introductory reading books used in school, was the nuclear family – Mummy at home, Daddy out at work, a girl, a boy and the family pet. Welfare State provision for health, education, housing, social services and so on grew rapidly and there were increasing numbers of professional groups with an interest in the upbringing of children, as well as a steadily rising quality of life for adults. The Plowden Report (CACE, 1967), with its advocacy of a child-centred curriculum, responsiveness to children's interests and flexible use of time through the 'integrated day', can be seen in this context. It reflected a faith in children's creativity and innate goodness which was to be drawn out by the skilful teacher through the provision of activity and direct experience. Partnerships with parents were seen as a considerable help in providing holistic support to the 'whole child'.

Modern English childhoods

In the last decades of the twentieth century new patterns emerged as women challenged the domestic roles into which they had been positioned and then entered the paid workforce in large numbers. Overall fertility continued to fall and the age at which women became mothers rose. The affluence of families with two wage-earners increased steadily, and new communication technologies and media brought easy access to the diversity of global cultures. There was sustained economic growth and new patterns of lifestyle consumption on clothes, cars, leisure, international travel, and so forth. Thus, for those in work it seemed possible that long hours, combined with new advances in science, communications and technology, would yield consistently rising living standards and thus underpin the diverse adult consumption patterns of the modern (and post-modern) world.

Importantly, however, Halsey and Young (1997) have questioned whether these 'gains for adults are at the expense of the interests of children'. In particular, they drew attention to the fallacy, assiduously promoted by Margaret Thatcher, that such individual freedom of choice is also a collective good. Such individualism has serious implications for children for, as Halsey and Young put it:

> Children thereby become commodities ... just like cars or videos or holidays, which adults can choose to have in preference to other consumables. And if they do, that is their choice and responsibility. Contraceptive control of our bodies enhances that illusion, so who needs a family or a community or, for that matter, a government other than to prevent ruin of the market for these good things by thieves and frauds? Surely Technology has conquered nature and we can safely allow individuals to choose a consuming style, limited only by their willingness to work for money. Everybody is then free to buy the good life of their own definition. Marriage becomes a mere contract.
>
> (p. 791)

Indeed, in the midst of this affluence and apparent progress, the traditional nuclear family began to show signs of considerable stress. The best-known indicator is the divorce rate which showed a significant increase. Thus by the 1990s, 40 per cent of new marriages were expected to break down and there was little associated stigma. Cohabitation prior to marriage had become commonplace, and one-third of children were born to couples who were not married. At the millennium, the proportion of children in one-parent families was almost 15 per cent – over one and a half million individuals. Thus the traditional nuclear family, though still idealized, was by no means the dominant manifestation of 'the family'.

Some children were rendered particularly vulnerable by these social changes in family forms. One-parent and workless families were especially likely to suffer from low incomes. Thus despite the general rise in incomes for those in work, income inequality rose throughout the 1980s and early 1990s. By 1996–7 over half of one-parent households received less than half of average income – the official definition of 'poverty'. In total, 4.3 million British children, one-third of the total, lived in households suffering from such poverty (Gregg *et al.*, 1999), and these households were increasingly concentrated in large cities and areas of public housing. In 1968 the comparable figure was 1.4 million. At the start of the new century, avoidance of child poverty is strongly associated with the capacity of an adult to sustain work, and this is more significant than the number of parents in a household. Ironically however, long hours worked by single parents reduces the available time to spend with their children.

Some major aspects of these structural changes over the past 200 years, and their implications for children, are highlighted here.

- The proportion of children in the population has dramatically decreased. There are now far fewer young people but many more of the retired and elderly. For instance, the number of households with children has decreased from around 90 per cent in 1900 to under a third today. Children thus have fewer direct advocates, and there is a much smaller proportion of the adult population with an immediate, daily interest in children's concerns.
- Women now spend a much smaller proportion of their lives in childbirth and childrearing, and are able to seek personal and economic fulfilment in new ways. Over 90 per cent of women now work outside the home during their working years. The ideology of the maternal homemaker has been challenged, and many women aspire to combine work, family and personal satisfaction. Children are a part of this, but not the only element.
- Family size and form have changed enormously. Large, stable, extended families gradually gave way to the smaller nuclear family, and this is now becoming fractured into a new diversity of household forms. Men have become less significant economically, and the underlying balance of power within families has thus altered.
- The economic contribution of children has significantly decreased. Children's agricultural work was valued and their labour was used (and exploited) in the industrial revolution, but compulsory education now prevents most children engaging in anything other than relatively marginal economic activity. Children are both more dependent on adults and, with the school leaving age at 16 and many young people remaining in colleges or universities until much later, they are more dependent for much longer. Children have therefore become a significant expense, rather than an economic asset.
- Legal, institutional and professional provision for the welfare of children has increased enormously, particularly in education, medicine and social welfare. However, this has also created large numbers of people and organizations who

have vested interests in defining 'childhood' and children's needs in ways that enable them to further their objectives. Teachers are one such group.

- Open, rural and communal environments in which children had considerable autonomy in their movements have been replaced by urban settings in which security and risk have become significant considerations for parents or carers. Modern play spaces now tend to be designated and controlled, whilst family life is becoming increasingly privatized. Simple toys and games have been superseded by a multiplicity of complex, mass-produced and gendered designs emphasizing excitement and innovation, whilst the continued development of multi-channel television, video and computer games furthers an individualistic, consumerist and privatizing trend.

- The conservative agricultural society of the eighteenth century with its entrenched religious values and social hierarchy has been replaced through the development of secular science and its capitalist application to industrial development. However, whilst its more divisive consequences have been ameliorated by the development of social democratic welfare provision, it can still produce extremes of inequality. Present society is more diverse, secular, mobile and individualistic than the past. It is more meritocratic, but can be just as cruel in terms of the distribution of wealth and life-chances.

- Old patterns of communal recreation, reflecting seasonal rhythms, cultural histories and relatively stable social structures, have been replaced by an incredible diversity of global, commercialized mass media. Thus, rather than inhabiting an ascribed social status and identity, it is now possible to experiment with lifestyles and entertain the notion of 'multiple selves'. Young people are particularly exposed and disposed to such experimentation as they strive to establish themselves in the adult world.

- The sphere of meaningful economic activity has moved from the locality to a global level. With the development of huge multinational companies, global production and marketing strategies mean that there is now a considerable degree of economic interdependence. However, on the labour supply side international competition is extremely fierce. In this context, the children of each country are seen as a vital national resource for the future – and the UK is a particular case in point.

So, if these are some of the major structural changes affecting family forms and children, how have they impacted on education policy?

14.3 STRUCTURAL CHANGE AND EDUCATION POLICY

In the specific case of the 1990s, which is the main focus of the PACE research, it is possible to identify three main sources of the education controls which have affected children and young people. We might term them: the indirect; the responsive; and the futuristic.

First, children were *indirectly* affected by the struggle between teachers and successive governments of the 1980s and 1990s. As we documented in the first PACE book (Pollard *et al.*, 1994), this essentially began as a battle between the government and the teaching profession, with parents being enlisted on the government's side through membership of governing bodies, promotion of a 'Parents' Charter', and encouragement to think of themselves as 'consumers'. Pupils were not consulted as consumers. Indeed, throughout the entire period very little regard was paid to their perspectives at all. In part this may have been a deliberate reaction against 'child-centred' ideas of the Plowden era – against which a discourse of derision was regularly mounted. More significantly however, pupil perspectives were simply not considered to be an issue of concern. This appears to have reflected the confident assumption amongst politicians that it was adults' responsibility to determine the curriculum and children's job to receive and respond to it. The real problem was to curtail the power of teachers, LEAs and educationists, and to restructure their work rather than worrying about pupils. Policy was thus essentially based on a delivery model of learning, with children cast in relatively passive positions.

However, the introduction of the National Curriculum and assessment procedures did have significant controlling effects on children and these have, of course, continued following the 1997 election of the Labour government. Blair's cry of 'education, education, education' brought a greater focus on literacy, numeracy, citizenship and ICT (Information and Communications Technology), but the emphasis on assessment and inspection remained and the new discipline of school target-setting intensified. We are not suggesting that 'constraining pupils' was an explicit aim of either Conservative or Labour education policy, but it seems apparent that it was a major consequence of their efforts to control teachers and force up standards of pupil attainment.

The second, more *responsive* motivation for public policy has been awareness of family and community breakdown, and the role of the state in providing practical support and even moral guidance. In particular, structural changes during the last decades of the twentieth century have seen the emergence of new patterns of family life, marriage and divorce, lifestyles, work participation, leisure, mass communication, and global economic competition. The world became a fast moving, highly complex and diverse place. Certainly, this environment enabled many people to flourish. However, there were problems too, for economic growth was bought by successive Conservative governments of the 1980s and 1990s at the price of increasing social differentiation. In particular, there was a considerable difference in the experience of those in paid employment and those out of it. The unemployed suffered multiple forms of social exclusion from our increasingly materialistic society, and this remains reflected in fields such as housing, leisure, transport, health, education, drug use and crime. These factors tend to overlay each other. For instance, in addition to being male, major risk factors for youth crime are low income, poor housing, living in an inner city, low school attainment, poor parental supervision with harsh but erratic discipline, parental conflict and divorce. Young offenders tend also to be involved in heavy drinking, drug use, dangerous driving, vandalism and promiscuous sex (Farrington, 1999).

Successive Conservative governments offered moral exhortation and stiffer sentencing, whilst emphasizing individual freedoms and market mechanisms, and denying the significance of social circumstances. More recently, the Labour government is directly addressing patterns of social exclusion. Policies such as the 'New Deal' and the introduction of 'Education Action Zones' are designed to tackle youth unemployment and regenerate run-down communities. Similarly, additional resources are being routed back to families through policies such as increased child benefit and pre-school provision. However, both the policies of condemnation and of amelioration have consequences that are firmly structuring of children's experiences. Campbell (1999) has expressed the role of schools:

> As modern society fractures morally, the state will need to reinforce the social and moral functions of schooling, primarily because it remains the only common site for moral socialisation, as respect for family, church, the law and other socialisation agencies weakens ... The role of primary teachers has become even more diffuse. In addition to teaching the curriculum, they are expected to be secretaries, social workers, community liaison officers, paramedics, priests, teacher trainers, expert spotters of drug abuse, advisers on safe sex and unsafe drugs.

> (p. 25)

Schooling is positioned on the front line of the fight against social fragmentation, not because it has sought this responsibility, but because it is one of very few public institutions that is nationally available to fulfil the necessary role. For many pupils schooling has been and is likely to continue to be seen as an institution of social control, whether at the level of 'healthy eating', challenging vandalism, checking up on homework, or policing a local 'curfew'.

The third, *futuristic*, way in which children are defined reflects adult preparations for the emergent economic, technological and social challenges of the twenty-first century. As Gordon Brown put it in his Budget speech of March 1999: 'children are 20 per cent of the British people, but 100 per cent of Britain's future'. New Labour has adopted immediate targets to increase the skill, knowledge and capability of school pupils to meet the needs of industry. With *Curriculum 2000* it has also reemphasized inclusivity and introduced a new emphasis on citizenship. On a longer, twenty-year, timescale, the government has also targeted the eradication of child poverty in the UK. However, their insistent emphasis is on the development of higher educational standards to provide a better supply of technologically skilled labour to enhance Britain's international competitiveness. Alan Prout, Director of ESRC's *Children 5 to 16* research programme, has argued this case as follows:

> Children are being constructed as a means of controlling the future. Precisely at a time when the intensification of global competition, the speed-up of economic processes and the intricate networking of national economies erodes possibilities for any state to control its own economic activity, so the shaping of the future labour force is seen as an increasingly important option. This is, after all, exactly what supply side economics is all about. Flexibility may be one of the aims, but that need for flexibility is being translated in the UK sphere of public education as a demand for a more standard and more reliable product.

> (Prout, 1999, p. 1)

As Prout indicates, there is a tension here in New Labour thinking between the basic skills agenda and the discourse of the flexible lifelong learner embracing new communication technologies. In the initial years of the National Curriculum, a similar tension existed between the rhetoric of 'the basics' and the desire to provide a broad and balanced curriculum in which ten subjects from the arts, sciences and humanities would echo the classic all-round education of the English gentleman. Whilst there is remarkable agreement about the importance of English and Mathematics, the emphasis of other curricular requirements clearly reflects political and value-led perspectives on the future. As James *et al.* (1998) put it:

> Curricula are more than the description of content. They are spatial theories of cognitive and bodily development and, as such, they contain world-views which are never accidental. They involve selections, choices, rules and conventions, all of which relate to questions of power, issues of personal identity and philosophies of human nature and potential ... In this sense, curricula are both social and political structures, containing assumptions about how people (that is, largely children) ought best to be.
>
> (p. 42)

And how ought children 'best be'? How does modern English society wish to bring up its children? Is it satisfactory to process them through an increasingly constrained education system focused on 'the basics', whilst also generating massive expectations that they should become 'flexible, creative learners'? The best hope for the success of this conflation of objectives at present may lie with teachers, for their creative mediation of government policy does go some way to weaken the damaging effects of over-structuring.

14.4 A CHALLENGE FOR THE FUTURE

The structural position of children in modern English society is one of profound weakness. Social conceptions of childhood and of what is deemed to be suitable provision for children are historically variable, but are strongly influenced by fundamental economic and social developments. In the recent decades of educational reform, direct considerations of children's learning needs, experiences or perspectives have been peripheral to government concerns. Rather, they have experienced the fallout of successive waves of the government's struggle with the teaching profession, whilst their home experiences are fundamentally shaped by the growing consequences of family and community fragmentation. Nevertheless, future hopes and aspirations are heaped upon the next generation, in waves of rhetoric, as we begin a new millennium. It is little wonder that the predominant response of pupils is to become increasingly strategic and pragmatic as they negotiate their lives in the adult world. Fortunately however, areas of autonomy remain – in play, friendship and imagination – where independent creativity still thrives.

From the adult point of view it might be time to pause and take stock. If we really believe that our future lies in the quality of the thinking, learning and capability of our children, then it is essential that we develop our education and family support systems to tap fundamental learning processes as physical, cognitive and affective development and socio-environmental experiences interact together. In particular, rather than ignoring, misunderstanding or undermining the spark of independent creativity in children, it is precisely what we need to foster for the future.

The real challenge is not whether we can improve on each and every measurement of performance in the basics, but how we can create policies and practices that enable a virtuous cycle to develop between standards, imagination, capability, flexibility and self-confidence. We must combine knowledge, skill, creativity and commitment to learning. Only then will we have an education system that is really providing what our citizens deserve and need for the twenty-first century.

Appendix 1

Systematic Observation: Definition of Categories

TEACHER OBSERVATION

1. Teacher activity

Coded at each ten-second interval. The code relates to what is happening at the 'beep', not to a summary of the previous ten seconds.

I Instruction: Teacher is involved with child/children directly on a curriculum activity (excluding hearing reading, encouraging and assessment, as defined below). This includes explaining a task and watching/listening to children doing a task. It does not include managing the task.

C Control: Control/discipline relating to children's behaviour, e.g. 'This room is getting noisy', 'Sit down Marilyn', 'Andrew!'. It does not include non-disciplinary directions, e.g. 'Stop what you are doing and listen to me'.

D Direction: Management of curriculum task activity, e.g. 'Blue group go to the library', 'Put your things away now', 'When you've finished you can colour it in'.

A Assessment: Explicit assessment, such as marking or correcting work, recording attainment or reviewing work with a pupil as an assessment activity.

E Encouragement: Positive praise, support or encouragement, e.g. 'That's really good', 'You have all worked really well today'. It does not include routine feedback, 'Yes, that's right' which is coded I.

N Negative: Negative feedback and comment on curriculum activity, e.g. 'That's no good at all', 'Why didn't you do it the way I told you?'. It does not include routine feedback, 'There are two hs in chrysanthemum'.

R Hearing children read: This refers to 'reading to teacher' as a one-to-one activity.

O Other: Including teacher talking to adult, teacher not involved with class and non-curriculum activities such as class administration. (*Note*: class administration is not included in planned observation but may occur unexpectedly.)

2. Teacher interaction

Coded every ten seconds. The code relates to what is happening at the beep. It is the teacher's interaction that is coded. Interaction includes verbal interaction (speaking and listening) and also other forms of interaction, such as touch, gesture and writing on the blackboard with the class watching.

O Alone means not interacting: Children may be physically present.

TC Teacher interaction with the whole class: It is coded whenever the teacher is working with all the children who are present in the room, even if some children from the class are missing. *But* if over half the children are out of the room, one of the group codes should be used. This code encompasses a range of settings, e.g. story time or discussions on class carpeted areas, as well as more direct instruction.

A Interaction with any other adult.

G With individual girl: One-to-one interaction with a single female pupil.

B With individual boy: One-to-one interaction with a single male pupil.

X With group of boys: Simultaneous interaction with more than one male pupil.

Y With group of girls: Simultaneous interaction with more than one female pupil.

M With a mixed group: Simultaneous interaction with a mixed group of pupils.

Note: A group is defined as two or more children but less than the whole class as defined above. For the teacher to be coded as interacting with a group, the children do not necessarily have to be working together.

3. Pedagogic context

This summarizes the teaching context *of the teacher* over the six minutes of observation. MAIN gives the overall summary of the teaching context and only one code should be used. PART is coded for any other teaching activity that took place and multiple codes may be used. Sometimes, if teaching is very varied or evenly balanced there may be no main context.

CLASS INTERACTION is defined as for TC above.

INDIVIDUAL WORK is when pupils are working individually on tasks. These may be the same tasks as other children.

COOPERATIVE GROUP WORK is when the teacher is working with a group of children who are also working cooperatively between themselves.

GROUP WORK WITH TEACHER is when the teacher is working with a group of children who are not otherwise working together (although they may be sitting together and doing similar tasks).

OTHER if none of the above contexts apply details are noted.

4. Curriculum context

This summarizes the curriculum content with which the teacher has been engaged in the preceding six minutes. MAIN gives the principal curriculum area, largely in terms of National Curriculum categories, and is normally coded once. PART refers to any other aspect of the curriculum that has been present. Sometimes, if the content is highly integrated with no subject category dominating, there may be no main code. Sometimes, if there has been a shift in the content the teacher is engaged with, there may be more than one main code. Clarification may be sought from the teacher if required.

CHILD OBSERVATION

1. Teacher activity

Coded as for teacher activity above.

2. Child interaction

Coded every ten seconds. The code refers to interactions of the target child at the beep. Interactions may be verbal (both speaking and listening) or by touch or gesture.
O Alone: The child is not interacting.
TC With teacher in whole class: The child is part of the teacher's class audience (teacher–whole-class interaction as defined above).
TO With teacher one-to-one: The child is the focus of the teacher's individual attention on a one-to-one basis (although other children may be listening).
TG With teacher in group: The child is part of a group with which the teacher is interacting (group as defined above).
AO With another adult one-to-one: Any interaction with an adult other than the teacher.
G With individual girl: One-to-one interaction with a female pupil.
B With individual boy: One-to-one interaction with a male pupil.
X With a group of boys: Simultaneous interaction with more than one male pupil.
Y With a group of girls: Simultaneous interaction with more than one female pupil.
M With a mixed group: Simultaneous interaction with a mixed group of pupils.
Note: If a child is notionally part of a class or group with the teacher but is actually interacting with one or more other children then the actual interaction should be coded.

3. Child activity

Coded every ten seconds. The code refers to the target child's activity at the beep.
TE Task engagement in curriculum task (excluding reading to teacher and being formally assessed): This includes listening to the teacher when the teacher could be coded as I.
TM Task management activity associated with a curriculum task, e.g. moving around the classroom, fetching or arranging books or materials, moving desks and

equipment, getting out or sharpening pencils, listening to the teacher when the content of the teacher's activity would be coded as D rather than I.

D Distracted: Includes behaviour that is not task-focused, messing around, talking to other children about something other than work, daydreaming, etc.

B Both distracted and task management.

A Assessment: Child being explicitly assessed by his or her own or another teacher. Assessment as defined for teacher activity.

W Waiting for teacher: Usually either as part of a queue or with hand up.

X Waiting (other): As above for another adult.

O Out of room/sight.

R Reading to teacher: Reading to the teacher as a one-to-one reading activity.

4. Pedagogic context

Summary of pedagogic situation of the target child for the six minutes of observation. MAIN is the overall summary of the child's teaching context and is coded once. PART refers to any other teaching context that occurred and may have multiple codes. Sometimes, if the teaching context is very varied or evenly balanced, there may be no main context. Categories are defined as in the teacher observation schedule. It is the context, not the actual activity, that is coded. If the child is part of a class lesson but has actually been interacting with other children, CLASS TEACHING is still coded. If the child is part of a cooperative group but has not contributed, COOP GROUP is still coded.

5. Curriculum context

This provides a summary of the curriculum content of the activities in which the target child was engaged. MAIN gives the principal curriculum context, mainly in terms of National Curriculum areas. PART refers to any other aspect of the curriculum that was present in the work being observed. Normally there will only be one code for MAIN and there may be several for PART. If the content is highly integrated, with no subject dominating, there may be no MAIN context. Occasionally, if the focus of a child's work has changed during the period of observation, there may be more than one MAIN code.

Appendix 2

A 'SAT Story': A Sample Comic Strip

(completed by Kim (at age 11) in relation to her Science SAT in which she scored Level 3)

☆ THE SAT STORY ☆

THIS IS ME

It was the 14ᵗʰ of May
It was the day of the Science A SAT

Appendix 3

Target Pupils Participating in PACE for Three or More Years

(by school, years of study and SAT results where known)

	Years in study	Name	English TA/SAT	Maths TA/SAT	Science TA/SAT
Greenmantle					
	6	Kate	5 5	5 5	5 5
	6	Sean	4 5	5 5	5 5
	5	Sharon	na	na	na
	5	Ben	5 5	5 4	5 5
	5	Juliet	5 4	3 4	4 4
	5	Tom	4 4	4 4	5 4
	4	Esther	4 4	3 4	4 4
Kenwood	6	Jessica	4 4	4 5	4 4
	6	Amanda	4 4	3 3	4 4
	5	Ewan	4 3	4 3	4 3
	4	Scott	3 3	3 3	3 3
	4	Dawn	4 4	4 4	4 4
	3	Jeremy	4 4	4 4	4 4
	3	Dean	3 3	3 3	4 5
St Bede's	6	Haley	3 3	3 3	3 3
	6	Sam	4 4	5 5	4 4
	6	Eliot	4 3	3 3	3 4
	6	Kim	4 5	5 5	4 4
	6	Samantha	4 3	3 3	3 3
	5	Harry	2 3	4 3	4 3
St Anne's	6	Philip	2 2	2 2	2 2
	6	Malcolm	2 3	2 3	2 3
	5	Susie	3 3	3 3	3 3

	5	Frances	A 4	3 3	A 3
	4	Jacquie	3 4	3 4	3 4
	4	Melanie	A 3	A 3	A 3
	3	Jenny	3 4	3 4	3 4
Audley	4	Brian	4 5	5 5	5 5
	4	Kevin	3 2	3 2	3 3
	4	Theresa	4 4	3 4	4 4
	4	Neil	4 4	4 5	4 4
	4	Mandy	5 5	4 5	4 5
	4	Maura	4 4	4 4	4 5
Orchard	5	Helen	3 4	4 4	4 4
	5	Laura	4 4	5 5	4 5
	5	Geoffrey	3 3	3 3	3 4
	4	Kelly	4 4	4 4	5 5
	4	Gavin	4 4	4 4	4 4
Lawnside	6	Martin	4 4	4 4	3 4
	6	Olivia	4 4	4 4	4 4
	6	Hugh	4 4	3 4	3 4
	5	Alice	5 5	5 5	4 4
	5	Rosie	4 4	3 4	3 4
	4	Lucy	4 4	4 4	4 4
Valley	6	Simon	4 4	3 4	3 4
	4	Jan	5 5	5 5	4 4
	4	Stella	4 4	4 4	4 4
	4	Richard	4 4	4 4	4 4
	3	Harriet	5 5	4 4	4 4
	3	Polly	na	na	na
	3	Trevor	na	na	na
Meadway	5	Corrine	4 4	4 4	3 3
	5	Wesley	na	na	na
	4	Kyle	2 3	2 3	3 3
	4	Ian	3 3	4 3	3 3
	3	Yasmin	N 2	N 2	2 2
	3	Shona	3 3	4 3	3 3
	3	Jane	5 5	5 5	4 4
	3	Celia	3 3	3 3	3 3

28 other children were studied as target pupils for one or two years.

References

Abbott, D. (1996) 'Teachers and Pupils: Expectations and Judgements', in P. Croll (ed.), *Teachers, Pupils and Primary Schooling: Continuity and Change.* London: Cassell.

Abbott, D., Broadfoot, P., Croll, P., Osborn, M. and Pollard, A. (1994) 'Some sink, some float: National Curriculum assessment and accountability', *British Educational Research Journal*, **20**(2), 155–76.

Acker, S. (1999) *The Realities of Teachers' Work: Never a Dull Moment.* London: Cassell.

Ahlberg, A. (1984) *Please, Mrs Butler.* Harmondsworth: Puffin Books.

Ahlberg, J. and Ahlberg, A. (1988) *Starting School.* London: Puffin Books.

Alderson, P. (1999) *Civil Rights in Schools Project Report.* London: London Institute of Education.

Alexander, R. (1984) *Primary Teaching.* London: Cassell.

Alexander, R. (1992) *Policy and Practice in Primary Education* (First edn). London: Routledge.

Alexander, R. (1995) *Versions of Primary Education.* London: Routledge.

Alexander, R. (1997) *Policy and Practice in Primary Education: Local Initiative, National Agenda* (Second edn). London: Routledge.

Alexander, R., Rose, J. and Woodhead, C. (1992) *Curriculum Organisation and Classroom Practice in Primary Schools: A Discussion Paper.* London: Department of Education and Science.

Alexander, R., Willcocks, J. and Nelson, N. (1996) 'Discourse, pedagogy and the National Curriculum: change and continuity in primary schools', *Research Papers in Education*, **11**(1), 81–120.

Apple, M. W. (1993) *Official Knowledge: Democratic Education in a Conservative Age.* London: Routledge.

Armstrong, M. (1980) *Closely Observed Children: The Diary of a Primary Classroom.* London: Writers and Readers.

Ball, S. J. (1990) *Politics and Policy Making in Education: Explorations in Policy Sociology*. London: Routledge.

Ball, S. J. (1994) *Education Reform: A Critical and Post-Structural Approach*. Buckingham: Open University Press.

Banks, M., Bates, I., Breakwell, G., Bynner, J., Emler, N., Jamieson, L. and Roberts, K. (1992) *Careers and Identities*. Buckingham: Open University Press.

Barber, M. (1997) *A Reading Revolution: How We Can Teach Every Child to Read Well*. London: The Labour Party's Literacy Task Group.

Bassey, M. (1978) *Nine Hundred Primary School Teachers*. Slough: NFER.

Bayliss, V. (1999) *Opening Minds: Education for the 21st Century*. London: RSA.

Bennett, N. (1976) *Teaching Styles and Pupil Progress*. London: Open Books.

Bennett, N., Andreae, J., Hegarty, P. and Wade, B. (1980) *Open Plan Schools: Teaching, Curriculum, Design*. Windsor: NFER.

Bennett, N., Wood, L. and Rogers, S. (1997) *Teaching Through Play: Teachers' Thinking and Classroom Practice*. Buckingham: Open University Press.

Bentley, T. (1998) *Learning Beyond the Classroom*. London: Routledge.

Bernstein, B. (1971) 'On the classification and framing of educational knowledge', in M. F. D. Young (ed.), *Knowledge and Control: New Directions for the Sociology of Education*. London: Collier-Macmillan.

Bernstein, B. (1975) *Class, Codes and Control: Towards a Theory of Educational Transmission* (Vol. 3). London: Routledge and Kegan Paul.

Bernstein, B. (1990) *The Structure of Pedagogic Discourse*. London: Routledge and Kegan Paul.

Bernstein, B. (1996) *Pedagogy, Symbolic Control and Identity: Theory, Research, Critique*. London: Taylor and Francis.

Blyth, W. A. L. (1965) *English Primary Education: Volume 1, Schools*. London: Routledge and Kegan Paul.

Blyth, W. A. L. (1984) *Development, Experience and Curriculum in Primary Education*. London: Croom Helm.

Blyth, W. A. L. (1998) 'English primary education: looking backward to look forward', in C. Richards and P. H. Taylor (eds), *How Shall We School Our Children? Primary Education and Its Future*. London: Falmer Press.

Bowlby, J. (1951) *Maternal Care and Mental Health*. London: HMSO.

Broadfoot, P., Gilly, M., Osborn, M. and Paillet, A. (1993) *Perceptions of Teaching: Primary School Teachers in England and France*. London: Cassell.

Broadfoot, P., Osborn, M., Planel, C. and Pollard, A. (1996) 'Teachers and Change: a study of primary school teachers' reactions to policy changes in England and France', in T. Winther-Jensen (ed.), *Challenges to European Education: cultural values, national identities and global responsibilities*. Berne: Peter Lang.

Broadfoot, P., Osborn, M., Planel, C. and Sharpe, K. (2000) *Promoting Quality in Learning: Does England Have the Answer?* London: Cassell.

Broadfoot, P. and Pollard, A. (1996) 'Continuity and Change in English Primary Education', in P. Croll (ed.), *Teachers, Pupils and Primary Schooling*. London: Cassell.

Broadfoot, P. and Pollard, A. (2000) 'The changing discourse of assessment policy: the case of English primary education', in A. Filer (ed.), *Assessment: Social*

Practice and Social Product. London: Falmer Press.

Broadfoot, P. M. (1996) *Education, Assessment and Society*. Buckingham: Open University Press.

CACE (1967) *Children and their Primary Schools* (Plowden Report). London: HMSO.

Callaghan, J. (1976) 'Towards a national debate', *Education*, **148**(17), 332–3.

Campbell, J. (1994) 'Curriculum manageability: the issue of time allocation', *Education 3–13*, **22**(1), 2–10.

Campbell, J. (1998) 'Primary teaching: roles and relationships', in R. Richards and P. H. Taylor (eds), *How Shall We School Our Children? Primary Education and Its Future*. London: Falmer Press.

Campbell, J. (1999) 'Recruitment, retention and reward: issues in the modernisation of primary teaching', *Education 3 to 13*, **27**(3), 24–31.

Campbell, J. and Emery, H. (1994) 'Curriculum policy for Key Stage 2: possibilities, contradictions and constraints', in A. Pollard (ed.), *Look Before You Leap? Research Evidence for the Curriculum at Key Stage 2*. London: Tufnell.

Campbell, J., Emery, H. and Stone, C. (1993) 'The Broad and Balanced Curriculum at Key Stage 2: some limitations on reform'. Paper presented at the BERA Annual Conference, University of Liverpool.

Campbell, J. and Neill, S. R. St. J. (1992) *Teacher Time and Curriculum Manageability at Key Stage 1*. London: AMMA.

Campbell, J. and Neill, S. R. St. J. (1994a) *Curriculum Reform at Key Stage 1: Teacher Commitment and Policy Failure*. Harlow: Longman.

Campbell, R. J. and Neill, S. R. St. J. (1994b) *Primary Teachers at Work*. London: Routledge.

Claxton, G. (1999) *Wise Up: The Challenge of Lifelong Learning*. London: Bloomsbury.

Claxton, G. (forthcoming) *Get Smarter: How to Have More Good Ideas*.

Coffield, F. (1999) 'Breaking the consensus: lifelong learning as social control', *British Educational Research Journal*, **25**(4), 479–500.

Connell, R. W., Ashden, D. J., Kessler, S. and Dowsett, G. W. (1982) *Making the Difference: Schools, Families and Social Division*. Sidney: Allen and Unwin.

Corsaro, W. (1997) *The Sociology of Childhood*. Thousand Oaks, California: Pine Forge Press.

Cox, C. B. and Boyson, R. (eds) (1975) *Black Paper 1975*. London: Dent.

Cox, C. B. and Boyson, R. (eds) (1977) *Black Paper 1977*. London: Temple Smith.

Cox, C. B. and Dyson, A. E. (eds) (1969) *Fight for Education, A Black Paper*. London: Critical Quarterly Society.

Craft, A. (ed.) (1996) *Primary Education: Assessing and Planning Learning*. London: Routledge.

Croll, P. (1986) *Systematic Classroom Observation*. London: Falmer Press.

Croll, P. (1996) *Teachers, Pupils and Primary Schooling: Continuity and Change*. London: Cassell.

Croll, P. and Hastings, N. (eds) (1996) *Effective Primary Teaching: Research-based Classroom Strategies*. London: David Fulton.

Croll, P. and Moses, D. (1985) *One in Five: The Assessment and Incidence of Special*

Educational Needs. London: Routledge and Kegan Paul.

Cullingford, C. (1991) *The Inner World of the School.* London: Cassell.

Dale, D. (1981) 'Control, accountability and William Tyndale', in R. Dale, G. Esland, R. Fergusson and M. MacDonald (eds), *Education and the State, Vol. 2.* Lewes: Falmer Press.

Dearing, R. (1993) *The National Curriculum and Its Assessment: Final Report.* London: School Curriculum and Assessment Authority.

Degenhart, R. E. (1990) *Thirty Years of International Research: An Annotated Bibliography of IEA Publications (1960–1990).* The Hague: IEA.

DES (1985) *Better Schools, A Summary.* London: HMSO.

DES (1987) *Primary Staffing Survey.* London: HMSO.

DfEE (1997) *Excellence in Schools.* London: HMSO.

Dweck, C. S. (1986) 'Motivational processes affecting learning', *American Psychologist* (October), 1040–6.

Dweck, C. S. (1999) *Self-Theories: Their Role in Motivation, Personality and Development.* Philadelphia: Psychology Press.

Egan, K. (1988) *Primary Understanding.* London: Routledge.

Elliott, J. (1998) *The Curriculum Experiment: Meeting the Challenge of Social Change.* Buckingham: Open University Press.

Farrington, D. (1999) *Understanding and Preventing Youth Crime.* York: York Publishing Services.

Filer, A. and Pollard, A. (2000) *The Social World of Pupil Assessment.* London: Continuum.

Firestone, S. (1979) 'Down with childhood', in M. Hoyles (ed.), *Changing Childhood.* London: Readers and Writers.

Franklin, B. (ed.) (1995) *The Handbook of Children's Rights.* London: Routledge.

Galton, M. (1995) *Crisis in the Primary Classroom.* London: David Fulton.

Galton, M., Hargreaves, L. and Comber, C. (1998) 'Classroom practice and the National Curriculum in small primary schools', *British Educational Research Journal,* **24**(1), 43–61.

Galton, M., Hargreaves, L., Comber, C., Wall, D. and Pell, A. (1999) *Inside the Primary Classroom: 20 years on.* London: Routledge.

Galton, M. and Patrick, H. (eds) (1990) *Curriculum Provision in the Small Primary School.* London: Routledge.

Galton, M., Simon, B. and Croll, P. (1980) *Inside the Primary Classroom.* London: Routledge and Kegan Paul.

Gardner, H. (1985) *Frames of Mind: The Theory of Multiple Intelligences.* London: Paladin Books.

Gillborn, D. and Youdell, D. (1999) *Rationing Education: Policy Reform and School Inequality.* Buckingham: Open University Press.

Gipps, C. V. (1994) 'What we know about effective teaching', in J. Bourne (ed.), *Thinking Through Primary Practice.* London: Routledge.

Gipps, C. V. and Tunstall, P. (1997) 'Effort, ability and the teacher: young children's explanations for success and failure.' York: BERA Conference Paper.

Gipps, C. V., Brown, M., McCallum, B. and McManus, S. (1995) *Intuition or Evidence? Teachers and National Assessment of Seven-Year-Olds.* Buckingham:

Open University Press.

Goleman, D. (1996) *Emotional Intelligence: Why it Can Matter More than IQ.* London: Bloomsbury.

Goleman, D. (1998) *Working with Emotional Intelligence.* London: Bloomsbury.

Goodnow, J. and Burns, A. (1985) *Home and School: A Child's Eye View.* Sydney: Allen and Unwin.

Goodson, I. F. (1987) *School Subject and Curriculum Change.* Lewes: Falmer Press.

Goodson, I. F. (1994) *Studying Curriculum.* Buckingham: Open University Press.

Greenfield, S. (1997) *The Human Brain: A Guided Tour.* London: Weidenfeld and Nicolson.

Gregg, P., Harkness, S. and Machlin, S. (1999) *Child Development and Family Income.* York: York Publishing Services.

Halsey, A. H. and Young, M. (1997) 'The family and social justice', in A. H. Halsey, H. Lauder, P. Brown and A. S. Wells (eds), *Education, Culture, Economy and Society.* Oxford: Oxford University Press.

Hargreaves, A. (1991) 'Contrived Collegiality: the micro-politics of teacher collaboration', in N. Bennett, M. Crawford and C. Riches (eds), *Managing Change in Education.* London: Chapman/Open University.

Hargreaves, A. (1999) 'The psychic rewards (and annoyances) of teaching', in M. Hammersley (ed.), *Researching School Experience: Ethnographic Studies of Teaching and Learning.* London: Falmer.

Hargreaves, D. H. (1978) 'Whatever happened to symbolic interactionism?', in L. Barton (ed.), *Meighan, R.* Driffield: Nafferton.

Hargreaves, D. H. (1994) 'The new professionalism: the synthesis of professional and institutional development', *Teaching and Teacher Education,* **10**(4), 423–38.

Hastings, N. (1998) 'Change and progress in primary teaching', in C. Richards and R. H. Taylor (eds), *How Shall We School Our Children? Primary Education and Its Future.* London: Falmer Press.

Hatcher, R. (1994) 'Market relationships and the management of teachers', *British Journal of the Sociology of Education,* **15**(1), 41–62.

Heider, F. (1958) *The Psychology of Interpersonal Relations.* New York: Wiley.

HMCI (1998) *The Annual Report of Her Majesty's Chief Inspector of Schools in England. Standards and Quality in Education 1996–97.* London: The Stationery Office.

HMI (1978) *Primary Education in England: A Survey by HMI.* London: HMSO.

Howe, M. J. A. (1990) *The Origins of Exceptional Abilities.* London: Basil Blackwell.

Hughes, M., Wikeley, F. and Nash, T. (1994) *Parents and Their Children's Schools.* Oxford: Basil Blackwell.

Isaacs, S. (1930) *Intellectual Growth in Young Children.* London: Routledge and Kegan Paul.

Isaacs, S. (1932) *The Children We Teach.* London: University of London Press.

Jackson, P. W. (1968) *Life in Classrooms.* New York: Holt, Rinehart and Winston.

James, A., Jenks, C. and Prout, A. (1998) *Theorising Childhood.* Cambridge: Polity Press.

Jeffrey, B. (1999) 'Side-stepping the substantial self: the fragmentation of the primary teachers' professionality through audit accountability', in M. Hammersley (ed.), *Researching School Experience: Ethnographic Studies of Teaching and Learning*. London: Falmer Press.

Jeffrey, B. and Woods, P. (1998) *Testing Teachers: The Effects of School Inspections on Primary Teachers*. London: Falmer.

Kalechstein, A. D. and Nowicki, S. (1987) 'A meta-analytic examination of the relationships between control expectancies and academic achievement', *Genetic, Social and General Psychology Monographs*, **123**, 27–57.

Keeves, J. P. (1995) *The World of School Learning: Selected Key Findings from 35 Years of IEA Research*. The Hague: IEA.

Kell, J. (1999) *The Learning Agenda: A Research Report*. London: The Industrial Society.

Kelly, A. V. (1994) *The National Curriculum: A Critical Review* (Second edn). London: Paul Chapman.

Keys, W., Harris, S. and Fernandes, C. (1996) *Third International Mathematics and Science Study (TIMSS)*. Slough: NFER.

Labour Party (1997) *Because Britain Deserves Better*. London: The Labour Party.

Leach, J. and Moon, B. (eds) (1999) *Learners and Pedagogy*. London: Paul Chapman.

Meadows, S. (1993) *The Child as Thinker: The Development and Acquisition of Cognition in Childhood*. London: Routledge.

Menter, I., Muschamp, Y., Nicolls, P., Ozga, J. and Pollard, A. (1996) *Work and Identity in the Primary School: a post-Fordist analysis*. Buckingham: Open University Press.

Mercer, N. (1995) *The Guided Construction of Knowledge: Talk Amongst Teachers and Learners*. Clevedon: Multilingual Matters.

Meyer, J. W., Kamens, D. H. and Benavot, A. (1992) *School Knowledge for the Masses: World Models of National Primary Curricular Categories in the Twentieth Century*. London: Falmer.

Mortimore, P., Sammons, P., Stoll, L., Lewis, D. and Ecob, R. (1988) *School Matters: The Junior Years*. Wells: Open Books.

Mugny, G. and Carugati, F. F. (1989) *Social Representation of Intelligence*. Cambridge: Cambridge University Press.

National Union of Teachers (1991) *Report of the Survey on Key Stage 1 SATs*. London: National Union of Teachers.

Nias, J. (1989) *Primary Teachers Talking: A Study of Teaching as Work*. London: Routledge.

Nias, J. (1991) 'Changing times, changing identities: grieving for a lost self', in R. B. Burgess (ed.), *Educational Research and Evaluation*. London: Falmer Press.

Nias, J., Southworth, G. and Campbell, P. (1992) *Whole-school Curriculum Development in the Primary School*. London: Falmer Press.

Nias, J., Southworth, G. and Yeomans, R. (1989) *Staff Relationships in the Primary School: A Study of Organisational Cultures*. London: Cassell.

Nixon, J., Martin, J., McKeown, P. and Ranson, S. (1997) 'Towards a Learning Profession; changing codes of occupational practice within the new management of education', *British Journal of Sociology of Education*, **18**(1), 5–28.

OFSTED (1999) *Primary Education 1994–98: A Review of Primary Schools in*

England. London: The Stationery Office.

Osborn, M. (1996a) 'Identity, Career and Change: a tale of two teachers', in P. Croll (ed.), *Teachers, Pupils and Primary Schooling*. London: Cassell.

Osborn, M. (1996b) 'Teachers Mediating Change: Key Stage 1 revisited', in P. Croll (ed.), *Teachers, Pupils and Primary Schooling*. London: Cassell.

Osborn, M., Croll, P., Broadfoot, P., Pollard, A., McNess, E. and Triggs, P. (1997) 'Policy into Practice and Practice into Policy: creative mediation in the primary classroom', in G. Helsby and G. McCulloch (eds) *Teachers and the National Curriculum*. London: Cassell.

Osborn, M., McNess, E. and Broadfoot, P., with Pollard, A. and Triggs, P. (2000) *What Teachers Do: Changing Policy and Practice in Primary Education*. London: Cassell.

Paley, V. G. (1981) *Wally's Stories*. Cambridge, Massachusetts: Harvard University Press.

Paley, V. G. (1990) *The Boy Who Would Be a Helicopter*. Cambridge, Massachusetts: Harvard University Press.

Pollard, A. (1985) *The Social World of the Primary School*. London: Cassell.

Pollard, A. (1990) 'Towards a sociology of learning in primary schools', *British Journal of Sociology of Education*, **11**(3), 241–56.

Pollard, A. (1999) 'Towards a new perspective on children's learning?', *Education 3–13*, **27**(3), 56–60.

Pollard, A., Broadfoot, P., Croll, P., Osborn, M. and Abbott, D. (1994) *Changing English Primary Schools? The Impact of the Education Reform Act at Key Stage One*. London: Cassell.

Pollard, A., Broadfoot, P., Osborn, M., McNess, E., Triggs, P. and Noble, J. (1997a) 'Primary Assessment, Curriculum and Experience: A Review'. Paper presented at the British Educational Research Association Conference, York.

Pollard, A. with Filer, A. (1996) *The Social World of Children's Learning: Case Studies of Pupils from Four to Seven*. London: Cassell.

Pollard, A. and Filer, A. (1999) *The Social World of Pupil Career: Strategic Biographies Through Primary School*. London: Cassell.

Pollard, A., Thiessen, D. and Filer, A. (eds) (1997b) *Children and Their Curriculum: The Perspectives of Primary and Elementary School Children*. London: Falmer Press.

Proctor, N. (1990) *The Aims of Primary Education and the National Curriculum*. London: Falmer Press.

Prout, A. (1999) 'Children's Participation: Control and self-realisation in late modern childhood'. Paper presented at the Sites of Learning Conference, Hull.

QCA (1999) *Curriculum 2000*. London: Qualifications and Curriculum Authority.

Quicke, J. (1999) *A Curriculum for Life: Schools for a Democratic Learning Society*. Buckingham: Open University Press.

Qvortrup, J. (1993) *Childhood as a Social Phenomenon: Lessons from an International Project* (47). Vienna: European Centre.

Qvortrup, J. (1997) 'Childhood and Societal Macrostructures'. Paper presented at the Conceptualising Childhood: Perspectives on Research Conference, University of Keele.

Reay, D. and Wiliam, D. (1999) ' "I'll be a nothing": structure, agency and the construction of identity through assessment', *British Educational Research Journal*, **25**(3), 343–54.

Reynolds, D. and Farrell, S. (1996) *Worlds Apart? A review of International Surveys of Educational Achievement Involving England.* London: OFSTED.

Richards, C. (1998) 'Curriculum and pedagogy in Key Stage 2: a survey of policy and practice in small rural primary schools', *The Curriculum Journal*, **9**(3), 319–32.

Richards, C. (1999) *Primary Education: At a Hinge of History?* London: Falmer Press.

Richards, C. and Taylor, P. H. (eds) (1998) *How Shall We School Our Children? Primary Education and Its Future.* London: Falmer Press.

Rosenthal, R. and Jacobsen, L. (1968) *Pygmalion in the Classroom.* New York: Holt, Rinehart and Winston.

Rotter, J. B. (1954) *Social Learning and Clinical Psychology.* New York: Knopf.

Rowland, S. (1984) *The Enquiring Classroom.* London: Falmer.

SCAA (1995) *Planning the Curriculum at Key Stages 1 and 2.* London: School Curriculum and Assessment Authority.

Silcock, P. (1999) *New Progressivism.* London: Falmer Press.

Snyder, B. R. (1971) *The Hidden Curriculum.* New York: Knopf.

Swann, J. and Brown, S. (1997) 'The implementation of a national curriculum and teachers' classroom thinking', *Research Papers in Education*, **12**(1), 91–114.

TGAT (1988) *National Curriculum, Report.* London: DES.

Tizard, B., Blatchford, P., Burke, J., Farquhar, C. and Plewis, I. (1988) *Young Children at School in the Inner City.* London: Lawrence Erlbaum.

Torrance, H. and Pryor, J. (1998) *Investigating Formative Assessment: Teaching, Learning and Assessment in the Classroom.* Buckingham: Open University Press.

Troman, G. (1996) 'The Rise of the New Professionals? The restructuring of primary teachers' work and professionalism', *British Journal of Sociology of Education*, **17**(4), 473–87.

Wallace, M. (1991) 'Coping with multiple innovations in schools', *School Organisation, Vol. 11 (2), 187–209.*

Waller, W. (1932) The *Sociology of Teaching.* New York: Russell and Russell.

Webb, R. and Vulliamy, G. (1996a) 'A Deluge of Directives: conflict between collegiality and managerialism in the post-ERA primary school', *British Educational Research Journal*, **22**(4), 441–5.

Webb, R. and Vulliamy, G. (1996b) *Roles and Responsibilities in the Primary School: Changing Demands, Changing Practices.* Buckingham: Open University Press.

Weiner, B. (1986) *An Attributional Theory of Motivation and Emotion.* New York: Springer-Verlag.

West, A., Hailes, J. and Sammons, P. (1997) 'Children's attitudes to the National Curriculum at Key Stage 1', *British Educational Research Journal*, **23**(5), 597–614.

Wood, D. (1988) *How Children Think and Learn.* Oxford: Blackwell.

Woods, P. (1995) *Creative Teachers in Primary Schools.* Buckingham: Open University Press.

Woods, P. and Jeffrey, B. (1996) *Teachable Moments: the Art of Teaching in Primary Schools.* Buckingham: Open University Press.

Woods, P., Jeffrey, B., Troman, G. and Boyle, M. (1997) *Restructuring Schools, Reconstructing Teachers: responding to change in the primary school*. Buckingham: Open University Press.

Young, M. (1971) *Knowledge and Control*. London: Collier-Macmillan.

Young, M. (1998) *The Curriculum of the Future*. London: Falmer Press.

Name Index

Abbott, D. 61, 288
Acker, S. 49, 56, 279
Ahlberg, Allan 34–5
Alderson, P. 13
Alexander, R. 51–2, 55, 60, 79, 281
Apple, M.W. 278
Armstrong, M. 53, 290

Ball, S.J. 278, 281
Banks, M. 304
Barber, M. 297
Bayliss, V. 297
Bennett, N. 6, 280
Bentley, T. 278
Bernstein, Basil 10–13, 16, 18, 53, 60, 63–4,132, 153, 277–8, 281
Blair, Tony 313
Blyth, A. 304
Blyth, W.A.L. 13, 15, 51
Bowlby, J. 309
Boyson, R. 6
Broadfoot, P. 6, 10, 20, 44, 47, 63, 293, 296, 302
Brown, Gordon 314
Brown, S. 281
Burns, A. 51

Callaghan, James 6, 289
Campbell, J. 49, 51–2, 279, 282–3, 314
Carugati, F.F. 296
Claxton, G. 14, 296–7, 300, 302
Coffield, F. 297
Connell, R.W. 304
Cox, C.B. 6
Craft, A. 280
Croll, P. 7, 11–12, 48–9, 86, 96, 133, 305
Cullingford, C. 284

Dahl, Roald 69
Dale, D. 6
Dearing, Sir Ron see Dearing Review in Subject Index
Degenhart, R.E. 6
Dweck, C.S. 295–6, 300
Dyson, A.E. 6

Egan, K. 53
Elliott, J. 278
Emery, H. 52

Farrington, D. 313
Filer, A. 14, 20, 44, 238, 293, 298, 303
Firestone, S. 309
Franklin, B. 13

Galton, M. 20, 49, 52, 55–7, 59–60, 64, 282, 305
Gardner, H. 296
Gillborn, D. 304
Gipps, C.V. 61–2, 280, 295, 305
Goleman, D. 296, 302–3
Goodnow, J. 51
Goodson, I.F. 278
Greenfield, S. 297
Gregg, P. 311

Halsey, A.H. 310
Hargreaves, A. 279
Hargreaves, D.H. 280, 297
Hastings, N. 305
Hatcher, R. 280
Heider, F. 294
Howe, M.J.A. 296
Hughes, M. 303

Isaacs, S. 290

Jackson, P.   61, 289–90
Jacobsen, L.   61
James, A.   315
Jeffrey, B.   279–80
Joseph, Sir Keith   6, 289

Kalechstein, A.D.   294
Keeves, J.P.   6
Kell, J.   297
Kelly, A.V.   53
Keys, W.   6

Leach, J.   281

Major, John   278
Meadows, S.   300
Menter, I.   280
Mercer, N.   302
Moon, B.   281
Mortimore, P.   20
Mugny, G.   296

Neill, S.R.St.J.   49
Nias, J.   49, 56, 279
Nixon, J.   280
Nowicki, S.   294

Osborn, M.   4, 13, 16, 20, 28, 42, 47–8, 53–4, 56, 63,106, 153, 278, 281, 298, 302–3

Paley, V.G.   290
Pollard, A.   7, 10, 13–14, 20, 44, 47, 58–9, 61–2, 64, 76, 86, 96, 133, 238, 277, 283–4, 287, 289, 293, 298, 301, 303, 305, 312–13
Proctor, N.   279
Prout, A.   307, 314

Pryor, J.   280

Quicke, J.   14, 278
Qvortrup, J.   306

Reay, D.   303
Reynolds, D.   6
Richards, C.   278–9, 305
Rosenthal, R.   61
Rotter, J.B.   294, 300
Rowland, S.   53

Silcock, P.   305
Snyder, B.R.   61
Swann, J.   281

Taylor, P.H.   278
Thatcher, Margaret   6, 278, 310
Torrance, H.   280
Troman, G.   279

Vulliamy, G.   279

Wallace, M.   42
Waller, Willard   289–90
Webb, R.   49, 279
Weiner, B.   294
West, A.   283
Wiliam, D.   303
Wood, P.   302
Woodhead, Chris   296–7
Woods, P.   49, 56, 279–80

Youdell, D.   304
Young, M.   278, 310

Subject Index

ability   148–51, 285
ability groups   155, 171–5, 178–9, 195, 296, 303
accountability   13, 49, 51, 62–3, 279, 282, 297
   to government   217–18
activity of pupils   32, 57–8, 90, 96–7, 101, 103, 197
affective factors   132, 279, 281, 294–5
aggression   268–72
anxiety of pupils   101, 103, 133–5, 181–2, 285
   about assessment   139, 153, 220–30, 237, 258
   about displeasing the teacher   178
   about grouping   177, 286
   about lack of success   213
   about lack of time   198
   about loss of concentration   210, 212
anxiety of teachers   258
Art   77–8, 84, 86–7, 94–5, 97, 100, 101, 103, 188, 199–200, 283
asking for help   183–4, 263–4
assessment   6–7, 10–11, 61–4
   criteria for   135, 139, 152, 258, 285
   formative as distinct from summative   133, 238;
      see also formative assessment; summative assessment
   intuitive or evidence-based   61–3, 153
   mode, purpose and frequency   61
   negative feelings about   134–8
   positive feelings about   138
   protection of pupils from effects of   132, 139, 214, 229, 281
   pupils views of   132–54, 157, 285
   relative use of different procedures   62
   routine forms of   133, 238, 285
   studies of   38–42
   teachers views of   62, 153

   see also categoric assessment; self-assessment;
      Standard Assessment Tasks
attainment
   pupils own explanations of   141–52, 246–7, 262, 265, 271
   in relation to pupils attitudes   98–103
   see also ability
attribution theory   294–5
Audley Junior School   26–7, 73, 77, 80, 82, 172, 175, 196, 221
   SATs at   234–7
authority of teachers   104, 122–3
   pupils acceptance of   284–5
autonomy
   of pupils   54, 60, 64–5, 81, 91, 94, 100–1, 103, 105, 114, 129–30, 164–5, 196–8, 270, 281, 284, 286, 315
   of teachers   5, 11, 48, 279, 281
avoidance of disliked or difficult activities   116–17, 130

basic skills   51–2, 63, 67, 83, 314–15;   see also literacy; numeracy
Blunkett, David   9
boredom   92–4, 116–17, 127, 145, 203–5, 208, 211–12, 264, 287
Bristaix project   20, 44

case studies of individual pupils   240–73, 288
categoric assessment   140, 145, 218–19, 221, 226, 237–8, 272, 281, 288
celebration of individual pieces of work   188
changes in education, multiplicity of   42
changes of teacher   127
child-centred education   7, 13, 61, 197, 310, 313
child labour   307–9, 311

childcare   309
childhood   13–15
  changing conceptions of   306–12, 315
choices
  made by teachers   118, 121, 261
  offered to pupils   91, 93, 111–17, 130, 266,
    283;   *see also* free choice
CICADA project   60
citizenship   313–14
classroom studies   29–38
'climate' of the classroom or school   125, 130, 168,
    178, 224, 288, 298
closed questions   60, 64, 282
collaboration between pupils   173, 191–7
collegiality   279–80
comic strips   see SAT stories
commodification of education   48, 279–81
communication skills   72; *see also* talking; writing
competence , concept of   277
competition
  between pupils   177, 179, 221, 266
  between schools   6
compliant attitudes in pupils   98, 165
computers, use of   82–3
concentration   152–3, 202; *see also* distraction
confidence-building   183
conformity and non-conformity in the
    classroom   122, 128–9, 169, 228
Conservative Party   313
constructivism   281, 302
continuity in research   43
control
  by pupils   115–17, 130, 165, 171, 198, 235
  pupils acceptance of   121–5
  by teachers   109–13, 130, 164, 208, 283–4
  of teachers (by government)   290, 313
core curriculum   7, 50–51, 63, 97, 101, 103, 137,
    198, 283, 300
  pupils views of   67–76, 83–4
correctness, preoccupation with   135, 153, 182,
    285–6
creative activities   197
cultural capital   253
culture conducive to learning   238
curriculum   48–53, 63–4
  pupils views of   66–84, 85–7, 96–7, 103, 283–4
  significance of   319
  see also core curriculum
curriculum overload   212, 302
Curriculum 2000   314

data-gathering schedule   21–2, 29–30
daydreaming   204–5, 208–9, 264
Dearing Review   7–8, 53, 212, 282
defensive responses of pupils   205, 213
delivery of performance   47, 64, 66, 279, 313; *see
    also* performance model
dependence of pupils
  on peers   195

  on teachers   119, 130, 165, 195, 208, 248, 260,
    270, 286
  see also learned helplessness
Design Technology   80–1
difficult subjects   92, 94–7, 103, 283
difficulties, overcoming of   188–90
discipline   59, 174; *see also* control by teachers
discussions in class   72
disliked subjects   92–5, 97–8, 100–103, 283
dispositions towards learning   98, 152–4, 241,
    249–51, 273, 288, 292–305
distraction of pupils   58–9, 153, 195, 202–3, 208–
    12, 270, 287
divorce   309–10, 313
doing your best , ethic of   233–4, 238, 288

Economic and Social Research Council   21–2
Education Acts (1870, 1944 and 1992)   5, 8, 13
Education Reform Act (1988)   3–12 *passim*, 18,
    44, 48–9, 281, 283, 289, 302
effort   132, 135, 147, 151, 153, 167, 188, 203, 211,
    233, 246–7, 285–6
eleven-plus testing   6–7
emotional intelligence and stability   303
empathy   110
employment
  and learning   159
  and testing   230
  see also child labour
encouragement for pupils
  from parents and family members   142–3, 206
  from teachers   59, 188, 233, 287
engagement with the learning process   199, 207,
    287, 290, 301, 305
English   67–8, 83, 94–5, 98, 100, 172, 300;   *see
    also* Reading; Writing
enjoyment of learning   143–4, 147, 152, 196, 203–
    6, 243, 287; *see also* fun
ethos   126, 267, 268, 288
expectations of teachers   164–71, 178, 286
extension tests   220–21, 228, 233–6, 252, 300

failing schools   9
failure in tests, pupils own explanations of   145–8,
    265
family background   see home influences; parental
    involvement
family breakdown   309–10, 313
family groups in school   173
family size and form, changes in   311–12
feedback on learning   238, 285; *see also* formative
    assessment
feelings of pupils about school learning   196–208
finishing off by pupils   111
formative assessment   139, 238, 282
framing   60, 64, 73, 83, 85, 96–7, 130, 197, 281,
    284, 301
  definition of   105
France   20, 293, 296
free choice for pupils   83–4, 112

friendliness of teachers 110
friendships of pupils 29, 34, 35, 57
    in relation to grouping 177, 179, 192
fun in the classroom 89–90, 94, 96–7, 101, 103, 116–17, 127, 195–6
funding of social science research 43

GCSE examination 7
gender differences 52, 54, 57–8, 97–8, 106–7, 127–9, 192–3, 260, 273, 300
Geography 78–9, 87–8, 94–5, 98, 172
Greenmantle Primary School 25, 77, 80, 127, 150, 172, 216
group process 177, 196
group work 53–4, 56–7
    pupils aptitude for 192–4
grouping of pupils 155, 192
    by ability *see* ability groups
    on the basis of behaviour 174–5
    on the basis of SATs 216
    pupils own views on 171–8, 286

handwriting 70, 140, 182
hierarchical model of learning 160
higher achievers
    curriculum preferences of 99–101
    experience of SATs 232–3
History 78–9, 87–8, 94–5, 172
home influences 142, 147–50, 153, 182–3, 206–7, 250, 253, 265, 287
homework 123, 250

ideal pieces of work 167
ideal pupils, pupils perceptions of 125–8, 130, 261–2, 265, 284
ideal teachers, pupils perceptions of 128–30, 244–5, 253, 261–2, 265, 284
identities of pupils
    as learners 147, 190, 201, 207, 209, 213, 226, 229, 233, 238, 241, 249, 251, 265–6, 273, 285, 288
    personal 273, 299–301, 304
    reconstruction of 268–71
Identity and Learning Programme (ILP) 44, 293, 298, 301, 305
improvements in standards of performance 289–90, 293
individual work by pupils 53–4, 56–7, 64, 73
industrial revolution 308, 311
Industrial Society 297
Information Technology 80, 82–3
innate characteristics of individual pupils 145–7, 150, 153, 285
inner-city schools 52, 127, 196, 224, 229, 288
innovations in education, multiplicity of 42
inspection of schools 8–9, 161, 170, 226, 229, 231, 238, 280
instruction by teachers 59–60, 64, 75, 108–9, 282
instrumentalism and instrumentality 17, 48, 118–19, 130, 159, 178, 199, 249, 262, 279, 281, 287, 290, 302
integration of subjects 79–80, 266, 282
intelligence, theories of 295–6, 300
intentions of learning activities, pupils
    understanding of 156–64, 178, 204, 284–7
interactions of pupils 31–2, 55–7, 59, 64, 190–1
    personal , instruction and control
        categories 108–10
    see also interpersonal interactions
interest of pupils in curriculum subjects 89, 94–6, 101, 103, 104, 117, 119, 121, 129, 196
international comparisons 5–6, 20
International Mathematics and Science Survey 6
interpersonal interactions and relationships 108, 110, 130
interviews
    embedding of 19, 34–5
    with pupils 31–40, 42, 66–7
    recording of 36–7
    with teachers 28–9, 37, 39–40
investigative activities 75, 83, 206, 283

Junior Schools Project 20

Kenwood Junior School 24, 73, 80, 82, 127, 170, 172, 196, 219–20, 238, 254, 288
    SATs at 229–32
key stages 6–7

Labour government 8–9, 14, 282, 293, 313–14
language for talking about learning 164, 178, 286
Lawnside Primary School 26, 72–3, 77, 80, 82, 127, 168–9, 172–3, 175, 196, 218, 238, 288
    SATs at 227–9
league tables 7–8, 302
learnacy 14
learned helplessness 248, 295
learner identity *see* identities of pupils as learners; role of pupil
learning environment and orientation 190, 195, 297–8, 303
learning power 296
learning processes 208, 238, 245, 249, 282, 302; *see also* engagement
liberal progressive model of education 49, 61, 65, 278, 282
lifelong learning 14–15, 17, 285, 293–4, 297, 314
likes and dislikes of pupils
    for subjects 88–97, 283–4
    for teachers 107
listening 72, 83
literacy 8–9, 50–1, 140, 148–9, 204, 282, 313
Literacy Hour 9, 13, 63–4, 68–9
locus of control, internal or external 294
longitudinal data 20, 23, 27, 44
lower achievers
    curriculum preferences of 101–3
    experience of SATs 229–32

managerial style   49
managerialism   48
market philosophy in education   42
masculinity   128
Mathematics   53, 67, 73–5, 83, 86, 88, 94–5, 97,
    99–102, 140–1, 172, 178–9, 181, 188, 262, 300
Meadway Junior School   24–5, 73, 80, 127, 171–2,
    178, 196, 215, 221, 288
    SATs at   224–6, 229
mediation of policy initiatives   12, 47, 281, 315
message systems   18, 63, 132, 281–2
mixed-ability groups   195
model of learning, identity and social setting   299–
    304; *see also* performance model; hierarchical
    model; liberal progressive model
moods of teachers   106, 123, 130, 139, 178, 284
morale of teachers   7–8, 281–2
motivation
    of pupils   17, 140, 144–5, 152, 180–1, 197, 206–
        7, 262, 266, 284, 287, 290, 294, 297, 300, 305
    of teachers   281
Music   77–8, 83, 94

naming and shaming   9, 231
National Curriculum   3–17 *passim*, 49–54, 61, 79,
    83, 101, 103, 198, 208, 279–80, 298, 307, 313–14
    pupils perception and experience of   12–15
negotiation between pupils and teachers   121–3,
    125, 130, 171, 284–6, 289, 301
noise in the classroom   202–3, 287
non-core subjects, pupils views of   76–83
norms of classroom life   127, 129
    deviations from   166
nuclear family, the   309–11
numeracy   8–9, 51, 282, 313
Numeracy Hour   9, 13, 63–4

observation in classrooms   19, 31, 39–40
open-ended tasks   204
ORACLE research   20, 60
Orchard School   25–6, 72–3, 80, 82, 196, 218
organization within the classroom   174–5
organizational forms for schools   49

PACE project   4–12, 16–17
    findings from earlier phases of   47–8, 106, 132–
        3, 153, 155, 277–8, 281, 290, 297–8, 301, 305,
        312–13
    goals of   9–10, 21
    problems for research team   43–4
    research design and data-gathering
        methods   18–44
paralysis in students induced by failure   200, 208
parental involvement   150, 182–3, 206, 305, 310
parental pressure   220, 228, 231
pedagogy   53–60, 64
peers
    help from   183–4, 194–5
    influence of   137, 304
    working with   *see* collaboration

performance, overemphasis on   295
performance model of education   47–9, 63, 65,
    278, 282
Physical Education (PE)   76–8, 86–7, 94, 100–1,
    103, 283–4
pictures   33–4; *see also* SAT stories
play-type activities   99, 101, 280
pleasure of pupils in their work   185, 188–9, 206;
    see also enjoyment
Plowden Report   5, 13, 55, 278, 310, 313
policy for education   312–15; *see also* mediation
post-modern society   10
post-mortems on tests   235
poverty   311, 314
power of teachers   104–5, 110, 122, 124, 130, 153,
    284–5, 301
practice
    with activities   160, 163–4, 204
    at tests   231
pragmatism of pupils   124, 290, 315
prescriptiveness   14, 119, 282
privileges for pupils   187, 266
professional development of teachers   63, 302
professional judgement   54
professionalism of teachers   12, 48–9, 62, 279–82;
    see also autonomy of teachers
progression in learning   159–60, 164, 217, 286
pseudonyms, use of   27
punctuation   181
pupil careers   44
pupil-centred approaches   *see* child-centred
    education
pupil products   64–5

quality, criteria of   182
questionnaires
    to pupils   40
    to teachers   19, 28, 39–42
questions
    pupils asking   183–4, 264–5
    teachers use of   60

rapport with children   34
Reading   68–70, 83, 86, 88
realities of classroom life as perceived by
    pupils   120, 286
recognition for effort and achievement   187–8
Religious Education (RE)   5, 50, 94–5
repetition of work   167–8, 286
repetition of years of schooling   215
representativeness of data   43
required activities   156–7, 164
research projects related to PACE   20
respect for the role of teacher   125, 130
responsibility for learning, pupils own   129, 213,
    285
revision activities   214, 234
reward systems   186–8, 287
rights of children   13

risk-taking by pupils 167–8, 197, 250, 265, 285–7, 302

role
  of pupil 152, 166, 300; *see also* identities of pupils
  of teacher 49, 123, 125, 130
role frame concept 301
Royal Society of Arts 297
rules of classroom behaviour 105
rules-in-play 301

St Anne's School 25, 73, 77, 80–1, 168, 175, 266
St Bede's School 24, 73, 77, 80, 170, 172, 196
salaries of teachers 9
sampling 21
  of pupils 27–8
  of schools 22–4
SAT stories 28, 40–1, 215, 220–2, 225, 228, 233–8 *passim*, 271
SATs see Standard Assessment Tasks
satisfaction
  intrinsic and extrinsic 186
  from overcoming challenges 189
  for teachers 281
schools selected for study 24–7
Science 51, 53, 67, 75–6, 87–8, 94–5, 98, 141, 172, 199, 210, 214, 300
  investigations in 75, 83, 283
secondary schools, pupils transfer to 215–16, 226, 268, 287
self-assessment by pupils 134–5, 140–1, 153, 243–5, 264, 285
self-awareness of pupils 196
self-confidence
  of pupils 141, 145, 213, 261, 263, 300, 305
  of teachers 280
self-esteem of pupils 272, 286, 294–5, 304
setting of pupils 53, 64, 73, 216, 241, 282, 303
shouting
  by pupils 202
  by teachers 110, 122–3, 168, 268
Singing 77–8, 98
skill development 161–2, 164, 286
social differentiation and social exclusion 266, 303–4, 313–15
social dimension of learning 196, 297
social expectations 301–2
social identity of pupils 125, 127, 130, 215
social logic 277–8
socio-cultural theory 305
sociograms 58, 269
sociology of childhood 15
sociometric data 19, 29–30, 38
speed of working 146, 149–50, 250; *see also* time pressures
spelling 70, 140, 149, 181
Standard Assessment Tasks (SATs) 7, 17, 27–8, 38–40, 58, 61–3, 140, 161, 198–9, 282, 285–9
  distortion of curriculum caused by 63
  experiences of low and high attainers 229–37

preparation for 214–15, 224, 227
pupils views of 214–39
taking of 224–29, 234
teachers boycott of 8
see also SAT stories
standards 8, 167
  international comparisons of 5–6
stories
  listening to 93, 103
  writing of 71–2, 83, 88, 100–1
  see also SAT stories
strategic attitudes to learning 151, 154, 193, 213, 245, 268, 270, 284, 301, 315
stress on teachers 279–80
success, pupils explanations of 141–8, 151–2, 246–7, 262, 271
summative assessment 134, 138, 152, 238, 285, 303
supportiveness of the learning context 301
surprise of pupils at their own success 190, 206

talking as a learning activity 72–3, 83
tape-recording 19, 36–7, 40
target-setting 9, 313
targeting of teaching 173
task engagement 57–9, 64, 208; *see also* distraction
task-focus 270
Task Group on Assessment and Testing (TGAT) 7, 61
Teacher Assessment 7, 61, 98, 214
  inter-school moderation of 62
Teacher Training Agency 9
teacher zone of influence 283
teacher-pupil relationships 53, 104–31, 168, 302
  positive, neutral, negative or ambivalent 105–6
  pupils perspectives on 284–5
teachers
  changes in perspectives of 20
  in conflict with government 312, 315
  experience of 278–82
  see also under more specific headings
teaching
  methods of 54; *see also* pedagogy
  pupils perspectives on 155–79, 285–7
teaching to the test 63–4
Technology 80–2, 84, 94, 103, 266–7
television watching 103
test technique 214, 231, 238
TGAT *see* Task Group on Assessment and Testing
thinking activities of pupils 91
Three Wise Men report 54–5
time management 115
time pressures 146, 198–200, 204, 208, 212, 273, 283, 287
  in tests 232
topic work 51, 79–80, 111, 157, 282
transcription of interviews 37–8
triangulation 38

Tyndale Junior School   6

uncertainty experienced by pupils   201–4, 208
    about assessment   135–6, 153
understanding, pupils perception of need for   182,
    249
University of Bristol   43
University of the West of England   43

Valley School   26, 72–3, 80, 171, 173, 175, 196,
    288
    SATs at   232–3
village schools   171–2, 227, 232

washback effect   63–4, 282
whole-class work   53–5, 57–8, 60, 64, 266, 282
whole-school curriculum planning   49, 53, 64, 282
Writing   70–2, 74, 83–4, 86, 88, 98, 100, 140, 149–
    50, 188